Urantia 2025 Part 4C

Urantia 2025 Part 4C

The Life and Teachings of Jesus

A Revised Urantia Book

Joel F Covey

Joel F Covey
Urantia 2025 Part 4C

Published by Spines
ISBN 979-8-89569-896-9

The Parts of the Urantia 2025 Book

PART 1

THE CENTRAL AND SUPERUNIVERSES

Sponsored by a Uversa Corps of Super-universe Personalities acting by authority of the Orvonton Ancients of Days

PART 2

THE LOCAL UNIVERSE

Sponsored by a Nebadon Corps of Local Universe Personalities acting by authority of Gabriel of Salvington

PART 3

THE HISTORY OF URANTIA

These papers were sponsored by a Corps of Local Universe Personalities acting by authority of Gabriel of Salvington

PART 4

THE LIFE AND TEACHINGS OF JESUS

This group of papers was sponsored by a commission of twelve Urantia midwayers acting under the supervision of a Melchizedek revelatory director.

The basis of this narrative was supplied by the superhuman watch-care of the Apostle Andrew.

Contents

Part 4C

The Life and Teachings of Jesus

Part IV C

The Life and Teachings of Jesus

This group of papers was sponsored by a commission of twelve Urantia Midwayers acting under the supervision of a Melchizedek Revelatory Director. The basis of this narrative was supplied by a secondary Midwayer who was onetime assigned to the superhuman watchcare of the Apostle Andrew.

PAPER 172
GOING INTO JERUSALEM

JESUS and the apostles arrived at Bethany shortly after four o'clock on Friday afternoon, March 31, A.D. 30. Lazarus, his sisters, and their friends were expecting them; and since so many people came every day to talk with Lazarus about his resurrection, Jesus was informed that arrangements had been made for him to stay with a neighboring believer, one Simon, the leading citizen of the little village since the death of Lazarus's father.

That evening, Jesus received many visitors, and the common folks of Bethany and Bethpage did their best to make him feel welcome. Although many thought Jesus was now going into Jerusalem, in utter defiance of the Sanhedrin's decree of death, to proclaim himself king of the Jews, the Bethany family — Lazarus, Martha, and Mary — more fully realized that the Master was not that kind of a king; they dimly felt that this might be his last visit to Jerusalem and Bethany.

The chief priests were informed that Jesus lodged at Bethany, but they thought best not to attempt to seize him among his friends; they decided to await his coming on into Jerusalem. Jesus knew about all this, but he was majestically calm; his friends had never seen him more composed and congenial; even the apostles were astounded that he should be so unconcerned when the Sanhedrin had called upon all Jewry to deliver him into their hands. While the Master slept that night, the apostles watched over him by twos, and many of them were girded with swords. Early the next morning they were awakened by hundreds of pilgrims who came out from Jerusalem, even on the Sabbath day, to see Jesus and Lazarus, whom he had raised from the dead.

1. SABBATH AT BETHANY

Pilgrims from outside of Judea, as well as the Jewish authorities, had all been asking: "What do you think? will Jesus come up to the feast?" Therefore, when the people heard that Jesus was at Bethany, they were glad, but the chief priests and Pharisees were somewhat perplexed. They were pleased to have him under their jurisdiction, but they were a trifle disconcerted by his boldness; they remembered that on his previous visit to Bethany, Lazarus had been raised from the dead, and Lazarus was becoming a big problem to the enemies of Jesus.

Six days before the Passover, on the evening after the Sabbath, all Bethany and Bethpage joined in celebrating the arrival of Jesus by a public banquet at the home of Simon. This supper was in honor of both Jesus and Lazarus; it was tendered in defiance of the Sanhedrin. Martha directed the serving of the food; her sister Mary was among the women onlookers as it was against the custom of the Jews for a woman to sit at a public banquet. The agents of the Sanhedrin were present, but they feared to apprehend Jesus in the midst of his friends.

Jesus talked with Simon about Joshua of old, whose namesake he was, and recited how Joshua and the Israelites had come up to Jerusalem through Jericho. In commenting on the legend of the walls of Jericho falling down, Jesus said: "I am not concerned with such walls of brick and stone; but I would cause the walls of prejudice, self-righteousness, and hate to crumble before this preaching of the Father's love for all men."

The banquet went along in a very cheerful and normal manner except that all the apostles were unusually sober. Jesus was exceptionally cheerful and had been playing with the children up to the time of coming to the table.

Nothing out of the ordinary happened until near the close of the feasting when Mary the sister of Lazarus stepped forward from among the group of women onlookers and, going up to where Jesus reclined as the guest of honor, proceeded to open a large alabaster cruse of very rare and costly ointment; and after anointing the Master's head, she began to pour it upon his feet as she took down her hair and wiped them with it. The whole house became filled with the odor of the ointment, and everybody present was amazed at what Mary had done. Lazarus said nothing, but when some of the people murmured, showing indignation that so costly an ointment should be thus used, Judas Iscariot stepped over to where Andrew reclined and said: "Why was this ointment not sold and the money bestowed to feed the poor? You should speak to the Master that he rebuke such waste."

Jesus, knowing what they thought and hearing what they said, put his hand upon Mary's head as she knelt by his side and, with a kindly expression upon his face, said: "Let her alone, every one of you. Why do you trouble her about this, seeing that she has done a good thing in her heart? To you who murmur and say that this ointment should have been sold and the money given to the poor, let me say that you have the poor always with you so that you may minister to them at any time it seems good to you; but I shall not always be with you; I go soon to my Father. This woman has long saved this ointment for my body at its burial, and now that it has seemed good to her to make this anointing in anticipation of my death, she shall not be denied such satisfaction. In the doing of this, Mary has reproved all of you in that by this act she evinces faith in what I have said about my death and ascension to my Father in heaven. This woman shall not be reproved for that which she has this night done; rather do I say to you that in the ages to come, wherever this gospel shall be preached throughout the whole world, what she has done will be spoken of in memory of her."

It was because of this rebuke, which he took as a personal reproof, that Judas Iscariot finally made up his mind to seek revenge for his hurt feelings. Many times had he entertained such ideas subconsciously, but now he dared to think such wicked thoughts in his open and conscious mind. And many others encouraged him in this attitude since the cost of this ointment was a sum equal to the earnings of one man for one year — enough to provide bread for five thousand persons. But Mary loved Jesus; she had provided this precious ointment with which to embalm his body in death, for she believed his words when he forewarned them that he must die, and it was not to be denied her if she changed her mind and chose to bestow this offering upon the Master while he yet lived.

Both Lazarus and Martha knew that Mary had long saved the money wherewith to buy this cruse of spikenard, and they heartily approved of her doing as her heart desired in such a matter, for they were well-to-do and could easily afford to make such an offering.

When the chief priests heard of this dinner in Bethany for Jesus and Lazarus, they began to take counsel among themselves as to what should be done with Lazarus. And presently they decided that Lazarus must also die. They rightly concluded that it would be useless to put Jesus to death if they permitted Lazarus, whom he had raised from the dead, to live.

2. SUNDAY MORNING WITH THE APOSTLES

On this Sunday morning, in Simon's beautiful garden, the Master called his twelve apostles around him and gave them their final instructions preparatory to entering Jerusalem. He told them that he would probably deliver many addresses and teach many lessons before returning to the Father but advised the apostles to refrain from doing any public work during this Passover sojourn in Jerusalem. He instructed them to remain near him and to "watch and pray." Jesus knew that many of his apostles and immediate followers even then carried swords concealed on their persons, but he made no reference to this fact.

This morning's instructions embraced a brief review of their ministry from the day of their ordination near Capernaum down to this day when they were preparing to enter Jerusalem. The apostles listened in silence; they asked no questions.

Early that morning David Zebedee had turned over to Judas the funds realized from the sale of the equipment of the Pella encampment, and Judas, in turn, had placed the greater part of this money in the hands of Simon, their host, for safekeeping in anticipation of the exigencies of their entry into Jerusalem.

After the conference with the apostles Jesus held converse with Lazarus and instructed him to avoid the sacrifice of his life to the vengefulness of the Sanhedrin. It was in obedience to this admonition that Lazarus, a few days later, fled to Philadelphia when the officers of the Sanhedrin sent men to arrest him.

In a way, all of Jesus' followers sensed the impending crisis, but they were prevented from fully realizing its seriousness by the unusual cheerfulness and exceptional good humor of the Master.

3. THE START FOR JERUSALEM

Bethany was about two miles from the temple, and it was half past one that Sunday afternoon when Jesus made ready to start for Jerusalem. He had feelings of profound affection for Bethany and its simple people. Nazareth, Capernaum, and Jerusalem had rejected him, but Bethany had accepted him, had believed in him. And it was in this small village, where almost every man, woman, and child were believers, that he chose to perform the mightiest work of his earth bestowal, the resurrection of Lazarus. He did not raise Lazarus that the villagers might believe, but rather because they already believed.

All morning Jesus had thought about his entry into Jerusalem. Heretofore he had always endeavored to suppress all public acclaim of him as the Messiah, but it was different now; he was nearing the end of his career in the flesh, his death had been decreed by the Sanhedrin, and no harm could come from allowing his disciples to give free expression to their feelings, just as might occur if he elected to make a formal and public entry into the city.

Jesus did not decide to make this public entrance into Jerusalem as a last bid for popular favor nor as a final grasp for power. Neither did he do it altogether to satisfy the human longings of his disciples and apostles. Jesus entertained none of the illusions of a fantastic dreamer; he well knew what was to be the outcome of this visit.

Having decided upon making a public entrance into Jerusalem, the Master was confronted with the necessity of choosing a proper method of executing such a resolve. Jesus thought over all of the many more or less contradictory so-called Messianic prophesies, but there seemed to be only one which was at all appropriate for him to follow. Most of these prophetic utterances depicted a king, the son and successor of David, a bold and aggressive temporal deliverer of all Israel from the yoke of foreign domination. But there was one Scripture that had sometimes been associated with the Messiah by those who held more to the spiritual concept of his mission, which Jesus thought might consistently be taken as a guide for his projected entry into Jerusalem. This Scripture was found in Zechariah, and it said: "Rejoice greatly, O daughter of Zion; shout, O daughter of Jerusalem. Behold, your king comes to you. He is just and he brings salvation. He comes as the lowly one, riding upon an ass, upon a colt, the foal of an ass."

A warrior king always entered a city riding upon a horse; a king on a mission of peace and friendship always entered riding upon an ass. Jesus would not enter Jerusalem as a man on horseback, but he was willing to enter peacefully and with good will as the Son of Man on a donkey.

Jesus had long tried by direct teaching to impress upon his apostles and his disciples that his kingdom was not of this world, that it was a purely spiritual matter; but he had not succeeded in this effort. Now, what he had failed to do by plain and personal teaching, he would attempt to accomplish by a symbolic appeal. Accordingly, right after the noon lunch, Jesus called Peter and John, and after directing them to go over to Bethpage, a neighboring village a little off the main road and a short distance northwest of Bethany, he further said: "Go to Bethpage, and when you come to the junction of the roads, you will find the colt of an ass tied there. Loose the colt and bring it back with you. If any one asks you why you do this, merely say, `The Master has need of him.'" And when the two apostles had gone into Bethpage as the Master had directed, they found the colt tied near his mother in the open street and close to a house on the corner. As Peter began to untie the colt, the owner came over and asked why they did this, and when Peter answered him as Jesus had directed, the man said: "If your Master is Jesus from Galilee, let him have the colt." And so they returned bringing the colt with them.

By this time several hundred pilgrims had gathered around Jesus and his apostles. Since midforenoon the visitors passing by on their way to the Passover had tarried. Meanwhile, David Zebedee and some of his former messenger associates took it upon themselves to hasten on down to Jerusalem, where they effectively spread the report among the throngs of visiting pilgrims about the temple that Jesus of Nazareth was making a triumphal entry into the city. Accordingly, several thousand of these visitors flocked forth to greet this much-talked-of prophet and wonder-worker, whom some believed to be the Messiah. This multitude, coming out from Jerusalem, met Jesus and the crowd going into the city just after they had passed over the brow of Olivet and had begun the descent into the city.

As the procession started out from Bethany, there was great enthusiasm among the festive crowd of disciples, believers, and visiting pilgrims, many hailing from Galilee and Perea. Just before they started, the twelve women of the original women's corps, accompanied by some of their associates, arrived on the scene and joined this unique procession as it moved on joyously toward the city.

Before they started, the Alpheus twins put their cloaks on the donkey and held him while the Master got on. As the procession moved toward the summit of Olivet, the festive crowd threw their garments on the ground and brought branches from the near-by trees in order to make a carpet of honor for the donkey bearing the royal Son, the promised Messiah. As the merry crowd moved on toward Jerusalem, they began to sing, or rather to shout in unison, the Psalm, "Hosanna to the son of David; blessed is he who comes in the name of the Lord. Hosanna in the highest. Blessed be the kingdom that comes down from heaven."

Jesus was lighthearted and cheerful as they moved along until he came to the brow of Olivet, where the city and the temple towers came into full view; there the Master stopped the procession, and a great silence came upon all as they beheld him weeping. Looking down upon the vast multitude coming forth from the city to greet him, the Master, with much emotion and with tearful voice, said: "O Jerusalem, if you had only known, even you, at least in this your day, the things which belong to your peace, and which you could so freely have had! But now are these glories about to be hid from your eyes. You are about to reject the Son of Peace and turn your backs upon the gospel of salvation. The days will soon come upon you wherein your enemies will cast a trench around about you and lay siege to you on every side; they shall utterly destroy you, insomuch that not one stone shall be left upon another. And all this shall befall you because you knew not the time of your divine visitation. You are about to reject the gift of God, and all men will reject you."

When he had finished speaking, they began the descent of Olivet and presently were joined by the multitude of visitors who had come from

Jerusalem waving palm branches, shouting hosannas, and otherwise expressing gleefulness and good fellowship. The Master had not planned that these crowds should come out from Jerusalem to meet them; that was the work of others. He never premeditated anything which was dramatic.

Along with the multitude which poured out to welcome the Master, there came also many of the Pharisees and his other enemies. They were so much perturbed by this sudden and unexpected outburst of popular acclaim that they feared to arrest him lest such action precipitate an open revolt of the populace. They greatly feared the attitude of the large numbers of visitors, who had heard much of Jesus, and who, many of them, believed in him.

As they neared Jerusalem, the crowd became more demonstrative, so much so that some of the Pharisees made their way up alongside Jesus and said: "Teacher, you should rebuke your disciples and exhort them to behave more seemly." Jesus answered: "It is only fitting that these children should welcome the Son of Peace, whom the chief priests have rejected. It would be useless to stop them lest in their stead these stones by the roadside cry out."

The Pharisees hastened on ahead of the procession to rejoin the Sanhedrin, which was then in session at the temple, and they reported to their associates: "Behold, all that we do is of no avail; we are confounded by this Galilean. The people have gone mad over him; if we do not stop these ignorant ones, all the world will go after him."

There really was no deep significance to be attached to this superficial and spontaneous outburst of popular enthusiasm. This welcome, although it was joyous and sincere, did not betoken any real or deep-seated conviction in the hearts of this festive multitude. These same crowds were equally as willing quickly to reject Jesus later on this week when the Sanhedrin once took a firm and decided stand against him, and when they became disillusioned — when they realized that Jesus was not going to establish the kingdom in accordance with their long-cherished expectations.

But the whole city was mightily stirred up, insomuch that everyone asked, "Who is this man?" And the multitude answered, "This is the prophet of Galilee, Jesus of Nazareth."

4. VISITING ABOUT THE TEMPLE

While the Alpheus twins returned the donkey to its owner, Jesus and the ten apostles detached themselves from their immediate associates and strolled about the temple, viewing the preparations for the Passover. No attempt was made to molest Jesus as the Sanhedrin greatly feared the people, and that was, after all, one of the reasons Jesus had for allowing the multitude thus to acclaim him. The apostles little understood that this was the only human procedure which could have been effective in preventing Jesus' immediate arrest upon entering the city. The Master desired to give the inhabitants of Jerusalem, high and low, as well as the tens of thousands of Passover visitors, this one more and last chance to hear the gospel and receive, if they would, the Son of Peace.

And now, as the evening drew on and the crowds went in quest of nourishment, Jesus and his immediate followers were left alone. What a strange day it had been! The apostles were thoughtful, but speechless. Never, in their years of association with Jesus, had they seen such a day. For a moment they sat down by the treasury, watching the people drop in their contributions: the rich putting much in the receiving box and all giving something in accordance with the extent of their possessions. At last there came along a poor widow, scantily attired, and they observed as she cast two mites (small coppers) into the trumpet. And then said Jesus, calling the attention of the apostles to the widow: "Heed well what you have just seen. This poor widow cast in more than all the others, for all these others, from their superfluity, cast in some trifle as a gift, but this poor woman, even though she is in want, gave all that she had, even her living."

As the evening drew on, they walked about the temple courts in silence, and after Jesus had surveyed these familiar scenes once more, recalling his emotions in connection with previous visits, not excepting the earlier ones, he said, "Let us go up to Bethany for our rest." Jesus, with Peter and John, went to the home of Simon, while the other apostles lodged among their friends in Bethany and Bethpage.

5. THE APOSTLES' ATTITUDE

This Sunday evening as they returned to Bethany, Jesus walked in front of the apostles. Not a word was spoken until they separated after arriving at Simon's house. No twelve human beings ever experienced such diverse and inexplicable emotions as now surged through the minds and souls of these ambassadors of the kingdom. These sturdy Galileans were confused and disconcerted; they did not know what to expect next; they were too surprised to be much afraid. They knew nothing of the Master's plans for the next day, and they asked no questions. They went to their lodgings, though they did not sleep much, save the twins. But they did not keep armed watch over Jesus at Simon's house.

Andrew was thoroughly bewildered, well-nigh confused. He was the one apostle who did not seriously undertake to evaluate the popular outburst of acclaim. He was too preoccupied with the thought of his responsibility as chief of the apostolic corps to give serious consideration to the meaning or significance of the loud hosannas of the multitude. Andrew was busy watching some of his associates whom he feared might be led away by their emotions during the excitement, particularly Peter, James, John, and Simon Zelotes. Throughout this day and those which immediately followed, Andrew was troubled with serious doubts, but he never expressed any of these misgivings to his apostolic associates. He was concerned about the attitude of some of the twelve whom he knew were armed with swords; but he did not know that his own brother, Peter, was carrying such a weapon. And so the procession into Jerusalem made a comparatively superficial impression upon Andrew; he was too busy with the responsibilities of his office to be otherwise affected.

Simon Peter was at first almost swept off his feet by this popular manifestation of enthusiasm; but he was considerably sobered by the time they returned to Bethany that night. Peter simply could not figure out what the Master was about. He was terribly disappointed that Jesus did not follow up this wave of popular favor with some kind of a pronouncement. Peter could not understand why Jesus did not speak to the multitude when they arrived at the temple, or at least permit one of the apostles to address the crowd. Peter was a great preacher, and he disliked to see such a large, receptive, and enthusiastic audience go to waste. He would so much have liked to preach the gospel of the kingdom to that throng right there in the temple; but the Master had specifically charged them that they were to do no teaching or preaching while in Jerusalem this Passover week. The reaction from the spectacular procession into the city was disastrous to Simon Peter; by night he was sobered and inexpressibly saddened.

To James Zebedee, this Sunday was a day of perplexity and profound confusion; he could not grasp the purport of what was going on; he could not comprehend the Master's purpose in permitting this wild acclaim and then in refusing to say a word to the people when they arrived at the temple. As the procession moved down Olivet toward Jerusalem, more especially when they were met by the thousands of pilgrims who poured forth to welcome the Master, James was cruelly torn by his conflicting emotions of elation and gratification at what he saw and by his profound feeling of fear as to what would happen when they reached the temple. And then was he downcast and overcome by disappointment when Jesus climbed off the donkey and proceeded to walk leisurely about the temple courts. James could not understand the reason for throwing away such a magnificent opportunity to proclaim the kingdom. By night, his mind was held firmly in the grip of a distressing and dreadful uncertainty.

John Zebedee came somewhere near understanding why Jesus did this; at least he grasped in part the spiritual significance of this so-called triumphal entry into Jerusalem. As the multitude moved on toward the temple, and as John beheld his Master sitting there astride the colt, he recalled hearing Jesus onetime quote the passage of Scripture, the utterance of Zechariah, which described the coming of the Messiah as a man of peace and riding into Jerusalem on an ass. As John turned this Scripture over in his mind, he began to comprehend the symbolic significance of this Sunday-afternoon pageant. At least, he grasped enough of the meaning of this Scripture to enable him somewhat to enjoy the episode and to prevent his becoming overmuch depressed by the apparent purposeless ending of the triumphal procession. John had a type of mind which naturally tended to think and feel in symbols.

Philip was entirely unsettled by the suddenness and spontaneity of the outburst. He could not collect his thoughts sufficiently while on the way down Olivet to arrive at any settled notion as to what all the demonstration was about. In a way, he enjoyed the performance because his Master was being honored. By the time they reached the temple, he was perturbed by the thought that Jesus might possibly ask him to feed the multitude, so that the conduct of Jesus in turning leisurely away from the crowds, which so sorely disappointed the majority of the apostles, was a great relief to Philip. Multitudes had sometimes been a great trial to the steward of the twelve. After he was relieved of these personal fears regarding the material needs of the crowds, Philip joined with Peter in the expression of disappointment that nothing was done to teach the multitude. That night Philip got to thinking over these experiences and was tempted to doubt the whole idea of the kingdom; he honestly wondered what all these things could mean, but he expressed his doubts to no one; he loved Jesus too much. He had great personal faith in the Master.

Nathaniel, aside from the symbolic and prophetic aspects, came the nearest to understanding the Master's reason for enlisting the popular support of the Passover pilgrims. He reasoned it out, before they reached the temple, that without such a demonstrative entry into Jerusalem Jesus would have been arrested by the Sanhedrin officials and cast into prison the moment he presumed to enter the city. He was not, therefore, in the least surprised that the Master made no further use of the cheering crowds when he had once got inside the walls of the city and had thus so forcibly impressed the Jewish leaders that they would refrain from placing him under immediate arrest. Understanding the real reason for the Master's entering the city in this manner, Nathaniel naturally followed along with more poise and was less perturbed and disappointed by Jesus' subsequent conduct than were the other apostles. Nathaniel had great confidence in Jesus' understanding of men as well as in his sagacity and cleverness in handling difficult situations.

Matthew was at first nonplused by this pageant performance. He did not grasp the meaning of what his eyes were seeing until he also recalled the Scripture in Zechariah where the prophet had alluded to the rejoicing of Jerusalem because her king had come bringing salvation and riding upon the colt of an ass. As the procession moved in the direction of the city and then drew on toward the temple, Matthew became ecstatic; he was certain that something extraordinary would happen when the Master arrived at the temple at the head of this shouting multitude. When one of the Pharisees mocked Jesus, saying, "Look, everybody, see who comes here, the king of the Jews riding on an ass!" Matthew kept his hands off of him only by exercising great restraint. None of the twelve was more depressed on the way back to Bethany that evening. Next to Simon Peter and Simon Zelotes, he experienced the highest nervous tension and was in a state of exhaustion by night. But by morning Matthew was much cheered; he was, after all, a cheerful loser.

Thomas was the most bewildered and puzzled man of all the twelve. Most of the time he just followed along, gazing at the spectacle and honestly wondering what could be the Master's motive for participating in such a peculiar demonstration. Down deep in his heart he regarded the whole performance as a little childish, if not downright foolish. He had never seen Jesus do anything like this and was at a loss to account for his strange conduct on this Sunday afternoon. By the time they reached the temple, Thomas had deduced that the purpose of this popular demonstration was so to frighten the Sanhedrin that they would not dare immediately to arrest the Master. On the way back to Bethany Thomas thought much but said nothing. By bedtime the Master's cleverness in staging the tumultuous entry into Jerusalem had begun to make a somewhat humorous appeal, and he was much cheered up by this reaction.

This Sunday started off as a great day for Simon Zelotes. He saw visions of wonderful doings in Jerusalem the next few days, and in that he was right, but Simon dreamed of the establishment of the new national rule of the Jews, with Jesus on the throne of David. Simon saw the nationalists springing into action as soon as the kingdom was announced, and himself in supreme command of the assembling military forces of the new kingdom. On the way down Olivet he even envisaged the Sanhedrin and all of their sympathizers dead before sunset of that day. He really believed something great was going to happen. He was the noisiest man in the whole multitude. By five o'clock that afternoon he was a silent, crushed, and disillusioned apostle. He never fully recovered from the depression which settled down on him as a result of this day's shock; at least not until long after the Master's resurrection.

To the Alpheus twins this was a perfect day. They really enjoyed it all the way through, and not being present during the time of quiet visitation about the temple, they escaped much of the anticlimax of the popular upheaval. They could not possibly understand the downcast behavior of the apostles when they came back to Bethany that evening. In the memory of the twins this was always their day of being nearest heaven on earth. This day was the satisfying climax of their whole career as apostles. And the memory of the elation of this Sunday afternoon carried them on through all of the tragedy of this eventful week, right up to the hour of the crucifixion. It was the most befitting entry of the king the twins could conceive; they enjoyed every moment of the whole pageant. They fully approved of all they saw and long cherished the memory.

Of all the apostles, Judas Iscariot was the most adversely affected by this processional entry into Jerusalem. His mind was in a disagreeable ferment because of the Master's rebuke the preceding day in connection with Mary's anointing at the feast in Simon's house. Judas was disgusted with the whole spectacle. To him it seemed childish, if not indeed ridiculous. As this vengeful apostle looked upon the proceedings of this Sunday afternoon, Jesus seemed to him more to resemble a clown than a king. He heartily resented the whole performance. He shared the views of the Greeks and Romans, who looked down upon anyone who would consent to ride upon an ass or the colt of an ass. By the time the triumphal procession had entered the city, Judas had about made up his mind to abandon the whole idea of such a kingdom; he was almost resolved to forsake all such farcical attempts to establish the kingdom of heaven. And then he thought of the resurrection of Lazarus, and many other things, and decided to stay on with the twelve, at least for another day. Besides, he carried the bag, and he would not desert with the apostolic funds in his possession. On the way back to Bethany that night his conduct did not seem strange since all of the apostles were equally downcast and silent.

Judas was tremendously influenced by the ridicule of his Sadducean friends. No other single factor exerted such a powerful influence on him, in his final determination to forsake Jesus and his fellow apostles, as a certain episode which occurred just as Jesus reached the gate of the city: A prominent Sadducee (a friend of Judas's family) rushed up to him in a spirit of gleeful ridicule and, slapping him on the back, said: "Why so troubled of countenance, my good friend; cheer up and join us all while we acclaim this Jesus of Nazareth the king of the Jews as he rides through the gates of Jerusalem seated on an ass." Judas had never shrunk from persecution, but he could not stand this sort of ridicule. With the long-nourished emotion of revenge there was now blended this fatal fear of ridicule, that terrible and fearful feeling of being ashamed of his Master and his fellow apostles. At heart, this ordained ambassador of the kingdom was already a deserter; it only remained for him to find some plausible excuse for an open break with the Master.

PAPER 173
MONDAY IN JERUSALEM

Early on this Monday morning, by prearrangement, Jesus and the apostles assembled at the home of Simon in Bethany, and after a brief conference they set out for Jerusalem. The twelve were strangely silent as they journeyed on toward the temple; they had not recovered from the experience of the preceding day. They were expectant, fearful, and profoundly affected by a certain feeling of detachment growing out of the Master's sudden change of tactics, coupled with his instruction that they were to engage in no public teaching throughout this Passover week.

As this group journeyed down Mount Olivet, Jesus led the way, the apostles following closely behind in meditative silence. There was just one thought uppermost in the minds of all save Judas Iscariot, and that was: What will the Master do today? The one absorbing thought of Judas was: What shall I do? Shall I go on with Jesus and my associates, or shall I withdraw? And if I am going to quit, how shall I break off?

It was about nine o'clock on this beautiful morning when these men arrived at the temple. They went at once to the large court where Jesus so often taught, and after greeting the believers who were awaiting him, Jesus mounted one of the teaching platforms and began to address the gathering crowd. The apostles withdrew for a short distance and awaited developments.

1. CLEANSING THE TEMPLE

A huge commercial traffic had grown up in association with the services and ceremonies of the temple worship. There was the business of providing suitable animals for the various sacrifices. Though it was permissible for a worshiper to provide his own sacrifice, the fact remained that this animal must be free from all "blemish" in the meaning of the Levitical law and as interpreted by official inspectors of the temple. Many a worshiper had experienced the humiliation of having his supposedly perfect animal rejected by the temple examiners. It therefore became the more general practice to purchase sacrificial animals at the temple, and although there were several stations on near-by Olivet where they could be bought, it had become the vogue to buy these animals directly from the temple pens. Gradually there had grown up this custom of selling all kinds of sacrificial animals in the temple courts. An extensive business, in which enormous profits were made, had thus been brought into existence. Part of these gains was reserved for the temple treasury, but the larger part went indirectly into the hands of the ruling high-priestly families.

This sale of animals in the temple prospered because, when the worshiper purchased such an animal, although the price might be somewhat high, no more fees had to be paid, and he could be sure the intended sacrifice would not be rejected on the ground of possessing real or technical blemishes. At one time or another systems of exorbitant overcharge were practiced upon the common people, especially during the great national feasts. At one time the greedy priests went so far as to demand the equivalent of the value of a week's labor for a pair of doves which should have been sold to the poor for a few pennies. The "sons of Annas" had already begun to establish their bazaars in the temple precincts, those very merchandise marts which persisted to the time of their final overthrow by a mob three years before the destruction of the temple itself.

But traffic in sacrificial animals and sundry merchandise was not the only way in which the courts of the temple were profaned. At this time there was fostered an extensive system of banking and commercial exchange which was carried on right within the temple precincts. And this all came about in the following manner: During the Asmonean dynasty the Jews coined their own silver money, and it had become the practice to require the temple dues of one-half shekel and all other temple fees to be paid with this Jewish coin. This regulation necessitated that money-changers be licensed to exchange the many sorts of currency in circulation throughout Palestine and other provinces of the Roman Empire for this orthodox shekel of Jewish coining. The temple head tax, payable by all except women, slaves, and minors, was one-half shekel, a coin about the size of a ten cent piece but twice as thick. By the times of Jesus the priests had also been exempted from the payment of temple dues. Accordingly, from the 15th to the 25th of the month preceding the Passover, accredited money-changers erected their booths in the principal cities of Palestine for the purpose of providing the Jewish people with proper money to meet the temple dues after they had reached Jerusalem. After this ten-day period these money-changers moved on to Jerusalem and proceeded to set up their exchange tables in the courts of the temple. They were permitted to charge the equivalent of from three to four cents commission for the exchange of a coin valued at about ten cents, and in case a coin of larger value was offered for exchange, they were allowed to collect double. Likewise did these temple bankers profit from the exchange of all money intended for the purchase of sacrificial animals and for the payment of vows and the making of offerings.

These temple money-changers not only conducted a regular banking business for profit in the exchange of more than twenty sorts of money which the visiting pilgrims would periodically bring to Jerusalem, but they also engaged in all other kinds of transactions pertaining to the banking business. Both the temple treasury and the temple rulers profited tremendously from these commercial activities. It was not uncommon for the temple treasury to hold upwards of ten million dollars while the common people languished in poverty and continued to pay these unjust levies.

In the midst of this noisy aggregation of money-changers, merchandisers, and cattle sellers, Jesus, on this Monday morning, attempted to teach the gospel of the heavenly kingdom. He was not alone in resenting this profanation of the temple; the common people, especially the Jewish visitors from foreign provinces, also heartily resented this profiteering desecration of their national house of worship. At this time the Sanhedrin itself held its regular meetings in a chamber surrounded by all this babble and confusion of trade and barter.

As Jesus was about to begin his address, two things happened to arrest his attention. At the money table of a near-by exchanger a violent and heated argument had arisen over the alleged overcharging of a Jew from Alexandria, while at the same moment the air was rent by the bellowing of a drove of some one hundred bullocks which was being driven from one section of the animal pens to another. As Jesus paused, silently but thoughtfully contemplating this scene of commerce and confusion, close by he beheld a simple-minded Galilean, a man he had once talked with in Iron, being ridiculed and jostled about by supercilious and would-be superior Judeans; and all of this combined to produce one of those strange and periodic uprisings of indignant emotion in the soul of Jesus.

To the amazement of his apostles, standing near at hand, who refrained from participation in what so soon followed, Jesus stepped down from the teaching platform and, going over to the lad who was driving the cattle through the court, took from him his whip of cords and swiftly drove the animals from the temple. But that was not all; he strode majestically before the wondering gaze of the thousands assembled in the temple court to the farthest cattle pen and proceeded to open the gates of every stall and to drive out the imprisoned animals. By this time the assembled pilgrims were electrified, and with uproarious shouting they moved toward the bazaars and began to overturn the tables of the money-changers. In less than five minutes all commerce had been swept from the temple. By the time the near-by Roman guards had appeared on the scene, all was quiet, and the crowds had become orderly; Jesus, returning to the speaker's stand, spoke to the multitude: "You have this day witnessed that which is written in the Scriptures: `My house shall be called a house of prayer for all nations, but you have made it a den of robbers.'"

But before he could utter other words, the great assembly broke out in hosannas of praise, and presently a throng of youths stepped out from the crowd to sing grateful hymns of appreciation that the profane and profiteering merchandisers had been ejected from the sacred temple. By this time certain of the priests had arrived on the scene, and one of them said to Jesus, "Do you not hear what the children of the Levites say?" And the Master replied, "Have you never read, `Out of the mouths of babes and sucklings has praise been perfected'?" And all the rest of that day while Jesus taught, guards set by the people stood watch at every archway, and they would not permit anyone to carry even an empty vessel across the temple courts.

When the chief priests and the scribes heard about these happenings, they were dumfounded. All the more they feared the Master, and all the more they determined to destroy him. But they were nonplused. They did not know how to accomplish his death, for they greatly feared the multitudes, who were now so outspoken in their approval of his overthrow of the profane profiteers. And all this day, a day of quiet and peace in the temple courts, the people heard Jesus' teaching and literally hung on his words.

This surprising act of Jesus was beyond the comprehension of his apostles. They were so taken aback by this sudden and unexpected move of their Master that they remained throughout the whole episode huddled together near the speaker's stand; they never lifted a hand to further this cleansing of the temple. If this spectacular event had occurred the day before, at the time of Jesus' triumphal arrival at the temple at the termination of his tumultuous procession through the gates of the city, all the while loudly acclaimed by the multitude, they would have been ready for it, but coming as it did, they were wholly unprepared to participate.

This cleansing of the temple discloses the Master's attitude toward commercializing the practices of religion as well as his detestation of all forms of unfairness and profiteering at the expense of the poor and the unlearned. This episode also demonstrates that Jesus did not look with approval upon the refusal to employ force to protect the majority of any given human group against the unfair and enslaving practices of unjust minorities who may be able to entrench themselves behind political, financial, or ecclesiastical power. Shrewd, wicked, and designing men are not to be permitted to organize themselves for the exploitation and oppression of those who, because of their idealism, are not disposed to resort to force for self-protection or for the furtherance of their laudable life projects.

2. CHALLENGING THE MASTER'S AUTHORITY

On Sunday the triumphal entry into Jerusalem so overawed the Jewish leaders that they refrained from placing Jesus under arrest. Today, this spectacular cleansing of the temple likewise effectively postponed the Master's apprehension. Day by day the rulers of the Jews were becoming more and more determined to destroy him, but they were distraught by two fears, which conspired to delay the hour of striking. The chief priests and the scribes were unwilling to arrest Jesus in public for fear the multitude might turn upon them in a fury of resentment; they also dreaded the possibility of the Roman guards being called upon to quell a popular uprising.

At the noon session of the Sanhedrin it was unanimously agreed that Jesus must be speedily destroyed, inasmuch as no friend of the Master attended this meeting. But they could not agree as to when and how he should be taken into custody. Finally they agreed upon appointing five groups to go out among the people and seek to entangle him in his teaching or otherwise to discredit him in the sight of those who listened to his instruction. Accordingly, about two o'clock, when Jesus had just begun his discourse on "The Liberty of Sonship," a group of these elders of Israel made their way up near Jesus and, interrupting him in the customary manner, asked this question: "By what authority do you do these things? Who gave you this authority?"

It was altogether proper that the temple rulers and the officers of the Jewish Sanhedrin should ask this question of anyone who presumed to teach and perform in the extraordinary manner which had been characteristic of Jesus, especially as concerned his recent conduct in clearing the temple of all commerce. These traders and money-changers all operated by direct license from the highest rulers, and a percentage of their gains was supposed to go directly into the temple treasury. Do not forget that *authority* was the watchword of all Jewry. The prophets were always stirring up trouble because they so boldly presumed to teach without authority, without having been duly instructed in the rabbinic academies and subsequently regularly ordained by the Sanhedrin. Lack of this authority in pretentious public teaching was looked upon as indicating either ignorant presumption or open rebellion. At this time only the Sanhedrin could ordain an elder or teacher, and such a ceremony had to take place in the presence of at least three persons who had previously been so ordained. Such an ordination conferred the title of "rabbi" upon the teacher and also qualified him to act as a judge, "binding and loosing such matters as might be brought to him for adjudication."

The rulers of the temple came before Jesus at this afternoon hour challenging not only his teaching but his acts. Jesus well knew that these very men had long publicly taught that his authority for teaching was Satanic, and that all his mighty works had been wrought by the power of the prince of devils. Therefore did the Master begin his answer to their question by asking them a counter-question. Said Jesus: "I would also like to ask you one question which, if you will answer me, I likewise will tell you by what authority I do these works. The baptism of John, whence was it? Did John get his authority from heaven or from men?"

And when his questioners heard this, they withdrew to one side to take counsel among themselves as to what answer they might give. They had thought to embarrass Jesus before the multitude, but now they found themselves much confused before all who were assembled at that time in the temple court. And their discomfiture was all the more apparent when they returned to Jesus, saying: "Concerning the baptism of John, we cannot answer; we do not know." And they so answered the Master because they had reasoned among themselves: If we shall say from heaven, then will he say, Why did you not believe him, and perchance will add that he received his authority from John; and if we shall say from men, then might the multitude turn upon us, for most of them hold that John was a prophet; and so they were compelled to come before Jesus and the people confessing that they, the religious teachers and leaders of Israel, could not (or would not) express an opinion about John's mission. And when they had spoken, Jesus, looking down upon them, said, "Neither will I tell you by what authority I do these things."

Jesus never intended to appeal to John for his authority; John had never been ordained by the Sanhedrin. Jesus' authority was in himself and in his Father's eternal supremacy.

In employing this method of dealing with his adversaries, Jesus did not mean to dodge the question. At first it may seem that he was guilty of a masterly evasion, but it was not so. Jesus was never disposed to take unfair advantage of even his enemies. In this apparent evasion he really supplied all his hearers with the answer to the Pharisees' question as to the authority behind his mission. They had asserted that he performed by authority of the prince of devils. Jesus had repeatedly asserted that all his teaching and works were by the power and authority of his Father in heaven. This the Jewish leaders refused to accept and were seeking to corner him into admitting that he was an irregular teacher since he had never been sanctioned by the Sanhedrin. In answering them as he did, while not claiming authority from John, he so satisfied the people with the inference that the effort of his enemies to ensnare him was effectively turned upon themselves and was much to their discredit in the eyes of all present.

And it was this genius of the Master for dealing with his adversaries that made them so afraid of him. They attempted no more questions that day; they retired to take further counsel among themselves. But the people were not slow to discern the dishonesty and insincerity in these questions asked by the Jewish rulers. Even the common folk could not fail to distinguish between the moral majesty of the Master and the designing hypocrisy of his enemies. But the cleansing of the temple had brought the Sadducees over to the side of the Pharisees in perfecting the plan to destroy Jesus. And the Sadducees now represented a majority of the Sanhedrin.

3. PARABLE OF THE TWO SONS

As the caviling Pharisees stood there in silence before Jesus, he looked down on them and said: "Since you are in doubt about John's mission and arrayed in enmity against the teaching and the works of the Son of Man, give ear while I tell you a parable: A certain great and respected landholder had two sons, and desiring the help of his sons in the management of his large estates, he came to one of them, saying, `Son, go work today in my vineyard.' And this unthinking son answered his father, saying, `I will not go'; but afterward he repented and went. When he had found his older son, likewise he said to him, `Son, go work in my vineyard.' And this hypocritical and unfaithful son answered, `Yes, my father, I will go.' But when his father had departed, he went not. Let me ask you, which of these sons really did his father's will?"

And the people spoke with one accord, saying, "The first son." And then said Jesus: "Even so; and now do I declare that the publicans and harlots, even though they appear to refuse the call to repentance, shall see the error of their way and go on into the kingdom of God before you, who make great pretensions of serving the Father in heaven while you refuse to do the works of the Father. It was not you, the Pharisees and scribes, who believed John, but rather the publicans and sinners; neither do you believe my teaching, but the common people hear my words gladly."

Jesus did not despise the Pharisees and Sadducees personally. It was their systems of teaching and practice which he sought to discredit. He was hostile to no man, but here was occurring the inevitable clash between a new and living religion of the spirit and the older religion of ceremony, tradition, and authority.

All this time the twelve apostles stood near the Master, but they did not in any manner participate in these transactions. Each one of the twelve was reacting in his own peculiar way to the events of these closing days of Jesus' ministry in the flesh, and each one likewise remained obedient to the Master's injunction to refrain from all public teaching and preaching during this Passover week.

4. PARABLE OF THE ABSENT LANDLORD

When the chief Pharisees and the scribes who had sought to entangle Jesus with their questions had finished listening to the story of the two sons, they withdrew to take further counsel, and the Master, turning his attention to the listening multitude, told another parable:

"There was a good man who was a householder, and he planted a vineyard. He set a hedge about it, dug a pit for the wine press, and built a watchtower for the guards. Then he let this vineyard out to tenants while he went on a long journey into another country. And when the season of the fruits drew near, he sent servants to the tenants to receive his rental. But they took counsel among themselves and refused to give these servants the fruits due their master; instead, they fell upon his servants, beating one, stoning another, and sending the others away empty-handed. And when the householder heard about all this, he sent other and more trusted servants to deal with these wicked tenants, and these they wounded and also treated shamefully. And then the householder sent his favorite servant, his steward, and him they killed. And still, in patience and with forbearance, he dispatched many other servants, but none would they receive. Some they beat, others they killed, and when the householder had been so dealt with, he decided to send his son to deal with these ungrateful tenants, saying to himself, `They may mistreat my servants, but they will surely show respect for my beloved son.' But when these unrepentant and wicked tenants saw the son, they reasoned among themselves: `This is the heir; come, let us kill him and then the inheritance will be ours.' So they laid hold on him, and after casting him out of the vineyard, they killed him. When the lord of that vineyard shall hear how they have rejected and killed his son, what will he do to those ungrateful and wicked tenants?"

And when the people heard this parable and the question Jesus asked, they answered, "He will destroy those miserable men and let out his vineyard to other and honest farmers who will render to him the fruits in their season." And when some of them who heard perceived that this parable referred to the Jewish nation and its treatment of the prophets and to the impending rejection of Jesus and the gospel of the kingdom, they said in sorrow, "God forbid that we should go on doing these things."

Jesus saw a group of the Sadducees and Pharisees making their way through the crowd, and he paused for a moment until they drew near him, when he said: "You know how your fathers rejected the prophets, and you well know that you are set in your hearts to reject the Son of Man." And then, looking with searching gaze upon those priests and elders who were standing near him, Jesus said: "Did you never read in the Scripture about the stone which the builders rejected, and which, when the people had discovered it, was made into the cornerstone? And so once more do I warn you that, if you continue to reject this gospel, presently will the kingdom of God be taken away from you and be given to a people willing to receive the good news and to bring forth the fruits of the spirit. And there is a mystery about this stone, seeing that whoso falls upon it, while he is thereby broken in pieces, shall be saved; but on whomsoever this stone falls, he will be ground to dust and his ashes scattered to the four winds."

When the Pharisees heard these words, they understood that Jesus referred to themselves and the other Jewish leaders. They greatly desired to lay hold on him then and there, but they feared the multitude. However, they were so angered by the Master's words that they withdrew and held further counsel among themselves as to how they might bring about his death. And that night both the Sadducees and the Pharisees joined hands in the plan to entrap him the next day.

5. PARABLE OF THE MARRIAGE FEAST

After the scribes and rulers had withdrawn, Jesus addressed himself again to the assembled crowd and spoke the parable of the wedding feast. He said:

"The kingdom of heaven may be likened to a certain king who made a marriage feast for his son and dispatched messengers to call those who had previously been invited to the feast to come, saying, `Everything is ready for the marriage supper at the king's palace.' Now, many of those who had once promised to attend, at this time refused to come. When the king heard of these rejections of his invitation, he sent other servants and messengers, saying: `Tell all those who were bidden, to come, for, behold, my dinner is ready. My oxen and my fatlings are killed, and all is in readiness for the celebration of the forthcoming marriage of my son.' But again did the thoughtless make light of this call of their king, and they went their ways, one to the farm, another to the pottery, and others to their merchandise. Still others were not content thus to slight the king's call, but in open rebellion they laid hands on the king's messengers and shamefully mistreated them, even killing some of them. And when the king perceived that his chosen guests, even those who had accepted his preliminary invitation and had promised to attend the wedding feast, had finally rejected his call and in rebellion had assaulted and slain his chosen messengers, he was exceedingly wroth. And then this insulted king ordered out his armies and the armies of his allies and instructed them to destroy these rebellious murderers and to burn down their city.

"And when he had punished those who spurned his invitation, he appointed yet another day for the wedding feast and said to his messengers: `They who were first bidden to the wedding were not worthy; so go now into the parting of the ways and into the highways and even beyond the borders of the city, and as many as you shall find, bid even these strangers to come in and attend this wedding feast.' And then these servants went out into the highways and the out-of-the-way places, and they gathered together as many as they found, good and bad, rich and poor, so that at last the wedding chamber was filled with willing guests. When all was ready, the king came in to view his guests, and much to his surprise he saw there a man without a wedding garment. The king , since he had freely provided wedding garments for all his guests, addressing this man, said: `Friend, how is it that you come into my guest chamber on this occasion without a wedding garment?' And this unprepared man was speechless. Then said the king to his servants: `Cast out this thoughtless guest from my house to share the lot of all the others who have spurned my hospitality and rejected my call. I will have none here except those who delight to accept my invitation, and who do me the honor to wear those guest garments so freely provided for all.'"

After speaking this parable, Jesus was about to dismiss the multitude when a sympathetic believer, making his way through the crowds toward him, asked: "But, Master, how shall we know about these things? how shall we be ready for the king's invitation? what sign will you give us whereby we shall know that you are the Son of God?" And when the Master heard this, he said, "Only one sign shall be given you." And then, pointing to his own body, he continued, "Destroy this temple, and in three days I will raise it up." But they did not understand him, and as they dispersed, they talked among themselves, saying, "Almost fifty years has this temple been in building, and yet he says he will destroy it and raise it up in three days." Even his own apostles did not comprehend the significance of this utterance, but subsequently, after his resurrection, they recalled what he had said.

About four o'clock this afternoon Jesus beckoned to his apostles and indicated that he desired to leave the temple and to go to Bethany for their evening meal and a night of rest. On the way up Olivet Jesus instructed Andrew, Philip, and Thomas that, on the morrow, they should establish a camp nearer the city which they could occupy during the remainder of the Passover week. In compliance with this instruction the following morning they pitched their tents in the hillside ravine overlooking the public camping park of Gethsemane, on a plot of ground belonging to Simon of Bethany.

Again it was a silent group of Jews who made their way up the western slope of Olivet on this Monday night. These twelve men, as never before, were beginning to sense that something tragic was about to happen. While the dramatic cleansing of the temple during the early morning had aroused their hopes of seeing the Master assert himself and manifest his mighty powers, the events of the entire afternoon only operated as an anticlimax in that they all pointed to the certain rejection of Jesus' teaching by the Jewish authorities. The apostles were gripped by suspense and were held in the firm grasp of a terrible uncertainty. They realized that only a few short days could intervene between the events of the day just passed and the crash of an impending doom. They all felt that something tremendous was about to happen, but they knew not what to expect. They went to their various places for rest, but they slept very little. Even the Alpheus twins were at last aroused to the realization that the events of the Master's life were moving swiftly toward their final culmination.

PAPER 174
TUESDAY MORNING IN THE TEMPLE

ABOUT SEVEN O'CLOCK on this Tuesday morning Jesus met the apostles, the women's corps, and some two dozen other prominent disciples at the home of Simon. At this meeting he said farewell to Lazarus, giving him that instruction which led him so soon to flee to Philadelphia in Perea, where he later became connected with the missionary movement having its headquarters in that city. Jesus also said good-bye to the aged Simon, and gave his parting advice to the women's corps, as he never again formally addressed them.

This morning he greeted each of the twelve with a personal salutation. To Andrew he said: "Be not dismayed by the events just ahead. Keep a firm hold on your brethren and see that they do not find you downcast." To Peter he said: "Put not your trust in the arm of flesh nor in weapons of steel. Establish yourself on the spiritual foundations of the eternal rocks." To James he said: "Falter not because of outward appearances. Remain firm in your faith, and you shall soon know of the reality of that which you believe." To John he said: "Be gentle; love even your enemies; be tolerant. And remember that I have trusted you with many things." To Nathaniel he said: "Judge not by appearances; remain firm in your faith when all appears to vanish; be true to your commission as an ambassador of the kingdom." To Philip he said: "Be unmoved by the events now impending. Remain unshaken, even when you cannot see the way. Be loyal to your oath of consecration." To Matthew he said: "Forget not the mercy that received you into the kingdom. Let no man cheat you of your eternal reward. As you have withstood the inclinations of the mortal nature, be willing to be steadfast." To Thomas he said: "No matter how difficult it may be, just now you must walk by faith and not by sight. Doubt not that I am able to finish the work I have begun, and that I shall eventually see all of my faithful ambassadors in the kingdom beyond." To the Alpheus twins he said: "Do not allow the things which you cannot understand to crush you. Be true to the affections of your hearts and put not your trust in either great men or the changing attitude of the people. Stand by your brethren." And to Simon Zelotes he said: "Simon, you may be crushed by disappointment, but your spirit shall rise above all that may come upon you. What you have failed to learn from me, my spirit will teach you. Seek the true realities of the spirit and cease to be attracted by unreal and material shadows."

And to Judas Iscariot he said: "Judas, I have loved you and have prayed that you would love your brethren. Be not weary in well doing; and I would warn you to beware the slippery paths of flattery and the poison darts of ridicule."

And when he had concluded these greetings, he departed for Jerusalem with Andrew, Peter, James, and John as the other apostles set about the establishment of the Gethsemane camp, where they were to go that night, and where they made their headquarters for the remainder of the Master's life in the flesh. About halfway down the slope of Olivet Jesus paused and visited more than an hour with the four apostles.

1. DIVINE FORGIVENESS

For several days Peter and James had been engaged in discussing their differences of opinion about the Master's teaching regarding the forgiveness of sin. They had both agreed to lay the matter before Jesus, and Peter embraced this occasion as a fitting opportunity for securing the Master's counsel. Accordingly, Simon Peter broke in on the conversation dealing with the differences between praise and worship, by asking: "Master, James and I are not in accord regarding your teachings having to do with the forgiveness of sin. James claims you teach that the Father forgives us even before we ask him, and I maintain that repentance and confession must precede the forgiveness. Which of us is right? what do you say?"

After a short silence Jesus looked significantly at all four and answered: "My brethren, you err in your opinions because you do not comprehend the nature of those intimate and loving relations between the creature and the Creator, between man and God. You fail to grasp that understanding sympathy which the wise parent entertains for his immature and sometimes erring child. It is indeed doubtful whether intelligent and affectionate parents are ever called upon to forgive an average and normal child. Understanding relationships associated with attitudes of love effectively prevent all those estrangements which later necessitate the readjustment of repentance by the child with forgiveness by the parent.

"A part of every father lives in the child. The father enjoys priority and superiority of understanding in all matters connected with the child-parent relationship. The parent is able to view the immaturity of the child in the light of the more advanced parental maturity, the riper experience of the older partner. With the earthly child and the heavenly Father, the divine parent possesses infinity and divinity of sympathy and capacity for loving understanding. Divine forgiveness is inevitable; it is inherent and inalienable in God's infinite understanding, in his perfect knowledge of all that concerns the mistaken judgment and erroneous choosing of the child. Divine justice is so eternally fair that it unfailingly embodies understanding mercy.

"When a wise man understands the inner impulses of his fellows, he will love them. And when you love your brother, you have already forgiven him. This capacity to understand man's nature and forgive his apparent wrong-doing is Godlike. If you are wise parents, this is the way you will love and understand your children, even forgive them when transient misunder-standing has apparently separated you. The child, being immature and lacking in the fuller understanding of the depth of the child-father relation-ship, must frequently feel a sense of guilty separation from a father's full approval, but the true father is never conscious of any such separation. Sin is an experience of creature consciousness; it is not a part of God's consciousness.

"Your inability or unwillingness to forgive your fellows is the measure of your immaturity, your failure to attain adult sympathy, understanding, and love. You hold grudges and nurse vengefulness in direct proportion to your ignorance of the inner nature and true longings of your children and your fellow beings. Love is the outworking of the divine and inner urge of life. It is founded on understanding, nurtured by unselfish service, and perfected in wisdom."

2. QUESTIONS BY THE JEWISH RULERS

On Monday evening there had been held a council between the Sanhedrin and some fifty additional leaders selected from among the scribes, Pharisees, and the Sadducees. It was the consensus of this meeting that it would be dangerous to arrest Jesus in public because of his hold upon the affections of the common people. It was also the opinion of the majority that a determined effort should be made to discredit him in the eyes of the multitude before he should be arrested and brought to trial. Accordingly, several groups of learned men were designated to be on hand the next morning in the temple to undertake to entrap him with difficult questions and otherwise to seek to embarrass him before the people. At last, the Pharisees, Sadducees, and even the Herodians were all united in this effort to discredit Jesus in the eyes of the Passover multitudes.

Tuesday morning, when Jesus arrived in the temple court and began to teach, he had uttered but few words when a group of the younger students from the academies, who had been rehearsed for this purpose, came forward and by their spokesman addressed Jesus: "Master, we know you are a righteous teacher, and we know that you proclaim the ways of truth, and that you serve only God, for you fear no man, and that you are no respecter of persons. We are only students, and we would know the truth about a matter which troubles us; our difficulty is this: Is it lawful for us to give tribute to Caesar? Shall we give or shall we not give?" Jesus, perceiving their hypocrisy and craftiness, said to them: "Why do you thus come to tempt me? Show me the tribute money, and I will answer you." And when they handed him a denarius, he looked at it and said, "Whose image and superscription does this coin bear?" And when they answered him, "Caesar's," Jesus said, "Render to Caesar the things that are Caesar's and render to God the things that are God's."

When he had thus answered these young scribes and their Herodian accomplices, they withdrew from his presence, and the people, even the Sadducees, enjoyed their discomfiture. Even the youths who had endeavored to entrap him marveled greatly at the unexpected sagacity of the Master's answer.

The previous day the rulers had sought to trip him before the multitude on matters of ecclesiastical authority, and having failed, they now sought to involve him in a damaging discussion of civil authority. Both Pilate and Herod were in Jerusalem at this time, and Jesus' enemies conjectured that, if he would dare to advise against the payment of tribute to Caesar, they could go at once before the Roman authorities and charge him with sedition. On the other hand, if he should advise the payment of tribute in so many words, they rightly calculated that such a pronouncement would greatly wound the national pride of his Jewish hearers, thereby alienating the good will and affection of the multitude.

In all this the enemies of Jesus were defeated since it was a well-known ruling of the Sanhedrin, made for the guidance of the Jews dispersed among the gentile nations, that the "right of coinage carried with it the right to levy taxes." In this manner Jesus avoided their trap. To have answered "No" to their question would have been equivalent to inciting rebellion; to have answered "Yes" would have shocked the deep-rooted nationalist sentiments of that day. The Master did not evade the question; he merely employed the wisdom of making a double reply. Jesus was never evasive, but he was always wise in his dealings with those who sought to harass and destroy him.

3. THE SADDUCEES AND THE RESURRECTION

Before Jesus could get started with his teaching, another group came forward to question him, this time a company of the learned and crafty Sadducees. Their spokesman, drawing near to him, said: "Master, Moses said that if a married man should die, leaving no children, his brother should take the wife and raise up seed for the deceased brother. Now there occurred a case where a certain man who had six brothers died childless; his next brother took his wife but also soon died, leaving no children. Likewise did the second brother take the wife, but he also died leaving no offspring. And so on until all six of the brothers had had her, and all six of them passed on without leaving children. And then, after them all, the woman herself died. Now, what we would like to ask you is this: In the resurrection whose wife will she be since all seven of these brothers had her?"

Jesus knew, and so did the people, that these Sadducees were not sincere in asking this question because it was not likely that such a case would really occur; and besides, this practice of the brothers of a dead man seeking to beget children for him was practically a dead letter at this time among the Jews. Nevertheless, Jesus condescended to reply to their mischievous question. He said: "You all do err in asking such questions because you know neither the Scriptures nor the living power of God. You know that the sons of this world can marry and are given in marriage, but you do not seem to understand that they who are accounted worthy to attain the worlds to come, through the resurrection of the righteous, neither marry nor are given in marriage. Those who experience the resurrection from the dead are more like the angels of heaven, and they never die. These resurrected ones are eternally the sons of God; they are the children of light resurrected into the progress of eternal life. And even your Father Moses understood this, for, in connection with his experiences at the burning bush, he heard the Father say, `I *am* the God of Abraham, the God of Isaac, and the God of Jacob.' And so, along with Moses, do I declare that my Father is not the God of the dead but of the living. In him you all do live, reproduce, and possess your mortal existence."

When Jesus had finished answering these questions, the Sadducees withdrew, and some of the Pharisees so far forgot themselves as to exclaim, "True, true, Master, you have well answered these unbelieving Sadducees." The Sadducees dared not ask him any more questions, and the common people marveled at the wisdom of his teaching.

Jesus appealed only to Moses in his encounter with the Sadducees because this religio-political sect acknowledged the validity of only the five so-called Books of Moses; they did not allow that the teachings of the prophets were admissible as a basis of doctrinal dogmas. The Master in his answer, though positively affirming the fact of the survival of mortal creatures by the technique of the resurrection, did not in any sense speak approvingly of the Pharisaic beliefs in the resurrection of the literal human body. The point Jesus wished to emphasize was: That the Father had said, "I *am* the God of Abraham, Isaac, and Jacob," not I *was* their God.

The Sadducees had thought to subject Jesus to the withering influence of *ridicule*, knowing full well that persecution in public would most certainly create further sympathy for him in the minds of the multitude.

4. THE GREAT COMMANDMENT

Another group of Sadducees had been instructed to ask Jesus entangling questions about angels, but when they beheld the fate of their comrades who had sought to entrap him with questions concerning the resurrection, they very wisely decided to hold their peace; they retired without asking a question. It was the prearranged plan of the confederated Pharisees, scribes, Sadducees, and Herodians to fill up the entire day with these entangling questions, hoping thereby to discredit Jesus before the people and at the same time effectively to prevent his having any time for the proclamation of his disturbing teachings.

Then came forward one of the groups of the Pharisees to ask harassing questions, and the spokesman, signaling to Jesus, said: "Master, I am a lawyer, and I would like to ask you which, in your opinion, is the greatest commandment?" Jesus answered: "There is but one commandment, and that one is the greatest of all, and that commandment is: `Hear O Israel, the Lord our God, the Lord is one; and you shall love the Lord your God with all your heart and with all your soul, with all your mind and with all your strength.' This is the first and great commandment. And the second commandment is like this first; indeed, it springs directly therefrom, and it is: `You shall love your neighbor as yourself.' There is no other commandment greater than these; on these two commandments hang all the law and the prophets."

When the lawyer perceived that Jesus had answered not only in accordance with the highest concept of Jewish religion, but that he had also answered wisely in the sight of the assembled multitude, he thought it the better part of valor openly to commend the Master's reply. Accordingly, he said: "Of a truth, Master, you have well said that God is one and there is none beside him; and that to love him with all the heart, understanding, and strength, and also to love one's neighbor as one's self, is the first and great commandment; and we are agreed that this great commandment is much more to be regarded than all the burnt offerings and sacrifices." When the lawyer answered thus discreetly, Jesus looked down upon him and said, "My friend, I perceive that you are not far from the kingdom of God."

Jesus spoke the truth when he referred to this lawyer as being "not far from the kingdom," for that very night he went out to the Master's camp near Gethsemane, professed faith in the gospel of the kingdom, and was baptized by Josiah, one of the disciples of Abner.

Two or three other groups of the scribes and Pharisees were present and had intended to ask questions, but they were either disarmed by Jesus' answer to the lawyer, or they were deterred by the discomfiture of all who had undertaken to ensnare him. After this no man dared to ask him another question in public.

When no more questions were forthcoming, and as the noon hour was near, Jesus did not resume his teaching but was content merely to ask the Pharisees and their associates a question. Said Jesus: "Since you ask no more questions, I would like to ask you one. What do you think of the Deliverer? That is, whose son is he?" After a brief pause one of the scribes answered, "The Messiah is the son of David." And since Jesus knew that there had been much debate, even among his own disciples, as to whether or not he was the son of David, he asked this further question: "If the Deliverer is indeed the son of David, how is it that, in the Psalm which you accredit to David, he himself, speaking in the spirit, says, `The Lord said to my lord, sit on my right hand until I make your enemies the footstool of your feet.' If David calls him Lord, how then can he be his son?" Although the rulers, the scribes, and the chief priests made no reply to this question, they likewise refrained from asking him any more questions in an effort to entangle him. They never answered this question which Jesus put to them, but after the Master's death they attempted to escape the difficulty by changing the interpretation of this Psalm so as to make it refer to Abraham instead of the Messiah. Others sought to escape the dilemma by disallowing that David was the author of this so-called Messianic Psalm.

A short time back the Pharisees had enjoyed the manner in which the

Sadducees had been silenced by the Master; now the Sadducees were delighted by the failure of the Pharisees; but such rivalry was only momentary; they speedily forgot their time-honored differences in the united effort to stop Jesus' teachings and doings. But throughout all of these experiences the common people heard him gladly.

5. THE INQUIRING GREEKS

About noontime, as Philip was purchasing supplies for the new camp which was that day being established near Gethsemane, he was accosted by a delegation of strangers, a group of believing Greeks from Alexandria, Athens, and Rome, whose spokesman said to the apostle: "You have been pointed out to us by those who know you; so we come to you, Sir, with the request to see Jesus, your Master." Philip was taken by surprise thus to meet these prominent and inquiring Greek gentiles in the market place, and, since Jesus had so explicitly charged all of the twelve not to engage in any public teaching during the Passover week, he was a bit perplexed as to the right way to handle this matter. He was also disconcerted because these men were foreign gentiles. If they had been Jews or near-by and familiar gentiles, he would not have hesitated so markedly. What he did was this: He asked these Greeks to remain right where they were. As he hastened away, they supposed that he went in search of Jesus, but in reality he hurried off to the home of Joseph, where he knew Andrew and the other apostles were at lunch; and calling Andrew out, he explained the purpose of his coming, and then, accompanied by Andrew, he returned to the waiting Greeks.

Since Philip had about finished the purchasing of supplies, he and Andrew returned with the Greeks to the home of Joseph, where Jesus received them; and they sat near while he spoke to his apostles and a number of leading disciples assembled at this luncheon. Said Jesus:

"My Father sent me to this world to reveal his loving-kindness to the children of men, but those to whom I first came have refused to receive me. True, indeed, many of you have believed my gospel for yourselves, but the children of Abraham and their leaders are about to reject me, and in so doing they will reject Him who sent me. I have freely proclaimed the gospel of salvation to this people; I have told them of sonship with joy, liberty, and life more abundant in the spirit. My Father has done many wonderful works among these fear-ridden sons of men. But truly did the Prophet Isaiah refer to this people when he wrote: `Lord, who has believed our teachings? And to whom has the Lord been revealed?' Truly have the leaders of my people deliberately blinded their eyes that they see not, and hardened their hearts lest they believe and be saved. All these years have I sought to heal them of their unbelief that they might be recipients of the Father's eternal salvation. I know that not all have failed me; some of you have indeed believed my message. In this room now are a full score of men who were once members of the Sanhedrin, or who were high in the councils of the nation, albeit even some of you still shrink from open confession of the truth lest they cast you out of the synagogue. Some of you are tempted to love the glory of men more than the glory of God. But I am constrained to show forbearance since I fear for the safety and loyalty of even some of those who have been so long near me, and who have lived so close by my side.

"In this banquet chamber I perceive there are assembled Jews and gentiles in about equal numbers, and I would address you as the first and last of such a group that I may instruct in the affairs of the kingdom before I go to my Father."

These Greeks had been in faithful attendance upon Jesus' teaching in the temple. On Monday evening they had held a conference at the home of Nicodemus, which lasted until the dawn of day, and thirty of them had elected to enter the kingdom.

As Jesus stood before them at this time, he perceived the end of one dispensation and the beginning of another. Turning his attention to the Greeks, the Master said:

"He who believes this gospel, believes not merely in me but in Him who sent me. When you look upon me, you see not only the Son of Man but also Him who sent me. I am the light of the world, and whosoever will believe my teaching shall no longer abide in darkness. If you gentiles will hear me, you shall receive the words of life and shall enter forthwith into the joyous liberty of the truth of sonship with God. If my fellow countrymen, the Jews, choose to reject me and to refuse my teachings, I will not sit in judgment on them, for I came not to judge the world but to offer it salvation. Nevertheless, they who reject me and refuse to receive my teaching shall be brought to judgment in due season by my Father and those whom he has appointed to sit in judgment on such as reject the gift of mercy and the truths of salvation. Remember, all of you, that I speak not of myself, but that I have faithfully declared to you that which the Father commanded I should reveal to the children of men. And these words which the Father directed me to speak to the world are words of divine truth, everlasting mercy, and eternal life.

"But to both Jew and gentile I declare the hour has about come when the Son of Man will be glorified. You well know that, except a grain of wheat falls into the earth and dies, it abides alone; but if it dies in good soil, it springs up again to life and bears much fruit. He who selfishly loves his life stands in danger of losing it; but he who is willing to lay down his life for my sake and the gospel's shall enjoy a more abundant existence on earth and in heaven, life eternal. If you will truly follow me, even after I have gone to my Father, then shall you become my disciples and the sincere servants of your fellow mortals.

"I know my hour is approaching, and I am troubled. I perceive that my people are determined to spurn the kingdom, but I am rejoiced to receive these truth-seeking gentiles who come here today inquiring for the way of light. Nevertheless, my heart aches for my people, and my soul is distraught by that which lies just before me. What shall I say as I look ahead and discern what is about to befall me? Shall I say, Father save me from this awful hour? No! For this very purpose have I come into the world and even to this hour. Rather will I say, and pray that you will join me: Father, glorify your name; your will be done."

When Jesus had thus spoken, the Personalized Adjuster of his indwelling during prebaptismal times appeared before him, and as he paused noticeably, this now mighty spirit of the Father's representation spoke to Jesus of Nazareth, saying: "I have glorified my name in your bestowals many times, and I will glorify it once more."

While the Jews and gentiles here assembled heard no voice, they could not fail to discern that the Master had paused in his speaking while a message came to him from some superhuman source. They all said, every man to the one who was by him, "An angel has spoken to him."

Then Jesus continued to speak: "All this has not happened for my sake but for yours. I know of a certainty that the Father will receive me and accept my mission in your behalf, but it is needful that you be encouraged and be made ready for the fiery trial which is just ahead. Let me assure you that victory shall eventually crown our united efforts to enlighten the world and liberate mankind. The old order is bringing itself to judgment; the Prince of this world I have cast down; and all men shall become free by the light of the spirit which I will pour out upon all flesh after I have ascended to my Father in heaven.

"And now I declare to you that I, if I be lifted up on earth and in your lives, will draw all men to myself and into the fellowship of my Father. You have believed that the Deliverer would abide on earth forever, but I declare that the Son of Man will be rejected by men, and that he will go back to the Father. Only a little while will I be with you; only a little time will the living light be among this darkened generation. Walk while you have this light so that the oncoming darkness and confusion may not overtake you. He who walks in the darkness knows not where he goes; but if you will choose to walk in the light, you shall all indeed become liberated sons of God. And now, all of you, come with me while we go back to the temple and I speak farewell words to the chief priests, the scribes, the Pharisees, the Sadducees, the Herodians, and the benighted rulers of Israel."

Having thus spoken, Jesus led the way over the narrow streets of Jerusalem back to the temple. They had just heard the Master say that this was to be his farewell discourse in the temple, and they followed him in silence and in deep meditation.

PAPER 175
THE LAST TEMPLE DISCOURSE

SHORTLY AFTER TWO o'clock on this Tuesday afternoon, Jesus, accompanied by eleven apostles, Joseph of Arimathea, the thirty Greeks, and certain other disciples, arrived at the temple and began the delivery of his last address in the courts of the sacred edifice. This discourse was intended to be his last appeal to the Jewish people and the final indictment of his vehement enemies and would-be destroyers — the scribes, Pharisees, Sadducees, and the chief rulers of Israel. Throughout the forenoon the various groups had had an opportunity to question Jesus; this afternoon no one asked him a question.

As the Master began to speak, the temple court was quiet and orderly. The money-changers and the merchandisers had not dared again to enter the temple since Jesus and the aroused multitude had driven them out the previous day. Before beginning the discourse, Jesus tenderly looked down upon this audience which was so soon to hear his farewell public address of mercy to mankind coupled with his last denunciation of the false teachers and the bigoted rulers of the Jews.

1. THE DISCOURSE

"This long time have I been with you, going up and down in the land proclaiming the Father's love for the children of men, and many have seen the light and, by faith, have entered into the kingdom of heaven. In connection with this teaching and preaching the Father has done many wonderful works, even to the resurrection of the dead. Many sick and afflicted have been made whole because they believed; but all of this proclamation of truth and healing of disease has not opened the eyes of those who refuse to see light, those who are determined to reject this gospel of the kingdom.

"In every manner consistent with doing my Father's will, I and my apostles have done our utmost to live in peace with our brethren, to conform with the reasonable requirements of the laws of Moses and the traditions of Israel. We have persistently sought peace, but the leaders of Israel will not have it. By rejecting the truth of God and the light of heaven, they are aligning themselves on the side of error and darkness. There cannot be peace between light and darkness, between life and death, between truth and error.

"Many of you have dared to believe my teachings and have already entered into the joy and liberty of the consciousness of sonship with God. And you will bear me witness that I have offered this same sonship with God to all the Jewish nation, even to these very men who now seek my destruction. And even now would my Father receive these blinded teachers and these hypocritical leaders if they would only turn to him and accept his mercy. Even now it is not too late for this people to receive the word of heaven and to welcome the Son of Man.

"My Father has long dealt in mercy with this people. Generation after generation have we sent our prophets to teach and warn them, and generation after generation have they killed these heaven-sent teachers. And now do your willful high priests and stubborn rulers go right on doing this same thing. As Herod brought about the death of John, you likewise now make ready to destroy the Son of Man.

"As long as there is a chance that the Jews will turn to my Father and seek salvation, the God of Abraham, Isaac, and Jacob will keep his hands of mercy outstretched toward you; but when you have once filled up your cup of impenitence, and when once you have finally rejected my Father's mercy, this nation will be left to its own counsels, and it shall speedily come to an inglorious end. This people was called to become the light of the world, to show forth the spiritual glory of a God-knowing race, but you have so far departed from the fulfillment of your divine privileges that your leaders are about to commit the supreme folly of all the ages in that they are on the verge of finally rejecting the gift of God to all men and for all ages — the revelation of the love of the Father in heaven for all his creatures on earth.

"And when you do once reject this revelation of God to man, the kingdom of heaven shall be given to other peoples, to those who will receive it with joy and gladness. In the name of the Father who sent me, I solemnly warn you that you are about to lose your position in the world as the standard-bearers of eternal truth and the custodians of the divine law. I am just now offering you your last chance to come forward and repent, to signify your intention to seek God with all your hearts and to enter, like little children and by sincere faith, into the security and salvation of the kingdom of heaven.

"My Father has long worked for your salvation, and I came down to live among you and personally show you the way. Many of both the Jews and the Samaritans, and even the gentiles, have believed the gospel of the kingdom, but those who should be first to come forward and accept the light of heaven have steadfastly refused to believe the revelation of the truth of God — God revealed in man and man uplifted to God.

"This afternoon my apostles stand here before you in silence, but you shall soon hear their voices ringing out with the call to salvation and with the urge to unite with the heavenly kingdom as the sons of the living God. And now I call to witness these, my disciples and believers in the gospel of the kingdom, as well as the unseen messengers by their sides, that I have once more offered Israel and her rulers deliverance and salvation. But you all behold how the Father's mercy is slighted and how the messengers of truth are rejected. Nevertheless, I admonish you that these scribes and Pharisees still sit in Moses' seat, and therefore, until the Most Highs who rule in the kingdoms of men shall finally overthrow this nation and destroy the place of these rulers, I bid you co-operate with these elders in Israel. You are not required to unite with them in their plans to destroy the Son of Man, but in everything related to the peace of Israel you are to be subject to them. In all these matters do whatsoever they bid you and observe the essentials of the law but do not pattern after their evil works. Remember, this is the sin of these rulers: They say that which is good, but they do it not. You well know how these leaders bind heavy burdens on your shoulders, burdens grievous to bear, and that they will not lift as much as one finger to help you bear these weighty burdens. They have oppressed you with ceremonies and enslaved you by traditions.

"Furthermore, these self-centered rulers delight in doing their good works so that they will be seen by men. They make broad their phylacteries and enlarge the borders of their official robes. They crave the chief places at the feasts and demand the chief seats in the synagogues. They covet laudatory salutations in the market places and desire to be called rabbi by all men. And even while they seek all this honor from men, they secretly lay hold of widows' houses and take profit from the services of the sacred temple. For a pretense these hypocrites make long prayers in public and give alms to attract the notice of their fellows.

"While you should honor your rulers and reverence your teachers, you should call no man Father in the spiritual sense, for there is one who is your Father, even God. Neither should you seek to lord it over your brethren in the kingdom. Remember, I have taught you that he who would be greatest among you should become the server of all. If you presume to exalt yourselves before God, you will certainly be humbled; but whoso truly humbles himself will surely be exalted. Seek in your daily lives, not self-glorification, but the glory of God. Intelligently subordinate your own wills to the will of the Father in heaven.

"Mistake not my words. I bear no malice toward these chief priests and rulers who even now seek my destruction; I have no ill will for these scribes and Pharisees who reject my teachings. I know that many of you believe in secret, and I know you will openly profess your allegiance to the kingdom when my hour comes. But how will your rabbis justify themselves since they profess to talk with God and then presume to reject and destroy him who comes to reveal the Father to the worlds?

"Woe upon you, scribes and Pharisees, hypocrites! You would shut the doors of the kingdom of heaven against sincere men because they happen to be unlearned in the ways of your teaching. You refuse to enter the kingdom and at the same time do everything within your power to prevent all others from entering. You stand with your backs to the doors of salvation and fight with all who would enter therein.

"Woe upon you, scribes and Pharisees, hypocrites that you are! for you do indeed encompass land and sea to make one proselyte, and when you have succeeded, you are not content until you have made him twofold worse than he was as a child of the heathen.

"Woe upon you, chief priests and rulers who lay hold of the property of the poor and demand heavy dues of those who would serve God as they think Moses ordained! You who refuse to show mercy, can you hope for mercy in the worlds to come?

"Woe upon you, false teachers, blind guides! What can be expected of a nation when the blind lead the blind? They both shall stumble into the pit of destruction.

"Woe upon you who dissimulate when you take an oath! You are tricksters since you teach that a man may swear by the temple and break his oath, but that whoso swears by the gold in the temple must remain bound. You are all fools and blind. You are not even consistent in your dishonesty, for which is the greater, the gold or the temple which has supposedly sanctified the gold? You also teach that, if a man swears by the altar, it is nothing; but that, if one swears by the gift that is upon the altar, then shall he be held as a debtor. Again are you blind to the truth, for which is the greater, the gift or the altar which sanctifies the gift? How can you justify such hypocrisy and dishonesty in the sight of the God of heaven?

"Woe upon you, scribes and Pharisees and all other hypocrites who make sure that they tithe mint, anise, and cumin and at the same time disregard the weightier matters of the law — faith, mercy, and judgment! Within reason, the one you ought to have done but not to have left the other undone. You are truly blind guides and dumb teachers; you strain out the gnat and swallow the camel.

"Woe upon you, scribes, Pharisees, and hypocrites! for you are scrupulous to cleanse the outside of the cup and the platter, but within there remains the filth of extortion, excesses, and deception. You are spiritually blind. Do you not recognize how much better it would be first to cleanse the inside of the cup, and then that which spills over would of itself cleanse the outside? You wicked reprobates! you make the outward performances of your religion to conform with the letter of your interpretation of Moses' law while your souls are steeped in iniquity and filled with murder.

"Woe upon all of you who reject truth and spurn mercy! Many of you are like whited sepulchres, which outwardly appear beautiful but within are full of dead men's bones and all sorts of uncleanness. Even so do you who knowingly reject the counsel of God appear outwardly to men as holy and righteous, but inwardly your hearts are filled with hypocrisy and iniquity.

"Woe upon you, false guides of a nation! Over yonder have you built a monument to the martyred prophets of old, while you plot to destroy Him of whom they spoke. You garnish the tombs of the righteous and flatter yourselves that, had you lived in the days of your fathers, you would not have killed the prophets; and then in the face of such self-righteous thinking you make ready to slay him of whom the prophets spoke, the Son of Man. Inasmuch as you do these things, are you witness to yourselves that you are the wicked sons of them who slew the prophets. Go on, then, and fill up the cup of your condemnation to the full!

"Woe upon you, children of evil! John did truly call you the offspring of vipers, and I ask how can you escape the judgment that John pronounced upon you?

"But even now I offer you in my Father's name mercy and forgiveness; even now I proffer the loving hand of eternal fellowship. My Father has sent you the wise men and the prophets; some you have persecuted and others you have killed. Then appeared John proclaiming the coming of the Son of Man, and him you destroyed after many had believed his teaching. And now you make ready to shed more innocent blood. Do you not comprehend that a terrible day of reckoning will come when the Judge of all the earth shall require of this people an accounting for the way they have rejected, persecuted, and destroyed these messengers of heaven? Do you not understand that you must account for all of this righteous blood, from the first prophet killed down to the times of Zechariah, who was slain between the sanctuary and the altar? And if you go on in your evil ways, this accounting may be required of this very generation.

"O Jerusalem and the children of Abraham, you who have stoned the prophets and killed the teachers that were sent to you, even now would I gather your children together as a hen gathers her chickens under her wings, but you will not!

"And now I take leave of you. You have heard my message and have made your decision. Those who have believed my gospel are even now safe within the kingdom of God. To you who have chosen to reject the gift of God, I say that you will no more see me teaching in the temple. My work for you is done. Behold, I now go forth with my children, and your house is left to you desolate!"

And then the Master beckoned his followers to depart from the temple.

2. STATUS OF INDIVIDUAL JEWS

The fact that the spiritual leaders and the religious teachers of the Jewish nation onetime rejected the teachings of Jesus and conspired to bring about his cruel death, does not in any manner affect the status of any individual Jew in his standing before God. And it should not cause those who profess to be followers of the Christ to be prejudiced against the Jew as a fellow mortal. The Jews, as a nation, as a sociopolitical group, paid in full the terrible price of rejecting the Prince of Peace. Long since they ceased to be the spiritual torchbearers of divine truth to the races of mankind, but this constitutes no valid reason why the individual descendants of these long-ago Jews should be made to suffer the persecutions which have been visited upon them by intolerant, unworthy, and bigoted professed followers of Jesus of Nazareth, who was, himself, a Jew by natural birth.

Many times has this unreasoning and un-Christlike hatred and persecution of modern Jews terminated in the suffering and death of some innocent and unoffending Jewish individual whose very ancestors, in the times of Jesus, heartily accepted his gospel and presently died unflinchingly for that truth which they so wholeheartedly believed. What a shudder of horror passes over the onlooking celestial beings as they behold the professed followers of Jesus indulge themselves in persecuting, harassing, and even murdering the later-day descendants of Peter, Philip, Matthew, and others of the Palestinian Jews who so gloriously yielded up their lives as the first martyrs of the gospel of the heavenly kingdom!

How cruel and unreasoning to compel innocent children to suffer for the sins of their progenitors, misdeeds of which they are wholly ignorant, and for which they could in no way be responsible! And to do such wicked deeds in the name of one who taught his disciples to love even their enemies! It has become necessary, in this recital of the life of Jesus, to portray the manner in which certain of his fellow Jews rejected him and conspired to bring about his ignominious death; but we would warn all who read this narrative that the presentation of such a historical recital in no way justifies the unjust hatred, nor condones the unfair attitude of mind, which so many professed Christians have maintained toward individual Jews for many centuries. Kingdom believers, those who follow the teachings of Jesus, must cease to mistreat the individual Jew as one who is guilty of the rejection and crucifixion of Jesus. The Father and his Creator Son have never ceased to love the Jews. God is no respecter of persons, and salvation is for the Jew as well as for the gentile.

3. THE FATEFUL SANHEDRIN MEETING

At eight o'clock on this Tuesday evening the fateful meeting of the Sanhedrin was called to order. On many previous occasions had this supreme court of the Jewish nation informally decreed the death of Jesus. Many times had this august ruling body determined to put a stop to his work, but never before had they resolved to place him under arrest and to bring about his death at any and all costs. It was just before midnight on this Tuesday, April 4, A.D. 30, that the Sanhedrin, as then constituted, officially and *unanimously* voted to impose the death sentence upon both Jesus and Lazarus. This was the answer to the Master's last appeal to the rulers of the Jews which he had made in the temple only a few hours before, and it represented their reaction of bitter resentment toward Jesus' last and vigorous indictment of these same chief priests and impenitent Sadducees and Pharisees. The passing of death sentence (even before his trial) upon the Son of God was the Sanhedrin's reply to the last offer of heavenly mercy ever to be extended to the Jewish nation, as such.

From this time on the Jews were left to finish their brief and short lease of national life wholly in accordance with their purely human status among the nations of Urantia. Israel had repudiated the Son of the God who made a covenant with Abraham, and the plan to make the children of Abraham the light-bearers of truth to the world had been shattered. The divine covenant had been abrogated, and the end of the Hebrew nation drew on apace.

The officers of the Sanhedrin were given the orders for Jesus' arrest early the next morning, but with instructions that he must not be apprehended in public. They were told to plan to take him in secret, preferably suddenly and at night. Understanding that he might not return that day (Wednesday) to teach in the temple, they instructed these officers of the Sanhedrin to "bring him before the high Jewish court sometime before midnight on Thursday."

4. THE SITUATION IN JERUSALEM

At the conclusion of Jesus' last discourse in the temple, the apostles once more were left in confusion and consternation. Before the Master began his terrible denunciation of the Jewish rulers, Judas had returned to the temple, so that all twelve heard this latter half of Jesus' last discourse in the temple. It is unfortunate that Judas Iscariot could not have heard the first and mercy-proffering half of this farewell address. He did not hear this last offer of mercy to the Jewish rulers because he was still in conference with a certain group of Sadducean relatives and friends with whom he had lunched, and with whom he was conferring as to the most fitting manner of dissociating himself from Jesus and his fellow apostles. It was while listening to the Master's final indictment of the Jewish leaders and rulers that Judas finally and fully made up his mind to forsake the gospel movement and wash his hands of the whole enterprise. Nevertheless, he left the temple in company with the twelve, went with them to Mount Olivet, where, with his fellow apostles, he listened to that fateful discourse on the destruction of Jerusalem and the end of the Jewish nation, and remained with them that Tuesday night at the new camp near Gethsemane.

The multitude who heard Jesus swing from his merciful appeal to the Jewish leaders into that sudden and scathing rebuke which bordered on ruthless denunciation, were stunned and bewildered. That night, while the Sanhedrin sat in death judgment upon Jesus, and while the Master sat with his apostles and certain of his disciples out on the Mount of Olives foretelling the death of the Jewish nation, all Jerusalem was given over to the serious and suppressed discussion of just one question: "What will they do with Jesus?"

At the home of Nicodemus more than thirty prominent Jews who were secret believers in the kingdom met and debated what course they would pursue in case an open break with the Sanhedrin should come. All present agreed that they would make open acknowledgment of their allegiance to the Master in the very hour they should hear of his arrest. And that is just what they did.

The Sadducees, who now controlled and dominated the Sanhedrin, were desirous of making away with Jesus for the following reasons:

1. They feared that the increased popular favor with which the multitude regarded him threatened to endanger the existence of the Jewish nation by possible involvement with the Roman authorities.

2. His zeal for temple reform struck directly at their revenues; the cleansing of the temple affected their pocketbooks.

3. They felt themselves responsible for the preservation of social order, and they feared the consequences of the further spread of Jesus' strange and new doctrine of the brotherhood of man.

The Pharisees had different motives for wanting to see Jesus put to death. They feared him because:

1. He was arrayed in telling opposition to their traditional hold upon the people. The Pharisees were ultraconservative, and they bitterly resented these supposedly radical attacks upon their vested prestige as religious teachers.

2. They held that Jesus was a lawbreaker; that he had shown utter disregard for the Sabbath and numerous other legal and ceremonial requirements.

3. They charged him with blasphemy because he alluded to God as his Father.

4. And now were they thoroughly angry with him because of his last discourse of bitter denunciation which he had this day delivered in the temple as the concluding portion of his farewell address.

The Sanhedrin, having formally decreed the death of Jesus and having issued orders for his arrest, adjourned on this Tuesday near midnight, after appointing to meet at ten o'clock the next morning at the home of Caiaphas the high priest for the purpose of formulating the charges on which Jesus should be brought to trial.

A small group of the Sadducees had actually proposed to dispose of Jesus by assassination, but the Pharisees utterly refused to countenance such a procedure.

And this was the situation in Jerusalem and among men on this eventful day while a vast concourse of celestial beings hovered over this momentous scene on earth, anxious to do something to assist their beloved Sovereign but powerless to act because they were effectively restrained by their commanding superiors.

PAPER 176
TUESDAY EVENING ON MOUNT OLIVET

THIS TUESDAY AFTERNOON, as Jesus and the apostles passed out of the temple on their way to the Gethsemane camp, Matthew, calling attention to the temple construction, said: "Master, observe what manner of buildings these are. See the massive stones and the beautiful adornment; can it be that these buildings are to be destroyed?" As they went on toward Olivet, Jesus said: "You see these stones and this massive temple; verily, verily, I say to you: In the days soon to come there shall not be left one stone upon another. They shall all be thrown down." These remarks depicting the destruction of the sacred temple aroused the curiosity of the apostles as they walked along behind the Master; they could conceive of no event short of the end of the world which would occasion the destruction of the temple.

In order to avoid the crowds passing along the Kidron valley toward Gethsemane, Jesus and his associates were minded to climb up the western slope of Olivet for a short distance and then follow a trail over to their private camp near Gethsemane located a short distance above the public camping ground. As they turned to leave the road leading on to Bethany, they observed the temple, glorified by the rays of the setting sun; and while they tarried on the mount, they saw the lights of the city appear and beheld the beauty of the illuminated temple; and there, under the mellow light of the full moon, Jesus and the twelve sat down. The Master talked with them, and presently Nathaniel asked this question: "Tell us, Master, how shall we know when these events are about to come to pass?"

1. THE DESTRUCTION OF JERUSALEM

In answering Nathaniel's question, Jesus said: "Yes, I will tell you about the times when this people shall have filled up the cup of their iniquity; when justice shall swiftly descend upon this city of our fathers. I am about to leave you; I go to the Father. After I leave you, take heed that no man deceive you, for many will come as deliverers and will lead many astray. When you hear of wars and rumors of wars, be not troubled, for though all these things will happen, the end of Jerusalem is not yet at hand. You should not be perturbed by famines or earthquakes; neither should you be concerned when you are delivered up to the civil authorities and are persecuted for the sake of the gospel. You will be thrown out of the synagogue and put in prison for my sake, and some of you will be killed. When you are brought up before governors and rulers, it shall be for a testimony of your faith and to show your steadfastness in the gospel of the kingdom. And when you stand before judges, be not anxious beforehand as to what you should say, for the spirit will teach you in that very hour what you should answer your adversaries. In these days of travail, even your own kinsfolk, under the leadership of those who have rejected the Son of Man, will deliver you up to prison and death. For a time you may be hated by all men for my sake, but even in these persecutions I will not forsake you; my spirit will not desert you. Be patient! doubt not that this gospel of the kingdom will triumph over all enemies and, eventually, be proclaimed to all nations."

Jesus paused while he looked down upon the city. The Master realized that the rejection of the spiritual concept of the Messiah, the determination to cling persistently and blindly to the material mission of the expected deliverer, would presently bring the Jews in direct conflict with the powerful Roman armies, and that such a contest could only result in the final and complete overthrow of the Jewish nation. When his people rejected his spiritual bestowal and refused to receive the light of heaven as it so mercifully shone upon them, they thereby sealed their doom as an independent people with a special spiritual mission on earth. Even the Jewish leaders subsequently recognized that it was this secular idea of the Messiah which directly led to the turbulence which eventually brought about their destruction.

Since Jerusalem was to become the cradle of the early gospel movement, Jesus did not want its teachers and preachers to perish in the terrible overthrow of the Jewish people in connection with the destruction of Jerusalem; wherefore did he give these instructions to his followers. Jesus was much concerned lest some of his disciples become involved in these soon-coming revolts and so perish in the downfall of Jerusalem.

Then Andrew inquired: "But, Master, if the Holy City and the temple are to be destroyed, and if you are not here to direct us, when should we forsake Jerusalem?" Said Jesus: "You may remain in the city after I have gone, even through these times of travail and bitter persecution, but when you finally see Jerusalem being encompassed by the Roman armies after the revolt of the false prophets, then will you know that her desolation is at hand; then must you flee to the mountains. Let none who are in the city and around about tarry to save aught, neither let those who are outside dare to enter therein. There will be great tribulation, for these will be the days of gentile vengeance. And after you have deserted the city, this disobedient people will fall by the edge of the sword and will be led captive into all nations; and so shall Jerusalem be trodden down by the gentiles. In the meantime, I warn you, be not deceived. If any man comes to you, saying, `Behold, here is the Deliverer,' or `Behold, there is he,' believe it not, for many false teachers will arise and many will be led astray; but you should not be deceived, for I have told you all this beforehand."

The apostles sat in silence in the moonlight for a considerable time while these astounding predictions of the Master sank into their bewildered minds. And it was in conformity with this very warning that practically the entire group of believers and disciples fled from Jerusalem upon the first appearance of the Roman troops, finding a safe shelter in Pella to the north.

Even after this explicit warning, many of Jesus' followers interpreted these predictions as referring to the changes which would obviously occur in Jerusalem when the reappearing of the Messiah would result in the establishment of the New Jerusalem and in the enlargement of the city to become the world's capital. In their minds these Jews were determined to connect the destruction of the temple with the "end of the world." They believed this New Jerusalem would fill all Palestine; that the end of the world would be followed by the immediate appearance of the "new heavens and the new earth." And so it was not strange that Peter should say: "Master, we know that all things will pass away when the new heavens and the new earth appear, but how shall we know when you will return to bring all this about?"

When Jesus heard this, he was thoughtful for some time and then said: "You ever err since you always try to attach the new teaching to the old; you are determined to misunderstand all my teaching; you insist on interpreting the gospel in accordance with your established beliefs. Nevertheless, I will try to enlighten you."

2. THE MASTER'S SECOND COMING

On several occasions Jesus had made statements which led his hearers to infer that, while he intended presently to leave this world, he would most certainly return to consummate the work of the heavenly kingdom. As the conviction grew on his followers that he was going to leave them, and after he had departed from this world, it was only natural for all believers to lay fast hold upon these promises to return. The doctrine of the second coming of Christ thus became early incorporated into the teachings of the Christians, and almost every subsequent generation of disciples has devoutly believed this truth and has confidently looked forward to his sometime coming.

If they were to part with their Master and Teacher, how much more did these first disciples and the apostles grasp at this promise to return, and they lost no time in associating the predicted destruction of Jerusalem with this promised second coming. And they continued thus to interpret his words notwithstanding that, throughout this evening of instruction on Mount Olivet, the Master took particular pains to prevent just such a mistake.

In further answer to Peter's question, Jesus said: "Why do you still look for the Son of Man to sit upon the throne of David and expect that the material dreams of the Jews will be fulfilled? Have I not told you all these years that my kingdom is not of this world? The things which you now look down upon are coming to an end, but this will be a new beginning out of which the gospel of the kingdom will go to all the world and this salvation will spread to all peoples. And when the kingdom shall have come to its full fruition, be assured that the Father in heaven will not fail to visit you with an enlarged revelation of truth and an enhanced demonstration of righteousness, even as he has already bestowed upon this world him who became the prince of darkness, and then Adam, who was followed by Melchizedek, and in these days, the Son of Man. And so will my Father continue to manifest his mercy and show forth his love, even to this dark and evil world. So also will I, after my Father has invested me with all power and authority, continue to follow your fortunes and to guide in the affairs of the kingdom by the presence of my spirit, who shall shortly be poured out upon all flesh. Even though I shall thus be present with you in spirit, I also promise that I will sometime return to this world, where I have lived this life in the flesh and achieved the experience of simultaneously revealing God to man and leading man to God. Very soon must I leave you and take up the work the Father has intrusted to my hands, but be of good courage, for I will sometime return. In the meantime, my Spirit of the Truth of a universe shall comfort and guide you.

"You behold me now in weakness and in the flesh, but when I return, it shall be with power and in the spirit. The eye of flesh beholds the Son of Man in the flesh, but only the eye of the spirit will behold the Son of Man glorified by the Father and appearing on earth in his own name.

"But the times of the reappearing of the Son of Man are known only in the councils of Paradise; not even the angels of heaven know when this will occur. However, you should understand that, when this gospel of the kingdom shall have been proclaimed to all the world for the salvation of all peoples, and when the fullness of the age has come to pass, the Father will send you another dispensational bestowal, or else the Son of Man will return to adjudge the age.

"And now concerning the travail of Jerusalem, about which I have spoken to you, even this generation will not pass away until my words are fulfilled; but concerning the times of the coming again of the Son of Man, no one in heaven or on earth may presume to speak. But you should be wise regarding the ripening of an age; you should be alert to discern the signs of the times. You know when the fig tree shows its tender branches and puts forth its leaves that summer is near. Likewise, when the world has passed through the long winter of material-mindedness and you discern the coming of the spiritual springtime of a new dispensation, should you know that the summertime of a new visitation draws near.

"But what is the significance of this teaching having to do with the coming of the Sons of God? Do you not perceive that, when each of you is called to lay down his life struggle and pass through the portal of death, you stand in the immediate presence of judgment, and that you are face to face with the facts of a new dispensation of service in the eternal plan of the infinite Father? What the whole world must face as a literal fact at the end of an age, you, as individuals, must each most certainly face as a personal experience when you reach the end of your natural life and thereby pass on to be confronted with the conditions and demands inherent in the next revelation of the eternal progression of the Father's kingdom."

Of all the discourses which the Master gave his apostles, none ever became so confused in their minds as this one, given this Tuesday evening on the Mount of Olives, regarding the twofold subject of the destruction of Jerusalem and his own second coming. There was, therefore, little agreement between the subsequent written accounts based on the memories of what the Master said on this extraordinary occasion. Consequently, when the records were left blank concerning much that was said that Tuesday evening, there grew up many traditions; and very early in the second century a Jewish apocalyptic about the Messiah written by one Selta, who was attached to the court of the Emperor Caligula, was bodily copied into the Matthew Gospel and subsequently added (in part) to the Mark and Luke records. It was in these writings of Selta that the parable of the ten virgins appeared. No part of the gospel record ever suffered such confusing misconstruction as this evening's teaching. But the Apostle John never became thus confused.

As these thirteen men resumed their journey toward the camp, they were speechless and under great emotional tension. Judas had finally confirmed his decision to abandon his associates. It was a late hour when David Zebedee, John Mark, and a number of the leading disciples welcomed Jesus and the twelve to the new camp, but the apostles did not want to sleep; they wanted to know more about the destruction of Jerusalem, the Master's departure, and the end of the world.

3. LATER DISCUSSION AT THE CAMP

As they gathered about the campfire, some twenty of them, Thomas asked: "Since you are to return to finish the work of the kingdom, what should be our attitude while you are away on the Father's business?" As Jesus looked them over by the firelight, he answered:

"And even you, Thomas, fail to comprehend what I have been saying. Have I not all this time taught you that your connection with the kingdom is spiritual and individual, wholly a matter of personal experience in the spirit by the faith-realization that you are a son of God? What more shall I say? The downfall of nations, the crash of empires, the destruction of the unbelieving Jews, the end of an age, even the end of the world, what have these things to do with one who believes this gospel, and who has established his life in the surety of the eternal kingdom? You who are God-knowing and gospel-believing have already received the assurances of eternal life. Since your lives have been lived in the spirit and for the Father, nothing can be of serious concern to you. Kingdom builders, the accredited citizens of the heavenly worlds, are not to be disturbed by temporal upheavals or perturbed by terrestrial cataclysms. What does it matter to you who believe this gospel of the kingdom if nations overturn, the age ends, or all things visible crash, since you know that your life is the gift of the Son, and that it is eternally secure in the Father? Having lived the temporal life by faith and having yielded the fruits of the spirit as the righteousness of loving service for your fellows, you can confidently look forward to the next step in the eternal career with the same survival faith that has carried you through your first and earthly adventure in sonship with God.

"Each generation of believers should carry on their work, in view of the possible return of the Son of Man, exactly as each individual believer carries forward his lifework in view of inevitable and ever-impending natural death. When you have by faith once established yourself as a son of God, nothing else matters as regards the surety of survival. But make no mistake! this survival faith is a living faith, and it increasingly manifests the fruits of that divine spirit which first inspired it in the human heart. That you have once accepted sonship in the heavenly kingdom will not save you in the face of the knowing and persistent rejection of those truths which have to do with the progressive spiritual fruit-bearing of the sons of God in the flesh. You who have been with me in the Father's business on earth can even now desert the kingdom if you find that you love not the way of the Father's service for mankind.

"As individuals, and as a generation of believers, hear me while I speak a parable: There was a certain great man who, before starting out on a long journey to another country, called all his trusted servants before him and delivered into their hands all his goods. To one he gave five talents, to another two, and to another one. And so on down through the entire group of honored stewards, to each he intrusted his goods according to their several abilities; and then he set out on his journey. When their lord had departed, his servants set themselves at work to gain profits from the wealth intrusted to them. Immediately he who had received five talents began to trade with them and very soon had made a profit of another five talents. In like manner he who had received two talents soon had gained two more. And so did all of these servants make gains for their master except he who received but one talent. He went away by himself and dug a hole in the earth where he hid his lord's money. Presently the lord of those servants unexpectedly returned and called upon his stewards for a reckoning. And when they had all been called before their master, he who had received the five talents came forward with the money which had been intrusted to him and brought five additional talents, saying, `Lord, you gave me five talents to invest, and I am glad to present five other talents as my gain.' And then his lord said to him: `Well done, good and faithful servant, you have been faithful over a few things; I will now set you as steward over many; enter forthwith into the joy of your lord.' And then he who had received the two talents came forward, saying: `Lord, you delivered into my hands two talents; behold, I have gained these other two talents.' And his lord then said to him: `Well done, good and faithful steward; you also have been faithful over a few things, and I will now set you over many; enter you into the joy of your lord.'

And then there came to the accounting he who had received the one talent. This servant came forward, saying, `Lord, I knew you and realized that you were a shrewd man in that you expected gains where you had not personally labored; therefore was I afraid to risk aught of that which was intrusted to me. I safely hid your talent in the earth; here it is; you now have what belongs to you.' But his lord answered: `You are an indolent and slothful steward. By your own words you confess that you knew I would require of you an accounting with reasonable profit, such as your diligent fellow servants have this day rendered. Knowing this, you ought, therefore, to have at least put my money into the hands of the bankers that on my return I might have received my own with interest.' And then to the chief steward this lord said: `Take away this one talent from this unprofitable servant and give it to him who has the ten talents.'

"To every one who has, more shall be given, and he shall have abundance; but from him who has not, even that which he has shall be taken away. You cannot stand still in the affairs of the eternal kingdom. My Father requires all his children to grow in grace and in a knowledge of the truth. You who know these truths must yield the increase of the fruits of the spirit and manifest a growing devotion to the unselfish service of your fellow servants. And remember that, inasmuch as you minister to one of the least of my brethren, you have done this service to me.

"And so should you go about the work of the Father's business, now and henceforth, even forevermore. Carry on until I come. In faithfulness do that which is intrusted to you, and thereby shall you be ready for the reckoning call of death. And having thus lived for the glory of the Father and the satisfaction of the Son, you shall enter with joy and exceedingly great pleasure into the eternal service of the everlasting kingdom."

Truth is living; the Spirit of Truth is ever leading the children of light into new realms of spiritual reality and divine service. You are not given truth to crystallize into settled, safe, and honored forms. Your revelation of truth must be so enhanced by passing through your personal experience that new beauty and actual spiritual gains will be disclosed to all who behold your spiritual fruits and in consequence thereof are led to glorify the Father who is in heaven. Only those faithful servants who thus grow in the knowledge of the truth, and who thereby develop the capacity for divine appreciation of spiritual realities, can ever hope to "enter fully into the joy of their Lord." What a sorry sight for successive generations of the professed followers of Jesus to say, regarding their stewardship of divine truth: "Here, Master, is the truth you committed to us a hundred or a thousand years ago. We have lost nothing; we have faithfully preserved all you gave us; we have allowed no changes to be made in that which you taught us; here is the truth you gave us." But such a plea concerning spiritual indolence will not justify the barren steward of truth in the presence of the Master. In accordance with the truth committed to your hands will the Master of truth require a reckoning.

In the next world you will be asked to give an account of the endowments and stewardships of this world. Whether inherent talents are few or many, a just and merciful reckoning must be faced. If endowments are used only in selfish pursuits and no thought is bestowed upon the higher duty of obtaining increased yield of the fruits of the spirit, as they are manifested in the ever-expanding service of men and the worship of God, such selfish stewards must accept the consequences of their deliberate choosing.

And how much like all selfish mortals was this unfaithful servant with the one talent in that he blamed his slothfulness directly upon his lord. How prone is man, when he is confronted with the failures of his own making, to put the blame upon others, oftentimes upon those who least deserve it!

Said Jesus that night as they went to their rest: "Freely have you received; therefore freely should you give of the truth of heaven, and in the giving will this truth multiply and show forth the increasing light of saving grace, even as you minister it."

4. THE RETURN OF MICHAEL

Of all the Master's teachings no one phase has been so misunderstood as his promise sometime to come back in person to this world. It is not strange that Michael should be interested in sometime returning to the planet whereon he experienced his seventh and last bestowal, as a mortal of the realm. It is only natural to believe that Jesus of Nazareth, now sovereign ruler of a vast universe, would be interested in coming back, not only once but even many times, to the world whereon he lived such a unique life and finally won for himself the Father's unlimited bestowal of universe power and authority. Urantia will eternally be one of the seven nativity spheres of Michael in the winning of universe sovereignty.

Jesus did, on numerous occasions and to many individuals, declare his intention of returning to this world. As his followers awakened to the fact that their Master was not going to function as a temporal deliverer, and as they listened to his predictions of the overthrow of Jerusalem and the downfall of the Jewish nation, they most naturally began to associate his promised return with these catastrophic events. But when the Roman armies leveled the walls of Jerusalem, destroyed the temple, and dispersed the Judean Jews, and still the Master did not reveal himself in power and glory, his followers began the formulation of that belief which eventually associated the second coming of Christ with the end of the age, even with the end of the world.

Jesus promised to do two things after he had ascended to the Father, and after all power in heaven and on earth had been placed in his hands. He promised, first, to send into the world, and in his stead, another teacher, the Spirit of Truth; and this he did on the day of Pentecost. Second, he most certainly promised his followers that he would sometime personally return to this world. But he did not say how, where, or when he would revisit this planet of his bestowal experience in the flesh. On one occasion he intimated that, whereas the eye of flesh had beheld him when he lived here in the flesh, on his return (at least on one of his possible visits) he would be discerned only by the eye of spiritual faith.

Many of us are inclined to believe that Jesus will return to Urantia many times during the ages to come. We do not have his specific promise to make these plural visits, but it seems most probable that he who carries among his universe titles that of Planetary Prince of Urantia will many times visit the world whose conquest conferred such a unique title upon him.

We most positively believe that Michael will again come in person to Urantia, but we have not the slightest idea as to when or in what manner he may choose to come. Will his second advent on earth be timed to occur in connection with the terminal judgment of this present age, either with or without the associated appearance of a Magisterial Son? Will he come in connection with the termination of some subsequent Urantian age? Will he come unannounced and as an isolated event? We do not know. Only one thing we are certain of, that is, when he does return, all the world will likely know about it, for he must come as the supreme ruler of a universe and not as the obscure babe of Bethlehem. But if every eye is to behold him, and if only spiritual eyes are to discern his presence, then must his advent be long deferred.

You would do well, therefore, to disassociate the Master's personal return to earth from any and all set events or settled epochs. We are sure of only one thing: He has promised to come back. We have no idea as to when he will fulfill this promise or in what connection. As far as we know, he may appear on earth any day, and he may not come until age after age has passed and been duly adjudicated by his associated Sons of the Paradise corps.

The second advent of Michael on earth is an event of tremendous sentimental value to both midwayers and humans; but otherwise it is of no immediate moment to midwayers and of no more practical importance to human beings than the common event of natural death, which so suddenly precipitates mortal man into the immediate grasp of that succession of universe events which leads directly to the presence of this same Jesus, the sovereign ruler of our universe. The children of light are all destined to see him, and it is of no serious concern whether we go to him or whether he should chance first to come to us. Be you therefore ever ready to welcome him on earth as he stands ready to welcome you in heaven. We confidently look for his glorious appearing, even for repeated comings, but we are wholly ignorant as to how, when, or in what connection he is destined to appear.

PAPER 177
WEDNESDAY, THE REST DAY

WHEN THE WORK of teaching the people did not press them, it was the custom of Jesus and his apostles to rest from their labors each Wednesday. On this particular Wednesday they ate breakfast somewhat later than usual, and the camp was pervaded by an ominous silence; little was said during the first half of this morning meal. At last Jesus spoke: "I desire that you rest today. Take time to think over all that has happened since we came to Jerusalem and meditate on what is just ahead, of which I have plainly told you. Make sure that the truth abides in your lives, and that you daily grow in grace."

After breakfast the Master informed Andrew that he intended to be absent for the day and suggested that the apostles be permitted to spend the time in accordance with their own choosing, except that under no circumstances should they go within the gates of Jerusalem.

When Jesus made ready to go into the hills alone, David Zebedee accosted him, saying: "You well know, Master, that the Pharisees and rulers seek to destroy you, and yet you make ready to go alone into the hills. To do this is folly; I will therefore send three men with you well prepared to see that no harm befalls you." Jesus looked over the three well-armed and stalwart Galileans and said to David: "You mean well, but you err in that you fail to understand that the Son of Man needs no one to defend him. No man will lay hands on me until that hour when I am ready to lay down my life in conformity to my Father's will. These men may not accompany me. I desire to go alone, that I may commune with the Father."

Upon hearing these words, David and his armed guards withdrew; but as Jesus started off alone, John Mark came forward with a small basket containing food and water and suggested that, if he intended to be away all day, he might find himself hungry. The Master smiled on John and reached down to take the basket.

1. ONE DAY ALONE WITH GOD

As Jesus was about to take the lunch basket from John's hand, the young man ventured to say: "But, Master, you may set the basket down while you turn aside to pray and go on without it. Besides, if I should go along to carry the lunch, you would be more free to worship, and I will surely be silent. I will ask no questions and will stay by the basket when you go apart by yourself to pray."

While making this speech, the temerity of which astonished some of the near-by listeners, John had made bold to hold on to the basket. There they stood, both John and Jesus holding the basket. Presently the Master let go and, looking down on the lad, said: "Since with all your heart you crave to go with me, it shall not be denied you. We will go off by ourselves and have a good visit. You may ask me any question that arises in your heart, and we will comfort and console each other. You may start out carrying the lunch, and when you grow weary, I will help you. Follow on with me."

Jesus did not return to the camp that evening until after sunset. The Master spent this last day of quiet on earth visiting with this truth-hungry youth and talking with his Paradise Father. This event has become known on high as "the day which a young man spent with God in the hills." Forever this occasion exemplifies the willingness of the Creator to fellowship the creature. Even a youth, if the desire of the heart is really supreme, can command the attention and enjoy the loving companionship of the God of a universe, actually experience the unforgettable ecstasy of being alone with God in the hills, and for a whole day. And such was the unique experience of John Mark on this Wednesday in the hills of Judea.

Jesus visited much with John, talking freely about the affairs of this world and the next. John told Jesus how much he regretted that he had not been old enough to be one of the apostles and expressed his great appreciation that he had been permitted to follow on with them since their first preaching at the Jordan ford near Jericho, except for the trip to Phoenicia. Jesus warned the lad not to become discouraged by impending events and assured him he would live to become a mighty messenger of the kingdom.

John Mark was thrilled by the memory of this day with Jesus in the hills, but he never forgot the Master's final admonition, spoken just as they were about to return to the Gethsemane camp, when he said: "Well, John, we have had a good visit, a real day of rest, but see to it that you tell no man the things which I told you." And John Mark never did reveal anything that transpired on this day which he spent with Jesus in the hills.

Throughout the few remaining hours of Jesus' earth life John Mark never permitted the Master for long to get out of his sight. Always was the lad in hiding near by; he slept only when Jesus slept.

2. EARLY HOME LIFE

In the course of this day's visiting with John Mark, Jesus spent considerable time comparing their early childhood and later boyhood experiences. Although John's parents possessed more of this world's goods than had Jesus' parents, there was much experience in their boyhood which was very similar. Jesus said many things which helped John better to understand his parents and other members of his family. When the lad asked the Master how he could know that he would turn out to be a "mighty messenger of the kingdom," Jesus said:

"I know you will prove loyal to the gospel of the kingdom because I can depend upon your present faith and love when these qualities are grounded upon such an early training as has been your portion at home. You are the product of a home where the parents bear each other a sincere affection, and therefore you have not been overloved so as injuriously to exalt your concept of self-importance. Neither has your personality suffered distortion in consequence of your parents' loveless maneuvering for your confidence and loyalty, the one against the other. You have enjoyed that parental love which insures laudable self-confidence and which fosters normal feelings of security. But you have also been fortunate in that your parents possessed wisdom as well as love; and it was wisdom which led them to withhold most forms of indulgence and many luxuries which wealth can buy while they sent you to the synagogue school along with your neighborhood playfellows, and they also encouraged you to learn how to live in this world by permitting you to have original experience. You came over to the Jordan, where we preached and John's disciples baptized, with your young friend Amos. Both of you desired to go with us. When you returned to Jerusalem, your parents consented; Amos's parents refused; they loved their son so much that they denied him the blessed experience which you have had, even such as you this day enjoy. By running away from home, Amos could have joined us, but in so doing he would have wounded love and sacrificed loyalty. Even if such a course had been wise, it would have been a terrible price to pay for experience, independence, and liberty. Wise parents, such as yours, see to it that their children do not have to wound love or stifle loyalty in order to develop independence and enjoy invigorating liberty when they have grown up to your age.

"Love, John, is the supreme reality of the universe when bestowed by all-wise beings, but it is a dangerous and oftentimes semiselfish trait as it is manifested in the experience of mortal parents. When you get married and have children of your own to rear, make sure that your love is admonished by wisdom and guided by intelligence.

"Your young friend Amos believes this gospel of the kingdom just as much as you, but I cannot fully depend upon him; I am not certain about what he will do in the years to come. His early home life was not such as would produce a wholly dependable person. Amos is too much like one of the apostles who failed to enjoy a normal, loving, and wise home training. Your whole afterlife will be more happy and dependable because you spent your first eight years in a normal and well-regulated home. You possess a strong and well-knit character because you grew up in a home where love prevailed and wisdom reigned. Such a childhood training produces a type of loyalty which assures me that you will go through with the course you have begun."

For more than an hour Jesus and John continued this discussion of home life. The Master went on to explain to John how a child is wholly dependent on his parents and the associated home life for all his early concepts of everything intellectual, social, moral, and even spiritual since the family represents to the young child all that he can first know of either human or divine relationships. The child must derive his first impressions of the universe from the mother's care; he is wholly dependent on the earthly father for his first ideas of the heavenly Father. The child's subsequent life is made happy or unhappy, easy or difficult, in accordance with his early mental and emotional life, conditioned by these social and spiritual relationships of the home. A human being's entire afterlife is enormously influenced by what happens during the first few years of existence.

It is our sincere belief that the gospel of Jesus' teaching, founded as it is on the father-child relationship, can hardly enjoy a world-wide acceptance until such a time as the home life of the modern civilized peoples embraces more of love and more of wisdom. Notwithstanding that parents of today possess great knowledge and increased truth for improving the home and ennobling the home life, it remains a fact that very few modern homes are such good places in which to nurture boys and girls as Jesus' home in Galilee and John Mark's home in Judea, albeit the acceptance of Jesus' gospel will result in the immediate improvement of home life. The love life of a wise home and the loyal devotion of true religion exert a profound reciprocal influence upon each other. Such a home life enhances religion, and genuine religion always glorifies the home.

It is true that many of the objectionable stunting influences and other cramping features of these olden Jewish homes have been virtually eliminated from many of the better-regulated modern homes. There is, indeed, more spontaneous freedom and far more personal liberty, but this liberty is not restrained by love, motivated by loyalty, nor directed by the intelligent discipline of wisdom. As long as we teach the child to pray, "Our Father who is in heaven," a tremendous responsibility rests upon all earthly fathers so to live and order their homes that the word *father* becomes worthily enshrined in the minds and hearts of all growing children.

3. THE DAY AT CAMP

The apostles spent most of this day walking about on Mount Olivet and visiting with the disciples who were encamped with them, but early in the afternoon they became very desirous of seeing Jesus return. As the day wore on, they grew increasingly anxious about his safety; they felt inexpressibly lonely without him. There was much debating throughout the day as to whether the Master should have been allowed to go off by himself in the hills, accompanied only by an errand boy. Though no man openly so expressed his thoughts, there was not one of them, save Judas Iscariot, who did not wish himself in John Mark's place.

It was about midafternoon when Nathaniel made his speech on "Supreme Desire" to about half a dozen of the apostles and as many disciples, the ending of which was: "What is wrong with most of us is that we are only halfhearted. We fail to love the Master as he loves us. If we had all wanted to go with him as much as John Mark did, he would surely have taken us all. We stood by while the lad approached the Master and offered him the basket, but when the Master took hold of it, the lad would not let go. And so the Master left us here while he went off to the hills with basket, boy, and all."

About four o'clock, runners came to David Zebedee bringing him word from his mother at Bethsaida and from Jesus' mother. Several days previously David had made up his mind that the chief priests and rulers were going to kill Jesus. David knew they were determined to destroy the Master, and he was about convinced that Jesus would neither exert his divine power to save himself nor permit his followers to employ force in his defense. Having reached these conclusions, he lost no time in dispatching a messenger to his mother, urging her to come at once to Jerusalem and to bring Mary the mother of Jesus and every member of his family.

David's mother did as her son requested, and now the runners came back to David bringing the word that his mother and Jesus' entire family were on the way to Jerusalem and should arrive sometime late on the following day or very early the next morning. Since David did this on his own initiative, he thought it wise to keep the matter to himself. He told no one, therefore, that Jesus' family was on the way to Jerusalem.

Shortly after noon, more than twenty of the Greeks who had met with Jesus and the twelve at the home of Joseph of Arimathea arrived at the camp, and Peter and John spent several hours in conference with them. These Greeks, at least some of them, were well advanced in the knowledge of the kingdom, having been instructed by Rodan at Alexandria.

That evening, after returning to the camp, Jesus visited with the Greeks, and had it not been that such a course would have greatly disturbed his apostles and many of his leading disciples, he would have ordained these twenty Greeks, even as he had the seventy.

While all of this was going on at the camp, in Jerusalem the chief priests and elders were amazed that Jesus did not return to address the multitudes. True, the day before, when he left the temple, he had said, "I leave your house to you desolate." But they could not understand why he would be willing to forego the great advantage which he had built up in the friendly attitude of the crowds. While they feared he would stir up a tumult among the people, the Master's last words to the multitude had been an exhortation to conform in every reasonable manner with the authority of those "who sit in Moses' seat." But it was a busy day in the city as they simultaneously prepared for the Passover and perfected their plans for destroying Jesus.

Not many people came to the camp, for its establishment had been kept a well-guarded secret by all who knew that Jesus was expecting to stay there in place of going out to Bethany every night.

4. JUDAS AND THE CHIEF PRIESTS

Shortly after Jesus and John Mark left the camp, Judas Iscariot disappeared from among his brethren, not returning until late in the afternoon. This confused and discontented apostle, notwithstanding his Master's specific request to refrain from entering Jerusalem, went in haste to keep his appointment with Jesus' enemies at the home of Caiaphas the high priest.

This was an informal meeting of the Sanhedrin and had been appointed for shortly after 10 o'clock that morning. This meeting was called to discuss the nature of the charges which should be lodged against Jesus and to decide upon the procedure to be employed in bringing him before the Roman authorities for the purpose of securing the necessary civil confirmation of the death sentence which they had already passed upon him.

On the preceding day Judas had disclosed to some of his relatives and to certain Sadducean friends of his father's family that he had reached the conclusion that, while Jesus was a well-meaning dreamer and idealist, he was not the expected deliverer of Israel. Judas stated that he would very much like to find some way of withdrawing gracefully from the whole movement. His friends flatteringly assured him that his withdrawal would be hailed by the Jewish rulers as a great event, and that nothing would be too good for him. They led him to believe that he would forthwith receive high honors from the Sanhedrin, and that he would at last be in a position to erase the stigma of his well-meant but "unfortunate association with untaught Galileans."

Judas could not quite believe that the mighty works of the Master had been wrought by the power of the prince of devils, but he was now fully convinced that Jesus would not exert his power in self-aggrandizement; he was at last convinced that Jesus would allow himself to be destroyed by the Jewish rulers, and he could not endure the humiliating thought of being identified with a movement of defeat. He refused to entertain the idea of apparent failure. He thoroughly understood the sturdy character of his Master and the keenness of that majestic and merciful mind, yet he derived pleasure from even the partial entertainment of the suggestion of one of his relatives that Jesus, while he was a well-meaning fanatic, was probably not really sound of mind; that he had always appeared to be a strange and misunderstood person.

And now, as never before, Judas found himself becoming strangely resentful that Jesus had never assigned him a position of greater honor. All along he had appreciated the honor of being the apostolic treasurer, but now he began to feel that he was not appreciated; that his abilities were unrecognized. He was suddenly overcome with indignation that Peter, James, and John should have been honored with close association with Jesus, and at this time, when he was on the way to the high priest's home, he was bent on getting even with Peter, James, and John more than he was concerned with any thought of betraying Jesus. But over and above all, just then, a new and dominating thought began to occupy the forefront of his conscious mind: He had set out to get honor for himself, and if this could be secured simultaneously with getting even with those who had contributed to the greatest disappointment of his life, all the better. He was seized with a terrible conspiracy of confusion, pride, desperation, and determination. And so it must be plain that it was not for money that Judas was then on his way to the home of Caiaphas to arrange for the betrayal of Jesus.

As Judas approached the home of Caiaphas, he arrived at the final decision to abandon Jesus and his fellow apostles; and having thus made up his mind to desert the cause of the kingdom of heaven, he was determined to secure for himself as much as possible of that honor and glory which he had thought would sometime be his when he first identified himself with Jesus and the new gospel of the kingdom. All of the apostles once shared this ambition with Judas, but as time passed they learned to admire truth and to love Jesus, at least more than did Judas.

The traitor was presented to Caiaphas and the Jewish rulers by his cousin, who explained that Judas, having discovered his mistake in allowing himself to be misled by the subtle teaching of Jesus, had arrived at the place where he wished to make public and formal renunciation of his association with the Galilean and at the same time to ask for reinstatement in the confidence and fellowship of his Judean brethren. This spokesman for Judas went on to explain that Judas recognized it would be best for the peace of Israel if Jesus should be taken into custody, and that, as evidence of his sorrow in having participated in such a movement of error and as proof of his sincerity in now returning to the teachings of Moses, he had come to offer himself to the Sanhedrin as one who could so arrange with the captain holding the orders for Jesus' arrest that he could be taken into custody quietly, thus avoiding any danger of stirring up the multitudes or the necessity of postponing his arrest until after the Passover.

When his cousin had finished speaking, he presented Judas, who, stepping forward near the high priest, said: "All that my cousin has promised, I will do, but what are you willing to give me for this service?" Judas did not seem to discern the look of disdain and even disgust that came over the face of the hardhearted and vainglorious Caiaphas; his heart was too much set on self-glory and the craving for the satisfaction of self-exaltation.

And then Caiaphas looked down upon the betrayer while he said: "Judas, you go to the captain of the guard and arrange with that officer to bring your Master to us either tonight or tomorrow night, and when he has been delivered by you into our hands, you shall receive your reward for this service." When Judas heard this, he went forth from the presence of the chief priests and rulers and took counsel with the captain of the temple guards as to the manner in which Jesus was to be apprehended. Judas knew that Jesus was then absent from the camp and had no idea when he would return that evening, and so they agreed among themselves to arrest Jesus the next evening (Thursday) after the people of Jerusalem and all of the visiting pilgrims had retired for the night.

Judas returned to his associates at the camp intoxicated with thoughts of grandeur and glory such as he had not had for many a day. He had enlisted with Jesus hoping some day to become a great man in the new kingdom. He at last realized that there was to be no new kingdom such as he had anticipated. But he rejoiced in being so sagacious as to trade off his disappointment in failing to achieve glory in an anticipated new kingdom for the immediate realization of honor and reward in the old order, which he now believed would survive, and which he was certain would destroy Jesus and all that he stood for. In its last motive of conscious intention, Judas's betrayal of Jesus was the cowardly act of a selfish deserter whose only thought was his own safety and glorification, no matter what might be the results of his conduct upon his Master and upon his former associates.

But it was ever just that way. Judas had long been engaged in this deliberate, persistent, selfish, and vengeful consciousness of progressively building up in his mind, and entertaining in his heart, these hateful and evil desires of revenge and disloyalty. Jesus loved and trusted Judas even as he loved and trusted the other apostles, but Judas failed to develop loyal trust and to experience wholehearted love in return. And how dangerous ambition can become when it is once wholly wedded to self-seeking and supremely motivated by sullen and long-suppressed vengeance! What a crushing thing is disappointment in the lives of those foolish persons who, in fastening their gaze on the shadowy and evanescent allurements of time, become blinded to the higher and more real achievements of the everlasting attainments of the eternal worlds of divine values and true spiritual realities. Judas craved worldly honor in his mind and grew to love this desire with his whole heart; the other apostles likewise craved this same worldly honor in their minds, but with their hearts they loved Jesus and were doing their best to learn to love the truths which he taught them.

Judas did not realize it at this time, but he had been a subconscious critic of Jesus ever since John the Baptist was beheaded by Herod. Deep down in his heart Judas always resented the fact that Jesus did not save John. You should not forget that Judas had been a disciple of John before he became a follower of Jesus. And all these accumulations of human resentment and bitter disappointment which Judas had laid by in his soul in habiliments of hate were now well organized in his subconscious mind and ready to spring up to engulf him when he once dared to separate himself from the supporting influence of his brethren while at the same time exposing himself to the clever insinuations and subtle ridicule of the enemies of Jesus. Every time Judas allowed his hopes to soar high and Jesus would do or say something to dash them to pieces, there was always left in Judas's heart a scar of bitter resentment; and as these scars multiplied, presently that heart, so often wounded, lost all real affection for the one who had inflicted this distasteful experience upon a well-intentioned but cowardly and self-centered personality. Judas did not realize it, but he was a coward. Accordingly was he always inclined to assign to Jesus cowardice as the motive which led him so often to refuse to grasp for power or glory when they were apparently within his easy reach. And every mortal man knows full well how love, even when once genuine, can, through disappointment, jealousy, and long-continued resentment, be eventually turned into actual hate.

At last the chief priests and elders could breathe easily for a few hours. They would not have to arrest Jesus in public, and the securing of Judas as a traitorous ally insured that Jesus would not escape from their jurisdiction as he had so many times in the past.

5. THE LAST SOCIAL HOUR

Since it was Wednesday, this evening at the camp was a social hour. The Master endeavored to cheer his downcast apostles, but that was well-nigh impossible. They were all beginning to realize that disconcerting and crushing events were impending. They could not be cheerful, even when the Master recounted their years of eventful and loving association. Jesus made careful inquiry about the families of all of the apostles and, looking over toward David Zebedee, asked if anyone had heard recently from his mother, his youngest sister, or other members of his family. David looked down at his feet; he was afraid to answer.

This was the occasion of Jesus' warning his followers to beware of the support of the multitude. He recounted their experiences in Galilee when time and again great throngs of people enthusiastically followed them around and then just as ardently turned against them and returned to their former ways of believing and living. And then he said: "And so you must not allow yourselves to be deceived by the great crowds who heard us in the temple, and who seemed to believe our teachings. These multitudes listen to the truth and believe it superficially with their minds, but few of them permit the word of truth to strike down into the heart with living roots. Those who know the gospel only in the mind, and who have not experienced it in the heart, cannot be depended upon for support when real trouble comes. When the rulers of the Jews reach an agreement to destroy the Son of Man, and when they strike with one accord, you will see the multitude either flee in dismay or else stand by in silent amazement while these maddened and blinded rulers lead the teachers of the gospel truth to their death. And then, when adversity and persecution descend upon you, still others whom you think love the truth will be scattered, and some will renounce the gospel and desert you. Some who have been very close to us have already made up their minds to desert. You have rested today in preparation for those times which are now upon us. Watch, therefore, and pray that on the morrow you may be strengthened for the days that are just ahead."

The atmosphere of the camp was charged with an inexplicable tension. Silent messengers came and went, communicating with only David Zebedee. Before the evening had passed, certain ones knew that Lazarus had taken hasty flight from Bethany. John Mark was ominously silent after returning to camp, notwithstanding he had spent the whole day in the Master's company. Every effort to persuade him to talk only indicated clearly that Jesus had told him not to talk.

Even the Master's good cheer and his unusual sociability frightened them. They all felt the certain drawing upon them of the terrible isolation which they realized was about to descend with crashing suddenness and inescapable terror. They vaguely sensed what was coming, and none felt prepared to face the test. The Master had been away all day; they had missed him tremendously.

This Wednesday evening was the low-tide mark of their spiritual status up to the actual hour of the Master's death. Although the next day was one more day nearer the tragic Friday, still, he was with them, and they passed through its anxious hours more gracefully.

It was just before midnight when Jesus, knowing this would be the last night he would ever sleep through with his chosen family on earth, said, as he dispersed them for the night: "Go to your sleep, my brethren, and peace be upon you till we rise on the morrow, one more day to do the Father's will and experience the joy of knowing that we are his sons."

PAPER 178
LAST DAY AT THE CAMP

JESUS PLANNED to spend this Thursday, his last free day on earth as a divine Son incarnated in the flesh, with his apostles and a few loyal and devoted disciples. Soon after the breakfast hour on this beautiful morning, the Master led them to a secluded spot a short distance above their camp and there taught them many new truths. Although Jesus delivered other discourses to the apostles during the early evening hours of the day, this talk of Thursday forenoon was his farewell address to the combined camp group of apostles and chosen disciples, both Jews and gentiles. The twelve were all present save Judas. Peter and several of the apostles remarked about his absence, and some of them thought Jesus had sent him into the city to attend to some matter, probably to arrange the details of their forthcoming celebration of the Passover. Judas did not return to the camp until midafternoon, a short time before Jesus led the twelve into Jerusalem to partake of the Last Supper.

1. DISCOURSE ON SONSHIP AND CITIZENSHIP

Jesus talked to about fifty of his trusted followers for almost two hours and answered a score of questions regarding the relation of the kingdom of heaven to the kingdoms of this world, concerning the relation of sonship with God to citizenship in earthly governments. This discourse, together with his answers to questions, may be summarized and restated in modern language as follows:

The kingdoms of this world, being material, may often find it necessary to employ physical force in the execution of their laws and for the maintenance of order. In the kingdom of heaven true believers will not resort to the employment of physical force. The kingdom of heaven, being a spiritual brotherhood of the spirit-born sons of God, may be promulgated only by the power of the spirit. This distinction of procedure refers to the relations of the kingdom of believers to the kingdoms of secular government and does not nullify the right of social groups of believers to maintain order in their ranks and administer discipline upon unruly and unworthy members.

There is nothing incompatible between sonship in the spiritual kingdom and citizenship in the secular or civil government. It is the believer's duty to render to Caesar the things which are Caesar's and to God the things which are God's. There cannot be any disagreement between these two requirements, the one being material and the other spiritual, unless it should develop that a Caesar presumes to usurp the prerogatives of God and demand that spiritual homage and supreme worship be rendered to him. In such a case you shall worship only God while you seek to enlighten such misguided earthly rulers and in this way lead them also to the recognition of the Father in heaven. You shall not render spiritual worship to earthly rulers; neither should you employ the physical forces of earthly governments, whose rulers may sometime become believers, in the work of furthering the mission of the spiritual kingdom.

Sonship in the kingdom, from the standpoint of advancing civilization, should assist you in becoming the ideal citizens of the kingdoms of this world since brotherhood and service are the cornerstones of the gospel of the kingdom. The love call of the spiritual kingdom should prove to be the effective destroyer of the hate urge of the unbelieving and war-minded citizens of the earthly kingdoms. But these material-minded sons in darkness will never know of your spiritual light of truth unless you draw very near them with that unselfish social service which is the natural outgrowth of the bearing of the fruits of the spirit in the life experience of each individual believer.

As mortal and material men, you are indeed citizens of the earthly kingdoms, and you should be good citizens, all the better for having become reborn spirit sons of the heavenly kingdom. As faith-enlightened and spirit-liberated sons of the kingdom of heaven, you face a double responsibility of duty to man and duty to God while you voluntarily assume a third and sacred obligation: service to the brotherhood of God-knowing believers.

You may not worship your temporal rulers, and you should not employ temporal power in the furtherance of the spiritual kingdom; but you should manifest the righteous ministry of loving service to believers and unbelievers alike. In the gospel of the kingdom there resides the mighty Spirit of Truth, and presently I will pour out this same spirit upon all flesh. The fruits of the spirit, your sincere and loving service, are the mighty social lever to uplift the races of darkness, and this Spirit of Truth will become your power-multiplying fulcrum.

Display wisdom and exhibit sagacity in your dealings with unbelieving civil rulers. By discretion show yourselves to be expert in ironing out minor disagreements and in adjusting trifling misunderstandings. In every possible way — in everything short of your spiritual allegiance to the rulers of the universe — seek to live peaceably with all men. Be you always as wise as serpents but as harmless as doves.

You should be made all the better citizens of the secular government as a result of becoming enlightened sons of the kingdom; so should the rulers of earthly governments become all the better rulers in civil affairs as a result of believing this gospel of the heavenly kingdom. The attitude of unselfish service of man and intelligent worship of God should make all kingdom believers better world citizens, while the attitude of honest citizenship and sincere devotion to one's temporal duty should help to make such a citizen the more easily reached by the spirit call to sonship in the heavenly kingdom.

So long as the rulers of earthly governments seek to exercise the authority of religious dictators, you who believe this gospel can expect only trouble, persecution, and even death. But the very light which you bear to the world, and even the very manner in which you will suffer and die for this gospel of the kingdom, will, in themselves, eventually enlighten the whole world and result in the gradual divorcement of politics and religion. The persistent preaching of this gospel of the kingdom will some day bring to all nations a new and unbelievable liberation, intellectual freedom, and religious liberty.

Under the soon-coming persecutions by those who hate this gospel of joy and liberty, you will thrive and the kingdom will prosper. But you will stand in grave danger in subsequent times when most men will speak well of kingdom believers and many in high places nominally accept the gospel of the heavenly kingdom. Learn to be faithful to the kingdom even in times of peace and prosperity. Tempt not the angels of your supervision to lead you in troublous ways as a loving discipline designed to save your ease-drifting souls.

Remember that you are commissioned to preach this gospel of the kingdom — the supreme desire to do the Father's will coupled with the supreme joy of the faith realization of sonship with God — and you must not allow anything to divert your devotion to this one duty. Let all mankind benefit from the overflow of your loving spiritual ministry, enlightening intellectual communion, and uplifting social service; but none of these humanitarian labors, nor all of them, should be permitted to take the place of proclaiming the gospel. These mighty ministrations are the social by-products of the still more mighty and sublime ministrations and transformations wrought in the heart of the kingdom believer by the living Spirit of Truth and by the personal realization that the faith of a spirit-born man confers the assurance of living fellowship with the eternal God.

You must not seek to promulgate truth nor to establish righteousness by the power of civil governments or by the enaction of secular laws. You may always labor to persuade men's minds, but you must never dare to compel them. You must not forget the great law of human fairness which I have taught you in positive form: Whatsoever you would that men should do to you, do even so to them.

When a kingdom believer is called upon to serve the civil government, let him render such service as a temporal citizen of such a government, albeit such a believer should display in his civil service all of the ordinary traits of citizenship as these have been enhanced by the spiritual enlightenment of the ennobling association of the mind of mortal man with the indwelling spirit of the eternal God. If the unbeliever can qualify as a superior civil servant, you should seriously question whether the roots of truth in your heart have not died from the lack of the living waters of combined spiritual communion and social service. The consciousness of sonship with God should quicken the entire life service of every man, woman, and child who has become the possessor of such a mighty stimulus to all the inherent powers of a human personality.

You are not to be passive mystics or colorless ascetics; you should not become dreamers and drifters, supinely trusting in a fictitious Providence to provide even the necessities of life. You are indeed to be gentle in your dealings with erring mortals, patient in your intercourse with ignorant men, and forbearing under provocation; but you are also to be valiant in defense of righteousness, mighty in the promulgation of truth, and aggressive in the preaching of this gospel of the kingdom, even to the ends of the earth.

This gospel of the kingdom is a living truth. I have told you it is like the leaven in the dough, like the grain of mustard seed; and now I declare that it is like the seed of the living being, which, from generation to generation, while it remains the same living seed, unfailingly unfolds itself in new manifestations and grows acceptably in channels of new adaptation to the peculiar needs and conditions of each successive generation. The revelation I have made to you is a *living revelation*, and I desire that it shall bear appropriate fruits in each individual and in each generation in accordance with the laws of spiritual growth, increase, and adaptative development. From generation to generation this gospel must show increasing vitality and exhibit greater depth of spiritual power. It must not be permitted to become merely a sacred memory, a mere tradition about me and the times in which we now live.

And forget not: We have made no direct attack upon the persons or upon the authority of those who sit in Moses' seat; we only offered them the new light, which they have so vigorously rejected. We have assailed them only by the denunciation of their spiritual disloyalty to the very truths which they profess to teach and safeguard. We clashed with these established leaders and recognized rulers only when they threw themselves directly in the way of the preaching of the gospel of the kingdom to the sons of men. And even now, it is not we who assail them, but they who seek our destruction. Do not forget that you are commissioned to go forth preaching only the good news. You are not to attack the old ways; you are skillfully to put the leaven of new truth in the midst of the old beliefs. Let the Spirit of Truth do his own work. Let controversy come only when they who despise the truth force it upon you. But when the willful unbeliever attacks you, do not hesitate to stand in vigorous defense of the truth which has saved and sanctified you.

Throughout the vicissitudes of life, remember always to love one another. Do not strive with men, even with unbelievers. Show mercy even to those who despitefully abuse you. Show yourselves to be loyal citizens, upright artisans, praiseworthy neighbors, devoted kinsmen, understanding parents, and sincere believers in the brotherhood of the Father's kingdom. And my spirit shall be upon you, now and even to the end of the world.

When Jesus had concluded his teaching, it was almost one o'clock, and they immediately went back to the camp, where David and his associates had lunch ready for them.

2. AFTER THE NOONTIME MEAL

Not many of the Master's hearers were able to take in even a part of his forenoon address. Of all who heard him, the Greeks comprehended most. Even the eleven apostles were bewildered by his allusions to future political kingdoms and to successive generations of kingdom believers. Jesus' most devoted followers could not reconcile the impending end of his earthly ministry with these references to an extended future of gospel activities. Some of these Jewish believers were beginning to sense that earth's greatest tragedy was about to take place, but they could not reconcile such an impending disaster with either the Master's cheerfully indifferent personal attitude or his forenoon discourse, wherein he repeatedly alluded to the future transactions of the heavenly kingdom, extending over vast stretches of time and embracing relations with many and successive temporal kingdoms on earth.

By noon of this day all the apostles and disciples had learned about the hasty flight of Lazarus from Bethany. They began to sense the grim determination of the Jewish rulers to exterminate Jesus and his teachings.

David Zebedee, through the work of his secret agents in Jerusalem, was fully advised concerning the progress of the plan to arrest and kill Jesus. He knew all about the part of Judas in this plot, but he never disclosed this knowledge to the other apostles nor to any of the disciples. Shortly after lunch he did lead Jesus aside and, making bold, asked him whether he knew — but he never got further with his question. The Master, holding up his hand, stopped him, saying: "Yes, David, I know all about it, and I know that you know, but see to it that you tell no man. Only doubt not in your own heart that the will of God will prevail in the end."

This conversation with David was interrupted by the arrival of a messenger from Philadelphia bringing word that Abner had heard of the plot to kill Jesus and asking if he should depart for Jerusalem. This runner hastened off for Philadelphia with this word for Abner: "Go on with your work. If I depart from you in the flesh, it is only that I may return in the spirit. I will not forsake you. I will be with you to the end."

About this time Philip came to the Master and asked: "Master, seeing that the time of the Passover draws near, where would you have us prepare to eat it?" And when Jesus heard Philip's question, he answered: "Go and bring Peter and John, and I will give you directions concerning the supper we will eat together this night. As for the Passover, that you will have to consider after we have first done this."

When Judas heard the Master speaking with Philip about these matters, he drew closer that he might overhear their conversation. But David Zebedee, who was standing near, stepped up and engaged Judas in conversation while Philip, Peter, and John went to one side to talk with the Master.

Said Jesus to the three: "Go immediately into Jerusalem, and as you enter the gate, you will meet a man bearing a water pitcher. He will speak to you, and then shall you follow him. When he leads you to a certain house, go in after him and ask of the good man of that house, `Where is the guest chamber wherein the Master is to eat supper with his apostles?' And when you have thus inquired, this householder will show you a large upper room all furnished and ready for us."

When the apostles reached the city, they met the man with the water pitcher near the gate and followed on after him to the home of John Mark, where the lad's father met them and showed them the upper room in readiness for the evening meal.

And all of this came to pass as the result of an understanding arrived at between the Master and John Mark during the afternoon of the preceding day when they were alone in the hills. Jesus wanted to be sure he would have this one last meal undisturbed with his apostles, and believing if Judas knew beforehand of their place of meeting he might arrange with his enemies to take him, he made this secret arrangement with John Mark. In this way Judas did not learn of their place of meeting until later on when he arrived there in company with Jesus and the other apostles.

David Zebedee had much business to transact with Judas so that he was easily prevented from following Peter, John, and Philip, as he so much desired to do. When Judas gave David a certain sum of money for provisions, David said to him: "Judas, might it not be well, under the circumstances, to provide me with a little money in advance of my actual needs?" And after Judas had reflected for a moment, he answered: "Yes, David, I think it would be wise. In fact, in view of the disturbed conditions in Jerusalem, I think it would be best for me to turn over all the money to you. They plot against the Master, and in case anything should happen to me, you would not be hampered."

And so David received all the apostolic cash funds and receipts for all money on deposit. Not until the evening of the next day did the apostles learn of this transaction.

It was about half past four o'clock when the three apostles returned and informed Jesus that everything was in readiness for the supper. The Master immediately prepared to lead his twelve apostles over the trail to the Bethany road and on into Jerusalem. And this was the last journey he ever made with all twelve of them.

3. ON THE WAY TO THE SUPPER

Seeking again to avoid the crowds passing through the Kidron valley back and forth between Gethsemane Park and Jerusalem, Jesus and the twelve walked over the western brow of Mount Olivet to meet the road leading from Bethany down to the city. As they drew near the place where Jesus had tarried the previous evening to discourse on the destruction of Jerusalem, they unconsciously paused while they stood and looked down in silence upon the city. As they were a little early, and since Jesus did not wish to pass through the city until after sunset, he said to his associates:

"Sit down and rest yourselves while I talk with you about what must shortly come to pass. All these years have I lived with you as brethren, and I have taught you the truth concerning the kingdom of heaven and have revealed to you the mysteries thereof. And my Father has indeed done many wonderful works in connection with my mission on earth. You have been witnesses of all this and partakers in the experience of being laborers together with God. And you will bear me witness that I have for some time warned you that I must presently return to the work the Father has given me to do; I have plainly told you that I must leave you in the world to carry on the work of the kingdom. It was for this purpose that I set you apart, in the hills of Capernaum. The experience you have had with me, you must now make ready to share with others. As the Father sent me into this world, so am I about to send you forth to represent me and finish the work I have begun.

"You look down on yonder city in sorrow, for you have heard my words telling of the end of Jerusalem. I have forewarned you lest you should perish in her destruction and so delay the proclamation of the gospel of the kingdom. Likewise do I warn you to take heed lest you needlessly expose yourselves to peril when they come to take the Son of Man. I must go, but you are to remain to witness to this gospel when I have gone, even as I directed that Lazarus flee from the wrath of man that he might live to make known the glory of God. If it is the Father's will that I depart, nothing you may do can frustrate the divine plan. Take heed to yourselves lest they kill you also. Let your souls be valiant in defense of the gospel by spirit power but be not misled into any foolish attempt to defend the Son of Man. I need no defense by the hand of man; the armies of heaven are even now near at hand; but I am determined to do the will of my Father in heaven, and therefore must we submit to that which is so soon to come upon us.

"When you see this city destroyed, forget not that you have entered already upon the eternal life of endless service in the ever-advancing kingdom of heaven, even of the heaven of heavens. You should know that in my Father's universe and in mine are many abodes, and that there awaits the children of light the revelation of cities whose builder is God and worlds whose habit of life is righteousness and joy in the truth. I have brought the kingdom of heaven to you here on earth, but I declare that all of you who by faith enter therein and remain therein by the living service of truth, shall surely ascend to the worlds on high and sit with me in the spirit kingdom of our Father. But first must you gird yourselves and complete the work which you have begun with me. You must first pass through much tribulation and endure many sorrows — and these trials are even now upon us — and when you have finished your work on earth, you shall come to my joy, even as I have finished my Father's work on earth and am about to return to his embrace."

When the Master had spoken, he arose, and they all followed him down Olivet and into the city. None of the apostles, save three, knew where they were going as they made their way along the narrow streets in the approaching darkness. The crowds jostled them, but no one recognized them nor knew that the Son of God was passing by on his way to the last mortal rendezvous with his chosen ambassadors of the kingdom. And neither did the apostles know that one of their own number had already entered into a conspiracy to betray the Master into the hands of his enemies.

John Mark had followed them all the way into the city, and after they had entered the gate, he hurried on by another street so that he was waiting to welcome them to his father's home when they arrived.

PAPER 179
THE LAST SUPPER

DURING THE AFTERNOON of this Thursday, when Philip reminded the Master about the approaching Passover and inquired concerning his plans for its celebration, he had in mind the Passover supper which was due to be eaten on the evening of the next day, Friday. It was the custom to begin the preparations for the celebration of the Passover not later than noon of the preceding day. And since the Jews reckoned the day as beginning at sunset, this meant that Saturday's Passover supper would be eaten on Friday night, sometime before the midnight hour.

The apostles were, therefore, entirely at a loss to understand the Master's announcement that they would celebrate the Passover one day early. They thought, at least some of them did, that he knew he would be placed under arrest before the time of the Passover supper on Friday night and was therefore calling them together for a special supper on this Thursday evening. Others thought that this was merely a special occasion which was to precede the regular Passover celebration.

The apostles knew that Jesus had celebrated other Passovers without the lamb; they knew that he did not personally participate in any sacrificial service of the Jewish system. He had many times partaken of the paschal lamb as a guest, but always, when he was the host, no lamb was served. It would not have been a great surprise to the apostles to have seen the lamb omitted even on Passover night, and since this supper was given one day earlier, they thought nothing of its absence.

After receiving the greetings of welcome extended by the father and mother of John Mark, the apostles went immediately to the upper chamber while Jesus lingered behind to talk with the Mark family.

It had been understood beforehand that the Master was to celebrate this occasion alone with his twelve apostles; therefore no servants were provided to wait upon them.

1. THE DESIRE FOR PREFERENCE

When the apostles had been shown upstairs by John Mark, they beheld a large and commodious chamber, which was completely furnished for the supper, and observed that the bread, wine, water, and herbs were all in readiness on one end of the table. Except for the end on which rested the bread and wine, this long table was surrounded by thirteen reclining couches, just such as would be provided for the celebration of the Passover in a well-to-do Jewish household.

As the twelve entered this upper chamber, they noticed, just inside the door, the pitchers of water, the basins, and towels for laving their dusty feet; and since no servant had been provided to render this service, the apostles began to look at one another as soon as John Mark had left them, and each began to think within himself, Who shall wash our feet? And each likewise thought that it would not be he who would thus seem to act as the servant of the others.

As they stood there, debating in their hearts, they surveyed the seating arrangement of the table, taking note of the higher divan of the host with one couch on the right and eleven arranged around the table on up to opposite this second seat of honor on the host's right.

They expected the Master to arrive any moment, but they were in a quandary as to whether they should seat themselves or await his coming and depend on him to assign them their places. While they hesitated, Judas stepped over to the seat of honor, at the left of the host, and signified that he intended there to recline as the preferred guest. This act of Judas immediately stirred up a heated dispute among the other apostles. Judas had no sooner seized the seat of honor than John Zebedee laid claim to the next preferred seat, the one on the right of the host. Simon Peter was so enraged at this assumption of choice positions by Judas and John that, as the other angry apostles looked on, he marched clear around the table and took his place on the lowest couch, the end of the seating order and just opposite to that chosen by John Zebedee. Since others had seized the high seats, Peter thought to choose the lowest, and he did this, not merely in protest against the unseemly pride of his brethren, but with the hope that Jesus, when he should come and see him in the place of least honor, would call him up to a higher one, thus displacing one who had presumed to honor himself.

With the highest and the lowest positions thus occupied, the rest of the apostles chose places, some near Judas and some near Peter, until all were located. They were seated about the U-shaped table on these reclining divans in the following order: on the right of the Master, John; on the left, Judas, Simon Zelotes, Matthew, James Zebedee, Andrew, the Alpheus twins, Philip, Nathaniel, Thomas, and Simon Peter.

They are gathered together to celebrate, at least in spirit, an institution which antedated even Moses and referred to the times when their fathers were slaves in Egypt. This supper is their last rendezvous with Jesus, and even in such a solemn setting, under the leadership of Judas the apostles are led once more to give way to their old predilection for honor, preference, and personal exaltation.

They were still engaged in voicing angry recriminations when the Master appeared in the doorway, where he hesitated a moment as a look of disappointment slowly crept over his face. Without comment he went to his place, and he did not disturb their seating arrangement.

They were now ready to begin the supper, except that their feet were still unwashed, and they were in anything but a pleasant frame of mind. When the Master arrived, they were still engaged in making uncomplimentary remarks about one another, to say nothing of the thoughts of some who had sufficient emotional control to refrain from publicly expressing their feelings.

2. BEGINNING THE SUPPER

For a few moments after the Master had gone to his place, not a word was spoken. Jesus looked them all over and, relieving the tension with a smile, said: "I have greatly desired to eat this Passover with you. I wanted to eat with you once more before I suffered, and realizing that my hour has come, I arranged to have this supper with you tonight, for, as concerns the morrow, we are all in the hands of the Father, whose will I have come to execute. I shall not again eat with you until you sit down with me in the kingdom which my Father will give me when I have finished that for which he sent me into this world."

After the wine and the water had been mixed, they brought the cup to Jesus, who, when he had received it from the hand of Thaddeus, held it while he offered thanks. And when he had finished offering thanks, he said: "Take this cup and divide it among yourselves and, when you partake of it, realize that I shall not again drink with you the fruit of the vine since this is our last supper. When we sit down again in this manner, it will be in the kingdom to come."

Jesus began thus to talk to his apostles because he knew that his hour had come. He understood that the time had come when he was to return to the Father, and that his work on earth was almost finished. The Master knew he had revealed the Father's love on earth and had shown forth his mercy to mankind, and that he had completed that for which he came into the world, even to the receiving of all power and authority in heaven and on earth. Likewise, he knew Judas Iscariot had fully made up his mind to deliver him that night into the hands of his enemies. He fully realized that this traitorous betrayal was the work of Judas, but that it also pleased Lucifer, Satan, and Caligastia the prince of darkness. But he feared none of those who sought his spiritual overthrow any more than he feared those who sought to accomplish his physical death. The Master had but one anxiety, and that was for the safety and salvation of his chosen followers. And so, with the full knowledge that the Father had put all things under his authority, the Master now prepared to enact the parable of brotherly love.

3. WASHING THE APOSTLES' FEET

After drinking the first cup of the Passover, it was the Jewish custom for the host to arise from the table and wash his hands. Later on in the meal and after the second cup, all of the guests likewise rose up and washed their hands. Since the apostles knew that their Master never observed these rites of ceremonial hand washing, they were very curious to know what he intended to do when, after they had partaken of this first cup, he arose from the table and silently made his way over to near the door, where the water pitchers, basins, and towels had been placed. And their curiosity grew into astonishment as they saw the Master remove his outer garment, gird himself with a towel, and begin to pour water into one of the foot basins. Imagine the amazement of these twelve men, who had so recently refused to wash one another's feet, and who had engaged in such unseemly disputes about positions of honor at the table, when they saw him make his way around the unoccupied end of the table to the lowest seat of the feast, where Simon Peter reclined, and, kneeling down in the attitude of a servant, make ready to wash Simon's feet. As the Master knelt, all twelve arose as one man to their feet; even the traitorous Judas so far forgot his infamy for a moment as to arise with his fellow apostles in this expression of surprise, respect, and utter amazement.

There stood Simon Peter, looking down into the upturned face of his Master. Jesus said nothing; it was not necessary that he should speak. His attitude plainly revealed that he was minded to wash Simon Peter's feet. Notwithstanding his frailties of the flesh, Peter loved the Master. This Galilean fisherman was the first human being wholeheartedly to believe in the divinity of Jesus *and* to make full and public confession of that belief. And Peter had never since really doubted the divine nature of the Master. Since Peter so revered and honored Jesus in his heart, it was not strange that his soul resented the thought of Jesus' kneeling there before him in the attitude of a menial servant and proposing to wash his feet as would a slave. When Peter presently collected his wits sufficiently to address the Master, he spoke the heart feelings of all his fellow apostles.

After a few moments of this great embarrassment, Peter said, "Master, do you really mean to wash my feet?" And then, looking up into Peter's face, Jesus said: "You may not fully understand what I am about to do, but hereafter you will know the meaning of all these things." Then Simon Peter, drawing a long breath, said, "Master, you shall never wash my feet!" And each of the apostles nodded their approval of Peter's firm declaration of refusal to allow Jesus thus to humble himself before them.

The dramatic appeal of this unusual scene at first touched the heart of even Judas Iscariot; but when his vainglorious intellect passed judgment upon the spectacle, he concluded that this gesture of humility was just one more episode which conclusively proved that Jesus would never qualify as Israel's deliverer, and that he had made no mistake in the decision to desert the Master's cause.

As they all stood there in breathless amazement, Jesus said: "Peter, I declare that, if I do not wash your feet, you will have no part with me in that which I am about to perform." When Peter heard this declaration, coupled with the fact that Jesus continued kneeling there at his feet, he made one of those decisions of blind acquiescence in compliance with the wish of one whom he respected and loved. As it began to dawn on Simon Peter that there was attached to this proposed enactment of service some signification that determined one's future connection with the Master's work, he not only became reconciled to the thought of allowing Jesus to wash his feet but, in his characteristic and impetuous manner, said: "Then, Master, wash not my feet only but also my hands and my head."

As the Master made ready to begin washing Peter's feet, he said: "He who is already clean needs only to have his feet washed. You who sit with me tonight are clean — but not all. But the dust of your feet should have been washed away before you sat down at meat with me. And besides, I would perform this service for you as a parable to illustrate the meaning of a new commandment which I will presently give you."

In like manner the Master went around the table, in silence, washing the feet of his twelve apostles, not even passing by Judas. When Jesus had finished washing the feet of the twelve, he donned his cloak, returned to his place as host, and after looking over his bewildered apostles, said:

"Do you really understand what I have done to you? You call me Master, and you say well, for so I am. If, then, the Master has washed your feet, why was it that you were unwilling to wash one another's feet? What lesson should you learn from this parable in which the Master so willingly does that service which his brethren were unwilling to do for one another? Verily, verily, I say to you: A servant is not greater than his master; neither is one who is sent greater than he who sends him. You have seen the way of service in my life among you, and blessed are you who will have the gracious courage so to serve. But why are you so slow to learn that the secret of greatness in the spiritual kingdom is not like the methods of power in the material world?

"When I came into this chamber tonight, you were not content proudly to refuse to wash one another's feet, but you must also fall to disputing among yourselves as to who should have the places of honor at my table. Such honors the Pharisees and the children of this world seek, but it should not be so among the ambassadors of the heavenly kingdom. Do you not know that there can be no place of preferment at my table? Do you not understand that I love each of you as I do the others? Do you not know that the place nearest me, as men regard such honors, can mean nothing concerning your standing in the kingdom of heaven? You know that the kings of the gentiles have lordship over their subjects, while those who exercise this authority are sometimes called benefactors. But it shall not be so in the kingdom of heaven. He who would be great among you, let him become as the younger; while he who would be chief, let him become as one who serves. Who is the greater, he who sits at meat, or he who serves? Is it not commonly regarded that he who sits at meat is the greater? But you will observe that I am among you as one who serves. If you are willing to become fellow servants with me in doing the Father's will, in the kingdom to come you shall sit with me in power, still doing the Father's will in future glory."

When Jesus had finished speaking, the Alpheus twins brought on the bread and wine, with the bitter herbs and the paste of dried fruits, for the next course of the Last Supper.

4. LAST WORDS TO THE BETRAYER

For some minutes the apostles ate in silence, but under the influence of the Master's cheerful demeanor they were soon drawn into conversation, and ere long the meal was proceeding as if nothing out of the ordinary had occurred to interfere with the good cheer and social accord of this extraordinary occasion. After some time had elapsed, in about the middle of this second course of the meal, Jesus, looking them over, said: "I have told you how much I desired to have this supper with you, and knowing how the evil forces of darkness have conspired to bring about the death of the Son of Man, I determined to eat this supper with you in this secret chamber and a day in advance of the Passover since I will not be with you by this time tomorrow night. I have repeatedly told you that I must return to the Father. Now has my hour come, but it was not required that one of you should betray me into the hands of my enemies."

When the twelve heard this, having already been robbed of much of their self-assertiveness and self-confidence by the parable of the feet washing and the Master's subsequent discourse, they began to look at one another while in disconcerted tones they hesitatingly inquired, "Is it I?" And when they had all so inquired, Jesus said: "While it is necessary that I go to the Father, it was not required that one of you should become a traitor to fulfill the Father's will. This is the coming to fruit of the concealed evil in the heart of one who failed to love the truth with his whole soul. How deceitful is the intellectual pride that precedes the spiritual downfall! My friend of many years, who even now eats my bread, will be willing to betray me, even as he now dips his hand with me in the dish."

And when Jesus had thus spoken, they all began again to ask, "Is it I?" And as Judas, sitting on the left of his Master, again asked, "Is it I?" Jesus, dipping the bread in the dish of herbs, handed it to Judas, saying, "You have said." But the others did not hear Jesus speak to Judas. John, who reclined on Jesus' right hand, leaned over and asked the Master: "Who is it? We should know who it is that has proved untrue to his trust." Jesus answered: "Already have I told you, even he to whom I gave the sop." But it was so natural for the host to give a sop to the one who sat next to him on the left that none of them took notice of this, even though the Master had so plainly spoken. But Judas was painfully conscious of the meaning of the Master's words associated with his act, and he became fearful lest his brethren were likewise now aware that he was the betrayer.

Peter was highly excited by what had been said, and leaning forward over the table, he addressed John, "Ask him who it is, or if he has told you, tell me who is the betrayer."

Jesus brought their whisperings to an end by saying: "I sorrow that this evil should have come to pass and hoped even up to this hour that the power of truth might triumph over the deceptions of evil, but such victories are not won without the faith of the sincere love of truth. I would not have told you these things at this, our last supper, but I desire to warn you of these sorrows and so prepare you for what is now upon us. I have told you of this because I desire that you should recall, after I have gone, that I knew about all these evil plottings, and that I forewarned you of my betrayal. And I do all this only that you may be strengthened for the temptations and trials which are just ahead."

When Jesus had thus spoken, leaning over toward Judas, he said: "What you have decided to do, do quickly." And when Judas heard these words, he arose from the table and hastily left the room, going out into the night to do what he had set his mind to accomplish. When the other apostles saw Judas hasten off after Jesus had spoken to him, they thought he had gone to procure something additional for the supper or to do some other errand for the Master since they supposed he still carried the bag.

Jesus now knew that nothing could be done to keep Judas from turning traitor. He started with twelve — now he had eleven. He chose six of these apostles, and though Judas was among those nominated by his first-chosen apostles, still the Master accepted him and had, up to this very hour, done everything possible to sanctify and save him, even as he had wrought for the peace and salvation of the others.

This supper, with its tender episodes and softening touches, was Jesus' last appeal to the deserting Judas, but it was of no avail. Warning, even when administered in the most tactful manner and conveyed in the most kindly spirit, as a rule, only intensifies hatred and fires the evil determination to carry out to the full one's own selfish projects, when love is once really dead.

5. ESTABLISHING THE REMEMBRANCE SUPPER

As they brought Jesus the third cup of wine, the "cup of blessing," he arose from the couch and, taking the cup in his hands, blessed it, saying: "Take this cup, all of you, and drink of it. This shall be the cup of my remembrance. This is the cup of the blessing of a new dispensation of grace and truth. This shall be to you the emblem of the bestowal and ministry of the divine Spirit of Truth. And I will not again drink this cup with you until I drink in new form with you in the Father's eternal kingdom."

The apostles all sensed that something out of the ordinary was transpiring as they drank of this cup of blessing in profound reverence and perfect silence. The old Passover commemorated the emergence of their fathers from a state of slavery into individual freedom; now the Master was instituting a new remembrance supper as a symbol of the new dispensation wherein the enslaved individual emerges from the bondage of ceremonialism and selfishness into the spiritual joy of the brotherhood and fellowship of the liberated faith sons of the living God.

When they had finished drinking this new cup of remembrance, the Master took up the bread and, after giving thanks, broke it in pieces and, directing them to pass it around, said: "Take this bread of remembrance and eat it. I have told you that I am the bread of life. And this bread of life is the united life of the Father and the Son in one gift. The word of the Father, as revealed in the Son, is indeed the bread of life." When they had partaken of the bread of remembrance, the symbol of the living word of truth incarnated in the likeness of mortal flesh, they all sat down.

In instituting this remembrance supper, the Master, as was always his habit, resorted to parables and symbols. He employed symbols because he wanted to teach certain great spiritual truths in such a manner as to make it difficult for his successors to attach precise interpretations and definite meanings to his words. In this way he sought to prevent successive generations from crystallizing his teaching and binding down his spiritual meanings by the dead chains of tradition and dogma. In the establishment of the only ceremony or sacrament associated with his whole life mission, Jesus took great pains to *suggest* his meanings rather than to commit himself to *precise definitions.* He did not wish to destroy the individual's concept of divine communion by establishing a precise form; neither did he desire to limit the believer's spiritual imagination by formally cramping it. He rather sought to set man's reborn soul free upon the joyous wings of a new and living spiritual liberty.

Notwithstanding the Master's effort thus to establish this new sacrament of the remembrance, those who followed after him in the intervening centuries saw to it that his express desire was effectively thwarted in that his simple spiritual symbolism of that last night in the flesh has been reduced to precise interpretations and subjected to the almost mathematical precision of a set formula. Of all Jesus' teachings none have become more tradition-standardized.

This supper of remembrance, when it is partaken of by those who are Son-believing and God-knowing, does not need to have associated with its symbolism any of man's puerile misinterpretations regarding the meaning of the divine presence, for upon all such occasions the Master is *really present.* The remembrance supper is the believer's symbolic rendezvous with Michael. When you become thus spirit-conscious, the Son is actually present, and his spirit fraternizes with the indwelling fragment of his Father.

After they had engaged in meditation for a few moments, Jesus continued speaking: "When you do these things, recall the life I have lived on earth among you and rejoice that I am to continue to live on earth with you and to serve through you. As individuals, contend not among yourselves as to who shall be greatest. Be you all as brethren. And when the kingdom grows to embrace large groups of believers, likewise should you refrain from contending for greatness or seeking preferment between such groups."

And this mighty occasion took place in the upper chamber of a friend. There was nothing of sacred form or of ceremonial consecration about either the supper or the building. The remembrance supper was established without ecclesiastical sanction.

When Jesus had thus established the supper of the remembrance, he said to the twelve: "And as often as you do this, do it in remembrance of me. And when you do remember me, first look back upon my life in the flesh, recall that I was once with you, and then, by faith, discern that you shall all some time sup with me in the Father's eternal kingdom. This is the new Passover which I leave with you, even the memory of my bestowal life, the word of eternal truth; and of my love for you, the outpouring of my Spirit of Truth upon all flesh."

And they ended this celebration of the old but bloodless Passover in connection with the inauguration of the new supper of the remembrance, by singing, all together, the one hundred and eighteenth Psalm.

PAPER 180
THE FAREWELL DISCOURSE

AFTER SINGING the Psalm at the conclusion of the Last Supper, the apostles thought that Jesus intended to return immediately to the camp, but he indicated that they should sit down. Said the Master:

"You well remember when I sent you forth without purse or wallet and even advised that you take with you no extra clothes. And you will all recall that you lacked nothing. But now have you come upon troublous times. No longer can you depend upon the good will of the multitudes. Henceforth, he who has a purse, let him take it with him. When you go out into the world to proclaim this gospel, make such provision for your support as seems best. I have come to bring peace, but it will not appear for a time."

"The time has now come for the Son of Man to be glorified, and the Father shall be glorified in me. My friends, I am to be with you only a little longer. Soon you will seek for me, but you will not find me, for I am going to a place to which you cannot, at this time, come. But when you have finished your work on earth as I have now finished mine, you shall then come to me even as I now prepare to go to my Father. In just a short time I am going to leave you, you will see me no more on earth, but you shall all see me in the age to come when you ascend to the kingdom which my Father has given to me."

1. THE NEW COMMANDMENT

After a few moments of informal conversation, Jesus stood up and said: "When I enacted for you a parable indicating how you should be willing to serve one another, I said that I desired to give you a new commandment; and I would do this now as I am about to leave you. You well know the commandment which directs that you love one another; that you love your neighbor even as yourself. But I am not wholly satisfied with even that sincere devotion on the part of my children. I would have you perform still greater acts of love in the kingdom of the believing brotherhood. And so I give you this new commandment: That you love one another even as I have loved you. And by this will all men know that you are my disciples if you thus love one another.

"When I give you this new commandment, I do not place any new burden upon your souls; rather do I bring you new joy and make it possible for you to experience new pleasure in knowing the delights of the bestowal of your heart's affection upon your fellow men. I am about to experience the supreme joy, even though enduring outward sorrow, in the bestowal of my affection upon you and your fellow mortals.

"When I invite you to love one another, even as I have loved you, I hold up before you the supreme measure of true affection, for greater love can no man have than this: that he will lay down his life for his friends. And you are my friends; you will continue to be my friends if you are but willing to do what I have taught you. You have called me Master, but I do not call you servants. If you will only love one another as I am loving you, you shall be my friends, and I will ever speak to you of that which the Father reveals to me.

"You have not merely chosen me, but I have also chosen you, and I have ordained you to go forth into the world to yield the fruit of loving service to your fellows even as I have lived among you and revealed the Father to you. The Father and I will both work with you, and you shall experience the divine fullness of joy if you will only obey my command to love one another, even as I have loved you."

If you would share the Master's joy, you must share his love. And to share his love means that you have shared his service. Such an experience of love does not deliver you from the difficulties of this world; it does not create a new world, but it most certainly does make the old world new.

Keep in mind: It is loyalty, not sacrifice, that Jesus demands. The consciousness of sacrifice implies the absence of that wholehearted affection which would have made such a loving service a supreme joy. The idea of *duty* signifies that you are servant-minded and hence are missing the mighty thrill of doing your service as a friend and for a friend. The impulse of friendship transcends all convictions of duty, and the service of a friend for a friend can never be called a sacrifice. The Master has taught the apostles that they are the sons of God. He has called them brethren, and now, before he leaves, he calls them his friends.

2. THE VINE AND THE BRANCHES

Then Jesus stood up again and continued teaching his apostles: "I am the true vine, and my Father is the husbandman. I am the vine, and you are the branches. And the Father requires of me only that you shall bear much fruit. The vine is pruned only to increase the fruitfulness of its branches. Every branch coming out of me which bears no fruit, the Father will take away. Every branch which bears fruit, the Father will cleanse that it may bear more fruit. Already are you clean through the word I have spoken, but you must continue to be clean. You must abide in me, and I in you; the branch will die if it is separated from the vine. As the branch cannot bear fruit except it abides in the vine, so neither can you yield the fruits of loving service except you abide in me. Remember: I am the real vine, and you are the living branches. He who lives in me, and I in him, will bear much fruit of the spirit and experience the supreme joy of yielding this spiritual harvest. If you will maintain this living spiritual connection with me, you will bear abundant fruit. If you abide in me and my words live in you, you will be able to commune freely with me, and then can my living spirit so infuse you that you may ask whatsoever my spirit wills and do all this with the assurance that the Father will grant us our petition. Herein is the Father glorified: that the vine has many living branches, and that every branch bears much fruit. And when the world sees these fruit-bearing branches — my friends who love one another, even as I have loved them — all men will know that you are truly my disciples.

"As the Father has loved me, so have I loved you. Live in my love even as I live in the Father's love. If you do as I have taught you, you shall abide in my love even as I have kept the Father's word and evermore abide in his love."

The Jews had long taught that the Messiah would be "a stem arising out of the vine" of David's ancestors, and in commemoration of this olden teaching a large emblem of the grape and its attached vine decorated the entrance to Herod's temple. The apostles all recalled these things while the Master talked to them this night in the upper chamber.

But great sorrow later attended the misinterpretation of the Master's inferences regarding prayer. There would have been little difficulty about these teachings if his exact words had been remembered and subsequently truthfully recorded. But as the record was made, believers eventually regarded prayer in Jesus' name as a sort of supreme magic, thinking that they would receive from the Father anything they asked for. For centuries honest souls have continued to wreck their faith against this stumbling block. How long will it take the world of believers to understand that prayer is not a process of getting your way but rather a program of taking God's way, an experience of learning how to recognize and execute the Father's will? It is entirely true that, when your will has been truly aligned with his, you can ask anything conceived by that will-union, and it will be granted. And such a will-union is effected by and through Jesus even as the life of the vine flows into and through the living branches.

When there exists this living connection between divinity and humanity, if humanity should thoughtlessly and ignorantly pray for selfish ease and vainglorious accomplishments, there could be only one divine answer: more and increased bearing of the fruits of the spirit on the stems of the living branches. When the branch of the vine is alive, there can be only one answer to all its petitions: increased grape bearing. In fact, the branch exists only for, and can do nothing except, fruit bearing, yielding grapes. So does the true believer exist only for the purpose of bearing the fruits of the spirit: to love man as he himself has been loved by God — that we should love one another, even as Jesus has loved us.

And when the Father's hand of discipline is laid upon the vine, it is done in love, in order that the branches may bear much fruit. And a wise husbandman cuts away only the dead and fruitless branches.

Jesus had great difficulty in leading even his apostles to recognize that prayer is a function of spirit-born believers in the spirit-dominated kingdom.

3. ENMITY OF THE WORLD

The eleven had scarcely ceased their discussions of the discourse on the vine and the branches when the Master, indicating that he was desirous of speaking to them further and knowing that his time was short, said: "When I have left you, be not discouraged by the enmity of the world. Be not downcast even when faint-hearted believers turn against you and join hands with the enemies of the kingdom. If the world shall hate you, you should recall that it hated me even before it hated you. If you were of this world, then would the world love its own, but because you are not, the world refuses to love you. You are in this world, but your lives are not to be worldlike. I have chosen you out of the world to represent the spirit of another world even to this world from which you have been chosen. But always remember the words I have spoken to you: The servant is not greater than his master. If they dare to persecute me, they will also persecute you. If my words offend the unbelievers, so also will your words offend the ungodly. And all of this will they do to you because they believe not in me nor in Him who sent me; so will you suffer many things for the sake of my gospel. But when you endure these tribulations, you should recall that I also suffered before you for the sake of this gospel of the heavenly kingdom.

"Many of those who will assail you are ignorant of the light of heaven, but this is not true of some who now persecute us. If we had not taught them the truth, they might do many strange things without falling under condemnation, but now, since they have known the light and presumed to reject it, they have no excuse for their attitude. He who hates me hates my Father. It cannot be otherwise; the light which would save you if accepted can only condemn you if it is knowingly rejected. And what have I done to these men that they should hate me with such a terrible hatred? Nothing, save to offer them fellowship on earth and salvation in heaven. But have you not read in the Scripture the saying: `And they hated me without a cause'?

"But I will not leave you alone in the world. Very soon, after I have gone, I will send you a spirit helper. You shall have with you one who will take my place among you, one who will continue to teach you the way of truth, who will even comfort you.

"Let not your hearts be troubled. You believe in God; continue to believe also in me. Even though I must leave you, I will not be far from you. I have already told you that in my Father's universe there are many tarrying-places. If this were not true, I would not have repeatedly told you about them. I am going to return to these worlds of light, stations in the Father's heaven to which you shall some time ascend. From these places I came into this world, and the hour is now at hand when I must return to my Father's work in the spheres on high.

"If I thus go before you into the Father's heavenly kingdom, so will I surely send for you that you may be with me in the places that were prepared for the mortal sons of God before this world was. Even though I must leave you, I will be present with you in spirit, and eventually you shall be with me in person when you have ascended to me in my universe even as I am about to ascend to my Father in his greater universe. And what I have told you is true and everlasting, even though you may not fully comprehend it. I go to the Father, and though you cannot now follow me, you shall certainly follow me in the ages to come."

When Jesus sat down, Thomas arose and said: "Master, we do not know where you are going; so of course we do not know the way. But we will follow you this very night if you will show us the way."

When Jesus heard Thomas, he answered: "Thomas, I am the way, the truth, and the life. No man goes to the Father except through me. All who find the Father, first find me. If you know me, you know the way to the Father. And you do know me, for you have lived with me and you now see me."

But this teaching was too deep for many of the apostles, especially for Philip, who, after speaking a few words with Nathaniel, arose and said: "Master, show us the Father, and everything you have said will be made plain."

And when Philip had spoken, Jesus said: "Philip, have I been so long with you and yet you do not even now know me? Again do I declare: He who has seen me has seen the Father. How can you then say, Show us the

Father? Do you not believe that I am in the Father and the Father in me? Have I not taught you that the words which I speak are not my words but the words of the Father? I speak for the Father and not of myself. I am in this world to do the Father's will, and that I have done. My Father abides in me and works through me. Believe me when I say that the Father is in me, and that I am in the Father, or else believe me for the sake of the very life I have lived — for the work's sake."

As the Master went aside to refresh himself with water, the eleven engaged in a spirited discussion of these teachings, and Peter was beginning to deliver himself of an extended speech when Jesus returned and beckoned them to be seated.

4. THE PROMISED HELPER

Jesus continued to teach, saying: "When I have gone to the Father, and after he has fully accepted the work I have done for you on earth, and after I have received the final sovereignty of my own domain, I shall say to my Father: Having left my children alone on earth, it is in accordance with my promise to send them another teacher. And when the Father shall approve, I will pour out the Spirit of Truth upon all flesh. Already is my Father's spirit in your hearts, and when this day shall come, you will also have me with you even as you now have the Father. This new gift is the spirit of living truth. The unbelievers will not at first listen to the teachings of this spirit, but the sons of light will all receive him gladly and with a whole heart. And you shall know this spirit when he comes even as you have known me, and you will receive this gift in your hearts, and he will abide with you. You thus perceive that I am not going to leave you without help and guidance. I will not leave you desolate. Today I can be with you only in person. In the times to come I will be with you and all other men who desire my presence, wherever you may be, and with each of you at the same time. Do you not discern that it is better for me to go away; that I leave you in the flesh so that I may the better and the more fully be with you in the spirit?

"In just a few hours the world will see me no more; but you will continue to know me in your hearts even until I send you this new teacher, the Spirit of Truth. As I have lived with you in person, then shall I live in you; I shall be one with your personal experience in the spirit kingdom. And when this has come to pass, you shall surely know that I am in the Father, and that, while your life is hid with the Father in me, I am also in you. I have loved the Father and have kept his word; you have loved me, and you will keep my word. As my Father has given me of his spirit, so will I give you of my spirit. And this Spirit of Truth which I will bestow upon you shall guide and comfort you and shall eventually lead you into all truth.

"I am telling you these things while I am still with you that you may be the better prepared to endure those trials which are even now right upon us. And when this new day comes, you will be indwelt by the Son as well as by the Father. And these gifts of heaven will ever work the one with the other even as the Father and I have wrought on earth and before your very eyes as one person, the Son of Man. And this spirit friend will bring to your remembrance everything I have taught you."

As the Master paused for a moment, Judas Alpheus made bold to ask one of the few questions which either he or his brother ever addressed to Jesus in public. Said Judas: "Master, you have always lived among us as a friend; how shall we know you when you no longer manifest yourself to us save by this spirit? If the world sees you not, how shall we be certain about you? How will you show yourself to us?"

Jesus looked down upon them all, smiled, and said: "My little children, I am going away, going back to my Father. In a little while you will not see me as you do here, as flesh and blood. In a very short time I am going to send you my spirit, just like me except for this material body. This new teacher is the Spirit of Truth who will live with each one of you, in your hearts, and so will all the children of light be made one and be drawn toward one another. And in this very manner will my Father and I be able to live in the souls of each one of you and also in the hearts of all other men who love us and make that love real in their experiences by loving one another, even as I am now loving you."

Judas Alpheus did not fully understand what the Master said, but he grasped the promise of the new teacher, and from the expression on Andrew's face, he perceived that his question had been satisfactorily answered.

5. THE SPIRIT OF TRUTH

The new helper which Jesus promised to send into the hearts of believers, to pour out upon all flesh, is the *Spirit of Truth.* This divine endowment is not the letter or law of truth, neither is it to function as the form or expression of truth. The new teacher is the *conviction of truth*, the consciousness and assurance of true meanings on real spirit levels. And this new teacher is the spirit of living and growing truth, expanding, unfolding, and adaptative truth.

Divine truth is a spirit-discerned and living reality. Truth exists only on high spiritual levels of the realization of divinity and the consciousness of communion with God. You can know the truth, and you can live the truth; you can experience the growth of truth in the soul and enjoy the liberty of its enlightenment in the mind, but you cannot imprison truth in formulas, codes, creeds, or intellectual patterns of human conduct. When you undertake the human formulation of divine truth, it speedily dies. The post-mortem salvage of imprisoned truth, even at best, can eventuate only in the realization of a peculiar form of intellectualized glorified wisdom. Static truth is dead truth, and only dead truth can be held as a theory. Living truth is dynamic and can enjoy only an experiential existence in the human mind.

Intelligence grows out of a material existence which is illuminated by the presence of the cosmic mind. Wisdom comprises the consciousness of knowledge elevated to new levels of meaning and activated by the presence of the universe endowment of the adjutant of wisdom. Truth is a spiritual reality value experienced only by spirit-endowed beings who function upon supermaterial levels of universe consciousness, and who, after the realization of truth, permit its spirit of activation to live and reign within their souls.

The true child of universe insight looks for the living Spirit of Truth in every wise saying. The God-knowing individual is constantly elevating wisdom to the living-truth levels of divine attainment; the spiritually unprogressive soul is all the while dragging the living truth down to the dead levels of wisdom and to the domain of mere exalted knowledge.

The golden rule, when divested of the superhuman insight of the Spirit of Truth, becomes nothing more than a rule of high ethical conduct. The golden rule, when literally interpreted, may become the instrument of great offense to one's fellows. Without a spiritual discernment of the golden rule of wisdom you might reason that, since you are desirous that all men speak the full and frank truth of their minds to you, you should therefore fully and frankly speak the full thought of your mind to your fellow beings. Such an unspiritual interpretation of the golden rule might result in untold unhappiness and no end of sorrow.

Some persons discern and interpret the golden rule as a purely intellectual affirmation of human fraternity. Others experience this expression of human relationship as an emotional gratification of the tender feelings of the human personality. Another mortal recognizes this same golden rule as the yardstick for measuring all social relations, the standard of social conduct. Still others look upon it as being the positive injunction of a great moral teacher who embodied in this statement the highest concept of moral obligation as regards all fraternal relationships. In the lives of such moral beings the golden rule becomes the wise center and circumference of all their philosophy.

In the kingdom of the believing brotherhood of God-knowing truth lovers, this golden rule takes on living qualities of spiritual realization on those higher levels of interpretation which cause the mortal sons of God to view this injunction of the Master as requiring them so to relate themselves to their fellows that they will receive the highest possible good as a result of the believer's contact with them. This is the essence of true religion: that you love your neighbor as yourself.

But the highest realization and the truest interpretation of the golden rule consists in the consciousness of the spirit of the truth of the enduring and living reality of such a divine declaration. The true cosmic meaning of this rule of universal relationship is revealed only in its spiritual realization, in the interpretation of the law of conduct by the spirit of the Son to the spirit of the Father that indwells the soul of mortal man. And when such spirit-led mortals realize the true meaning of this golden rule, they are filled to overflowing with the assurance of citizenship in a friendly universe, and their ideals of spirit reality are satisfied only when they love their fellows as Jesus loved us all, and that is the reality of the realization of the love of God.

This same philosophy of the living flexibility and cosmic adaptability of divine truth to the individual requirements and capacity of every son of God, must be perceived before you can hope adequately to understand the

Master's teaching and practice of nonresistance to evil. The Master's teaching is basically a spiritual pronouncement. Even the material implications of his philosophy cannot be helpfully considered apart from their spiritual correlations. The spirit of the Master's injunction consists in the nonresistance of all selfish reaction to the universe, coupled with the aggressive and progressive attainment of righteous levels of true spirit values: divine beauty, infinite goodness, and eternal truth — to know God and to become increasingly like him.

Love, unselfishness, must undergo a constant and living readaptative interpretation of relationships in accordance with the leading of the Spirit of Truth. Love must thereby grasp the ever-changing and enlarging concepts of the highest cosmic good of the individual who is loved. And then love goes on to strike this same attitude concerning all other individuals who could possibly be influenced by the growing and living relationship of one spirit-led mortal's love for other citizens of the universe. And this entire living adaptation of love must be effected in the light of both the environment of present evil and the eternal goal of the perfection of divine destiny.

And so must we clearly recognize that neither the golden rule nor the teaching of nonresistance can ever be properly understood as dogmas or precepts. They can only be comprehended by living them, by realizing their meanings in the living interpretation of the Spirit of Truth, who directs the loving contact of one human being with another.

And all this clearly indicates the difference between the old religion and the new. The old religion taught self-sacrifice; the new religion teaches only self-forgetfulness, enhanced self-realization in conjoined social service and universe comprehension. The old religion was motivated by fear-consciousness; the new gospel of the kingdom is dominated by truth-conviction, the spirit of eternal and universal truth. And no amount of piety or creedal loyalty can compensate for the absence in the life experience of kingdom believers of that spontaneous, generous, and sincere friendliness which characterizes the spirit-born sons of the living God. Neither tradition nor a ceremonial system of formal worship can atone for the lack of genuine compassion for one's fellows.

6. THE NECESSITY FOR LEAVING

After Peter, James, John, and Matthew had asked the Master numerous questions, he continued his farewell discourse by saying: "And I am telling you about all this before I leave you in order that you may be so prepared for what is coming upon you that you will not stumble into serious error. The authorities will not be content with merely putting you out of the synagogues; I warn you the hour draws near when they who kill you will think they are doing a service to God. And all of these things they will do to you and to those whom you lead into the kingdom of heaven because they do not know the Father. They have refused to know the Father by refusing to receive me; and they refuse to receive me when they reject you, provided you have kept my new commandment that you love one another even as I have loved you. I am telling you in advance about these things so that, when your hour comes, as mine now has, you may be strengthened in the knowledge that all was known to me, and that my spirit shall be with you in all your sufferings for my sake and the gospel's. It was for this purpose that I have been talking so plainly to you from the very beginning. I have even warned you that a man's foes may be those of his own household. Although this gospel of the kingdom never fails to bring great peace to the soul of the individual believer, it will not bring peace on earth until man is willing to believe my teaching wholeheartedly and to establish the practice of doing the Father's will as the chief purpose in living the mortal life.

"Now that I am leaving you, seeing that the hour has come when I am about to go to the Father, I am surprised that none of you have asked me, Why do you leave us? Nevertheless, I know that you ask such questions in your hearts. I will speak to you plainly, as one friend to another. It is really profitable for you that I go away. If I go not away, the new teacher cannot come into your hearts. I must be divested of this mortal body and be restored to my place on high before I can send this spirit teacher to live in your souls and lead your spirits into the truth. And when my spirit comes to indwell you, he will illuminate the difference between sin and righteousness and will enable you to judge wisely in your hearts concerning them.

"I have yet much to say to you, but you cannot stand any more just now.

Albeit, when he, the Spirit of Truth, comes, he shall eventually guide you into all truth as you pass through the many abodes in my Father's universe.

"This spirit will not speak of himself, but he will declare to you that which the Father has revealed to the Son, and he will even show you things to come; he will glorify me even as I have glorified my Father. This spirit comes forth from me, and he will reveal my truth to you. Everything which the Father has in this domain is now mine; wherefore did I say that this new teacher would take of that which is mine and reveal it to you.

"In just a little while I will leave you for a short time. Afterward, when you again see me, I shall already be on my way to the Father so that even then you will not see me for long."

While he paused for a moment, the apostles began to talk with each other: "What is this that he tells us? `In just a little while I will leave you,' and `When you see me again it will not be for long, for I will be on my way to the Father.' What can he mean by this `little while' and `not for long'? We cannot understand what he is telling us."

And since Jesus knew they asked these questions, he said: "Do you inquire among yourselves about what I meant when I said that in a little while I would not be with you, and that, when you would see me again, I would be on my way to the Father? I have plainly told you that the Son of Man must die, but that he will rise again. Can you not then discern the meaning of my words? You will first be made sorrowful, but later on will you rejoice with many who will understand these things after they have come to pass. A woman is indeed sorrowful in the hour of her travail, but when she is once delivered of her child, she immediately forgets her anguish in the joy of the knowledge that a baby has been born into the world. And so are you about to sorrow over my departure, but I will soon see you again, and then will your sorrow be turned into rejoicing, and there shall come to you a new revelation of the salvation of God which no man can ever take away from you. And all the worlds will be blessed in this same revelation of life in effecting the overthrow of death. Hitherto have you made all your requests in my Father's name. After you see me again, you may also ask in my name, and I will hear you.

"Down here I have taught you in proverbs and spoken to you in parables. I did so because you were only children in the spirit; but the time is coming when I will talk to you plainly concerning the Father and his kingdom. And I shall do this because the Father himself loves you and desires to be more fully revealed to you. Mortal man cannot see the spirit Father; therefore have I come into the world to show the Father to your creature eyes. But when you have become perfected in spirit growth, you shall then see the Father himself."

When the eleven had heard him speak, they said to each other: "Behold, he does speak plainly to us. Surely the Master did come forth from God. But why does he say he must return to the Father?" And Jesus saw that they did not even yet comprehend him. These eleven men could not get away from their long-nourished ideas of the Jewish concept of the Messiah. The more fully they believed in Jesus as the Messiah, the more troublesome became these deep-rooted notions regarding the glorious material triumph of the kingdom on earth.

PAPER 181
FINAL ADMONITIONS AND WARNINGS

After the conclusion of the farewell discourse to the eleven, Jesus visited informally with them and recounted many experiences which concerned them as a group and as individuals. At last it was beginning to dawn upon these Galileans that their friend and teacher was going to leave them, and their hope grasped at the promise that, after a little while, he would again be with them, but they were prone to forget that this return visit was also for a little while. Many of the apostles and the leading disciples really thought that this promise to return for a short season (the short interval between the resurrection and the ascension) indicated that Jesus was just going away for a brief visit with his Father, after which he would return to establish the kingdom. And such an interpretation of his teaching conformed both with their preconceived beliefs and with their ardent hopes. Since their lifelong beliefs and hopes of wish fulfillment were thus agreed, it was not difficult for them to find an interpretation of the Master's words which would justify their intense longings.

After the farewell discourse had been discussed and had begun to settle down in their minds, Jesus again called the apostles to order and began the impartation of his final admonitions and warnings.

1. LAST WORDS OF COMFORT

When the eleven had taken their seats, Jesus stood and addressed them: "As long as I am with you in the flesh, I can be but one individual in your midst or in the entire world. But when I have been delivered from this investment of mortal nature, I will be able to return as a spirit indweller of each of you and of all other believers in this gospel of the kingdom. In this way the Son of Man will become a spiritual incarnation in the souls of all true believers.

"When I have returned to live in you and work through you, I can the better lead you on through this life and guide you through the many abodes in the future life in the heaven of heavens. Life in the Father's eternal creation is not an endless rest of idleness and selfish ease but rather a ceaseless progression in grace, truth, and glory. Each of the many, many stations in my Father's house is a stopping place, a life designed to prepare you for the next one ahead. And so will the children of light go on from glory to glory until they attain the divine estate wherein they are spiritually perfected even as the Father is perfect in all things.

"If you would follow after me when I leave you, put forth your earnest efforts to live in accordance with the spirit of my teachings and with the ideal of my life — the doing of my Father's will. This do instead of trying to imitate my natural life in the flesh as I have, perforce, been required to live it on this world.

"The Father sent me into this world, but only a few of you have chosen fully to receive me. I will pour out my spirit upon all flesh, but all men will not choose to receive this new teacher as the guide and counselor of the soul. But as many as do receive him shall be enlightened, cleansed, and comforted. And this Spirit of Truth will become in them a well of living water springing up into eternal life.

"And now, as I am about to leave you, I would speak words of comfort. Peace I leave with you; my peace I give to you. I make these gifts not as the world gives — by measure — I give each of you all you will receive. Let not your heart be troubled, neither let it be fearful. I have overcome the world, and in me you shall all triumph through faith. I have warned you that the Son of Man will be killed, but I assure you I will come back before I go to the Father, even though it be for only a little while. And after I have ascended to the Father, I will surely send the new teacher to be with you and to abide in your very hearts. And when you see all this come to pass, be not dismayed, but rather believe, inasmuch as you knew it all beforehand. I have loved you with a great affection, and I would not leave you, but it is the Father's will. My hour has come.

"Doubt not any of these truths even after you are scattered abroad by persecution and are downcast by many sorrows. When you feel that you are alone in the world, I will know of your isolation even as, when you are scattered every man to his own place, leaving the Son of Man in the hands of his enemies, you will know of mine. But I am never alone; always is the Father with me. Even at such a time I will pray for you. And all of these things have I told you that you might have peace and have it more abundantly. In this world you will have tribulation, but be of good cheer; I have triumphed in the world and shown you the way to eternal joy and everlasting service."

Jesus gives peace to his fellow doers of the will of God but not on the order of the joys and satisfactions of this material world. Unbelieving materialists and fatalists can hope to enjoy only two kinds of peace and soul comfort: Either they must be stoics, with steadfast resolution determined to face the inevitable and to endure the worst; or they must be optimists, ever indulging that hope which springs eternal in the human breast, vainly longing for a peace which never really comes.

A certain amount of both stoicism and optimism are serviceable in living a life on earth, but neither has aught to do with that superb peace which the Son of God bestows upon his brethren in the flesh. The peace which Michael gives his children on earth is that very peace which filled his own soul when he himself lived the mortal life in the flesh and on this very world. The peace of Jesus is the joy and satisfaction of a God-knowing individual who has achieved the triumph of learning fully how to do the will of God while living the mortal life in the flesh. The peace of Jesus' mind was founded on an absolute human faith in the actuality of the divine Father's wise and sympathetic overcare. Jesus had trouble on earth, he has even been falsely called the "man of sorrows," but in and through all of these experiences he enjoyed the comfort of that confidence which ever empowered him to proceed with his life purpose in the full assurance that he was achieving the Father's will.

Jesus was determined, persistent, and thoroughly devoted to the accomplishment of his mission, but he was not an unfeeling and calloused stoic; he ever sought for the cheerful aspects of his life experiences, but he was not a blind and self-deceived optimist. The Master knew all that was to befall him, and he was unafraid. After he had bestowed this peace upon each of his followers, he could consistently say, "Let not your heart be troubled, neither let it be afraid."

The peace of Jesus is, then, the peace and assurance of a son who fully believes that his career for time and eternity is safely and wholly in the care and keeping of an all-wise, all-loving, and all-powerful spirit Father. And this is, indeed, a peace which passes the understanding of mortal mind, but which can be enjoyed to the full by the believing human heart.

2. FAREWELL PERSONAL ADMONITIONS

The Master had finished giving his farewell instructions and imparting his final admonitions to the apostles as a group. He then addressed himself to saying good-bye individually and to giving each a word of personal advice, together with his parting blessing. The apostles were still seated about the table as when they first sat down to partake of the Last Supper, and as the Master went around the table talking to them, each man rose to his feet when Jesus addressed him.

To John, Jesus said: "You, John, are the youngest of my brethren. You have been very near me, and while I love you all with the same love which a father bestows upon his sons, you were designated by Andrew as one of the three who should always be near me. Besides this, you have acted for me and must continue so to act in many matters concerning my earthly family. And I go to the Father, John, having full confidence that you will continue to watch over those who are mine in the flesh. See to it that their present confusion regarding my mission does not in any way prevent your extending to them all sympathy, counsel, and help even as you know I would if I were to remain in the flesh. And when they all come to see the light and enter fully into the kingdom, while you all will welcome them joyously, I depend upon you, John, to welcome them for me.

"And now, as I enter upon the closing hours of my earthly career, remain near at hand that I may leave any message with you regarding my family. As concerns the work put in my hands by the Father, it is now finished except for my death in the flesh, and I am ready to drink this last cup. But as for the responsibilities left to me by my earthly father, Joseph, while I have attended to these during my life, I must now depend upon you to act in my stead in all these matters. And I have chosen you to do this for me, John, because you are the youngest and will therefore very likely outlive these other apostles.

"Once we called you and your brother sons of thunder. You started out with us strong-minded and intolerant, but you have changed much since you wanted me to call fire down upon the heads of ignorant and thoughtless unbelievers. And you must change yet more. You should become the apostle of the new commandment which I have this night given you. Dedicate your life to teaching your brethren how to love one another, even as I have loved you."

As John Zebedee stood there in the upper chamber, the tears rolling down his cheeks, he looked into the Master's face and said: "And so I will, my Master, but how can I learn to love my brethren more?" And then answered Jesus: "You will learn to love your brethren more when you first learn to love their Father in heaven more, and after you have become truly more interested in their welfare in time and in eternity. And all such human interest is fostered by understanding sympathy, unselfish service, and unstinted forgiveness. No man should despise your youth, but I exhort you always to give due consideration to the fact that age oftentimes represents experience, and that nothing in human affairs can take the place of actual experience. Strive to live peaceably with all men, especially your friends in the brotherhood of the heavenly kingdom. And, John, always remember, strive not with the souls you would win for the kingdom."

And then the Master, passing around his own seat, paused a moment by the side of the place of Judas Iscariot. The apostles were rather surprised that Judas had not returned before this, and they were very curious to know the significance of Jesus' sad countenance as he stood by the betrayer's vacant seat. But none of them, except possibly Andrew, entertained even the slightest thought that their treasurer had gone out to betray his Master, as Jesus had intimated to them earlier in the evening and during the supper. So much had been going on that, for the time being, they had quite forgotten about the Master's announcement that one of them would betray him.

Jesus now went over to Simon Zelotes, who stood up and listened to this admonition: "You are a true son of Abraham, but what a time I have had trying to make you a son of this heavenly kingdom. I love you and so do all of your brethren. I know that you love me, Simon, and that you also love the kingdom, but you are still set on making this kingdom come according to your liking. I know full well that you will eventually grasp the spiritual nature and meaning of my gospel, and that you will do valiant work in its proclamation, but I am distressed about what may happen to you when I depart. I would rejoice to know that you would not falter; I would be made happy if I could know that, after I go to the Father, you would not cease to be my apostle, and that you would acceptably deport yourself as an ambassador of the heavenly kingdom."

Jesus had hardly ceased speaking to Simon Zelotes when the fiery patriot, drying his eyes, replied: "Master, have no fears for my loyalty. I have turned my back upon everything that I might dedicate my life to the establishment of your kingdom on earth, and I will not falter. I have survived every disappointment so far, and I will not forsake you."

And then, laying his hand on Simon's shoulder, Jesus said: "It is indeed refreshing to hear you talk like that, especially at such a time as this, but, my good friend, you still do not know what you are talking about. Not for one moment would I doubt your loyalty, your devotion; I know you would not hesitate to go forth in battle and die for me, as all these others would" (and they all nodded a vigorous approval), "but that will not be required of you. I have repeatedly told you that my kingdom is not of this world, and that my disciples will not fight to effect its establishment. I have told you this many times, Simon, but you refuse to face the truth. I am not concerned with your loyalty to me and to the kingdom, but what will you do when I go away and you at last wake up to the realization that you have failed to grasp the meaning of my teaching, and that you must adjust your misconceptions to the reality of another and spiritual order of affairs in the kingdom?"

Simon wanted to speak further, but Jesus raised his hand and, stopping him, went on to say: "None of my apostles are more sincere and honest at heart than you, but not one of them will be so upset and disheartened as you, after my departure. In all of your discouragement my spirit shall abide with you, and these, your brethren, will not forsake you. Do not forget what I have taught you regarding the relation of citizenship on earth to sonship in the Father's spiritual kingdom. Ponder well all that I have said to you about rendering to Caesar the things which are Caesar's and to God that which is God's. Dedicate your life, Simon, to showing how acceptably mortal man may fulfill my injunction concerning the simultaneous recognition of temporal duty to civil powers and spiritual service in the brotherhood of the kingdom. If you will be taught by the Spirit of Truth, never will there be conflict between the requirements of citizenship on earth and sonship in heaven unless the temporal rulers presume to require of you the homage and worship which belong only to God.

"And now, Simon, when you do finally see all of this, and after you have shaken off your depression and have gone forth proclaiming this gospel in great power, never forget that I was with you even through all of your season of discouragement, and that I will go on with you to the very end. You shall always be my apostle, and after you become willing to see by the eye of the spirit and more fully to yield your will to the will of the Father in heaven, then will you return to labor as my ambassador, and no one shall take away from you the authority which I have conferred upon you, because of your slowness of comprehending the truths I have taught you. And so, Simon, once more I warn you that they who fight with the sword perish with the sword, while they who labor in the spirit achieve life everlasting in the kingdom to come with joy and peace in the kingdom which now is. And when the work given into your hands is finished on earth, you, Simon, shall sit down with me in my kingdom over there. You shall really see the kingdom you have longed for, but not in this life. Continue to believe in me and in that which I have revealed to you, and you shall receive the gift of eternal life."

When Jesus had finished speaking to Simon Zelotes, he stepped over to Matthew Levi and said: "No longer will it devolve upon you to provide for the treasury of the apostolic group. Soon, very soon, you will all be scattered; you will not be permitted to enjoy the comforting and sustaining association of even one of your brethren. As you go onward preaching this gospel of the kingdom, you will have to find for yourselves new associates. I have sent you forth two and two during the times of your training, but now that I am leaving you, after you have recovered from the shock, you will go out alone, and to the ends of the earth, proclaiming this good news: That faith-quickened mortals are the sons of God."

Then spoke Matthew: "But, Master, who will send us, and how shall we know where to go? Will Andrew show us the way?" And Jesus answered: "No, Levi, Andrew will no longer direct you in the proclamation of the gospel. He will, indeed, continue as your friend and counselor until that day whereon the new teacher comes, and then shall the Spirit of Truth lead each of you abroad to labor for the extension of the kingdom. Many changes have come over you since that day at the customhouse when you first set out to follow me; but many more must come before you will be able to see the vision of a brotherhood in which gentile sits alongside Jew in fraternal association. But go on with your urge to win your Jewish brethren until you are fully satisfied and then turn with power to the gentiles. One thing you may be certain of, Levi: You have won the confidence and affection of your brethren; they all love you." (And all ten of them signified their acquiescence in the Master's words.)

"Levi, I know much about your anxieties, sacrifices, and labors to keep the treasury replenished which your brethren do not know, and I am rejoiced that, though he who carried the bag is absent, the publican ambassador is here at my farewell gathering with the messengers of the kingdom. I pray that you may discern the meaning of my teaching with the eyes of the spirit. And when the new teacher comes into your heart, follow on as he will lead you and let your brethren see — even all the world — what the Father can do for a hated tax-gatherer who dared to follow the Son of Man and to believe the gospel of the kingdom. Even from the first, Levi, I loved you as I did these other Galileans. Knowing then so well that neither the Father nor the Son has respect of persons, see to it that you make no such distinctions among those who become believers in the gospel through your ministry. And so, Matthew, dedicate your whole future life service to showing all men that God is no respecter of persons; that, in the sight of God and in the fellowship of the kingdom, all men are equal, all believers are the sons of God."

Jesus then stepped over to James Zebedee, who stood in silence as the Master addressed him, saying: "James, when you and your younger brother once came to me seeking preferment in the honors of the kingdom, and I told you such honors were for the Father to bestow, I asked if you were able to drink my cup, and both of you answered that you were. Even if you were not then able, and if you are not now able, you will soon be prepared for such a service by the experience you are about to pass through. By such behavior you angered your brethren at that time. If they have not already fully forgiven you, they will when they see you drink my cup. Whether your ministry be long or short, possess your soul in patience. When the new teacher comes, let him teach you the poise of compassion and that sympathetic tolerance which is born of sublime confidence in me and of perfect submission to the Father's will. Dedicate your life to the demonstration of that combined human affection and divine dignity of the God-knowing and Son-believing disciple. And all who thus live will reveal the gospel even in the manner of their death. You and your brother John will go different ways, and one of you may sit down with me in the eternal kingdom long before the other. It would help you much if you would learn that true wisdom embraces discretion as well as courage. You should learn sagacity to go along with your aggressiveness. There will come those supreme moments wherein my disciples will not hesitate to lay down their lives for this gospel, but in all ordinary circumstances it would be far better to placate the wrath of unbelievers that you might live and continue to preach the glad tidings. As far as lies in your power, live long on the earth that your life of many years may be fruitful in souls won for the heavenly kingdom."

When the Master had finished speaking to James Zebedee, he stepped around to the end of the table where Andrew sat and, looking his faithful helper in the eyes, said: "Andrew, you have faithfully represented me as acting head of the ambassadors of the heavenly kingdom. Although you have sometimes doubted and at other times manifested dangerous timidity, still, you have always been sincerely just and eminently fair in dealing with your associates. Ever since the ordination of you and your brethren as messengers of the kingdom, you have been self-governing in all group administrative affairs except that I designated you as the acting head of these chosen ones. In no other temporal matter have I acted to direct or to influence your decisions. And this I did in order to provide for leadership in the direction of all your subsequent group deliberations. In my universe and in my Father's universe of universes, our brethren-sons are dealt with as individuals in all their spiritual relations, but in all group relationships we unfailingly provide for definite leadership. Our kingdom is a realm of order, and where two or more will creatures act in co-operation, there is always provided the authority of leadership.

"And now, Andrew, since you are the chief of your brethren by authority of my appointment, and since you have thus served as my personal representative, and as I am about to leave you and go to my Father, I release you from all responsibility as regards these temporal and administrative affairs. From now on you may exercise no jurisdiction over your brethren except that which you have earned in your capacity as spiritual leader, and which your brethren therefore freely recognize. From this hour you may exercise no authority over your brethren unless they restore such jurisdiction to you by their definite legislative action after I shall have gone to the Father. But this release from responsibility as the administrative head of this group does not in any manner lessen your moral responsibility to do everything in your power to hold your brethren together with a firm and loving hand during the trying time just ahead, those days which must intervene between my departure in the flesh and the sending of the new teacher who will live in your hearts, and who ultimately will lead you into all truth. As I prepare to leave you, I would liberate you from all administrative responsibility which had its inception and authority in my presence as one among you. Henceforth I shall exercise only spiritual authority over you and among you.

"If your brethren desire to retain you as their counselor, I direct that you should, in all matters temporal and spiritual, do your utmost to promote peace and harmony among the various groups of sincere gospel believers. Dedicate the remainder of your life to promoting the practical aspects of brotherly love among your brethren. Be kind to my brothers in the flesh when they come fully to believe this gospel; manifest loving and impartial devotion to the Greeks in the West and to Abner in the East. Although these, my apostles, are soon going to be scattered to the four corners of the earth, there to proclaim the good news of the salvation of sonship with God, you are to hold them together during the trying time just ahead, that season of intense testing during which you must learn to believe this gospel without my personal presence while you patiently await the arrival of the new teacher, the Spirit of Truth. And so, Andrew, though it may not fall to you to do the great works as seen by men, be content to be the teacher and counselor of those who do such things. Go on with your work on earth to the end, and then shall you continue this ministry in the eternal kingdom, for have I not many times told you that I have other sheep not of this flock?"

Jesus then went over to the Alpheus twins and, standing between them, said: "My little children, you are one of the three groups of brothers who chose to follow after me. All six of you have done well to work in peace with your own flesh and blood, but none have done better than you. Hard times are just ahead of us. You may not understand all that will befall you and your brethren, but never doubt that you were once called to the work of the kingdom. For some time there will be no multitudes to manage, but do not become discouraged; when your lifework is finished, I will receive you on high, where in glory you shall tell of your salvation to seraphic hosts and to multitudes of the high Sons of God. Dedicate your lives to the enhancement of commonplace toil. Show all men on earth and the angels of heaven how cheerfully and courageously mortal man can, after having been called to work for a season in the special service of God, return to the labors of former days. If, for the time being, your work in the outward affairs of the kingdom should be completed, you should go back to your former labors with the new enlightenment of the experience of sonship with God and with the exalted realization that, to him who is God-knowing, there is no such thing as common labor or secular toil. To you who have worked with me, all things have become sacred, and all earthly labor has become a service even to God the Father. And when you hear the news of the doings of your former apostolic associates, rejoice with them and continue your daily work as those who wait upon God and serve while they wait. You have been my apostles, and you always shall be, and I will remember you in the kingdom to come."

And then Jesus went over to Philip, who, standing up, heard this message from his Master: "Philip, you have asked me many foolish questions, but I have done my utmost to answer every one, and now would I answer the last of such questionings which have arisen in your most honest but unspiritual mind. All the time I have been coming around toward you, have you been saying to yourself, `What shall I ever do if the Master goes away and leaves us alone in the world?' O, you of little faith! And yet you have almost as much as many of your brethren. You have been a good steward, Philip. You failed us only a few times, and one of those failures we utilized to manifest the Father's glory. Your office of stewardship is about over. You must soon more fully do the work you were called to do — the preaching of this gospel of the kingdom. Philip, you have always wanted to be shown, and very soon shall you see great things. Far better that you should have seen all this by faith, but since you were sincere even in your material sightedness, you will live to see my words fulfilled. And then, when you are blessed with spiritual vision, go forth to your work, dedicating your life to the cause of leading mankind to search for God and to seek eternal realities with the eye of spiritual faith and not with the eyes of the material mind. Remember, Philip, you have a great mission on earth, for the world is filled with those who look at life just as you have tended to. You have a great work to do, and when it is finished in faith, you shall come to me in my kingdom, and I will take great pleasure in showing you that which eye has not seen, ear heard, nor the mortal mind conceived. In the meantime, become as a little child in the kingdom of the spirit and permit me, as the spirit of the new teacher, to lead you forward in the spiritual kingdom. And in this way will I be able to do much for you which I was not able to accomplish when I sojourned with you as a mortal of the realm. And always remember, Philip, he who has seen me has seen the Father."

Then went the Master over to Nathaniel. As Nathaniel stood up, Jesus bade him be seated and, sitting down by his side, said: "Nathaniel, you have learned to live above prejudice and to practice increased tolerance since you became my apostle. But there is much more for you to learn. You have been a blessing to your fellows in that they have always been admonished by your consistent sincerity. When I have gone, it may be that your frankness will interfere with your getting along well with your brethren, both old and new. You should learn that the expression of even a good thought must be modulated in accordance with the intellectual status and spiritual development of the hearer. Sincerity is most serviceable in the work of the kingdom when it is wedded to discretion.

"If you would learn to work with your brethren, you might accomplish more permanent things, but if you find yourself going off in quest of those who think as you do, in that event dedicate your life to proving that the God-knowing disciple can become a kingdom builder even when alone in the world and wholly isolated from his fellow believers. I know you will be faithful to the end, and I will some day welcome you to the enlarged service of my kingdom on high."

Then Nathaniel spoke, asking Jesus this question: "I have listened to your teaching ever since you first called me to the service of this kingdom, but I honestly cannot understand the full meaning of all you tell us. I do not know what to expect next, and I think most of my brethren are likewise perplexed, but they hesitate to confess their confusion. Can you help me?" Jesus, putting his hand on Nathaniel's shoulder, said: "My friend, it is not strange that you should encounter perplexity in your attempt to grasp the meaning of my spiritual teachings since you are so handicapped by your preconceptions of Jewish tradition and so confused by your persistent tendency to interpret my gospel in accordance with the teachings of the scribes and Pharisees.

"I have taught you much by word of mouth, and I have lived my life among you. I have done all that can be done to enlighten your minds and liberate your souls, and what you have not been able to get from my teachings and my life, you must now prepare to acquire at the hand of that master of all teachers — actual experience. And in all of this new experience which now awaits you, I will go before you and the Spirit of Truth shall be with you. Fear not; that which you now fail to comprehend, the new teacher, when he has come, will reveal to you throughout the remainder of your life on earth and on through your training in the eternal ages."

And then the Master, turning to all of them, said: "Be not dismayed that you fail to grasp the full meaning of the gospel. You are but finite, mortal men, and that which I have taught you is infinite, divine, and eternal. Be patient and of good courage since you have the eternal ages before you in which to continue your progressive attainment of the experience of becoming perfect, even as your Father in Paradise is perfect."

And then Jesus went over to Thomas, who, standing up, heard him say: "Thomas, you have often lacked faith; however, when you have had your seasons with doubt, you have never lacked courage. I know well that the false prophets and spurious teachers will not deceive you. After I have gone, your brethren will the more appreciate your critical way of viewing new teachings. And when you all are scattered to the ends of the earth in the times to come, remember that you are still my ambassador. Dedicate your life to the great work of showing how the critical material mind of man can triumph over the inertia of intellectual doubting when faced by the demonstration of the manifestation of living truth as it operates in the experience of spirit-born men and women who yield the fruits of the spirit in their lives, and who love one another, even as I have loved you. Thomas, I am glad you joined us, and I know, after a short period of perplexity, you will go on in the service of the kingdom. Your doubts have perplexed your brethren, but they have never troubled me. I have confidence in you, and I will go before you even to the uttermost parts of the earth."

Then the Master went over to Simon Peter, who stood up as Jesus addressed him: "Peter, I know you love me, and that you will dedicate your life to the public proclamation of this gospel of the kingdom to Jew and gentile, but I am distressed that your years of such close association with me have not done more to help you think before you speak. What experience must you pass through before you will learn to set a guard upon your lips? How much trouble have you made for us by your thoughtless speaking, by your presumptuous self-confidence! And you are destined to make much more trouble for yourself if you do not master this frailty. You know that your brethren love you in spite of this weakness, and you should also understand that this shortcoming in no way impairs my affection for you, but it lessens your usefulness and never ceases to make trouble for you. But you will undoubtedly receive great help from the experience you will pass through this very night. And what I now say to you, Simon Peter, I likewise say to all your brethren here assembled: This night you will all be in great danger of stumbling over me. You know it is written, `The shepherd will be smitten and the sheep will be scattered abroad.' When I am absent, there is great danger that some of you will succumb to doubts and stumble because of what befalls me. But I promise you now that I will come back to you for a little while, and that I will then go before you into Galilee."

Then said Peter, placing his hand on Jesus' shoulder: "No matter if all my brethren should succumb to doubts because of you, I promise that I will not stumble over anything you may do. I will go with you and, if need be, die for you."

As Peter stood there before his Master, all atremble with intense emotion and overflowing with genuine love for him, Jesus looked straight into his moistened eyes as he said: "Peter, verily, verily, I say to you, this night the cock will not crow until you have denied me three or four times. And thus what you have failed to learn from peaceful association with me, you will learn through much trouble and many sorrows. And after you have really learned this needful lesson, you should strengthen your brethren and go on living a life dedicated to preaching this gospel, though you may fall into prison and, perhaps, follow me in paying the supreme price of loving service in the building of the Father's kingdom.

"But remember my promise: When I am raised up, I will tarry with you for a season before I go to the Father. And even this night will I make supplication to the Father that he strengthen each of you for that which you must now so soon pass through. I love you all with the love wherewith the Father loves me, and therefore should you henceforth love one another, even as I have loved you."

And then, when they had sung a hymn, they departed for the camp on the Mount of Olives.

PAPER 182
IN GETHSEMANE

It was about ten o'clock this Thursday night when Jesus led the eleven apostles from the home of Elijah and Mary Mark on their way back to the Gethsemane camp. Ever since that day in the hills, John Mark had made it his business to keep a watchful eye on Jesus. John, being in need of sleep, had obtained several hours of rest while the Master had been with his apostles in the upper room, but on hearing them coming downstairs, he arose and, quickly throwing a linen coat about himself, followed them through the city, over the brook Kidron, and on to their private encampment adjacent to Gethsemane Park. And John Mark remained so near the Master throughout this night and the next day that he witnessed everything and overheard much of what the Master said from this time on to the hour of the crucifixion.

As Jesus and the eleven made their way back to camp, the apostles began to wonder about the meaning of Judas's prolonged absence, and they spoke to one another concerning the Master's prediction that one of them would betray him, and for the first time they suspected that all was not well with Judas Iscariot. But they did not engage in open comment about Judas until they reached the camp and observed that he was not there, waiting to receive them. When they all besieged Andrew to know what had become of Judas, their chief remarked only, "I do not know where Judas is, but I fear he has deserted us."

1. THE LAST GROUP PRAYER

A few moments after arriving at camp, Jesus said to them: "My friends and brethren, my time with you is now very short, and I desire that we draw apart by ourselves while we pray to our Father in heaven for strength to sustain us in this hour and henceforth in all the work we must do in his name."

When Jesus had thus spoken, he led the way a short distance up on Olivet, and in full view of Jerusalem he bade them kneel on a large flat rock in a circle about him as they had done on the day of their ordination; and then, as he stood there in the midst of them glorified in the mellow moonlight, he lifted up his eyes toward heaven and prayed:

"Father, my hour has come; now glorify your Son that the Son may glorify you. I know that you have given me full authority over all living creatures in my realm, and I will give eternal life to all who will become faith sons of God. And this is eternal life, that my creatures should know you as the only true God and Father of all, and that they should believe in him whom you sent into the world. Father, I have exalted you on earth and have accomplished the work which you gave me to do. I have almost finished my bestowal upon the children of our own creation; there remains only for me to lay down my life in the flesh. And now, O my Father, glorify me with the glory which I had with you before this world was and receive me once more at your right hand.

"I have manifested you to the men whom you chose from the world and gave to me. They are yours — as all life is in your hands — you gave them to me, and I have lived among them, teaching them the way of life, and they have believed. These men are learning that all I have comes from you, and that the life I live in the flesh is to make known my Father to the worlds. The truth which you have given to me I have revealed to them. These, my friends and ambassadors, have sincerely willed to receive your word. I have told them that I came forth from you, that you sent me into this world, and that I am about to return to you. Father, I do pray for these chosen men. And I pray for them not as I would pray for the world, but as for those whom I have chosen out of the world to represent me to the world after I have returned to your work, even as I have represented you in this world during my sojourn in the flesh. These men are mine; you gave them to me; but all things which are mine are ever yours, and all that which was yours you have now caused to be mine. You have been exalted in me, and I now pray that I may be honored in these men. I can no longer be in this world; I am about to return to the work you have given me to do. I must leave these men behind to represent us and our kingdom among men. Father, keep these men faithful as I prepare to yield up my life in the flesh. Help these, my friends, to be one in spirit, even as we are one. As long as I could be with them, I could watch over them and guide them, but now am I about to go away. Be near them, Father, until we can send the new teacher to comfort and strengthen them.

"You gave me twelve men, and I have kept them all save one, the son of revenge, who would not have further fellowship with us. These men are weak and frail, but I know we can trust them; I have proved them; they love me, even as they reverence you. While they must suffer much for my sake, I desire that they should also be filled with the joy of the assurance of sonship in the heavenly kingdom. I have given these men your word and have taught them the truth. The world may hate them, even as it has hated me, but I do not ask that you take them out of the world, only that you keep them from the evil in the world. Sanctify them in the truth; your word is truth. And as you sent me into this world, even so am I about to send these men into the world. For their sakes I have lived among men and have consecrated my life to your service that I might inspire them to be purified through the truth I have taught them and the love I have revealed to them. I well know, my Father, that there is no need for me to ask you to watch over these brethren after I have gone; I know you love them even as I, but I do this that they may the better realize the Father loves mortal men even as does the Son.

"And now, my Father, I would pray not only for these eleven men but also for all others who now believe, or who may hereafter believe the gospel of the kingdom through the word of their future ministry. I want them all to be one, even as you and I are one. You are in me and I am in you, and I desire that these believers likewise be in us; that both of our spirits indwell them. If my children are one as we are one, and if they love one another as I have loved them, all men will then believe that I came forth from you and be willing to receive the revelation of truth and glory which I have made. The glory which you gave me I have revealed to these believers. As you have lived with me in spirit, so have I lived with them in the flesh. As you have been one with me, so have I been one with them, and so will the new teacher ever be one with them and in them. And all this have I done that my brethren in the flesh may know that the Father loves them even as does the Son, and that you love them even as you love me. Father, work with me to save these believers that they may presently come to be with me in glory and then go on to join you in the Paradise embrace. Those who serve with me in humiliation, I would have with me in glory so that they may see all you have given into my hands as the eternal harvest of the seed sowing of time in the likeness of mortal flesh. I long to show my earthly brethren the glory I had with you before the founding of this world. This world knows very little of you, righteous Father, but I know you, and I have made you known to these believers, and they will make known your name to other generations. And now I promise them that you will be with them in the world even as you have been with me — even so."

The eleven remained kneeling in this circle about Jesus for several minutes before they arose and in silence made their way back to the near-by camp.

Jesus prayed for *unity* among his followers, but he did not desire uniformity. Sin creates a dead level of evil inertia, but righteousness nourishes the creative spirit of individual experience in the living realities of eternal truth and in the progressive communion of the divine spirits of the Father and the Son. In the spiritual fellowship of the believer-son with the divine Father there can never be doctrinal finality and sectarian superiority of group consciousness.

The Master, during the course of this final prayer with his apostles, alluded to the fact that he had manifested the Father's *name* to the world. And that is truly what he did by the revelation of God through his perfected life in the flesh. The Father in heaven had sought to reveal himself to Moses, but he could proceed no further than to cause it to be said, "I AM." And when pressed for further revelation of himself, it was only disclosed, "I AM that I AM." But when Jesus had finished his earth life, this name of the Father had been so revealed that the Master, who was the Father incarnate, could truly say:

I am the bread of life.

I am the living water.

I am the light of the world.
I am the desire of all ages.
I am the open door to eternal salvation.
I am the reality of endless life.
I am the good shepherd.
I am the pathway of infinite perfection.
I am the resurrection and the life.
I am the secret of eternal survival.
I am the way, the truth, and the life.
I am the infinite Father of my finite children.
I am the true vine; you are the branches.
I am the hope of all who know the living truth.
I am the living bridge from one world to another.
I am the living link between time and eternity.

Thus did Jesus enlarge the living revelation of the name of God to all generations. As divine love reveals the nature of God, eternal truth discloses his name in ever-enlarging proportions.

2. LAST HOUR BEFORE THE BETRAYAL

The apostles were greatly shocked when they returned to their camp and found Judas absent. While the eleven were engaged in a heated discussion of their traitorous fellow apostle, David Zebedee and John Mark took Jesus to one side and revealed that they had kept Judas under observation for several days, and that they knew he intended to betray him into the hands of his enemies. Jesus listened to them but only said: "My friends, nothing can happen to the Son of Man unless the Father in heaven so wills. Let not your hearts be troubled; all things will work together for the glory of God and the salvation of men."

The cheerful attitude of Jesus was waning. As the hour passed, he grew more and more serious, even sorrowful. The apostles, being much agitated, were loath to return to their tents even when requested to do so by the Master himself. Returning from his talk with David and John, he addressed his last words to all eleven, saying: "My friends, go to your rest. Prepare yourselves for the work of tomorrow. Remember, we should all submit ourselves to the will of the Father in heaven. My peace I leave with you." And having thus spoken, he motioned them to their tents, but as they went, he called to Peter, James, and John, saying, "I desire that you remain with me for a little while."

The apostles fell asleep only because they were literally exhausted; they had been running short on sleep ever since their arrival in Jerusalem. Before they went to their separate sleeping quarters, Simon Zelotes led them all over to his tent, where were stored the swords and other arms, and supplied each of them with this fighting equipment. All of them received these arms and girded themselves therewith except Nathaniel. Nathaniel, in refusing to arm himself, said: "My brethren, the Master has repeatedly told us that his kingdom is not of this world, and that his disciples should not fight with the sword to bring about its establishment. I believe this; I do not think the Master needs to have us employ the sword in his defense. We have all seen his mighty power and know that he could defend himself against his enemies if he so desired. If he will not resist his enemies, it must be that such a course represents his attempt to fulfill his Father's will. I will pray, but I will not wield the sword." When Andrew heard Nathaniel's speech, he handed his sword back to Simon Zelotes. And so nine of them were armed as they separated for the night.

Resentment of Judas's being a traitor for the moment eclipsed everything else in the apostles' minds. The Master's comment in reference to Judas, spoken in the course of the last prayer, opened their eyes to the fact that he had forsaken them.

After the eight apostles had finally gone to their tents, and while Peter, James, and John were standing by to receive the Master's orders, Jesus called to David Zebedee, "Send to me your most fleet and trustworthy messenger." When David brought to the Master one Jacob, once a runner on the overnight messenger service between Jerusalem and Bethsaida, Jesus, addressing him, said: "In all haste, go to Abner at Philadelphia and say: `The Master sends greetings of peace to you and says that the hour has come when he will be delivered into the hands of his enemies, who will put him to death, but that he will rise from the dead and appear to you shortly, before he goes to the Father, and that he will then give you guidance to the time when the new teacher shall come to live in your hearts.'" And when Jacob had rehearsed this message to the Master's satisfaction, Jesus sent him on his way, saying: "Fear not what any man may do to you, Jacob, for this night an unseen messenger will run by your side."

Then Jesus turned to the chief of the visiting Greeks who were encamped with them, and said: "My brother, be not disturbed by what is about to take place since I have already forewarned you. The Son of Man will be put to death at the instigation of his enemies, the chief priests and the rulers of the Jews, but I will rise to be with you a short time before I go to the Father. And when you have seen all this come to pass, glorify God and strengthen your brethren."

In ordinary circumstances the apostles would have bidden the Master a personal good night, but this evening they were so preoccupied with the sudden realization of Judas's desertion and so overcome by the unusual nature of the Master's farewell prayer that they listened to his good-bye salutation and went away in silence.

Jesus did say this to Andrew as he left his side that night: "Andrew, do what you can to keep your brethren together until I come again to you after I have drunk this cup. Strengthen your brethren, seeing that I have already told you all. Peace be with you."

None of the apostles expected anything out of the ordinary to happen that night since it was already so late. They sought sleep that they might rise up early in the morning and be prepared for the worst. They thought that the chief priests would seek to apprehend their Master early in the morning as no secular work was ever done after noon on the preparation day for the Passover. Only David Zebedee and John Mark understood that the enemies of Jesus were coming with Judas that very night.

David had arranged to stand guard that night on the upper trail which led to the Bethany-Jerusalem road, while John Mark was to watch along the road coming up by the Kidron to Gethsemane. Before David went to his self-imposed task of outpost duty, he bade farewell to Jesus, saying: "Master, I have had great joy in my service with you. My brothers are your apostles, but I have delighted to do the lesser things as they should be done, and I shall miss you with all my heart when you are gone." And then said Jesus to

David: "David, my son, others have done that which they were directed to do, but this service have you done of your own heart, and I have not been unmindful of your devotion. You, too, shall some day serve with me in the eternal kingdom."

And then, as he prepared to go on watch by the upper trail, David said to Jesus: "You know, Master, I sent for your family, and I have word by a messenger that they are tonight in Jericho. They will be here early tomorrow forenoon since it would be dangerous for them to come up the bloody way by night." And Jesus, looking down upon David, only said: "Let it be so, David."

When David had gone up Olivet, John Mark took up his vigil near the road which ran by the brook down to Jerusalem. And John would have remained at this post but for his great desire to be near Jesus and to know what was going on. Shortly after David left him, and when John Mark observed Jesus withdraw, with Peter, James, and John, into a near-by ravine, he was so overcome with combined devotion and curiosity that he forsook his sentinel post and followed after them, hiding himself in the bushes, from which place he saw and overheard all that transpired during those last moments in the garden and just before Judas and the armed guards appeared to arrest Jesus.

While all this was in progress at the Master's camp, Judas Iscariot was in conference with the captain of the temple guards, who had assembled his men preparatory to setting out, under the leadership of the betrayer, to arrest Jesus.

3. ALONE IN GETHSEMANE

After all was still and quiet about the camp, Jesus, taking Peter, James, and John, went a short way up a near-by ravine where he had often before gone to pray and commune. The three apostles could not help recognizing that he was grievously oppressed; never before had they observed their Master to be so heavy-laden and sorrowful. When they arrived at the place of his devotions, he bade the three sit down and watch with him while he went off about a stone's throw to pray. And when he had fallen down on his face, he prayed: "My Father, I came into this world to do your will, and so have I. I know that the hour has come to lay down this life in the flesh, and I do not shrink therefrom, but I would know that it is your will that I drink this cup. Send me the assurance that I will please you in my death even as I have in my life."

The Master remained in a prayerful attitude for a few moments, and then, going over to the three apostles, he found them sound asleep, for their eyes were heavy and they could not remain awake. As Jesus awoke them, he said: "What! can you not watch with me even for one hour? Cannot you see that my soul is exceedingly sorrowful, even to death, and that I crave your companionship?" After the three had aroused from their slumber, the Master again went apart by himself and, falling down on the ground, again prayed: "Father, I know it is possible to avoid this cup — all things are possible with you — but I have come to do your will, and while this is a bitter cup, I would drink it if it is your will." And when he had thus prayed, a mighty angel came down by his side and, speaking to him, touched him and strengthened him.

When Jesus returned to speak with the three apostles, he again found them fast asleep. He awakened them, saying: "In such an hour I need that you should watch and pray with me — all the more do you need to pray that you enter not into temptation — wherefore do you fall asleep when I leave you?"

And then, for a third time, the Master withdrew and prayed: "Father, you see my sleeping apostles; have mercy upon them. The spirit is indeed willing, but the flesh is weak. And now, O Father, if this cup may not pass, then would I drink it. Not my will, but yours, be done." And when he had finished praying, he lay for a moment prostrate on the ground. When he arose and went back to his apostles, once more he found them asleep. He surveyed them and, with a pitying gesture, tenderly said: "Sleep on now and take your rest; the time of decision is past. The hour is now upon us wherein the Son of Man will be betrayed into the hands of his enemies." As he reached down to shake them that he might awaken them, he said: "Arise, let us be going back to the camp, for, behold, he who betrays me is at hand, and the hour has come when my flock shall be scattered. But I have already told you about these things."

During the years that Jesus lived among his followers, they did, indeed, have much proof of his divine nature, but just now are they about to witness new evidences of his humanity. Just before the greatest of all the revelations of his divinity, his resurrection, must now come the greatest proofs of his mortal nature, his humiliation and crucifixion.

Each time he prayed in the garden, his humanity laid a firmer faith-hold upon his divinity; his human will more completely became one with the divine will of his Father. Among other words spoken to him by the mighty angel was the message that the Father desired his Son to finish his earth bestowal by passing through the creature experience of death just as all mortal creatures must experience material dissolution in passing from the existence of time into the progression of eternity.

Earlier in the evening it had not seemed so difficult to drink the cup, but as the human Jesus bade farewell to his apostles and sent them to their rest, the trial grew more appalling. Jesus experienced that natural ebb and flow of feeling which is common to all human experience, and just now he was weary from work, exhausted from the long hours of strenuous labor and painful anxiety concerning the safety of his apostles. While no mortal can presume to understand the thoughts and feelings of the incarnate Son of God at such a time as this, we know that he endured great anguish and suffered untold sorrow, for the perspiration rolled off his face in great drops. He was at last convinced that the Father intended to allow natural events to take their course; he was fully determined to employ none of his sovereign power as the supreme head of a universe to save himself.

The assembled hosts of a vast creation are now hovered over this scene under the transient joint command of Gabriel and the Personalized Adjuster of Jesus. The division commanders of these armies of heaven have repeatedly been warned not to interfere with these transactions on earth unless Jesus himself should order them to intervene.

The experience of parting with the apostles was a great strain on the human heart of Jesus; this sorrow of love bore down on him and made it more difficult to face such a death as he well knew awaited him. He realized how weak and how ignorant his apostles were, and he dreaded to leave them. He well knew that the time of his departure had come, but his human heart longed to find out whether there might not possibly be some legitimate avenue of escape from this terrible plight of suffering and sorrow. And when it had thus sought escape, and failed, it was willing to drink the cup. The divine mind of Michael knew he had done his best for the twelve apostles; but the human heart of Jesus wished that more might have been done for them before they should be left alone in the world. Jesus' heart was being crushed; he truly loved his brethren. He was isolated from his family in the flesh; one of his chosen associates was betraying him. His father Joseph's people had rejected him and thereby sealed their doom as a people with a special mission on earth. His soul was tortured by baffled love and rejected mercy. It was just one of those awful human moments when everything seems to bear down with crushing cruelty and terrible agony.

Jesus' humanity was not insensible to this situation of private loneliness, public shame, and the appearance of the failure of his cause. All these sentiments bore down on him with indescribable heaviness. In this great sorrow his mind went back to the days of his childhood in Nazareth and to his early work in Galilee. At the time of this great trial there came up in his mind many of those pleasant scenes of his earthly ministry. And it was from these old memories of Nazareth, Capernaum, Mount Hermon, and of the sunrise and sunset on the shimmering Sea of Galilee, that he soothed himself as he made his human heart strong and ready to encounter the traitor who should so soon betray him.

Before Judas and the soldiers arrived, the Master had fully regained his customary poise; the spirit had triumphed over the flesh; faith had asserted itself over all human tendencies to fear or entertain doubt. The supreme test of the full realization of the human nature had been met and acceptably passed. Once more the Son of Man was prepared to face his enemies with equanimity and in the full assurance of his invincibility as a mortal man unreservedly dedicated to the doing of his Father's will.

PAPER 183
THE BETRAYAL AND ARREST OF JESUS

AFTER JESUS HAD FINALLY AWAKENED Peter, James, and John, he suggested that they go to their tents and seek sleep in preparation for the duties of the morrow. But by this time the three apostles were wide awake; they had been refreshed by their short naps, and besides, they were stimulated and aroused by the arrival on the scene of two excited messengers who inquired for David Zebedee and quickly went in quest of him when Peter informed them where he kept watch.

Although eight of the apostles were sound asleep, the Greeks who were encamped alongside them were more fearful of trouble, so much so that they had posted a sentinel to give the alarm in case danger should arise. When these two messengers hurried into camp, the Greek sentinel proceeded to arouse all of his fellow countrymen, who streamed forth from their tents, fully dressed and fully armed. All the camp was now aroused except the eight apostles. Peter desired to call his associates, but Jesus definitely forbade him. The Master mildly admonished them all to return to their tents, but they were reluctant to comply with his suggestion.

Failing to disperse his followers, the Master left them and walked down toward the olive press near the entrance to Gethsemane Park. Although the three apostles, the Greeks, and the other members of the camp hesitated immediately to follow him, John Mark hastened around through the olive trees and secreted himself in a small shed near the olive press. Jesus withdrew from the camp and from his friends in order that his apprehenders, when they arrived, might arrest him without disturbing his apostles. The Master feared to have his apostles awake and present at the time of his arrest lest the spectacle of Judas's betraying him should so arouse their animosity that they would offer resistance to the soldiers and would be taken into custody with him. He feared that, if they should be arrested with him, they might also perish with him.

Though Jesus knew that the plan for his death had its origin in the councils of the rulers of the Jews, he was also aware that all such nefarious schemes had the full approval of Lucifer, Satan, and Caligastia. And he well knew that these rebels of the realms would also be pleased to see all of the apostles destroyed with him.

Jesus sat down, alone, on the olive press, where he awaited the coming of the betrayer, and he was seen at this time only by John Mark and an innumerable host of celestial observers.

1. THE FATHER'S WILL

There is great danger of misunderstanding the meaning of numerous sayings and many events associated with the termination of the Master's career in the flesh. The cruel treatment of Jesus by the ignorant servants and the calloused soldiers, the unfair conduct of his trials, and the unfeeling attitude of the professed religious leaders, must not be confused with the fact that Jesus, in patiently submitting to all this suffering and humiliation, was truly doing the will of the Father in Paradise. It was, indeed and in truth, the will of the Father that his Son should drink to the full the cup of mortal experience, from birth to death, but the Father in heaven had nothing whatever to do with instigating the barbarous behavior of those supposedly civilized human beings who so brutally tortured the Master and so horribly heaped successive indignities upon his nonresisting person. These inhuman and shocking experiences which Jesus was called upon to endure in the final hours of his mortal life were not in any sense a part of the divine will of the Father, which his human nature had so triumphantly pledged to carry out at the time of the final surrender of man to God as signified in the threefold prayer which he indited in the garden while his weary apostles slept the sleep of physical exhaustion.

The Father in heaven desired the bestowal Son to finish his earth career *naturally*, just as all mortals must finish up their lives on earth and in the flesh. Ordinary men and women cannot expect to have their last hours on earth and the supervening episode of death made easy by a special dispensation. Accordingly, Jesus elected to lay down his life in the flesh in the manner which was in keeping with the outworking of natural events, and he steadfastly refused to extricate himself from the cruel clutches of a wicked conspiracy of inhuman events which swept on with horrible certainty toward his unbelievable humiliation and ignominious death. And every bit of all this astounding manifestation of hatred and this unprecedented demonstration of cruelty was the work of evil men and wicked mortals. God in heaven did not will it, neither did the archenemies of Jesus dictate it, though they did much to insure that unthinking and evil mortals would thus reject the bestowal Son. Even the father of sin turned his face away from the excruciating horror of the scene of the crucifixion.

2. JUDAS IN THE CITY

After Judas so abruptly left the table while eating the Last Supper, he went directly to the home of his cousin, and then did the two go straight to the captain of the temple guards. Judas requested the captain to assemble the guards and informed him that he was ready to lead them to Jesus. Judas having appeared on the scene a little before he was expected, there was some delay in getting started for the Mark home, where Judas expected to find Jesus still visiting with the apostles. The Master and the eleven left the home of Elijah Mark fully fifteen minutes before the betrayer and the guards arrived. By the time the apprehenders reached the Mark home, Jesus and the eleven were well outside the walls of the city and on their way to the Olivet camp.

Judas was much perturbed by this failure to find Jesus at the Mark residence and in the company of eleven men, only two of whom were armed for resistance. He happened to know that, in the afternoon when they had left camp, only Simon Peter and Simon Zelotes were girded with swords; Judas had hoped to take Jesus when the city was quiet, and when there was little chance of resistance. The betrayer feared that, if he waited for them to return to their camp, more than threescore of devoted disciples would be encountered, and he also knew that Simon Zelotes had an ample store of arms in his possession. Judas was becoming increasingly nervous as he meditated how the eleven loyal apostles would detest him, and he feared they would all seek to destroy him. He was not only disloyal, but he was a real coward at heart.

When they failed to find Jesus in the upper chamber, Judas asked the captain of the guard to return to the temple. By this time the rulers had begun to assemble at the high priest's home preparatory to receiving Jesus, seeing that their bargain with the traitor called for Jesus' arrest by midnight of that day. Judas explained to his associates that they had missed Jesus at the Mark home, and that it would be necessary to go to Gethsemane to arrest him. The betrayer then went on to state that more than threescore devoted followers were encamped with him, and that they were all well armed. The rulers of the Jews reminded Judas that Jesus had always preached nonresistance, but Judas replied that they could not depend upon all Jesus' followers obeying such teaching. He really feared for himself and therefore made bold to ask for a company of forty armed soldiers. Since the Jewish authorities had no such force of armed men under their jurisdiction, they went at once to the fortress of Antonia and requested the Roman commander to give them this guard; but when he learned that they intended to arrest Jesus, he promptly refused to accede to their request and referred them to his superior officer. In this way more than an hour was consumed in going from one authority to another until they finally were compelled to go to Pilate himself in order to obtain permission to employ the armed Roman guards. It was late when they arrived at Pilate's house, and he had retired to his private chambers with his wife. He hesitated to have anything to do with the enterprise, all the more so since his wife had asked him not to grant the request. But inasmuch as the presiding officer of the Jewish Sanhedrin was present and making personal request for this assistance, the governor thought it wise to grant the petition, thinking he could later on right any wrong they might be disposed to commit.

Accordingly, when Judas Iscariot started out from the temple, about half after eleven o'clock, he was accompanied by more than sixty persons —

temple guards, Roman soldiers, and curious servants of the chief priests and rulers.

3. THE MASTER'S ARREST

As this company of armed soldiers and guards, carrying torches and lanterns, approached the garden, Judas stepped well out in front of the band that he might be ready quickly to identify Jesus so that the apprehenders could easily lay hands on him before his associates could rally to his defense. And there was yet another reason why Judas chose to be ahead of the Master's enemies: He thought it would appear that he had arrived on the scene ahead of the soldiers so that the apostles and others gathered about Jesus might not directly connect him with the armed guards following so closely upon his heels. Judas had even thought to pose as having hastened out to warn them of the coming of the apprehenders, but this plan was thwarted by Jesus' blighting greeting of the betrayer. Though the Master spoke to Judas kindly, he greeted him as a traitor.

As soon as Peter, James, and John, with some thirty of their fellow campers, saw the armed band with torches swing around the brow of the hill, they knew that these soldiers were coming to arrest Jesus, and they all rushed down to near the olive press where the Master was sitting in moonlit solitude. As the company of soldiers approached on one side, the three apostles and their associates approached on the other. As Judas strode forward to accost the Master, there the two groups stood, motionless, with the Master between them and Judas making ready to impress the traitorous kiss upon his brow.

It had been the hope of the betrayer that he could, after leading the guards to Gethsemane, simply point Jesus out to the soldiers, or at most carry out the promise to greet him with a kiss, and then quickly retire from the scene. Judas greatly feared that the apostles would all be present, and that they would concentrate their attack upon him in retribution for his daring to betray their beloved teacher. But when the Master greeted him as a betrayer, he was so confused that he made no attempt to flee.

Jesus made one last effort to save Judas from actually betraying him in that, before the traitor could reach him, he stepped to one side and, addressing the foremost soldier on the left, the captain of the Romans, said, "Whom do you seek?" The captain answered, "Jesus of Nazareth." Then Jesus stepped up immediately in front of the officer and, standing there in the calm majesty of the God of all this creation, said, "I am he." Many of this armed band had heard Jesus teach in the temple, others had learned about his mighty works, and when they heard him thus boldly announce his identity, those in the front ranks fell suddenly backward. They were overcome with surprise at his calm and majestic announcement of identity. There was, therefore, no need for Judas to go on with his plan of betrayal. The Master had boldly revealed himself to his enemies, and they could have taken him without Judas's assistance. But the traitor had to do something to account for his presence with this armed band, and besides, he wanted to make a show of carrying out his part of the betrayal bargain with the rulers of the Jews in order to be eligible for the great reward and honors which he believed would be heaped upon him in compensation for his promise to deliver Jesus into their hands.

As the guards rallied from their first faltering at the sight of Jesus and at the sound of his unusual voice, and as the apostles and disciples drew nearer, Judas stepped up to Jesus and, placing a kiss upon his brow, said, "Hail, Master and Teacher." And as Judas thus embraced his Master, Jesus said, "Friend, is it not enough to do this! Would you even betray the Son of Man with a kiss?"

The apostles and disciples were literally stunned by what they saw. For a moment no one moved. Then Jesus, disengaging himself from the traitorous embrace of Judas, stepped up to the guards and soldiers and again asked, "Whom do you seek?" And again the captain said, "Jesus of Nazareth." And again answered Jesus: "I have told you that I am he. If, therefore, you seek me, let these others go their way. I am ready to go with you."

Jesus was ready to go back to Jerusalem with the guards, and the captain of the soldiers was altogether willing to allow the three apostles and their associates to go their way in peace. But before they were able to get started, as Jesus stood there awaiting the captain's orders, one Malchus, the Syrian bodyguard of the high priest, stepped up to Jesus and made ready to bind his hands behind his back, although the Roman captain had not directed that Jesus should be thus bound. When Peter and his associates saw their Master being subjected to this indignity, they were no longer able to restrain themselves. Peter drew his sword and with the others rushed forward to smite Malchus. But before the soldiers could come to the defense of the high priest's servant, Jesus raised a forbidding hand to Peter and, speaking sternly, said: "Peter, put up your sword. They who take the sword shall perish by the sword. Do you not understand that it is the Father's will that I drink this cup? And do you not further know that I could even now command more than twelve legions of angels and their associates, who would deliver me from the hands of these few men?"

While Jesus thus effectively put a stop to this show of physical resistance by his followers, it was enough to arouse the fear of the captain of the guards, who now, with the help of his soldiers, laid heavy hands on Jesus and quickly bound him. And as they tied his hands with heavy cords, Jesus said to them: "Why do you come out against me with swords and with staves as if to seize a robber? I was daily with you in the temple, publicly teaching the people, and you made no effort to take me."

When Jesus had been bound, the captain, fearing that the followers of the Master might attempt to rescue him, gave orders that they be seized; but the soldiers were not quick enough since, having overheard the captain's orders to arrest them, Jesus' followers fled in haste back into the ravine. All this time John Mark had remained secluded in the near-by shed. When the guards started back to Jerusalem with Jesus, John Mark attempted to steal out of the shed in order to catch up with the fleeing apostles and disciples; but just as he emerged, one of the last of the returning soldiers who had pursued the fleeing disciples was passing near and, seeing this young man in his linen coat, gave chase, almost overtaking him. In fact, the soldier got near enough to John to lay hold upon his coat, but the young man freed himself from the garment, escaping naked while the soldier held the empty coat. John Mark made his way in all haste to David Zebedee on the upper trail. When he had told David what had happened, they both hastened back to the tents of the sleeping apostles and informed all eight of the Master's betrayal and arrest.

At about the time the eight apostles were being awakened, those who had fled up the ravine were returning, and they all gathered together near the olive press to debate what should be done. In the meantime, Simon Peter and John Zebedee, who had hidden among the olive trees, had already gone on after the mob of soldiers, guards, and servants, who were now leading Jesus back to Jerusalem as they would have led a desperate criminal. John followed close behind the mob, but Peter followed afar off. After John Mark's escape from the clutch of the soldier, he provided himself with a cloak which he found in the tent of Simon Peter and John Zebedee. He suspected the guards were going to take Jesus to the home of Annas, the high priest emeritus; so he skirted around through the olive orchards and was there ahead of the mob, hiding near the entrance to the gate of the high priest's palace.

4. DISCUSSION AT THE OLIVE PRESS

James Zebedee found himself separated from Simon Peter and his brother John, and so he now joined the other apostles and their fellow campers at the olive press to deliberate on what should be done in view of the Master's arrest.

Andrew had been released from all responsibility in the group management of his fellow apostles; accordingly, in this greatest of all crises in their lives, he was silent. After a short informal discussion, Simon Zelotes stood up on the stone wall of the olive press and, making an impassioned plea for loyalty to the Master and the cause of the kingdom, exhorted his fellow apostles and the other disciples to hasten on after the mob and effect the rescue of Jesus. The majority of the company would have been disposed to follow his aggressive leadership had it not been for the advice of Nathaniel, who stood up the moment Simon had finished speaking and called their attention to Jesus' oft-repeated teachings regarding nonresistance. He further reminded them that Jesus had that very night instructed them that they should preserve their lives for the time when they should go forth into the world proclaiming the good news of the gospel of the heavenly kingdom. And Nathaniel was encouraged in this stand by James Zebedee, who now told how Peter and others drew their swords to defend the Master against arrest, and that Jesus bade Simon Peter and his fellow swordsmen sheathe their blades. Matthew and Philip also made speeches, but nothing definite came of this discussion until Thomas, calling their attention to the fact that Jesus had counseled Lazarus against exposing himself to death, pointed out that they could do nothing to save their Master inasmuch as he refused to allow his friends to defend him, and since he persisted in refraining from the use of his divine powers to frustrate his human enemies. Thomas persuaded them to scatter, every man for himself, with the understanding that David Zebedee would remain at the camp to maintain a clearinghouse and messenger headquarters for the group. By half past two o'clock that morning the camp was deserted; only David remained on hand with three or four messengers, the others having been dispatched to secure information as to where Jesus had been taken, and what was going to be done with him.

Five of the apostles, Nathaniel, Matthew, Philip, and the twins, went into hiding at Bethpage and Bethany. Thomas, Andrew, James, and Simon Zelotes were hiding in the city. Simon Peter and John Zebedee followed along to the home of Annas.

Shortly after daybreak, Simon Peter wandered back to the Gethsemane camp, a dejected picture of deep despair. David sent him in charge of a messenger to join his brother, Andrew, who was at the home of Nicodemus in Jerusalem.

Until the very end of the crucifixion, John Zebedee remained, as Jesus had directed him, always near at hand, and it was he who supplied David's messengers with information from hour to hour which they carried to David at the garden camp, and which was then relayed to the hiding apostles and to Jesus' family.

Surely, the shepherd is smitten and the sheep are scattered! While they all vaguely realize that Jesus has forewarned them of this very situation, they are too severely shocked by the Master's sudden disappearance to be able to use their minds normally.

It was shortly after daylight and just after Peter had been sent to join his brother, that Jude, Jesus' brother in the flesh, arrived in the camp, almost breathless and in advance of the rest of Jesus' family, only to learn that the Master had already been placed under arrest; and he hastened back down the Jericho road to carry this information to his mother and to his brothers and sisters. David Zebedee sent word to Jesus' family, by Jude, to forgather at the house of Martha and Mary in Bethany and there await news which his messengers would regularly bring them.

This was the situation during the last half of Thursday night and the early morning hours of Friday as regards the apostles, the chief disciples, and the earthly family of Jesus. And all these groups and individuals were kept in touch with each other by the messenger service which David Zebedee continued to operate from his headquarters at the Gethsemane camp.

5. ON THE WAY TO THE HIGH PRIEST'S PALACE

Before they started away from the garden with Jesus, a dispute arose between the Jewish captain of the temple guards and the Roman captain of the company of soldiers as to where they were to take Jesus. The captain of the temple guards gave orders that he should be taken to Caiaphas, the acting high priest. The captain of the Roman soldiers directed that Jesus be taken to the palace of Annas, the former high priest and father-in-law of Caiaphas. And this he did because the Romans were in the habit of dealing directly with Annas in all matters having to do with the enforcement of the Jewish ecclesiastical laws. And the orders of the Roman captain were obeyed; they took Jesus to the home of Annas for his preliminary examination.

Judas marched along near the captains, overhearing all that was said, but took no part in the dispute, for neither the Jewish captain nor the Roman officer would so much as speak to the betrayer — they held him in such contempt.

About this time John Zebedee, remembering his Master's instructions to remain always near at hand, hurried up near Jesus as he marched along between the two captains. The commander of the temple guards, seeing John come up alongside, said to his assistant: "Take this man and bind him. He is one of this fellow's followers." But when the Roman captain heard this and, looking around, saw John, he gave orders that the apostle should come over by him, and that no man should molest him. Then the Roman captain said to the Jewish captain: "This man is neither a traitor nor a coward. I saw him in the garden, and he did not draw a sword to resist us. He has the courage to come forward to be with his Master, and no man shall lay hands on him. The Roman law allows that any prisoner may have at least one friend to stand with him before the judgment bar, and this man shall not be prevented from standing by the side of his Master, the prisoner." And when Judas heard this, he was so ashamed and humiliated that he dropped back behind the marchers, coming up to the palace of Annas alone.

And this explains why John Zebedee was permitted to remain near Jesus all the way through his trying experiences this night and the next day. The Jews feared to say aught to John or to molest him in any way because he had something of the status of a Roman counselor designated to act as observer of the transactions of the Jewish ecclesiastical court. John's position of privilege was made all the more secure when, in turning Jesus over to the captain of the temple guards at the gate of Annas's palace, the Roman, addressing his assistant, said: "Go along with this prisoner and see that these Jews do not kill him without Pilate's consent. Watch that they do not assassinate him, and see that his friend, the Galilean, is permitted to stand by and observe all that goes on." And thus was John able to be near Jesus right on up to the time of his death on the cross, though the other ten apostles were compelled to remain in hiding. John was acting under Roman protection, and the Jews dared not molest him until after the Master's death.

And all the way to the palace of Annas, Jesus opened not his mouth. From the time of his arrest to the time of his appearance before Annas, the Son of Man spoke no word.

PAPER 184
BEFORE THE SANHEDRIN COURT

Representatives of Annas had secretly instructed the captain of the Roman soldiers to bring Jesus immediately to the palace of Annas after he had been arrested. The former high priest desired to maintain his prestige as the chief ecclesiastical authority of the Jews. He also had another purpose in detaining Jesus at his house for several hours, and that was to allow time for legally calling together the court of the Sanhedrin. It was not lawful to convene the Sanhedrin court before the time of the offering of the morning sacrifice in the temple, and this sacrifice was offered about three o'clock in the morning.

Annas knew that a court of Sanhedrists was in waiting at the palace of his son-in-law, Caiaphas. Some thirty members of the Sanhedrin had gathered at the home of the high priest by midnight so that they would be ready to sit in judgment on Jesus when he might be brought before them. Only those members were assembled who were strongly and openly opposed to Jesus and his teaching since it required only twenty-three to constitute a trial court.

Jesus spent about three hours at the palace of Annas on Mount Olivet, not far from the garden of Gethsemane, where they arrested him. John Zebedee was free and safe in the palace of Annas not only because of the word of the Roman captain, but also because he and his brother James were well known to the older servants, having many times been guests at the palace as the former high priest was a distant relative of their mother, Salome.

1. EXAMINATION BY ANNAS

Annas, enriched by the temple revenues, his son-in-law the acting high priest, and with his relations to the Roman authorities, was indeed the most powerful single individual in all Jewry. He was a suave and politic planner and plotter. He desired to direct the matter of disposing of Jesus; he feared to trust such an important undertaking wholly to his brusque and aggressive son-in-law. Annas wanted to make sure that the Master's trial was kept in the hands of the Sadducees; he feared the possible sympathy of some of the Pharisees, seeing that practically all of those members of the Sanhedrin who had espoused the cause of Jesus were Pharisees.

Annas had not seen Jesus for several years, not since the time when the Master called at his house and immediately left upon observing his coldness and reserve in receiving him. Annas had thought to presume on this early acquaintance and thereby attempt to persuade Jesus to abandon his claims and leave Palestine. He was reluctant to participate in the murder of a good man and had reasoned that Jesus might choose to leave the country rather than to suffer death. But when Annas stood before the stalwart and determined Galilean, he knew at once that it would be useless to make such proposals. Jesus was even more majestic and well poised than Annas remembered him.

When Jesus was young, Annas had taken a great interest in him, but now his revenues were threatened by what Jesus had so recently done in driving the money-changers and other commercial traders out of the temple. This act had aroused the enmity of the former high priest far more than had Jesus' teachings.

Annas entered his spacious audience chamber, seated himself in a large chair, and commanded that Jesus be brought before him. After a few moments spent in silently surveying the Master, he said: "You realize that something must be done about your teaching since you are disturbing the peace and order of our country." As Annas looked inquiringly at Jesus, the

Master looked full into his eyes but made no reply. Again Annas spoke, "What are the names of your disciples, besides Simon Zelotes, the agitator?" Again Jesus looked down upon him, but he did not answer.

Annas was considerably disturbed by Jesus' refusal to answer his questions, so much so that he said to him: "Do you have no care as to whether I am friendly to you or not? Do you have no regard for the power I have in determining the issues of your coming trial?" When Jesus heard this, he said: "Annas, you know that you could have no power over me unless it were permitted by my Father. Some would destroy the Son of Man because they are ignorant; they know no better, but you, friend, know what you are doing. How can you, therefore, reject the light of God?"

The kindly manner in which Jesus spoke to Annas almost bewildered him. But he had already determined in his mind that Jesus must either leave Palestine or die; so he summoned up his courage and asked: "Just what is it you are trying to teach the people? What do you claim to be?" Jesus answered: "You know full well that I have spoken openly to the world. I have taught in the synagogues and many times in the temple, where all the Jews and many of the gentiles have heard me. In secret I have spoken nothing; why, then, do you ask me about my teaching? Why do you not summon those who have heard me and inquire of them? Behold, all Jerusalem has heard that which I have spoken even if you have not yourself heard these teachings." But before Annas could make reply, the chief steward of the palace, who was standing near, struck Jesus in the face with his hand, saying, "How dare you answer the high priest with such words?" Annas spoke no words of rebuke to his steward, but Jesus addressed him, saying, "My friend, if I have spoken evil, bear witness against the evil; but if I have spoken the truth, why, then, should you smite me?"

Although Annas regretted that his steward had struck Jesus, he was too proud to take notice of the matter. In his confusion he went into another room, leaving Jesus alone with the household attendants and the temple guards for almost an hour.

When he returned, going up to the Master's side, he said, "Do you claim to be the Messiah, the deliverer of Israel?" Said Jesus: "Annas, you have known me from the times of my youth. You know that I claim to be nothing except that which my Father has appointed, and that I have been sent to all men, gentile as well as Jew." Then said Annas: "I have been told that you have claimed to be the Messiah; is that true?" Jesus looked upon Annas but only replied, "So you have said."

About this time messengers arrived from the palace of Caiaphas to inquire what time Jesus would be brought before the court of the Sanhedrin, and since it was nearing the break of day, Annas thought best to send Jesus bound and in the custody of the temple guards to Caiaphas. He himself followed after them shortly.

2. PETER IN THE COURTYARD

As the band of guards and soldiers approached the entrance to the palace of Annas, John Zebedee was marching by the side of the captain of the Roman soldiers. Judas had dropped some distance behind, and Simon Peter followed afar off. After John had entered the palace courtyard with Jesus and the guards, Judas came up to the gate but, seeing Jesus and John, went on over to the home of Caiaphas, where he knew the real trial of the Master would later take place. Soon after Judas had left, Simon Peter arrived, and as he stood before the gate, John saw him just as they were about to take Jesus into the palace. The portress who kept the gate knew John, and when he spoke to her, requesting that she let Peter in, she gladly assented.

Peter, upon entering the courtyard, went over to the charcoal fire and sought to warm himself, for the night was chilly. He felt very much out of place here among the enemies of Jesus, and indeed he was out of place. The Master had not instructed him to keep near at hand as he had admonished John. Peter belonged with the other apostles, who had been specifically warned not to endanger their lives during these times of the trial and crucifixion of their Master.

Peter threw away his sword shortly before he came up to the palace gate so that he entered the courtyard of Annas unarmed. His mind was in a whirl of confusion; he could scarcely realize that Jesus had been arrested. He could not grasp the reality of the situation — that he was here in the courtyard of Annas, warming himself beside the servants of the high priest. He wondered what the other apostles were doing and, in turning over in his mind as to how John came to be admitted to the palace, concluded that it was because he was known to the servants, since he had bidden the gate-keeper admit him.

Shortly after the portress let Peter in, and while he was warming himself by the fire, she went over to him and mischievously said, "Are you not also one of this man's disciples?" Now Peter should not have been surprised at this recognition, for it was John who had requested that the girl let him pass through the palace gates; but he was in such a tense nervous state that this identification as a disciple threw him off his balance, and with only one thought uppermost in his mind — the thought of escaping with his life — he promptly answered the maid's question by saying, "I am not."

Very soon another servant came up to Peter and asked: "Did I not see you in the garden when they arrested this fellow? Are you not also one of his followers?" Peter was now thoroughly alarmed; he saw no way of safely escaping from these accusers; so he vehemently denied all connection with Jesus, saying, "I know not this man, neither am I one of his followers."

About this time the portress of the gate drew Peter to one side and said: "I am sure you are a disciple of this Jesus, not only because one of his followers bade me let you in the courtyard, but my sister here has seen you in the temple with this man. Why do you deny this?" When Peter heard the maid accuse him, he denied all knowledge of Jesus with much cursing and swearing, again saying, "I am not this man's follower; I do not even know him; I never heard of him before."

Peter left the fireside for a time while he walked about the courtyard. He would have liked to have escaped, but he feared to attract attention to himself. Getting cold, he returned to the fireside, and one of the men standing near him said: "Surely you are one of this man's disciples. This Jesus is a Galilean, and your speech betrays you, for you also speak as a Galilean." And again Peter denied all connection with his Master.

Peter was so perturbed that he sought to escape contact with his accusers by going away from the fire and remaining by himself on the porch. After more than an hour of this isolation, the gate-keeper and her sister chanced to meet him, and both of them again teasingly charged him with being a follower of Jesus. And again he denied the accusation. Just as he had once more denied all connection with Jesus, the cock crowed, and Peter remembered the words of warning spoken to him by his Master earlier that same night. As he stood there, heavy of heart and crushed with the sense of guilt, the palace doors opened, and the guards led Jesus past on the way to Caiaphas. As the Master passed Peter, he saw, by the light of the torches, the look of despair on the face of his former self-confident and superficially brave apostle, and he turned and looked upon Peter. Peter never forgot that look as long as he lived. It was such a glance of commingled pity and love as mortal man had never beheld in the face of the Master.

After Jesus and the guards passed out of the palace gates, Peter followed them, but only for a short distance. He could not go farther. He sat down by the side of the road and wept bitterly. And when he had shed these tears of agony, he turned his steps back toward the camp, hoping to find his brother, Andrew. On arriving at the camp, he found only David Zebedee, who sent a messenger to direct him to where his brother had gone to hide in Jerusalem.

Peter's entire experience occurred in the courtyard of the palace of Annas on Mount Olivet. He did not follow Jesus to the palace of the high priest, Caiaphas. That Peter was brought to the realization that he had repeatedly denied his Master by the crowing of a cock indicates that this all occurred outside of Jerusalem since it was against the law to keep poultry within the city proper.

Until the crowing of the cock brought Peter to his better senses, he had only thought, as he walked up and down the porch to keep warm, how cleverly he had eluded the accusations of the servants, and how he had frustrated their purpose to identify him with Jesus. For the time being, he had only considered that these servants had no moral or legal right thus to question him, and he really congratulated himself over the manner in which he thought he had avoided being identified and possibly subjected to arrest and imprisonment. Not until the cock crowed did it occur to Peter that he had denied his Master. Not until Jesus looked upon him, did he realize that he had failed to live up to his privileges as an ambassador of the kingdom.

Having taken the first step along the path of compromise and least resistance, there was nothing apparent to Peter but to go on with the course of conduct decided upon. It requires a great and noble character, having started out wrong, to turn about and go right. All too often one's own mind tends to justify continuance in the path of error when once it is entered upon.

Peter never fully believed that he could be forgiven until he met his

Master after the resurrection and saw that he was received just as before the experiences of this tragic night of the denials.

3. BEFORE THE COURT OF SANHEDRISTS

It was about half past three o'clock this Friday morning when the chief priest, Caiaphas, called the Sanhedrist court of inquiry to order and asked that Jesus be brought before them for his formal trial. On three previous occasions the Sanhedrin, by a large majority vote, had decreed the death of Jesus, had decided that he was worthy of death on informal charges of law-breaking, blasphemy, and flouting the traditions of the fathers of Israel.

This was not a regularly called meeting of the Sanhedrin and was not held in the usual place, the chamber of hewn stone in the temple. This was a special trial court of some thirty Sanhedrists and was convened in the palace of the high priest. John Zebedee was present with Jesus throughout this so-called trial.

How these chief priests, scribes, Sadducees, and some of the Pharisees flattered themselves that Jesus, the disturber of their position and the challenger of their authority, was now securely in their hands! And they were resolved that he should never live to escape their vengeful clutches.

Ordinarily, the Jews, when trying a man on a capital charge, proceeded with great caution and provided every safeguard of fairness in the selection of witnesses and the entire conduct of the trial. But on this occasion, Caiaphas was more of a prosecutor than an unbiased judge.

Jesus appeared before this court clothed in his usual garments and with his hands bound together behind his back. The entire court was startled and somewhat confused by his majestic appearance. Never had they gazed upon such a prisoner nor witnessed such composure in a man on trial for his life.

The Jewish law required that at least two witnesses must agree upon any point before a charge could be laid against the prisoner. Judas could not be used as a witness against Jesus because the Jewish law specifically forbade the testimony of a traitor. More than a score of false witnesses were on hand to testify against Jesus, but their testimony was so contradictory and so evidently trumped up that the Sanhedrists themselves were very much ashamed of the performance. Jesus stood there, looking down benignly upon these perjurers, and his very countenance disconcerted the lying witnesses. Throughout all this false testimony the Master never said a word; he made no reply to their many false accusations.

The first time any two of their witnesses approached even the semblance of an agreement was when two men testified that they had heard Jesus say in the course of one of his temple discourses that he would "destroy this temple made with hands and in three days make another temple without hands." That was not exactly what Jesus said, regardless of the fact that he pointed to his own body when he made the remark referred to.

Although the high priest shouted at Jesus, "Do you not answer any of these charges?" Jesus opened not his mouth. He stood there in silence while all of these false witnesses gave their testimony. Hatred, fanaticism, and unscrupulous exaggeration so characterized the words of these perjurers that their testimony fell in its own entanglements. The very best refutation of their false accusations was the Master's calm and majestic silence.

Shortly after the beginning of the testimony of the false witnesses, Annas arrived and took his seat beside Caiaphas. Annas now arose and argued that this threat of Jesus to destroy the temple was sufficient to warrant three charges against him:

1. That he was a dangerous traducer of the people. That he taught them impossible things and otherwise deceived them.

2. That he was a fanatical revolutionist in that he advocated laying violent hands on the sacred temple, else how could he destroy it?

3. That he taught magic inasmuch as he promised to build a new temple, and that without hands.

Already had the full Sanhedrin agreed that Jesus was guilty of death-deserving transgressions of the Jewish laws, but they were now more concerned with developing charges regarding his conduct and teachings which would justify Pilate in pronouncing the death sentence upon their prisoner. They knew that they must secure the consent of the Roman governor before Jesus could legally be put to death. And Annas was minded to proceed along the line of making it appear that Jesus was a dangerous teacher to be abroad among the people.

But Caiaphas could not longer endure the sight of the Master standing there in perfect composure and unbroken silence. He thought he knew at least one way in which the prisoner might be induced to speak. Accordingly, he rushed over to the side of Jesus and, shaking his accusing finger in the Master's face, said: "I adjure you, in the name of the living God, that you tell us whether you are the Deliverer, the Son of God." Jesus answered Caiaphas: "I am. Soon I go to the Father, and presently shall the Son of Man be clothed with power and once more reign over the hosts of heaven."

When the high priest heard Jesus utter these words, he was exceedingly angry, and rending his outer garments, he exclaimed: "What further need have we of witnesses? Behold, now have you all heard this man's blasphemy. What do you now think should be done with this law-breaker and blasphemer?" And they all answered in unison, "He is worthy of death; let him be crucified."

Jesus manifested no interest in any question asked him when before Annas or the Sanhedrists except the one question relative to his bestowal mission. When asked if he were the Son of God, he instantly and unequivocally answered in the affirmative.

Annas desired that the trial proceed further, and that charges of a definite nature regarding Jesus' relation to the Roman law and Roman institutions be formulated for subsequent presentation to Pilate. The councilors were anxious to carry these matters to a speedy termination, not only because it was the preparation day for the Passover and no secular work should be done after noon, but also because they feared Pilate might any time return to the Roman capital of Judea, Caesarea, since he was in Jerusalem only for the Passover celebration.

But Annas did not succeed in keeping control of the court. After Jesus had so unexpectedly answered Caiaphas, the high priest stepped forward and smote him in the face with his hand. Annas was truly shocked as the other members of the court, in passing out of the room, spit in Jesus' face, and many of them mockingly slapped him with the palms of their hands. And thus in disorder and with such unheard-of confusion this first session of the Sanhedrist trial of Jesus ended at half past four o'clock.

Thirty prejudiced and tradition-blinded false judges, with their false witnesses, are presuming to sit in judgment on the righteous Creator of a universe. And these impassioned accusers are exasperated by the majestic silence and superb bearing of this God-man. His silence is terrible to endure; his speech is fearlessly defiant. He is unmoved by their threats and undaunted by their assaults. Man sits in judgment on God, but even then he loves them and would save them if he could.

4. THE HOUR OF HUMILIATION

The Jewish law required that, in the matter of passing the death sentence, there should be two sessions of the court. This second session was to be held on the day following the first, and the intervening time was to be spent in fasting and mourning by the members of the court. But these men could not await the next day for the confirmation of their decision that Jesus must die. They waited only one hour. In the meantime Jesus was left in the audience chamber in the custody of the temple guards, who, with the servants of the high priest, amused themselves by heaping every sort of indignity upon the Son of Man. They mocked him, spit upon him, and cruelly buffeted him. They would strike him in the face with a rod and then say, "Prophesy to us, you the Deliverer, who it was that struck you." And thus they went on for one full hour, reviling and mistreating this unresisting man of Galilee.

During this tragic hour of suffering and mock trials before the ignorant and unfeeling guards and servants, John Zebedee waited in lonely terror in an adjoining room. When these abuses first started, Jesus indicated to John, by a nod of his head, that he should retire. The Master well knew that, if he permitted his apostle to remain in the room to witness these indignities, John's resentment would be so aroused as to produce such an outbreak of protesting indignation as would probably result in his death.

Throughout this awful hour Jesus uttered no word. To this gentle and sensitive soul of humankind, joined in personality relationship with the God of all this universe, there was no more bitter portion of his cup of humiliation than this terrible hour at the mercy of these ignorant and cruel guards and servants, who had been stimulated to abuse him by the example of the members of this so-called Sanhedrist court.

The human heart cannot possibly conceive of the shudder of indignation that swept out over a vast universe as the celestial intelligences witnessed this sight of their beloved Sovereign submitting himself to the will of his ignorant and misguided creatures on the sin-darkened sphere of unfortunate Urantia.

What is this trait of the animal in man which leads him to want to insult and physically assault that which he cannot spiritually attain or intellectually achieve? In the half-civilized man there still lurks an evil brutality which seeks to vent itself upon those who are superior in wisdom and spiritual attainment. Witness the evil coarseness and the brutal ferocity of these supposedly civilized men as they derived a certain form of animal pleasure from this physical attack upon the unresisting Son of Man. As these insults, taunts, and blows fell upon Jesus, he was undefending but not defenseless. Jesus was not vanquished, merely uncontending in the material sense.

These are the moments of the Master's greatest victories in all his long and eventful career as maker, upholder, and savior of a vast and far-flung universe. Having lived to the full a life of revealing God to man, Jesus is now engaged in making a new and unprecedented revelation of man to God. Jesus is now revealing to the worlds the final triumph over all fears of creature personality isolation. The Son of Man has finally achieved the realization of identity as the Son of God. Jesus does not hesitate to assert that he and the Father are one; and on the basis of the fact and truth of that supreme and supernal experience, he admonishes every kingdom believer to become one with him even as he and his Father are one. The living experience in the religion of Jesus thus becomes the sure and certain technique whereby the spiritually isolated and cosmically lonely mortals of earth are enabled to escape personality isolation, with all its consequences of fear and associated feelings of helplessness. In the fraternal realities of the kingdom of heaven the faith sons of God find final deliverance from the isolation of the self, both personal and planetary. The God-knowing believer increasingly experiences the ecstasy and grandeur of spiritual socialization on a universe scale — citizenship on high in association with the eternal realization of the divine destiny of perfection attainment.

. . .

5. THE SECOND MEETING OF THE COURT

At five-thirty o'clock the court reassembled, and Jesus was led into the adjoining room, where John was waiting. Here the Roman soldier and the temple guards watched over Jesus while the court began the formulation of the charges which were to be presented to Pilate. Annas made it clear to his associates that the charge of blasphemy would carry no weight with Pilate. Judas was present during this second meeting of the court, but he gave no testimony.

This session of the court lasted only a half hour, and when they adjourned to go before Pilate, they had drawn up the indictment of Jesus, as being worthy of death, under three heads:

1. That he was a perverter of the Jewish nation; he deceived the people and incited them to rebellion.

2. That he taught the people to refuse to pay tribute to Caesar.

3. That, by claiming to be a king and the founder of a new sort of kingdom, he incited treason against the emperor.

This entire procedure was irregular and wholly contrary to the Jewish laws. No two witnesses had agreed on any matter except those who testified regarding Jesus' statement about destroying the temple and raising it again in three days. And even concerning that point, no witnesses spoke for the defense, and neither was Jesus asked to explain his intended meaning.

The only point the court could have consistently judged him on was that of blasphemy, and that would have rested entirely on his own testimony. Even concerning blasphemy, they failed to cast a formal ballot for the death sentence.

And now they presumed to formulate three charges, with which to go before Pilate, on which no witnesses had been heard, and which were agreed upon while the accused prisoner was absent. When this was done, three of the Pharisees took their leave; they wanted to see Jesus destroyed, but they would not formulate charges against him without witnesses and in his absence.

Jesus did not again appear before the Sanhedrist court. They did not want again to look upon his face as they sat in judgment upon his innocent life. Jesus did not know (as a man) of their formal charges until he heard them recited by Pilate.

While Jesus was in the room with John and the guards, and while the court was in its second session, some of the women about the high priest's palace, together with their friends, came to look upon the strange prisoner, and one of them asked him, "Are you the Messiah, the Son of God?" And Jesus answered: "If I tell you, you will not believe me; and if I ask you, you will not answer."

At six o'clock that morning Jesus was led forth from the home of Caiaphas to appear before Pilate for confirmation of the sentence of death which this Sanhedrist court had so unjustly and irregularly decreed.

PAPER 185
THE TRIAL BEFORE PILATE

SHORTLY AFTER SIX o'clock on this Friday morning, April 7, A.D. 30, Jesus was brought before Pilate, the Roman procurator who governed Judea, Samaria, and Idumea under the immediate supervision of the legatus of Syria. The Master was taken into the presence of the Roman governor by the temple guards, bound, and was accompanied by about fifty of his accusers, including the Sanhedrist court (principally Sadduceans), Judas Iscariot, and the high priest, Caiaphas, and by the Apostle John. Annas did not appear before Pilate.

Pilate was up and ready to receive this group of early morning callers, having been informed by those who had secured his consent, the previous evening, to employ the Roman soldiers in arresting the Son of Man, that Jesus would be early brought before him. This trial was arranged to take place in front of the praetorium, an addition to the fortress of Antonia, where Pilate and his wife made their headquarters when stopping in Jerusalem.

Though Pilate conducted much of Jesus' examination within the praetorium halls, the public trial was held outside on the steps leading up to the main entrance. This was a concession to the Jews, who refused to enter any gentile building where leaven might be used on this day of preparation for the Passover. Such conduct would not only render them ceremonially unclean and thereby debar them from partaking of the afternoon feast of thanksgiving but would also necessitate their subjection to purification ceremonies after sundown, before they would be eligible to partake of the Passover supper.

Although these Jews were not at all bothered in conscience as they intrigued to effect the judicial murder of Jesus, they were nonetheless scrupulous regarding all these matters of ceremonial cleanness and traditional regularity. And these Jews have not been the only ones to fail in the recognition of high and holy obligations of a divine nature while giving meticulous attention to things of trifling importance to human welfare in both time and eternity.

1. PONTIUS PILATE

If Pontius Pilate had not been a reasonably good governor of the minor provinces, Tiberius would hardly have suffered him to remain as procurator of Judea for ten years. Although he was a fairly good administrator, he was a moral coward. He was not a big enough man to comprehend the nature of his task as governor of the Jews. He failed to grasp the fact that these Hebrews had a *real* religion, a faith for which they were willing to die, and that millions upon millions of them, scattered here and there throughout the empire, looked to Jerusalem as the shrine of their faith and held the Sanhedrin in respect as the highest tribunal on earth.

Pilate did not love the Jews, and this deep-seated hatred early began to manifest itself. Of all the Roman provinces, none was more difficult to govern than Judea. Pilate never really understood the problems involved in the management of the Jews and, therefore, very early in his experience as governor, made a series of almost fatal and well-nigh suicidal blunders. And it was these blunders that gave the Jews such power over him. When they wanted to influence his decisions, all they had to do was to threaten an uprising, and Pilate would speedily capitulate. And this apparent vacillation, or lack of moral courage, of the procurator was chiefly due to the memory of a number of controversies he had had with the Jews and because in each instance they had worsted him. The Jews knew that Pilate was afraid of them, that he feared for his position before Tiberius, and they employed this knowledge to the great disadvantage of the governor on numerous occasions.

Pilate's disfavor with the Jews came about as a result of a number of unfortunate encounters. First, he failed to take seriously their deep-seated prejudice against all images as symbols of idol worship. Therefore he permitted his soldiers to enter Jerusalem without removing the images of Caesar from their banners, as had been the practice of the Roman soldiers under his predecessor. A large deputation of Jews waited upon Pilate for five days, imploring him to have these images removed from the military standards. He flatly refused to grant their petition and threatened them with instant death. Pilate, himself being a skeptic, did not understand that men of strong religious feelings will not hesitate to die for their religious convictions; and therefore was he dismayed when these Jews drew themselves up defiantly before his palace, bowed their faces to the ground, and sent word that they were ready to die. Pilate then realized that he had made a threat which he was unwilling to carry out. He surrendered, ordered the images removed from the standards of his soldiers in Jerusalem, and found himself from that day on to a large extent subject to the whims of the Jewish leaders, who had in this way discovered his weakness in making threats which he feared to execute.

Pilate subsequently determined to regain this lost prestige and accordingly had the shields of the emperor, such as were commonly used in Caesar worship, put up on the walls of Herod's palace in Jerusalem. When the Jews protested, he was adamant. When he refused to listen to their protests, they promptly appealed to Rome, and the emperor as promptly ordered the offending shields removed. And then was Pilate held in even lower esteem than before.

Another thing which brought him into great disfavor with the Jews was that he dared to take money from the temple treasury to pay for the construction of a new aqueduct to provide increased water supply for the millions of visitors to Jerusalem at the times of the great religious feasts. The Jews held that only the Sanhedrin could disburse the temple funds, and they never ceased to inveigh against Pilate for this presumptuous ruling. No less than a score of riots and much bloodshed resulted from this decision. The last of these serious outbreaks had to do with the slaughter of a large company of Galileans even as they worshiped at the altar.

It is significant that, while this vacillating Roman ruler sacrificed Jesus to his fear of the Jews and to safeguard his personal position, he finally was deposed as a result of the needless slaughter of Samaritans in connection with the pretensions of a false Messiah who led troops to Mount Gerizim, where he claimed the temple vessels were buried; and fierce riots broke out when he failed to reveal the hiding place of the sacred vessels, as he had promised. As a result of this episode, the legatus of Syria ordered Pilate to Rome. Tiberius died while Pilate was on the way to Rome, and he was not reappointed as procurator of Judea. He never fully recovered from the regretful condemnation of having consented to the crucifixion of Jesus. Finding no favor in the eyes of the new emperor, he retired to the province of Lausanne, where he subsequently committed suicide.

Claudia Procula, Pilate's wife, had heard much of Jesus through the word of her maid-in-waiting, who was a Phoenician believer in the gospel of the kingdom. After the death of Pilate, Claudia became prominently identified with the spread of the good news.

And all this explains much that transpired on this tragic Friday forenoon. It is easy to understand why the Jews presumed to dictate to Pilate — to get him up at six o'clock to try Jesus — and also why they did not hesitate to threaten to charge him with treason before the emperor if he dared to refuse their demands for Jesus' death.

A worthy Roman governor who had not become disadvantageously involved with the rulers of the Jews would never have permitted these bloodthirsty religious fanatics to bring about the death of a man whom he himself had declared to be innocent of their false charges and without fault. Rome made a great blunder, a far-reaching error in earthly affairs, when she sent the second-rate Pilate to govern Palestine. Tiberius had better have sent to the Jews the best provincial administrator in the empire.

2. JESUS APPEARS BEFORE PILATE

When Jesus and his accusers had gathered in front of Pilate's judgment hall, the Roman governor came out and, addressing the company assembled, asked, "What accusation do you bring against this fellow?" The Sadducees and councilors who had taken it upon themselves to put Jesus out of the way had determined to go before Pilate and ask for confirmation of the death sentence pronounced upon Jesus, without volunteering any definite charge. Therefore did the spokesman for the Sanhedrist court answer Pilate: "If this man were not an evildoer, we should not have delivered him up to you."

When Pilate observed that they were reluctant to state their charges against Jesus, although he knew they had been all night engaged in deliberations regarding his guilt, he answered them: "Since you have not agreed on any definite charges, why do you not take this man and pass judgment on him in accordance with your own laws?"

Then spoke the clerk of the Sanhedrin court to Pilate: "It is not lawful for us to put any man to death, and this disturber of our nation is worthy to die for the things which he has said and done. Therefore have we come before you for confirmation of this decree."

To come before the Roman governor with this attempt at evasion discloses both the ill-will and the ill-humor of the Sanhedrists toward Jesus as well as their lack of respect for the fairness, honor, and dignity of Pilate. What effrontery for these subject citizens to appear before their provincial governor asking for a decree of execution against a man before affording him a fair trial and without even preferring definite criminal charges against him!

Pilate knew something of Jesus' work among the Jews, and he surmised that the charges which might be brought against him had to do with infringements of the Jewish ecclesiastical laws; therefore he sought to refer the case back to their own tribunal. Again, Pilate took delight in making them publicly confess that they were powerless to pronounce and execute the death sentence upon even one of their own race whom they had come to despise with a bitter and envious hatred.

It was a few hours previously, shortly before midnight and after he had granted permission to use Roman soldiers in effecting the secret arrest of Jesus, that Pilate had heard further concerning Jesus and his teaching from his wife, Claudia, who was a partial convert to Judaism, and who later on became a full-fledged believer in Jesus' gospel.

Pilate would have liked to postpone this hearing, but he saw the Jewish leaders were determined to proceed with the case. He knew that this was not only the forenoon of preparation for the Passover, but that this day, being Friday, was also the preparation day for the Jewish Sabbath of rest and worship.

Pilate, being keenly sensitive to the disrespectful manner of the approach of these Jews, was not willing to comply with their demands that Jesus be sentenced to death without a trial. When, therefore, he had waited a few moments for them to present their charges against the prisoner, he turned to them and said: "I will not sentence this man to death without a trial; neither will I consent to examine him until you have presented your charges against him in writing."

When the high priest and the others heard Pilate say this, they signaled to the clerk of the court, who then handed to Pilate the written charges against Jesus. And these charges were:

"We find in the Sanhedrist tribunal that this man is an evildoer and a disturber of our nation in that he is guilty of:

"1. Perverting our nation and stirring up our people to rebellion.

"2. Forbidding the people to pay tribute to Caesar.

"3. Calling himself the king of the Jews and teaching the founding of a new kingdom."

Jesus had not been regularly tried nor legally convicted on any of these charges. He did not even hear these charges when first stated, but Pilate had him brought from the praetorium, where he was in the keeping of the guards, and he insisted that these charges be repeated in Jesus' hearing.

When Jesus heard these accusations, he well knew that he had not been heard on these matters before the Jewish court, and so did John Zebedee and his accusers, but he made no reply to their false charges. Even when Pilate bade him answer his accusers, he opened not his mouth. Pilate was so astonished at the unfairness of the whole proceeding and so impressed by Jesus' silent and masterly bearing that he decided to take the prisoner inside the hall and examine him privately.

Pilate was confused in mind, fearful of the Jews in his heart, and mightily stirred in his spirit by the spectacle of Jesus' standing there in majesty before his bloodthirsty accusers and gazing down on them, not in silent contempt, but with an expression of genuine pity and sorrowful affection.

3. THE PRIVATE EXAMINATION BY PILATE

Pilate took Jesus and John Zebedee into a private chamber, leaving the guards outside in the hall, and requesting the prisoner to sit down, he sat down by his side and asked several questions. Pilate began his talk with Jesus by assuring him that he did not believe the first count against him: that he was a perverter of the nation and an inciter to rebellion. Then he asked, "Did you ever teach that tribute should be refused Caesar?" Jesus, pointing to John, said, "Ask him or any other man who has heard my teaching." Then Pilate questioned John about this matter of tribute, and John testified concerning his Master's teaching and explained that Jesus and his apostles paid taxes both to Caesar and to the temple. When Pilate had questioned John, he said, "See that you tell no man that I talked with you." And John never did reveal this matter.

Pilate then turned around to question Jesus further, saying: "And now about the third accusation against you, are you the king of the Jews?" Since there was a tone of possibly sincere inquiry in Pilate's voice, Jesus smiled on the procurator and said: "Pilate, do you ask this for yourself, or do you take this question from these others, my accusers?" Whereupon, in a tone of partial indignation, the governor answered: "Am I a Jew? Your own people and the chief priests delivered you up and asked me to sentence you to death. I question the validity of their charges and am only trying to find out for myself what you have done. Tell me, have you said that you are the king of the Jews, and have you sought to found a new kingdom?"

Then said Jesus to Pilate: "Do you not perceive that my kingdom is not of this world? If my kingdom were of this world, surely would my disciples fight that I should not be delivered into the hands of the Jews. My presence here before you in these bonds is sufficient to show all men that my kingdom is a spiritual dominion, even the brotherhood of men who, through faith and by love, have become the sons of God. And this salvation is for the gentile as well as for the Jew."

"Then you are a king after all?" said Pilate. And Jesus answered: "Yes, I am such a king, and my kingdom is the family of the faith sons of my Father who is in heaven. For this purpose was I born into this world, even that I should show my Father to all men and bear witness to the truth of God. And even now do I declare to you that every one who loves the truth hears my voice."

Then said Pilate, half in ridicule and half in sincerity, "Truth, what is truth — who knows?"

Pilate was not able to fathom Jesus' words, nor was he able to understand the nature of his spiritual kingdom, but he was now certain that the prisoner had done nothing worthy of death. One look at Jesus, face to face, was enough to convince even Pilate that this gentle and weary, but majestic and upright, man was no wild and dangerous revolutionary who aspired to establish himself on the temporal throne of Israel. Pilate thought he understood something of what Jesus meant when he called himself a king, for he was familiar with the teachings of the Stoics, who declared that "the wise man is king." Pilate was thoroughly convinced that, instead of being a dangerous seditionmonger, Jesus was nothing more or less than a harmless visionary, an innocent fanatic.

After questioning the Master, Pilate went back to the chief priests and the accusers of Jesus and said: "I have examined this man, and I find no fault in him. I do not think he is guilty of the charges you have made against him; I think he ought to be set free." And when the Jews heard this, they were moved with great anger, so much so that they wildly shouted that Jesus should die; and one of the Sanhedrists boldly stepped up by the side of Pilate, saying: "This man stirs up the people, beginning in Galilee and continuing throughout all Judea. He is a mischief-maker and an evildoer. You will long regret it if you let this wicked man go free."

Pilate was hard pressed to know what to do with Jesus; therefore, when he heard them say that he began his work in Galilee, he thought to avoid the responsibility of deciding the case, at least to gain time for thought, by sending Jesus to appear before Herod, who was then in the city attending the Passover. Pilate also thought that this gesture would help to antidote some of the bitter feeling which had existed for some time between himself and Herod, due to numerous misunderstandings over matters of jurisdiction.

Pilate, calling the guards, said: "This man is a Galilean. Take him forthwith to Herod, and when he has examined him, report his findings to me." And they took Jesus to Herod.

4. JESUS BEFORE HEROD

When Herod Antipas stopped in Jerusalem, he dwelt in the old Maccabean palace of Herod the Great, and it was to this home of the former king that Jesus was now taken by the temple guards, and he was followed by his accusers and an increasing multitude. Herod had long heard of Jesus, and he was very curious about him. When the Son of Man stood before him, on this Friday morning, the wicked Idumean never for one moment recalled the lad of former years who had appeared before him in Sepphoris pleading for a just decision regarding the money due his father, who had been accidentally killed while at work on one of the public buildings. As far as Herod knew, he had never seen Jesus, although he had worried a great deal about him when his work had been centered in Galilee. Now that he was in custody of Pilate and the Judeans, Herod was desirous of seeing him, feeling secure against any trouble from him in the future. Herod had heard much about the miracles wrought by Jesus, and he really hoped to see him do some wonder.

When they brought Jesus before Herod, the tetrarch was startled by his stately appearance and the calm composure of his countenance. For some fifteen minutes Herod asked Jesus questions, but the Master would not answer. Herod taunted and dared him to perform a miracle, but Jesus would not reply to his many inquiries or respond to his taunts.

Then Herod turned to the chief priests and the Sadducees and, giving ear to their accusations, heard all and more than Pilate had listened to regarding the alleged evil doings of the Son of Man. Finally, being convinced that Jesus would neither talk nor perform a wonder for him, Herod, after making fun of him for a time, arrayed him in an old purple royal robe and sent him back to Pilate. Herod knew he had no jurisdiction over Jesus in Judea. Though he was glad to believe that he was finally to be rid of Jesus in Galilee, he was thankful that it was Pilate who had the responsibility of putting him to death. Herod never had fully recovered from the fear that cursed him as a result of killing John the Baptist. Herod had at certain times even feared that Jesus was John risen from the dead. Now he was relieved of that fear since he observed that Jesus was a very different sort of person from the outspoken and fiery prophet who dared to expose and denounce his private life.

5. JESUS RETURNS TO PILATE

When the guards had brought Jesus back to Pilate, he went out on the front steps of the praetorium, where his judgment seat had been placed, and calling together the chief priests and Sanhedrists, said to them: "You brought this man before me with charges that he perverts the people, forbids the payment of taxes, and claims to be king of the Jews. I have examined him and fail to find him guilty of these charges. In fact, I find no fault in him. Then I sent him to Herod, and the tetrarch must have reached the same conclusion since he has sent him back to us. Certainly, nothing worthy of death has been done by this man. If you still think he needs to be disciplined, I am willing to chastise him before I release him."

Just as the Jews were about to engage in shouting their protests against the release of Jesus, a vast crowd came marching up to the praetorium for the purpose of asking Pilate for the release of a prisoner in honor of the Passover feast. For some time it had been the custom of the Roman governors to allow the populace to choose some imprisoned or condemned man for pardon at the time of the Passover. And now that this crowd had come before him to ask for the release of a prisoner, and since Jesus had so recently been in great favor with the multitudes, it occurred to Pilate that he might possibly extricate himself from his predicament by proposing to this group that, since Jesus was now a prisoner before his judgment seat, he release to them this man of Galilee as the token of Passover good will.

As the crowd surged up on the steps of the building, Pilate heard them calling out the name of one Barabbas. Barabbas was a noted political agitator and murderous robber, the son of a priest, who had recently been apprehended in the act of robbery and murder on the Jericho road. This man was under sentence to die as soon as the Passover festivities were over.

Pilate stood up and explained to the crowd that Jesus had been brought to him by the chief priests, who sought to have him put to death on certain charges, and that he did not think the man was worthy of death. Said Pilate: "Which, therefore, would you prefer that I release to you, this Barabbas, the murderer, or this Jesus of Galilee?" And when Pilate had thus spoken, the chief priests and the Sanhedrin councilors all shouted at the top of their voices, "Barabbas, Barabbas!" And when the people saw that the chief priests were minded to have Jesus put to death, they quickly joined in the clamor for his life while they loudly shouted for the release of Barabbas.

A few days before this the multitude had stood in awe of Jesus, but the mob did not look up to one who, having claimed to be the Son of God, now found himself in the custody of the chief priests and the rulers and on trial before Pilate for his life. Jesus could be a hero in the eyes of the populace when he was driving the money-changers and the traders out of the temple, but not when he was a nonresisting prisoner in the hands of his enemies and on trial for his life.

Pilate was angered at the sight of the chief priests clamoring for the pardon of a notorious murderer while they shouted for the blood of Jesus. He saw their malice and hatred and perceived their prejudice and envy. Therefore he said to them: "How could you choose the life of a murderer in preference to this man's whose worst crime is that he figuratively calls himself the king of the Jews?" But this was not a wise statement for Pilate to make. The Jews were a proud people, now subject to the Roman political yoke but hoping for the coming of a Messiah who would deliver them from gentile bondage with a great show of power and glory. They resented, more than Pilate could know, the intimation that this meek-mannered teacher of strange doctrines, now under arrest and charged with crimes worthy of death, should be referred to as "the king of the Jews." They looked upon such a remark as an insult to everything which they held sacred and honorable in their national existence, and therefore did they all let loose their mighty shouts for Barabbas's release and Jesus' death.

Pilate knew Jesus was innocent of the charges brought against him, and had he been a just and courageous judge, he would have acquitted him and turned him loose. But he was afraid to defy these angry Jews, and while he hesitated to do his duty, a messenger came up and presented him with a sealed message from his wife, Claudia.

Pilate indicated to those assembled before him that he wished to read the communication which he had just received before he proceeded further with the matter before him. When Pilate opened this letter from his wife, he read: "I pray you have nothing to do with this innocent and just man whom they call Jesus. I have suffered many things in a dream this night because of him." This note from Claudia not only greatly upset Pilate and thereby delayed the adjudication of this matter, but it unfortunately also provided considerable time in which the Jewish rulers freely circulated among the crowd and urged the people to call for the release of Barabbas and to clamor for the crucifixion of Jesus.

Finally, Pilate addressed himself once more to the solution of the problem which confronted him, by asking the mixed assembly of Jewish rulers and the pardon-seeking crowd, "What shall I do with him who is called the king of the Jews?" And they all shouted with one accord, "Crucify him! Crucify him!" The unanimity of this demand from the mixed multitude startled and alarmed Pilate, the unjust and fear-ridden judge.

Then once more Pilate said: "Why would you crucify this man? What evil has he done? Who will come forward to testify against him?" But when they heard Pilate speak in defense of Jesus, they only cried out all the more, "Crucify him! Crucify him!"

Then again Pilate appealed to them regarding the release of the Passover prisoner, saying: "Once more I ask you, which of these prisoners shall I release to you at this, your Passover time?" And again the crowd shouted, "Give us Barabbas!"

Then said Pilate: "If I release the murderer, Barabbas, what shall I do with Jesus?" And once more the multitude shouted in unison, "Crucify him! Crucify him!"

Pilate was terrorized by the insistent clamor of the mob, acting under the direct leadership of the chief priests and the councilors of the Sanhedrin; nevertheless, he decided upon at least one more attempt to appease the crowd and save Jesus.

6. PILATE'S LAST APPEAL

In all that is transpiring early this Friday morning before Pilate, only the enemies of Jesus are participating. His many friends either do not yet know of his night arrest and early morning trial or are in hiding lest they also be apprehended and adjudged worthy of death because they believe Jesus' teachings. In the multitude which now clamors for the Master's death are to be found only his sworn enemies and the easily led and unthinking populace.

Pilate would make one last appeal to their pity. Being afraid to defy the clamor of this misled mob who cried for the blood of Jesus, he ordered the Jewish guards and the Roman soldiers to take Jesus and scourge him. This was in itself an unjust and illegal procedure since the Roman law provided that only those condemned to die by crucifixion should be thus subjected to scourging. The guards took Jesus into the open courtyard of the praetorium for this ordeal. Though his enemies did not witness this scourging, Pilate did, and before they had finished this wicked abuse, he directed the scourgers to desist and indicated that Jesus should be brought to him. Before the scourgers laid their knotted whips upon Jesus as he was bound to the whipping post, they again put upon him the purple robe, and plaiting a crown of thorns, they placed it upon his brow. And when they had put a reed in his hand as a mock scepter, they knelt before him and mocked him, saying, "Hail, king of the Jews!" And they spit upon him and struck him in the face with their hands. And one of them, before they returned him to Pilate, took the reed from his hand and struck him upon the head.

Then Pilate led forth this bleeding and lacerated prisoner and, presenting him before the mixed multitude, said: "Behold the man! Again I declare to you that I find no crime in him, and having scourged him, I would release him."

There stood Jesus of Nazareth, clothed in an old purple royal robe with a crown of thorns piercing his kindly brow. His face was bloodstained and his form bowed down with suffering and grief. But nothing can appeal to the unfeeling hearts of those who are victims of intense emotional hatred and slaves to religious prejudice. This sight sent a mighty shudder through the realms of a vast universe, but it did not touch the hearts of those who had set their minds to effect the destruction of Jesus.

When they had recovered from the first shock of seeing the Master's plight, they only shouted the louder and the longer, "Crucify him! Crucify him! Crucify him!"

And now did Pilate comprehend that it was futile to appeal to their supposed feelings of pity. He stepped forward and said: "I perceive that you are determined this man shall die, but what has he done to deserve death? Who will declare his crime?"

Then the high priest himself stepped forward and, going up to Pilate, angrily declared: "We have a sacred law, and by that law this man ought to die because he made himself out to be the Son of God." When Pilate heard this, he was all the more afraid, not only of the Jews, but recalling his wife's note and the Greek mythology of the gods coming down on earth, he now trembled at the thought of Jesus possibly being a divine personage. He waved to the crowd to hold its peace while he took Jesus by the arm and again led him inside the building that he might further examine him. Pilate was now confused by fear, bewildered by superstition, and harassed by the stubborn attitude of the mob.

7. PILATE'S LAST INTERVIEW

As Pilate, trembling with fearful emotion, sat down by the side of Jesus, he inquired: "Where do you come from? Really, who are you? What is this they say, that you are the Son of God?"

But Jesus could hardly answer such questions when asked by a man-fearing, weak, and vacillating judge who was so unjust as to subject him to flogging even when he had declared him innocent of all crime, and before he had been duly sentenced to die. Jesus looked Pilate straight in the face, but he did not answer him. Then said Pilate: "Do you refuse to speak to me? Do you not realize that I still have power to release you or to crucify you?" Then said Jesus: "You could have no power over me except it were permitted from above. You could exercise no authority over the Son of Man unless the Father in heaven allowed it. But you are not so guilty since you are ignorant of the gospel. He who betrayed me and he who delivered me to you, they have the greater sin."

This last talk with Jesus thoroughly frightened Pilate. This moral coward and judicial weakling now labored under the double weight of the superstitious fear of Jesus and mortal dread of the Jewish leaders.

Again Pilate appeared before the crowd, saying: "I am certain this man is only a religious offender. You should take him and judge him by your law.

Why should you expect that I would consent to his death because he has clashed with your traditions?"

Pilate was just about ready to release Jesus when Caiaphas, the high priest, approached the cowardly Roman judge and, shaking an avenging finger in Pilate's face, said with angry words which the entire multitude could hear: "If you release this man, you are not Caesar's friend, and I will see that the emperor knows all." This public threat was too much for Pilate. Fear for his personal fortunes now eclipsed all other considerations, and the cowardly governor ordered Jesus brought out before the judgment seat. As the Master stood there before them, he pointed to him and tauntingly said, "Behold your king." And the Jews answered, "Away with him. Crucify him!" And then Pilate said, with much irony and sarcasm, "Shall I crucify your king?" And the Jews answered, "Yes, crucify him! We have no king but Caesar." And then did Pilate realize that there was no hope of saving Jesus since he was unwilling to defy the Jews.

8. PILATE'S TRAGIC SURRENDER

Here stood the Son of God incarnate as the Son of Man. He was arrested without indictment; accused without evidence; adjudged without witnesses; punished without a verdict; and now was soon to be condemned to die by an unjust judge who confessed that he could find no fault in him. If Pilate had thought to appeal to their patriotism by referring to Jesus as the "king of the Jews," he utterly failed. The Jews were not expecting any such a king. The declaration of the chief priests and the Sadducees, "We have no king but Caesar," was a shock even to the unthinking populace, but it was too late now to save Jesus even had the mob dared to espouse the Master's cause.

Pilate was afraid of a tumult or a riot. He dared not risk having such a disturbance during Passover time in Jerusalem. He had recently received a reprimand from Caesar, and he would not risk another. The mob cheered when he ordered the release of Barabbas. Then he ordered a basin and some water, and there before the multitude he washed his hands, saying: "I am innocent of the blood of this man. You are determined that he shall die, but I have found no guilt in him. See you to it. The soldiers will lead him forth."

PAPER 186
JUST BEFORE THE CRUCIFIXION

As Jesus and his accusers started off to see Herod, the Master turned to the Apostle John and said: "John, you can do no more for me. Go to my mother and bring her to see me ere I die." When John heard his Master's request, although reluctant to leave him alone among his enemies, he hastened off to Bethany, where the entire family of Jesus was assembled in waiting at the home of Martha and Mary, the sisters of Lazarus whom Jesus raised from the dead.

Several times during the morning, messengers had brought news to Martha and Mary concerning the progress of Jesus' trial. But the family of Jesus did not reach Bethany until just a few minutes before John arrived bearing the request of Jesus to see his mother before he was put to death. After John Zebedee had told them all that had happened since the midnight arrest of Jesus, Mary his mother went at once in the company of John to see her eldest son. By the time Mary and John reached the city, Jesus, accompanied by the Roman soldiers who were to crucify him, had already arrived at Golgotha.

When Mary the mother of Jesus started out with John to go to her son, his sister Ruth refused to remain behind with the rest of the family. Since she was determined to accompany her mother, her brother Jude went with her. The rest of the Master's family remained in Bethany under the direction of

James, and almost every hour the messengers of David Zebedee brought them reports concerning the progress of that terrible business of putting to death their eldest brother, Jesus of Nazareth.

1. THE END OF JUDAS ISCARIOT

It was about half past eight o'clock this Friday morning when the hearing of Jesus before Pilate was ended and the Master was placed in the custody of the Roman soldiers who were to crucify him. As soon as the Romans took possession of Jesus, the captain of the Jewish guards marched with his men back to their temple headquarters. The chief priest and his Sanhedrist associates followed close behind the guards, going directly to their usual meeting place in the hall of hewn stone in the temple. Here they found many other members of the Sanhedrin waiting to learn what had been done with Jesus. As Caiaphas was engaged in making his report to the Sanhedrin regarding the trial and condemnation of Jesus, Judas appeared before them to claim his reward for the part he had played in his Master's arrest and sentence of death.

All of these Jews loathed Judas; they looked upon the betrayer with only feelings of utter contempt. Throughout the trial of Jesus before Caiaphas and during his appearance before Pilate, Judas was pricked in his conscience about his traitorous conduct. And he was also beginning to become somewhat disillusioned regarding the reward he was to receive as payment for his services as Jesus' betrayer. He did not like the coolness and aloofness of the Jewish authorities; nevertheless, he expected to be liberally rewarded for his cowardly conduct. He anticipated being called before the full meeting of the Sanhedrin and there hearing himself eulogized while they conferred upon him suitable honors in token of the great service which he flattered himself he had rendered his nation. Imagine, therefore, the great surprise of this egotistic traitor when a servant of the high priest, tapping him on the shoulder, called him just outside the hall and said: "Judas, I have been appointed to pay you for the betrayal of Jesus. Here is your reward." And thus speaking, the servant of Caiaphas handed Judas a bag containing thirty pieces of silver — the current price of a good, healthy slave.

Judas was stunned, dumfounded. He rushed back to enter the hall but was debarred by the doorkeeper. He wanted to appeal to the Sanhedrin, but they would not admit him. Judas could not believe that these rulers of the Jews would allow him to betray his friends and his Master and then offer him as a reward thirty pieces of silver. He was humiliated, disillusioned, and utterly crushed. He walked away from the temple, as it were, in a trance. He automatically dropped the money bag in his deep pocket, that same pocket wherein he had so long carried the bag containing the apostolic funds. And he wandered out through the city after the crowds who were on their way to witness the crucifixions.

From a distance Judas saw them raise the cross piece with Jesus nailed thereon, and upon sight of this he rushed back to the temple and, forcing his way past the doorkeeper, found himself standing in the presence of the Sanhedrin, which was still in session. The betrayer was well-nigh breathless and highly distraught, but he managed to stammer out these words: "I have sinned in that I have betrayed innocent blood. You have insulted me. You have offered me as a reward for my service, money — the price of a slave. I repent that I have done this; here is your money. I want to escape the guilt of this deed."

When the rulers of the Jews heard Judas, they scoffed at him. One of them sitting near where Judas stood, motioned that he should leave the hall and said: "Your Master has already been put to death by the Romans, and as for your guilt, what is that to us? See you to that — and begone!"

As Judas left the Sanhedrin chamber, he removed the thirty pieces of silver from the bag and threw them broadcast over the temple floor. When the betrayer left the temple, he was almost beside himself. Judas was now passing through the experience of the realization of the true nature of sin. All the glamor, fascination, and intoxication of wrongdoing had vanished. Now the evildoer stood alone and face to face with the judgment verdict of his disillusioned and disappointed soul. Sin was bewitching and adventurous in the committing, but now must the harvest of the naked and unromantic facts be faced.

This onetime ambassador of the kingdom of heaven on earth now walked through the streets of Jerusalem, forsaken and alone. His despair was desperate and well-nigh absolute. On he journeyed through the city and outside the walls, on down into the terrible solitude of the valley of Hinnom, where he climbed up the steep rocks and, taking the girdle of his cloak, fastened one end to a small tree, tied the other about his neck, and cast himself over the precipice. Ere he was dead, the knot which his nervous hands had tied gave way, and the betrayer's body was dashed to pieces as it fell on the jagged rocks below.

2. THE MASTER'S ATTITUDE

When Jesus was arrested, he knew that his work on earth, in the likeness of mortal flesh, was finished. He fully understood the sort of death he would die, and he was little concerned with the details of his so-called trials.

Before the Sanhedrist court Jesus declined to make replies to the testimony of perjured witnesses. There was but one question which would always elicit an answer, whether asked by friend or foe, and that was the one concerning the nature and divinity of his mission on earth. When asked if he were the Son of God, he unfailingly made reply. He steadfastly refused to speak when in the presence of the curious and wicked Herod. Before Pilate he spoke only when he thought that Pilate or some other sincere person might be helped to a better knowledge of the truth by what he said. Jesus had taught his apostles the uselessness of casting their pearls before swine, and he now dared to practice what he had taught. His conduct at this time exemplified the patient submission of the human nature coupled with the majestic silence and solemn dignity of the divine nature. He was altogether willing to discuss with Pilate any question related to the political charges brought against him — any question which he recognized as belonging to the governor's jurisdiction.

Jesus was convinced that it was the will of the Father that he submit himself to the natural and ordinary course of human events just as every other mortal creature must, and therefore he refused to employ even his purely human powers of persuasive eloquence to influence the outcome of the machinations of his socially nearsighted and spiritually blinded fellow mortals. Although Jesus lived and died on Urantia, his whole human career, from first to last, was a spectacle designed to influence and instruct the entire universe of his creation and unceasing upholding.

Jesus had acquired that type of human character which could preserve its composure and assert its dignity in the face of continued and gratuitous insult. He could not be intimidated. When first assaulted by the servant of Annas, he had only suggested the propriety of calling witnesses who might duly testify against him.

From first to last, in his so-called trial before Pilate, the onlooking celestial hosts could not refrain from broadcasting to the universe the depiction of the scene of "Pilate on trial before Jesus."

When before Caiaphas, and when all the perjured testimony had broken down, Jesus did not hesitate to answer the question of the chief priest, thereby providing in his own testimony that which they desired as a basis for convicting him of blasphemy.

The Master never displayed the least interest in Pilate's well-meant but halfhearted efforts to effect his release. He really pitied Pilate and sincerely endeavored to enlighten his darkened mind. He was wholly passive to all the Roman governor's appeals to the Jews to withdraw their criminal charges against him. Throughout the whole sorrowful ordeal he bore himself with simple dignity and unostentatious majesty.

Jesus said little during these trials, but he said enough to show all mortals the kind of human character man can perfect in partnership with God and to reveal to all the universe the manner in which God can become manifest in the life of the creature when such a creature truly chooses to do the will of the Father, thus becoming an active son of the living God.

His love for ignorant mortals is fully disclosed by his patience and great self-possession in the face of the jeers, blows, and buffetings of the coarse soldiers and the unthinking servants. He was not even angry when they blindfolded him and, derisively striking him in the face, exclaimed: "Prophesy to us who it was that struck you."

Pilate spoke more truly than he knew when, after Jesus had been scourged, he presented him before the multitude, exclaiming, "Behold the man!" Indeed, the fear-ridden Roman governor little dreamed that at just that moment the universe stood at attention, gazing upon this unique scene of its beloved Sovereign thus subjected in humiliation to the taunts and blows of his darkened and degraded mortal subjects. And as Pilate spoke, there echoed throughout all Nebadon, "Behold God and man!" Throughout a universe, untold millions have ever since that day continued to behold that man, while the God of Havona, the supreme ruler of the universe of universes, accepts the man of Nazareth as the satisfaction of the ideal of the mortal creatures of this local universe of time and space. In his matchless life he never failed to reveal God to man. Now, in these final episodes of his mortal career and in his subsequent death, he made a new and touching revelation of man to God.

3. THE DEPENDABLE DAVID ZEBEDEE

Shortly after Jesus was turned over to the Roman soldiers at the conclusion of the hearing before Pilate, a detachment of the temple guards hastened out to Gethsemane to disperse or arrest the followers of the Master. But long before their arrival these followers had scattered. The apostles had retired to designated hiding places; the Greeks had separated and gone to various homes in Jerusalem; the other disciples had likewise disappeared. David Zebedee believed that Jesus' enemies would return; so he early removed some five or six tents up the ravine near where the Master so often retired to pray and worship. Here he proposed to hide and at the same time maintain a center, or co-ordinating station, for his messenger service. David had hardly left the camp when the temple guards arrived. Finding no one there, they contented themselves with burning the camp and then hastened back to the temple. On hearing their report, the Sanhedrin was satisfied that the followers of Jesus were so thoroughly frightened and subdued that there would be no danger of an uprising or any attempt to rescue Jesus from the hands of his executioners. They were at last able to breathe easily, and so they adjourned, every man going his way to prepare for the Passover.

As soon as Jesus was turned over to the Roman soldiers by Pilate for crucifixion, a messenger hastened away to Gethsemane to inform David, and within five minutes runners were on their way to Bethsaida, Pella, Philadelphia, Sidon, Schechem, Hebron, Damascus, and Alexandria. And these messengers carried the news that Jesus was about to be crucified by the Romans at the insistent behest of the rulers of the Jews.

Throughout this tragic day, until the message finally went forth that the Master had been laid in the tomb, David sent messengers about every half hour with reports to the apostles, the Greeks, and Jesus' earthly family, assembled at the home of Lazarus in Bethany. When the messengers departed with the word that Jesus had been buried, David dismissed his corps of local runners for the Passover celebration and for the coming Sabbath of rest, instructing them to report to him quietly on Sunday morning at the home of Nicodemus, where he proposed to go in hiding for a few days with Andrew and Simon Peter.

This peculiar-minded David Zebedee was the only one of the leading disciples of Jesus who was inclined to take a literal and plain matter-of-fact view of the Master's assertion that he would die and "rise again on the third day." David had once heard him make this prediction and, being of a literal turn of mind, now proposed to assemble his messengers early Sunday morning at the home of Nicodemus so that they would be on hand to spread the news in case Jesus rose from the dead. David soon discovered that none of Jesus' followers were looking for him to return so soon from the grave; therefore did he say little about his belief and nothing about the mobilization of all his messenger force on early Sunday morning except to the runners who had been dispatched on Friday forenoon to distant cities and believer centers.

And so these followers of Jesus, scattered throughout Jerusalem and its environs, that night partook of the Passover and the following day remained in seclusion.

4. PREPARATION FOR THE CRUCIFIXION

After Pilate had washed his hands before the multitude, thus seeking to escape the guilt of delivering up an innocent man to be crucified just because he feared to resist the clamor of the rulers of the Jews, he ordered the Master turned over to the Roman soldiers and gave the word to their captain that he was to be crucified immediately. Upon taking charge of Jesus, the soldiers led him back into the courtyard of the praetorium, and after removing the robe which Herod had put on him, they dressed him in his own garments. These soldiers mocked and derided him, but they did not inflict further physical punishment. Jesus was now alone with these Roman soldiers. His friends were in hiding; his enemies had gone their way; even John Zebedee was no longer by his side.

It was a little after eight o'clock when Pilate turned Jesus over to the soldiers and a little before nine o'clock when they started for the scene of the crucifixion. During this period of more than half an hour Jesus never spoke a word. The executive business of a great universe was practically at a standstill. Gabriel and the chief rulers of Nebadon were either assembled here on Urantia, or else they were closely attending upon the space reports of the archangels in an effort to keep advised as to what was happening to the Son of Man on Urantia.

By the time the soldiers were ready to depart with Jesus for Golgotha, they had begun to be impressed by his unusual composure and extraordinary dignity, by his uncomplaining silence.

Much of the delay in starting off with Jesus for the site of the crucifixion was due to the last-minute decision of the captain to take along two thieves who had been condemned to die; since Jesus was to be crucified that morning, the Roman captain thought these two might just as well die with him as wait for the end of the Passover festivities.

As soon as the thieves could be made ready, they were led into the courtyard, where they gazed upon Jesus, one of them for the first time, but the other had often heard him speak, both in the temple and many months before at the Pella camp.

5. JESUS' DEATH IN RELATION TO THE PASSOVER

There is no direct relation between the death of Jesus and the Jewish Passover. True, the Master did lay down his life in the flesh on this day, the day of the preparation for the Jewish Passover, and at about the time of the sacrificing of the Passover lambs in the temple. But this coincidental occurrence does not in any manner indicate that the death of the Son of Man on earth has any connection with the Jewish sacrificial system. Jesus was a Jew, but as the Son of Man he was a mortal of the realms. The events already narrated and leading up to this hour of the Master's impending crucifixion are sufficient to indicate that his death at about this time was a purely natural and man-managed affair.

It was man and not God who planned and executed the death of Jesus on the cross. True, the Father refused to interfere with the march of human events on Urantia, but the Father in Paradise did not decree, demand, or require the death of his Son as it was carried out on earth. It is a fact that in some manner, sooner or later, Jesus would have had to divest himself of his mortal body, his incarnation in the flesh, but he could have executed such a task in countless ways without dying on a cross between two thieves. All of this was man's doing, not God's.

At the time of the Master's baptism he had already completed the technique of the required experience on earth and in the flesh which was necessary for the completion of his seventh and last universe bestowal. At this very time Jesus' duty on earth was done. All the life he lived thereafter, and even the manner of his death, was a purely personal ministry on his part for the welfare and uplifting of his mortal creatures on this world and on other worlds.

The gospel of the good news that mortal man may, by faith, become spirit-conscious that he is a son of God, is not dependent on the death of Jesus. True, indeed, all this gospel of the kingdom has been tremendously illuminated by the Master's death, but even more so by his life.

All that the Son of Man said or did on earth greatly embellished the doctrines of sonship with God and of the brotherhood of men, but these essential relationships of God and men are inherent in the universe facts of God's love for his creatures and the innate mercy of the divine Sons. These touching and divinely beautiful relations between man and his Maker on this world and on all others throughout the universe of universes, have existed from eternity; and they are not in any sense dependent on these periodic bestowal enactments of the Creator Sons of God, who thus assume the nature and likeness of their created intelligences as a part of the price which they must pay for the final acquirement of unlimited sovereignty over their respective local universes.

The Father in heaven loved mortal man on earth just as much before the life and death of Jesus on Urantia as he did after this transcendent exhibition of the copartnership of man and God. This mighty transaction of the incarnation of the God of Nebadon as a man on Urantia could not augment the attributes of the eternal, infinite, and universal Father, but it did enrich and enlighten all other administrators and creatures of the universe of Nebadon. While the Father in heaven loves us no more because of this bestowal of

Michael, all other celestial intelligences do. And this is because Jesus not only made a revelation of God to man, but he also likewise made a new revelation of man to the Gods and to the celestial intelligences of the universe of universes.

Jesus is not about to die as a sacrifice for sin. He is not going to atone for the inborn moral guilt of the human race. Mankind has no such guilt before God. Guilt is purely a matter of personal sin and knowing, deliberate rebellion against the will of the Father and the administration of his Sons.

Sin and rebellion have nothing to do with the fundamental bestowal plan of the Paradise Sons of God, albeit it does appear to us that the salvage plan is a provisional feature of the bestowal plan.

The salvation of God for the mortals of Urantia would have been just as effective and unerringly certain if Jesus had not been put to death by the cruel hands of ignorant mortals. If the Master had been favorably received by the mortals of earth and had departed from Urantia by the voluntary relinquishment of his life in the flesh, the fact of the love of God and the mercy of the Son — the fact of sonship with God — would have in no wise been affected. You mortals are the sons of God, and only one thing is required to make such a truth factual in your personal experience, and that is your spirit-born faith.

PAPER 187
THE CRUCIFIXION

AFTER THE TWO brigands had been made ready, the soldiers, under the direction of a centurion, started for the scene of the crucifixion. The centurion in charge of these twelve soldiers was the same captain who had led forth the Roman soldiers the previous night to arrest Jesus in Gethsemane. It was the Roman custom to assign four soldiers for each person to be crucified. The two brigands were properly scourged before they were taken out to be crucified, but Jesus was given no further physical punishment; the captain undoubtedly thought he had already been sufficiently scourged, even before his condemnation.

The two thieves crucified with Jesus were associates of Barabbas and would later have been put to death with their leader if he had not been released as the Passover pardon of Pilate. Jesus was thus crucified in the place of Barabbas.

What Jesus is now about to do, submit to death on the cross, he does of his own free will. In foretelling this experience, he said: "The Father loves and sustains me because I am willing to lay down my life. But I will take it up again. No one takes my life away from me — I lay it down of myself. I have authority to lay it down, and I have authority to take it up. I have received such a commandment from my Father."

It was just before nine o'clock this morning when the soldiers led Jesus from the praetorium on the way to Golgotha. They were followed by many who secretly sympathized with Jesus, but most of this group of two hundred or more were either his enemies or curious idlers who merely desired to enjoy the shock of witnessing the crucifixions. Only a few of the Jewish leaders went out to see Jesus die on the cross. Knowing that he had been turned over to the Roman soldiers by Pilate, and that he was condemned to die, they busied themselves with their meeting in the temple, whereat they discussed what should be done with his followers.

1. ON THE WAY TO GOLGOTHA

Before leaving the courtyard of the praetorium, the soldiers placed the crossbeam on Jesus' shoulders. It was the custom to compel the condemned man to carry the crossbeam to the site of the crucifixion. Such a condemned man did not carry the whole cross, only this shorter timber. The longer and upright pieces of timber for the three crosses had already been transported to Golgotha and, by the time of the arrival of the soldiers and their prisoners, had been firmly implanted in the ground.

According to custom the captain led the procession, carrying small white boards on which had been written with charcoal the names of the criminals and the nature of the crimes for which they had been condemned. For the two thieves the centurion had notices which gave their names, underneath which was written the one word, "Brigand." It was the custom, after the victim had been nailed to the crossbeam and hoisted to his place on the upright timber, to nail this notice to the top of the cross, just above the head of the criminal, that all witnesses might know for what crime the condemned man was being crucified. The legend which the centurion carried to put on the cross of Jesus had been written by Pilate himself in Latin, Greek, and Aramaic, and it read: "Jesus of Nazareth — the King of the Jews."

Some of the Jewish authorities who were yet present when Pilate wrote this legend made vigorous protest against calling Jesus the "king of the Jews." But Pilate reminded them that such an accusation was part of the charge which led to his condemnation. When the Jews saw they could not prevail upon Pilate to change his mind, they pleaded that at least it be modified to read, "He said, `I am the king of the Jews.'" But Pilate was adamant; he would not alter the writing. To all further supplication he only replied, "What I have written, I have written."

Ordinarily, it was the custom to journey to Golgotha by the longest road in order that a large number of persons might view the condemned criminal, but on this day they went by the most direct route to the Damascus gate, which led out of the city to the north, and following this road, they soon arrived at Golgotha, the official crucifixion site of Jerusalem. Beyond Golgotha were the villas of the wealthy, and on the other side of the road were the tombs of many well-to-do Jews.

Crucifixion was not a Jewish mode of punishment. Both the Greeks and the Romans learned this method of execution from the Phoenicians. Even Herod, with all his cruelty, did not resort to crucifixion. The Romans never crucified a Roman citizen; only slaves and subject peoples were subjected to this dishonorable mode of death. During the siege of Jerusalem, just forty years after the crucifixion of Jesus, all of Golgotha was covered by thousands upon thousands of crosses upon which, from day to day, there perished the flower of the Jewish race. A terrible harvest, indeed, of the seed-sowing of this day.

As the death procession passed along the narrow streets of Jerusalem, many of the tenderhearted Jewish women who had heard Jesus' words of good cheer and compassion, and who knew of his life of loving ministry, could not refrain from weeping when they saw him being led forth to such an ignoble death. As he passed by, many of these women bewailed and lamented. And when some of them even dared to follow along by his side, the Master turned his head toward them and said: "Daughters of Jerusalem, weep not for me, but rather weep for yourselves and for your children. My work is about done — soon I go to my Father — but the times of terrible trouble for Jerusalem are just beginning. Behold, the days are coming in which you shall say: Blessed are the barren and those whose breasts have never suckled their young. In those days will you pray the rocks of the hills to fall on you in order that you may be delivered from the terrors of your troubles."

These women of Jerusalem were indeed courageous to manifest sympathy for Jesus, for it was strictly against the law to show friendly feelings for one who was being led forth to crucifixion. It was permitted the rabble to jeer, mock, and ridicule the condemned, but it was not allowed that any sympathy should be expressed. Though Jesus appreciated the manifestation of sympathy in this dark hour when his friends were in hiding, he did not want these kindhearted women to incur the displeasure of the authorities by daring to show compassion in his behalf. Even at such a time as this Jesus thought little about himself, only of the terrible days of tragedy ahead for Jerusalem and the whole Jewish nation.

As the Master trudged along on the way to the crucifixion, he was very weary; he was nearly exhausted. He had had neither food nor water since the Last Supper at the home of Elijah Mark; neither had he been permitted to enjoy one moment of sleep. In addition, there had been one hearing right after another up to the hour of his condemnation, not to mention the abusive scourgings with their accompanying physical suffering and loss of blood. Superimposed upon all this was his extreme mental anguish, his acute spiritual tension, and a terrible feeling of human loneliness.

Shortly after passing through the gate on the way out of the city, as Jesus staggered on bearing the crossbeam, his physical strength momentarily gave way, and he fell beneath the weight of his heavy burden. The soldiers shouted at him and kicked him, but he could not arise. When the captain saw this, knowing what Jesus had already endured, he commanded the soldiers to desist. Then he ordered a passerby, one Simon from Cyrene, to take the crossbeam from Jesus' shoulders and compelled him to carry it the rest of the way to Golgotha.

This man Simon had come all the way from Cyrene, in northern Africa, to attend the Passover. He was stopping with other Cyrenians just outside the city walls and was on his way to the temple services in the city when the Roman captain commanded him to carry Jesus' crossbeam. Simon lingered all through the hours of the Master's death on the cross, talking with many of his friends and with his enemies. After the resurrection and before leaving Jerusalem, he became a valiant believer in the gospel of the kingdom, and when he returned home, he led his family into the heavenly kingdom. His two sons, Alexander and Rufus, became very effective teachers of the new gospel in Africa. But Simon never knew that Jesus, whose burden he bore, and the Jewish tutor who once befriended his injured son, were the same person.

It was shortly after nine o'clock when this procession of death arrived at Golgotha, and the Roman soldiers set themselves about the task of nailing the two brigands and the Son of Man to their respective crosses.

2. THE CRUCIFIXION

The soldiers first bound the Master's arms with cords to the crossbeam, and then they nailed his hands to the wood. When they had hoisted this crossbeam up on the post, and after they had nailed it securely to the upright timber of the cross, they bound and nailed his feet to the wood, using one long nail to penetrate both feet. The upright timber had a large peg, inserted at the proper height, which served as a sort of saddle for supporting the body weight. The cross was not high, the Master's feet being only about three feet from the ground. He was therefore able to hear all that was said of him in derision and could plainly see the expression on the faces of all those who so thoughtlessly mocked him. And also could those present easily hear all that Jesus said during these hours of lingering torture and slow death.

It was the custom to remove all clothes from those who were to be crucified, but since the Jews greatly objected to the public exposure of the naked human form, the Romans always provided a suitable loin cloth for all persons crucified at Jerusalem. Accordingly, after Jesus' clothes had been removed, he was thus garbed before he was put upon the cross.

Crucifixion was resorted to in order to provide a cruel and lingering punishment, the victim sometimes not dying for several days. There was considerable sentiment against crucifixion in Jerusalem, and there existed a society of Jewish women who always sent a representative to crucifixions for the purpose of offering drugged wine to the victim in order to lessen his suffering. But when Jesus tasted this narcotized wine, as thirsty as he was, he refused to drink it. The Master chose to retain his human consciousness until the very end. He desired to meet death, even in this cruel and inhuman form, and conquer it by voluntary submission to the full human experience.

Before Jesus was put on his cross, the two brigands had already been placed on their crosses, all the while cursing and spitting upon their executioners. Jesus' only words, as they nailed him to the crossbeam, were, "Father, forgive them, for they know not what they do." He could not have so mercifully and lovingly interceded for his executioners if such thoughts of affectionate devotion had not been the mainspring of all his life of unselfish service. The ideas, motives, and longings of a lifetime are openly revealed in a crisis.

After the Master was hoisted on the cross, the captain nailed the title up above his head, and it read in three languages, "Jesus of Nazareth — the King of the Jews." The Jews were infuriated by this believed insult. But Pilate was chafed by their disrespectful manner; he felt he had been intimidated and humiliated, and he took this method of obtaining petty revenge. He could have written "Jesus, a rebel." But he well knew how these Jerusalem Jews detested the very name of Nazareth, and he was determined thus to humiliate them. He knew that they would also be cut to the very quick by seeing this executed Galilean called "The King of the Jews."

Many of the Jewish leaders, when they learned how Pilate had sought to deride them by placing this inscription on the cross of Jesus, hastened out to Golgotha, but they dared not attempt to remove it since the Roman soldiers were standing on guard. Not being able to remove the title, these leaders mingled with the crowd and did their utmost to incite derision and ridicule, lest any give serious regard to the inscription.

The Apostle John, with Mary the mother of Jesus, Ruth, and Jude, arrived on the scene just after Jesus had been hoisted to his position on the cross, and just as the captain was nailing the title above the Master's head. John was the only one of the eleven apostles to witness the crucifixion, and even he was not present all of the time since he ran into Jerusalem to bring back his mother and her friends soon after he had brought Jesus' mother to the scene.

As Jesus saw his mother, with John and his brother and sister, he smiled but said nothing. Meanwhile the four soldiers assigned to the Master's crucifixion, as was the custom, had divided his clothes among them, one taking the sandals, one the turban, one the girdle, and the fourth the cloak. This left the tunic, or seamless vestment reaching down to near the knees, to be cut up into four pieces, but when the soldiers saw what an unusual garment it was, they decided to cast lots for it. Jesus looked down on them while they divided his garments, and the thoughtless crowd jeered at him.

It was well that the Roman soldiers took possession of the Master's clothing. Otherwise, if his followers had gained possession of these garments, they would have been tempted to resort to superstitious relic worship. The Master desired that his followers should have nothing material to associate with his life on earth. He wanted to leave mankind only the memory of a human life dedicated to the high spiritual ideal of being consecrated to doing the Father's will.

3. THOSE WHO SAW THE CRUCIFIXION

At about half past nine o'clock this Friday morning, Jesus was hung upon the cross. Before eleven o'clock, upward of one thousand persons had assembled to witness this spectacle of the crucifixion of the Son of Man. Throughout these dreadful hours the unseen hosts of a universe stood in silence while they gazed upon this extraordinary phenomenon of the Creator as he was dying the death of the creature, even the most ignoble death of a condemned criminal.

Standing near the cross at one time or another during the crucifixion were Mary, Ruth, Jude, John, Salome (John's mother), and a group of earnest women believers including Mary the wife of Clopas and sister of Jesus' mother, Mary Magdalene, and Rebecca, onetime of Sepphoris. These and other friends of Jesus held their peace while they witnessed his great patience and fortitude and gazed upon his intense sufferings.

Many who passed by wagged their heads and, railing at him, said: "You who would destroy the temple and build it again in three days, save yourself. If you are the Son of God, why do you not come down from your cross?" In like manner some of the rulers of the Jews mocked him, saying, "He saved others, but himself he cannot save." Others said, "If you are the king of the Jews, come down from the cross, and we will believe in you." And later on they mocked him the more, saying: "He trusted in God to deliver him. He even claimed to be the Son of God — look at him now — crucified between two thieves." Even the two thieves also railed at him and cast reproach upon him.

Inasmuch as Jesus would make no reply to their taunts, and since it was nearing noontime of this special preparation day, by half past eleven o'clock most of the jesting and jeering crowd had gone its way; less than fifty persons remained on the scene. The soldiers now prepared to eat lunch and drink their cheap, sour wine as they settled down for the long deathwatch. As they partook of their wine, they derisively offered a toast to Jesus, saying, "Hail and good fortune! to the king of the Jews." And they were astonished at the Master's tolerant regard of their ridicule and mocking.

When Jesus saw them eat and drink, he looked down upon them and said, "I thirst." When the captain of the guard heard Jesus say, "I thirst," he took some of the wine from his bottle and, putting the saturated sponge stopper upon the end of a javelin, raised it to Jesus so that he could moisten his parched lips.

Jesus had purposed to live without resort to his supernatural power, and he likewise elected to die as an ordinary mortal upon the cross. He had lived as a man, and he would die as a man — doing the Father's will.

4. THE THIEF ON THE CROSS

One of the brigands railed at Jesus, saying, "If you are the Son of God, why do you not save yourself and us?" But when he had reproached Jesus, the other thief, who had many times heard the Master teach, said: "Do you have no fear even of God? Do you not see that we are suffering justly for our deeds, but that this man suffers unjustly? Better that we should seek forgiveness for our sins and salvation for our souls." When Jesus heard the thief say this, he turned his face toward him and smiled approvingly. When the malefactor saw the face of Jesus turned toward him, he mustered up his courage, fanned the flickering flame of his faith, and said, "Lord, remember me when you come into your kingdom." And then Jesus said, "Verily, verily, I say to you today, you shall sometime be with me in Paradise."

The Master had time amidst the pangs of mortal death to listen to the faith confession of the believing brigand. When this thief reached out for salvation, he found deliverance. Many times before this he had been constrained to believe in Jesus, but only in these last hours of consciousness did he turn with a whole heart toward the Master's teaching. When he saw the manner in which Jesus faced death upon the cross, this thief could no longer resist the conviction that this Son of Man was indeed the Son of God.

During this episode of the conversion and reception of the thief into the kingdom by Jesus, the Apostle John was absent, having gone into the city to bring his mother and her friends to the scene of the crucifixion. Luke subsequently heard this story from the converted Roman captain of the guard.

The Apostle John told about the crucifixion as he remembered the event two thirds of a century after its occurrence. The other records were based upon the recital of the Roman centurion on duty who, because of what he saw and heard, subsequently believed in Jesus and entered into the full fellowship of the kingdom of heaven on earth.

This young man, the penitent brigand, had been led into a life of violence and wrongdoing by those who extolled such a career of robbery as an effective patriotic protest against political oppression and social injustice. And this sort of teaching, plus the urge for adventure, led many otherwise well-meaning youths to enlist in these daring expeditions of robbery. This young man had looked upon Barabbas as a hero. Now he saw that he had been mistaken. Here on the cross beside him he saw a really great man, a true hero. Here was a hero who fired his zeal and inspired his highest ideas of moral self-respect and quickened all his ideals of courage, manhood, and bravery. In beholding Jesus, there sprang up in his heart an overwhelming sense of love, loyalty, and genuine greatness.

And if any other person among the jeering crowd had experienced the birth of faith within his soul and had appealed to the mercy of Jesus, he would have been received with the same loving consideration that was displayed toward the believing brigand.

Just after the repentant thief heard the Master's promise that they should sometime meet in Paradise, John returned from the city, bringing with him his mother and a company of almost a dozen women believers. John took up his position near Mary the mother of Jesus, supporting her. Her son Jude stood on the other side. As Jesus looked down upon this scene, it was noontide, and he said to his mother, "Woman, behold your son!" And speaking to John, he said, "My son, behold your mother!" And then he addressed them both, saying, "I desire that you depart from this place." And so John and Jude led Mary away from Golgotha. John took the mother of Jesus to the place where he tarried in Jerusalem and then hastened back to the scene of the crucifixion. After the Passover Mary returned to Bethsaida, where she lived at John's home for the rest of her natural life. Mary did not live quite one year after the death of Jesus.

After Mary left, the other women withdrew for a short distance and remained in attendance upon Jesus until he expired on the cross, and they were yet standing by when the body of the Master was taken down for burial.

5. LAST HOUR ON THE CROSS

Although it was early in the season for such a phenomenon, shortly after twelve o'clock the sky darkened by reason of the fine sand in the air. The people of Jerusalem knew that this meant the coming of one of those hot-wind sandstorms from the Arabian desert. Before one o'clock the sky was so dark the sun was hid, and the remainder of the crowd hastened back to the city. When the Master gave up his life shortly after this hour, less than thirty people were present, only the thirteen Roman soldiers and a group of about fifteen believers. These believers were all women except two, Jude, Jesus' brother, and John Zebedee, who returned to the scene just before the Master expired.

Shortly after one o'clock, amidst the increasing darkness of the fierce sandstorm, Jesus began to fail in human consciousness. His last words of mercy, forgiveness, and admonition had been spoken. His last wish — concerning the care of his mother — had been expressed. During this hour of approaching death the human mind of Jesus resorted to the repetition of many passages in the Hebrew scriptures, particularly the Psalms. The last conscious thought of the human Jesus was concerned with the repetition in his mind of a portion of the Book of Psalms now known as the twentieth, twenty-first, and twenty-second Psalms. While his lips would often move, he was too weak to utter the words as these passages, which he so well knew by heart, would pass through his mind. Only a few times did those standing by catch some utterance, such as, "I know the Lord will save his anointed," "Your hand shall find out all my enemies," and "My God, my God, why have you forsaken me?" Jesus did not for one moment entertain the slightest doubt that he had lived in accordance with the Father's will; and he never doubted that he was now laying down his life in the flesh in accordance with his Father's will. He did not feel that the Father had forsaken him; he was merely reciting in his vanishing consciousness many Scriptures, among them this twenty-second Psalm, which begins with "My God, my God, why have you forsaken me?" And this happened to be one of the three passages which were spoken with sufficient clearness to be heard by those standing by.

The last request which the mortal Jesus made of his fellows was about half past one o'clock when, a second time, he said, "I thirst," and the same captain of the guard again moistened his lips with the same sponge wet in the sour wine, in those days commonly called vinegar.

The sandstorm grew in intensity and the heavens increasingly darkened. Still the soldiers and the small group of believers stood by. The soldiers crouched near the cross, huddled together to protect themselves from the cutting sand. The mother of John and others watched from a distance where they were somewhat sheltered by an overhanging rock. When the Master finally breathed his last, there were present at the foot of his cross John Zebedee, his brother Jude, his sister Ruth, Mary Magdalene, and Rebecca, onetime of Sepphoris.

It was just before three o'clock when Jesus, with a loud voice, cried out, "It is finished! Father, into your hands I commend my spirit." And when he had thus spoken, he bowed his head and gave up the life struggle. When the Roman centurion saw how Jesus died, he smote his breast and said: "This was indeed a righteous man; truly he must have been a Son of God." And from that hour he began to believe in Jesus.

Jesus died royally — as he had lived. He freely admitted his kingship and remained master of the situation throughout the tragic day. He went willingly to his ignominious death, after he had provided for the safety of his chosen apostles. He wisely restrained Peter's trouble-making violence and provided that John might be near him right up to the end of his mortal existence. He revealed his true nature to the murderous Sanhedrin and reminded Pilate of the source of his sovereign authority as a Son of God. He started out to Golgotha bearing his own crossbeam and finished up his loving bestowal by handing over his spirit of mortal acquirement to the Paradise Father. After such a life — and at such a death — the Master could truly say, "It is finished."

Because this was the preparation day for both the Passover and the Sabbath, the Jews did not want these bodies to be exposed on Golgotha. Therefore they went before Pilate asking that the legs of these three men be broken, that they be dispatched, so that they could be taken down from their crosses and cast into the criminal burial pits before sundown. When Pilate heard this request, he forthwith sent three soldiers to break the legs and dispatch Jesus and the two brigands.

When these soldiers arrived at Golgotha, they did accordingly to the two thieves, but they found Jesus already dead, much to their surprise. However, in order to make sure of his death, one of the soldiers pierced his left side with his spear. Though it was common for the victims of crucifixion to linger alive upon the cross for even two or three days, the overwhelming emotional agony and the acute spiritual anguish of Jesus brought an end to his mortal life in the flesh in a little less than five and one-half hours.

6. AFTER THE CRUCIFIXION

In the midst of the darkness of the sandstorm, about half past three o'clock, David Zebedee sent out the last of the messengers carrying the news of the Master's death. The last of his runners he dispatched to the home of Martha and Mary in Bethany, where he supposed the mother of Jesus stopped with the rest of her family.

After the death of the Master, John sent the women, in charge of Jude, to the home of Elijah Mark, where they tarried over the Sabbath day. John himself, being well known by this time to the Roman centurion, remained at

Golgotha until Joseph and Nicodemus arrived on the scene with an order from Pilate authorizing them to take possession of the body of Jesus.

Thus ended a day of tragedy and sorrow for a vast universe whose myriads of intelligences had shuddered at the shocking spectacle of the crucifixion of the human incarnation of their beloved Sovereign; they were stunned by this exhibition of mortal callousness and human perversity.

PAPER 188
THE TIME OF THE TOMB

THE DAY AND A HALF THAT JESUS' mortal body lay in the tomb of Joseph, the period between his death on the cross and his resurrection, is a chapter in the earth career of Michael which is little known to us. We can narrate the burial of the Son of Man and put in this record the events associated with his resurrection, but we cannot supply much information of an authentic nature about what really transpired during this epoch of about thirty-six hours, from three o'clock Friday afternoon to three o'clock Sunday morning. This period in the Master's career began shortly before he was taken down from the cross by the Roman soldiers. He hung upon the cross about one hour after his death. He would have been taken down sooner but for the delay in dispatching the two brigands.

The rulers of the Jews had planned to have Jesus' body thrown in the open burial pits of Gehenna, south of the city; it was the custom thus to dispose of the victims of crucifixion. If this plan had been followed, the body of the Master would have been exposed to the wild beasts.

In the meantime, Joseph of Arimathea, accompanied by Nicodemus, had gone to Pilate and asked that the body of Jesus be turned over to them for proper burial. It was not uncommon for friends of crucified persons to offer bribes to the Roman authorities for the privilege of gaining possession of such bodies. Joseph went before Pilate with a large sum of money, in case it became necessary to pay for permission to remove Jesus' body to a private burial tomb. But Pilate would not take money for this. When he heard the request, he quickly signed the order which authorized Joseph to proceed to Golgotha and take immediate and full possession of the Master's body. In the meantime, the sandstorm having considerably abated, a group of Jews representing the Sanhedrin had gone out to Golgotha for the purpose of making sure that Jesus' body accompanied those of the brigands to the open public burial pits.

1. THE BURIAL OF JESUS

When Joseph and Nicodemus arrived at Golgotha, they found the soldiers taking Jesus down from the cross and the representatives of the Sanhedrin standing by to see that none of Jesus' followers prevented his body from going to the criminal burial pits. When Joseph presented Pilate's order for the Master's body to the centurion, the Jews raised a tumult and clamored for its possession. In their raving they sought violently to take possession of the body, and when they did this, the centurion ordered four of his soldiers to his side, and with drawn swords they stood astride the Master's body as it lay there on the ground. The centurion ordered the other soldiers to leave the two thieves while they drove back this angry mob of infuriated Jews. When order had been restored, the centurion read the permit from Pilate to the Jews and, stepping aside, said to Joseph: "This body is yours to do with as you see fit. I and my soldiers will stand by to see that no man interferes."

A crucified person could not be buried in a Jewish cemetery; there was a strict law against such a procedure. Joseph and Nicodemus knew this law, and on the way out to Golgotha they had decided to bury Jesus in Joseph's new family tomb, hewn out of solid rock, located a short distance north of Golgotha and across the road leading to Samaria. No one had ever lain in this tomb, and they thought it appropriate that the Master should rest there. Joseph really believed that Jesus would rise from the dead, but Nicodemus was very doubtful. These former members of the Sanhedrin had kept their faith in Jesus more or less of a secret, although their fellow Sanhedrists had long suspected them, even before they withdrew from the council. From now on they were the most outspoken disciples of Jesus in all Jerusalem.

At about half past four o'clock the burial procession of Jesus of Nazareth started from Golgotha for Joseph's tomb across the way. The body was wrapped in a linen sheet as the four men carried it, followed by the faithful women watchers from Galilee. The mortals who bore the material body of Jesus to the tomb were: Joseph, Nicodemus, John, and the Roman centurion.

They carried the body into the tomb, a chamber about ten feet square, where they hurriedly prepared it for burial. The Jews did not really bury their dead; they actually embalmed them. Joseph and Nicodemus had brought with them large quantities of myrrh and aloes, and they now wrapped the body with bandages saturated with these solutions. When the embalming was completed, they tied a napkin about the face, wrapped the body in a linen sheet, and reverently placed it on a shelf in the tomb.

After placing the body in the tomb, the centurion signaled for his soldiers to help roll the doorstone up before the entrance to the tomb. The soldiers then departed for Gehenna with the bodies of the thieves while the others returned to Jerusalem, in sorrow, to observe the Passover feast according to the laws of Moses.

There was considerable hurry and haste about the burial of Jesus because this was preparation day and the Sabbath was drawing on apace. The men hurried back to the city, but the women lingered near the tomb until it was very dark.

While all this was going on, the women were hiding near at hand so that they saw it all and observed where the Master had been laid. They thus secreted themselves because it was not permissible for women to associate with men at such a time. These women did not think Jesus had been properly prepared for burial, and they agreed among themselves to go back to the home of Joseph, rest over the Sabbath, make ready spices and ointments, and return on Sunday morning properly to prepare the Master's body for the death rest. The women who thus tarried by the tomb on this Friday evening were: Mary Magdalene, Mary the wife of Clopas, Martha another sister of Jesus' mother, and Rebecca of Sepphoris.

Aside from David Zebedee and Joseph of Arimathea, very few of Jesus' disciples really believed or understood that he was due to arise from the tomb on the third day.

2. SAFEGUARDING THE TOMB

If Jesus' followers were unmindful of his promise to rise from the grave on the third day, his enemies were not. The chief priests, Pharisees, and Sadducees recalled that they had received reports of his saying he would rise from the dead.

This Friday night, after the Passover supper, about midnight a group of the Jewish leaders gathered at the home of Caiaphas, where they discussed their fears concerning the Master's assertions that he would rise from the dead on the third day. This meeting ended with the appointment of a committee of Sanhedrists who were to visit Pilate early the next day, bearing the official request of the Sanhedrin that a Roman guard be stationed before Jesus' tomb to prevent his friends from tampering with it. Said the spokesman of this committee to Pilate: "Sir, we remember that this deceiver, Jesus of Nazareth, said, while he was yet alive, `After three days I will rise again.' We have, therefore, come before you to request that you issue such orders as will make the sepulchre secure against his followers, at least until after the third day. We greatly fear lest his disciples come and steal him away by night and then proclaim to the people that he has risen from the dead. If we should permit this to happen, this mistake would be far worse than to have allowed him to live."

When Pilate heard this request of the Sanhedrists, he said: "I will give you a guard of ten soldiers. Go your way and make the tomb secure." They went back to the temple, secured ten of their own guards, and then marched out to Joseph's tomb with these ten Jewish guards and ten Roman soldiers, even on this Sabbath morning, to set them as watchmen before the tomb. These men rolled yet another stone before the tomb and set the seal of Pilate on and around these stones, lest they be disturbed without their knowledge. And these twenty men remained on watch up to the hour of the resurrection, the Jews carrying them their food and drink.

3. DURING THE SABBATH DAY

Throughout this Sabbath day the disciples and the apostles remained in hiding, while all Jerusalem discussed the death of Jesus on the cross. There were almost one and one-half million Jews present in Jerusalem at this time, hailing from all parts of the Roman Empire and from Mesopotamia. This was the beginning of the Passover week, and all these pilgrims would be in the city to learn of the resurrection of Jesus and to carry the report back to their homes.

Late Saturday night, John Mark summoned the eleven apostles secretly to come to the home of his father, where, just before midnight, they all assembled in the same upper chamber where they had partaken of the Last Supper with their Master two nights previously.

Mary the mother of Jesus, with Ruth and Jude, returned to Bethany to join their family this Saturday evening just before sunset. David Zebedee remained at the home of Nicodemus, where he had arranged for his messengers to assemble early Sunday morning. The women of Galilee, who prepared spices for the further embalming of Jesus' body, tarried at the home of Joseph of Arimathea.

We are not able fully to explain just what happened to Jesus of Nazareth during this period of a day and a half when he was supposed to be resting in Joseph's new tomb. Apparently he died the same natural death on the cross as would any other mortal in the same circumstances. We heard him say, "Father, into your hands I commend my spirit." We do not fully understand the meaning of such a statement inasmuch as his Thought Adjuster had long since been personalized and so maintained an existence apart from Jesus' mortal being. The Master's Personalized Adjuster could in no sense be affected by his physical death on the cross. That which Jesus put in the Father's hands for the time being must have been the spirit counterpart of the Adjuster's early work in spiritizing the mortal mind so as to provide for the transfer of the transcript of the human experience to the mansion worlds. There must have been some spiritual reality in the experience of Jesus which was analogous to the spirit nature, or soul, of the faith-growing mortals of the spheres. But this is merely our opinion — we do not really know what Jesus commended to his Father.

We know that the physical form of the Master rested there in Joseph's tomb until about three o'clock Sunday morning, but we are wholly uncertain regarding the status of the personality of Jesus during that period of thirty-six hours. We have sometimes dared to explain these things to ourselves somewhat as follows:

1. The Creator consciousness of Michael must have been at large and wholly free from its associated mortal mind of the physical incarnation.

2. The former Thought Adjuster of Jesus we know to have been present on earth during this period and in personal command of the assembled celestial hosts.

3. The acquired spirit identity of the man of Nazareth which was built up during his lifetime in the flesh, first, by the direct efforts of his Thought Adjuster, and later, by his own perfect adjustment between the physical necessities and the spiritual requirements of the ideal mortal existence, as it was effected by his never-ceasing choice of the Father's will, must have been consigned to the custody of the Paradise Father. Whether or not this spirit reality returned to become a part of the resurrected personality, we do not know, but we believe it did. But there are those in the universe who hold that this soul-identity of Jesus now reposes in the "bosom of the Father," to be subsequently released for leadership of the Nebadon Corps of the Finality in their undisclosed destiny in connection with the uncreated universes of the unorganized realms of outer space.

4. We think the human or mortal consciousness of Jesus slept during these thirty-six hours. We have reason to believe that the human Jesus knew nothing of what transpired in the universe during this period. To the mortal consciousness there appeared no lapse of time; the resurrection of life followed the sleep of death as of the same instant.

And this is about all we can place on record regarding the status of Jesus during this period of the tomb. There are a number of correlated facts to which we can allude, although we are hardly competent to undertake their interpretation.

In the vast court of the resurrection halls of the first mansion world of Satania, there may now be observed a magnificent material-morontia structure known as the "Michael Memorial," now bearing the seal of Gabriel.

This memorial was created shortly after Michael departed from this world, and it bears this inscription: "In commemoration of the mortal transit of Jesus of Nazareth on Urantia."

There are records extant which show that during this period the supreme council of Salvington held an executive meeting on Urantia under the presidency of Gabriel. There are also records showing that the Ancients of Days of Uversa communicated with Michael regarding the status of the universe of Nebadon during this time.

We know that at least one message passed between Michael and Immanuel on Salvington while the Master's body lay in the tomb.

There is good reason for believing that some personality sat in the seat of Caligastia in the system council of the Planetary Princes on Jerusem which convened while the body of Jesus rested in the tomb.

The records of Edentia indicate that the Constellation Father of Norlatiadek was on Urantia, and that he received instructions from Michael during this time of the tomb.

And there is much other evidence which suggests that not all of the personality of Jesus was asleep and unconscious during this time of apparent physical death.

4. MEANING OF THE DEATH ON THE CROSS

Although Jesus did not die this death on the cross to atone for the guilt of mortal man nor to provide some sort of effective approach to an otherwise offended and unforgiving God; even though the Son of Man did not offer himself as a sacrifice to appease the wrath of God and to open the way for sinful man to obtain salvation; notwithstanding that these ideas of atonement and propitiation are erroneous, nonetheless, there are significances attached to this death of Jesus on the cross which should not be overlooked. It is a fact that Urantia has become known among other neighboring inhabited planets as the "World of the Cross."

Jesus desired to live a full mortal life in the flesh on Urantia. Death is, ordinarily, a part of life. Death is the last act in the mortal drama. In your well-meant efforts to escape the superstitious errors of the false interpretation of the meaning of the death on the cross, you should be careful not to make the great mistake of failing to perceive the true significance and the genuine import of the Master's death.

Mortal man was never the property of the archdeceivers. Jesus did not die to ransom man from the clutch of the apostate rulers and fallen princes of the spheres. The Father in heaven never conceived of such crass injustice as damning a mortal soul because of the evildoing of his ancestors. Neither was the Master's death on the cross a sacrifice which consisted in an effort to pay God a debt which the race of mankind had come to owe him.

Before Jesus lived on earth, you might possibly have been justified in believing in such a God, but not since the Master lived and died among your fellow mortals. Moses taught the dignity and justice of a Creator God; but Jesus portrayed the love and mercy of a heavenly Father.

The animal nature — the tendency toward evildoing — may be hereditary, but sin is not transmitted from parent to child. Sin is the act of conscious and deliberate rebellion against the Father's will and the Sons' laws by an individual will creature.

Jesus lived and died for a whole universe, not just for the beings of this one world. While the mortals of the realms had salvation even before Jesus lived and died on Urantia, it is nevertheless a fact that his bestowal on this world greatly illuminated the way of salvation; his death did much to make forever plain the certainty of mortal survival after death in the flesh.

Though it is hardly proper to speak of Jesus as a sacrificer, a ransomer, or a redeemer, it is wholly correct to refer to him as a *savior*. He forever made the way of salvation (survival) more clear and certain; he did better and more surely show the way of salvation for all the mortals of all the worlds of the universe of Nebadon.

When once you grasp the idea of God as a true and loving Father, the only concept which Jesus ever taught, you must forthwith, in all consistency, utterly abandon all those primitive notions about God as an offended monarch, a stern and all-powerful ruler whose chief delight is to detect his subjects in wrongdoing and to see that they are adequately punished, unless some being almost equal to himself should volunteer to suffer for them, to die as a substitute and in their stead. The whole idea of ransom and atonement is incompatible with the concept of God as it was taught and exemplified by Jesus of Nazareth. The infinite love of God is not secondary to anything in the divine nature.

All this concept of atonement and sacrificial salvation is rooted and grounded in selfishness. Jesus taught that *service* to one's fellows is the highest concept of the brotherhood of spirit believers. Salvation should be taken for granted by those who believe in the fatherhood of God. The believer's chief concern should not be the selfish desire for personal salvation but rather the unselfish urge to love and, therefore, serve one's fellows even as Jesus loved and served mortal men.

Neither do genuine believers trouble themselves so much about the future punishment of sin. The real believer is only concerned about present separation from God. True, wise fathers may chasten their sons, but they do all this in love and for corrective purposes. They do not punish in anger, neither do they chastise in retribution.

Even if God were the stern and legal monarch of a universe in which justice ruled supreme, he certainly would not be satisfied with the childish scheme of substituting an innocent sufferer for a guilty offender.

The great thing about the death of Jesus, as it is related to the enrichment of human experience and the enlargement of the way of salvation, is not the *fact* of his death but rather the superb manner and the matchless spirit in which he met death.

This entire idea of the ransom of the atonement places salvation upon a plane of unreality; such a concept is purely philosophic. Human salvation is *real*; it is based on two realities which may be grasped by the creature's faith and thereby become incorporated into individual human experience: the fact of the fatherhood of God and its correlated truth, the brotherhood of man. It is true, after all, that you are to be "forgiven your debts, even as you forgive your debtors."

5. LESSONS FROM THE CROSS

The cross of Jesus portrays the full measure of the supreme devotion of the true shepherd for even the unworthy members of his flock. It forever places all relations between God and man upon the family basis. God is the Father; man is his son. Love, the love of a father for his son, becomes the central truth in the universe relations of Creator and creature — not the justice of a king which seeks satisfaction in the sufferings and punishment of the evil-doing subject.

The cross forever shows that the attitude of Jesus toward sinners was neither condemnation nor condonation, but rather eternal and loving salvation. Jesus is truly a savior in the sense that his life and death do win men over to goodness and righteous survival. Jesus loves men so much that his love awakens the response of love in the human heart. Love is truly contagious and eternally creative. Jesus' death on the cross exemplifies a love which is sufficiently strong and divine to forgive sin and swallow up all evil-doing. Jesus disclosed to this world a higher quality of righteousness than justice — mere technical right and wrong. Divine love does not merely forgive wrongs; it absorbs and actually destroys them. The forgiveness of love utterly transcends the forgiveness of mercy. Mercy sets the guilt of evil-doing to one side; but love destroys forever the sin and all weakness resulting therefrom. Jesus brought a new method of living to Urantia. He taught us not to resist evil but to find through him a goodness which effectually destroys evil. The forgiveness of Jesus is not condonation; it is salvation from condemnation. Salvation does not slight wrongs; *it makes them right.* True love does not compromise nor condone hate; it destroys it. The love of Jesus is never satisfied with mere forgiveness. The Master's love implies rehabilitation, eternal survival. It is altogether proper to speak of salvation as redemption if you mean this eternal rehabilitation.

Jesus, by the power of his personal love for men, could break the hold of sin and evil. He thereby set men free to choose better ways of living. Jesus portrayed a deliverance from the past which in itself promised a triumph for the future. Forgiveness thus provided salvation. The beauty of divine love, once fully admitted to the human heart, forever destroys the charm of sin and the power of evil.

The sufferings of Jesus were not confined to the crucifixion. In reality, Jesus of Nazareth spent upward of twenty-five years on the cross of a real and intense mortal existence. The real value of the cross consists in the fact that it was the supreme and final expression of his love, the completed revelation of his mercy.

On countless inhabited worlds, enormous numbers of evolving creatures who may have been tempted to give up the moral struggle and abandon the good fight of faith, have taken one more look at Jesus on the cross and then have forged on ahead, inspired by the sight of God's laying down his incarnate life in devotion to the unselfish service of man.

The triumph of the death on the cross is all summed up in the spirit of Jesus' attitude toward those who assailed him. He made the cross an eternal symbol of the triumph of love over hate and the victory of truth over evil when he prayed, "Father, forgive them, for they know not what they do." That devotion of love was contagious throughout a vast universe; the disciples caught it from their Master. The very first teacher of his gospel who was called upon to lay down his life in this service, said, as they stoned him to death, "Lay not this sin to their charge."

The cross makes a supreme appeal to the best in man because it discloses one who was willing to lay down his life in the service of his fellow men. Greater love no man can have than this: that he would be willing to lay down his life for his friends — and Jesus had such a love that he was willing to lay down his life for his enemies, a love greater than any which had hitherto been known on earth.

On other worlds, as well as on Urantia, this sublime spectacle of the death of the human Jesus on the cross of Golgotha has stirred the emotions of mortals, while it has aroused the highest devotion of the angels.

The cross is that high symbol of sacred service, the devotion of one's life to the welfare and salvation of one's fellows. The cross is not the symbol of the sacrifice of the innocent Son of God in the place of guilty sinners and in order to appease the wrath of an offended God, but it does stand forever, on earth and throughout a vast universe, as a sacred symbol of the good bestowing themselves upon the evil and thereby saving them by this very devotion of love. The cross does stand as the token of the highest form of unselfish service, the supreme devotion of the full bestowal of a righteous life in the service of wholehearted ministry, even in death, the death of the cross. And the very sight of this great symbol of the bestowal life of Jesus truly inspires all of us to want to go and do likewise.

When thinking men and women look upon Jesus as he offers up his life on the cross, they will hardly again permit themselves to complain at even the severest hardships of life, much less at petty harassments and their many purely fictitious grievances. His life was so glorious and his death so triumphant that we are all enticed to a willingness to share both. There is true drawing power in the whole bestowal of Michael, from the days of his youth to this overwhelming spectacle of his death on the cross.

Make sure, then, that when you view the cross as a revelation of God, you do not look with the eyes of the primitive man nor with the viewpoint of the later barbarian, both of whom regarded God as a relentless Sovereign of stern justice and rigid law-enforcement. Rather, make sure that you see in the cross the final manifestation of the love and devotion of Jesus to his life mission of bestowal upon the mortal races of his vast universe. See in the death of the Son of Man the climax of the unfolding of the Father's divine love for his sons of the mortal spheres. The cross thus portrays the devotion of willing affection and the bestowal of voluntary salvation upon those who are willing to receive such gifts and devotion. There was nothing in the cross which the Father required — only that which Jesus so willingly gave, and which he refused to avoid.

If man cannot otherwise appreciate Jesus and understand the meaning of his bestowal on earth, he can at least comprehend the fellowship of his mortal sufferings. No man can ever fear that the Creator does not know the nature or extent of his temporal afflictions.

We know that the death on the cross was not to effect man's reconciliation to God but to stimulate man's *realization* of the Father's eternal love and his Son's unending mercy, and to broadcast these universal truths to a whole universe.

PAPER 189
THE RESURRECTION

SOON AFTER THE burial of Jesus on Friday afternoon, the chief of the archangels of Nebadon, then present on Urantia, summoned his council of the resurrection of sleeping will creatures and entered upon the consideration of a possible technique for the restoration of Jesus. These assembled sons of the local universe, the creatures of Michael, did this on their own responsibility; Gabriel had not assembled them. By midnight they had arrived at the conclusion that the creature could do nothing to facilitate the resurrection of the Creator. They were disposed to accept the advice of Gabriel, who instructed them that, since Michael had "laid down his life of his own free will, he also had power to take it up again in accordance with his own determination." Shortly after the adjournment of this council of the archangels, the Life Carriers, and their various associates in the work of creature rehabilitation and morontia creation, the Personalized Adjuster of Jesus, being in personal command of the assembled celestial hosts then on Urantia, spoke these words to the anxious waiting watchers:

"Not one of you can do aught to assist your Creator-father in the return to life. As a mortal of the realm he has experienced mortal death; as the Sovereign of a universe he still lives. That which you observe is the mortal transit of Jesus of Nazareth from life in the flesh to life in the morontia. The spirit transit of this Jesus was completed at the time I separated myself from his personality and became your temporary director. Your Creator-father has elected to pass through the whole of the experience of his mortal creatures, from birth on the material worlds, on through natural death and the resurrection of the morontia, into the status of true spirit existence. A certain phase of this experience you are about to observe, but you may not participate in it. Those things which you ordinarily do for the creature, you may not do for the Creator. A Creator Son has within himself the power to bestow himself in the likeness of any of his created sons; he has within himself the power to lay down his observable life and to take it up again; and he has this power because of the direct command of the Paradise Father, and I know whereof I speak."

When they heard the Personalized Adjuster so speak, they all assumed the attitude of anxious expectancy, from Gabriel down to the most humble cherubim. They saw the mortal body of Jesus in the tomb; they detected evidences of the universe activity of their beloved Sovereign; and not understanding such phenomena, they waited patiently for developments.

1. THE MORONTIA TRANSIT

At two forty-five Sunday morning, the Paradise incarnation commission, consisting of seven unidentified Paradise personalities, arrived on the scene and immediately deployed themselves about the tomb. At ten minutes before three, intense vibrations of commingled material and morontia activities began to issue from Joseph's new tomb, and at two minutes past three o'clock, this Sunday morning, April 9, A.D. 30, the resurrected morontia form and personality of Jesus of Nazareth came forth from the tomb.

After the resurrected Jesus emerged from his burial tomb, the body of flesh in which he had lived and wrought on earth for almost thirty-six years was still lying there in the sepulchre niche, undisturbed and wrapped in the linen sheet, just as it had been laid to rest by Joseph and his associates on Friday afternoon. Neither was the stone before the entrance of the tomb in any way disturbed; the seal of Pilate was still unbroken; the soldiers were still on guard. The temple guards had been on continuous duty; the Roman guard had been changed at midnight. None of these watchers suspected that the object of their vigil had risen to a new and higher form of existence, and that the body which they were guarding was now a discarded outer covering which had no further connection with the delivered and resurrected morontia personality of Jesus.

Mankind is slow to perceive that, in all that is personal, matter is the skeleton of morontia, and that both are the reflected shadow of enduring spirit reality. How long before you will regard time as the moving image of eternity and space as the fleeting shadow of Paradise realities?

As far as we can judge, no creature of this universe nor any personality from another universe had anything to do with this morontia resurrection of Jesus of Nazareth. On Friday he laid down his life as a mortal of the realm; on Sunday morning he took it up again as a morontia being of the system of Satania in Norlatiadek. There is much about the resurrection of Jesus which we do not understand. But we know that it occurred as we have stated and at about the time indicated. We can also record that all known phenomena associated with this mortal transit, or morontia resurrection, occurred right there in Joseph's new tomb, where the mortal material remains of Jesus lay wrapped in burial cloths.

We know that no creature of the local universe participated in this morontia awakening. We perceived the seven personalities of Paradise surround the tomb, but we did not see them do anything in connection with the Master's awakening. Just as soon as Jesus appeared beside Gabriel, just above the tomb, the seven personalities from Paradise signalized their intention of immediate departure for Uversa.

Let us forever clarify the concept of the resurrection of Jesus by making the following statements:

1. His material or physical body was not a part of the resurrected personality. When Jesus came forth from the tomb, his body of flesh remained undisturbed in the sepulchre. He emerged from the burial tomb without moving the stones before the entrance and without disturbing the seals of Pilate.

2. He did not emerge from the tomb as a spirit nor as Michael of Nebadon; he did not appear in the form of the Creator Sovereign, such as he had had before his incarnation in the likeness of mortal flesh on Urantia.

3. He did come forth from this tomb of Joseph in the very likeness of the morontia personalities of those who, as resurrected morontia ascendant beings, emerge from the resurrection halls of the first mansion world of this local system of Satania. And the presence of the Michael memorial in the center of the vast court of the resurrection halls of mansonia number one leads us to conjecture that the Master's resurrection on Urantia was in some way fostered on this, the first of the system mansion worlds.

The first act of Jesus on arising from the tomb was to greet Gabriel and instruct him to continue in executive charge of universe affairs under Immanuel, and then he directed the chief of the Melchizedeks to convey his brotherly greetings to Immanuel. He thereupon asked the Most High of Edentia for the certification of the Ancients of Days as to his mortal transit; and turning to the assembled morontia groups of the seven mansion worlds, here gathered together to greet and welcome their Creator as a creature of their order, Jesus spoke the first words of the postmortal career. Said the morontia Jesus: "Having finished my life in the flesh, I would tarry here for a short time in transition form that I may more fully know the life of my ascendant creatures and further reveal the will of my Father in Paradise."

After Jesus had spoken, he signaled to the Personalized Adjuster, and all universe intelligences who had been assembled on Urantia to witness the resurrection were immediately dispatched to their respective universe assignments.

Jesus now began the contacts of the morontia level, being introduced, as a creature, to the requirements of the life he had chosen to live for a short time on Urantia. This initiation into the morontia world required more than an hour of earth time and was twice interrupted by his desire to communicate with his former associates in the flesh as they came out from Jerusalem wonderingly to peer into the empty tomb to discover what they considered evidence of his resurrection.

Now is the mortal transit of Jesus — the morontia resurrection of the Son of Man — completed. The transitory experience of the Master as a personality midway between the material and the spiritual has begun. And he has done all this through power inherent within himself; no personality has rendered him any assistance. He now lives as Jesus of morontia, and as he begins this morontia life, the material body of his flesh lies there undisturbed in the tomb. The soldiers are still on guard, and the seal of the governor about the rocks has not yet been broken.

2. THE MATERIAL BODY OF JESUS

At ten minutes past three o'clock, as the resurrected Jesus fraternized with the assembled morontia personalities from the seven mansion worlds of Satania, the chief of archangels — the angels of the resurrection — approached Gabriel and asked for the mortal body of Jesus. Said the chief of the archangels: "We may not participate in the morontia resurrection of the bestowal experience of Michael our sovereign, but we would have his mortal remains put in our custody for immediate dissolution. We do not propose to employ our technique of dematerialization; we merely wish to invoke the process of accelerated time. It is enough that we have seen the Sovereign live and die on Urantia; the hosts of heaven would be spared the memory of enduring the sight of the slow decay of the human form of the Creator and Upholder of a universe. In the name of the celestial intelligences of all Nebadon, I ask for a mandate giving me the custody of the mortal body of Jesus of Nazareth and empowering us to proceed with its immediate dissolution."

And when Gabriel had conferred with the senior Most High of Edentia, the archangel spokesman for the celestial hosts was given permission to make such disposition of the physical remains of Jesus as he might determine.

After the chief of archangels had been granted this request, he summoned to his assistance many of his fellows, together with a numerous host of the representatives of all orders of celestial personalities, and then, with the aid of the Urantia midwayers, proceeded to take possession of Jesus' physical body. This body of death was a purely material creation; it was physical and literal; it could not be removed from the tomb as the morontia form of the resurrection had been able to escape the sealed sepulchre. By the aid of certain morontia auxiliary personalities, the morontia form can be made at one time as of the spirit so that it can become indifferent to ordinary matter, while at another time it can become discernible and contactable to material beings, such as the mortals of the realm.

As they made ready to remove the body of Jesus from the tomb preparatory to according it the dignified and reverent disposal of near-instantaneous dissolution, it was assigned the secondary Urantia midwayers to roll away the stones from the entrance of the tomb. The larger of these two stones was a huge circular affair, much like a millstone, and it moved in a groove chiseled out of the rock, so that it could be rolled back and forth to open or close the tomb. When the watching Jewish guards and the Roman soldiers, in the dim light of the morning, saw this huge stone begin to roll away from the entrance of the tomb, apparently of its own accord — without any visible means to account for such motion — they were seized with fear and panic, and they fled in haste from the scene. The Jews fled to their homes, afterward going back to report these doings to their captain at the temple. The Romans fled to the fortress of Antonia and reported what they had seen to the centurion as soon as he arrived on duty.

The Jewish leaders began the sordid business of supposedly getting rid of Jesus by offering bribes to the traitorous Judas, and now, when confronted with this embarrassing situation, instead of thinking of punishing the guards who deserted their post, they resorted to bribing these guards and the Roman soldiers. They paid each of these twenty men a sum of money and instructed them to say to all: "While we slept during the nighttime, his disciples came upon us and took away the body." And the Jewish leaders made solemn promises to the soldiers to defend them before Pilate in case it should ever come to the governor's knowledge that they had accepted a bribe.

The Christian belief in the resurrection of Jesus has been based on the fact of the "empty tomb." It was indeed a *fact* that the tomb was empty, but this is not the *truth* of the resurrection. The tomb was truly empty when the first believers arrived, and this fact, associated with that of the undoubted resurrection of the Master, led to the formulation of a belief which was not true: the teaching that the material and mortal body of Jesus was raised from the grave. Truth having to do with spiritual realities and eternal values cannot always be built up by a combination of apparent facts. Although individual facts may be materially true, it does not follow that the association of a group of facts must necessarily lead to truthful spiritual conclusions.

The tomb of Joseph was empty, not because the body of Jesus had been rehabilitated or resurrected, but because the celestial hosts had been granted their request to afford it a special and unique dissolution, a return of the "dust to dust," without the intervention of the delays of time and without the operation of the ordinary and visible processes of mortal decay and material corruption.

The mortal remains of Jesus underwent the same natural process of elemental disintegration as characterizes all human bodies on earth except that, in point of time, this natural mode of dissolution was greatly accelerated, hastened to that point where it became well-nigh instantaneous.

The true evidences of the resurrection of Michael are spiritual in nature, albeit this teaching is corroborated by the testimony of many mortals of the realm who met, recognized, and communed with the resurrected morontia Master. He became a part of the personal experience of almost one thousand human beings before he finally took leave of Urantia.

3. THE DISPENSATIONAL RESURRECTION

A little after half past four o'clock this Sunday morning, Gabriel summoned the archangels to his side and made ready to inaugurate the general resurrection of the termination of the Adamic dispensation on Urantia. When the vast host of the seraphim and the cherubim concerned in this great event had been marshaled in proper formation, the morontia Michael appeared before Gabriel, saying: "As my Father has life in himself, so has he given it to the Son to have life in himself. Although I have not yet fully resumed the exercise of universe jurisdiction, this self-imposed limitation does not in any manner restrict the bestowal of life upon my sleeping sons; let the roll call of the planetary resurrection begin."

The circuit of the archangels then operated for the first time from Urantia. Gabriel and the archangel hosts moved to the place of the spiritual polarity of the planet; and when Gabriel gave the signal, there flashed to the first of the system mansion worlds the voice of Gabriel, saying: "By the mandate of Michael, let the dead of a Urantia dispensation rise!" Then all the survivors of the human races of Urantia who had fallen asleep since the days of Adam, and who had not already gone on to judgment, appeared in the resurrection halls of mansonia in readiness for morontia investiture. And in an instant of time the seraphim and their associates made ready to depart for the mansion worlds. Ordinarily these seraphic guardians, onetime assigned to the group custody of these surviving mortals, would have been present at the moment of their awaking in the resurrection halls of mansonia, but they were on this world itself at this time because of the necessity of Gabriel's presence here in connection with the morontia resurrection of Jesus.

Notwithstanding that countless individuals having personal seraphic guardians and those achieving the requisite attainment of spiritual personality progress had gone on to mansonia during the ages subsequent to the times of Adam and Eve, and though there had been many special and millennial resurrections of Urantia sons, this was the third of the planetary roll calls, or complete dispensational resurrections. The first occurred at the time of the arrival of the Planetary Prince, the second during the time of Adam, and this, the third, signalized the morontia resurrection, the mortal transit, of Jesus of Nazareth.

When the signal of the planetary resurrection had been received by the chief of archangels, the Personalized Adjuster of the Son of Man relinquished his authority over the celestial hosts assembled on Urantia, turning all these sons of the local universe back to the jurisdiction of their respective commanders. And when he had done this, he departed for Salvington to register with Immanuel the completion of the mortal transit of Michael. And he was immediately followed by all the celestial host not required for duty on Urantia. But Gabriel remained on Urantia with the morontia Jesus.

And this is the recital of the events of the resurrection of Jesus as viewed by those who saw them as they really occurred, free from the limitations of partial and restricted human vision.

4. DISCOVERY OF THE EMPTY TOMB

As we approach the time of the resurrection of Jesus on this early Sunday morning, it should be recalled that the ten apostles were sojourning at the home of Elijah and Mary Mark, where they were asleep in the upper chamber, resting on the very couches whereon they reclined during the last supper with their Master. This Sunday morning they were all there assembled except Thomas. Thomas was with them for a few minutes late Saturday night when they first got together, but the sight of the apostles, coupled with the thought of what had happened to Jesus, was too much for him. He looked his associates over and immediately left the room, going to the home of Simon in Bethpage, where he thought to grieve over his troubles in solitude. The apostles all suffered, not so much from doubt and despair as from fear, grief, and shame.

At the home of Nicodemus there were gathered together, with David Zebedee and Joseph of Arimathea, some twelve or fifteen of the more prominent of the Jerusalem disciples of Jesus. At the home of Joseph of Arimathea there were some fifteen or twenty of the leading women believers. Only these women abode in Joseph's house, and they had kept close within during the hours of the Sabbath day and the evening after the Sabbath, so that they were ignorant of the military guard on watch at the tomb; neither did they know that a second stone had been rolled in front of the tomb, and that both of these stones had been placed under the seal of Pilate.

A little before three o'clock this Sunday morning, when the first signs of day began to appear in the east, five of the women started out for the tomb of Jesus. They had prepared an abundance of special embalming lotions, and they carried many linen bandages with them. It was their purpose more thoroughly to give the body of Jesus its death anointing and more carefully to wrap it up with the new bandages.

The women who went on this mission of anointing Jesus' body were: Mary Magdalene, Mary the mother of the Alpheus twins, Salome the mother of the Zebedee brothers, Joanna the wife of Chuza, and Susanna the daughter of Ezra of Alexandria.

It was about half past three o'clock when the five women, laden with their ointments, arrived before the empty tomb. As they passed out of the Damascus gate, they encountered a number of soldiers fleeing into the city more or less panic-stricken, and this caused them to pause for a few minutes; but when nothing more developed, they resumed their journey.

They were greatly surprised to see the stone rolled away from the entrance to the tomb, inasmuch as they had said among themselves on the way out, "Who will help us roll away the stone?" They set down their burdens and began to look upon one another in fear and with great amazement. While they stood there, atremble with fear, Mary Magdalene ventured around the smaller stone and dared to enter the open sepulchre. This tomb of Joseph was in his garden on the hillside on the eastern side of the road, and it also faced toward the east. By this hour there was just enough of the dawn of a new day to enable Mary to look back to the place where the Master's body had lain and to discern that it was gone. In the recess of stone where they had laid Jesus, Mary saw only the folded napkin where his head had rested and the bandages wherewith he had been wrapped lying intact and as they had rested on the stone before the celestial hosts removed the body. The covering sheet lay at the foot of the burial niche.

After Mary had tarried in the doorway of the tomb for a few moments (she did not see distinctly when she first entered the tomb), she saw that Jesus' body was gone and in its place only these grave cloths, and she uttered a cry of alarm and anguish. All the women were exceedingly nervous; they had been on edge ever since meeting the panicky soldiers at the city gate, and when Mary uttered this scream of anguish, they were terror-stricken and fled in great haste. And they did not stop until they had run all the way to the Damascus gate. By this time Joanna was conscience-stricken that they had deserted Mary; she rallied her companions, and they started back for the tomb.

As they drew near the sepulchre, the frightened Magdalene, who was even more terrorized when she failed to find her sisters waiting when she came out of the tomb, now rushed up to them, excitedly exclaiming: "He is not there — they have taken him away!" And she led them back to the tomb, and they all entered and saw that it was empty.

All five of the women then sat down on the stone near the entrance and talked over the situation. It had not yet occurred to them that Jesus had been resurrected. They had been by themselves over the Sabbath, and they conjectured that the body had been moved to another resting place. But when they pondered such a solution of their dilemma, they were at a loss to account for the orderly arrangement of the grave cloths; how could the body have been removed since the very bandages in which it was wrapped were left in position and apparently intact on the burial shelf?

As these women sat there in the early hours of the dawn of this new day, they looked to one side and observed a silent and motionless stranger. For a moment they were again frightened, but Mary Magdalene, rushing toward him and addressing him as if she thought he might be the caretaker of the garden, said, "Where have you taken the Master? Where have they laid him? Tell us that we may go and get him." When the stranger did not answer Mary, she began to weep. Then spoke Jesus to them, saying, "Whom do you seek?" Mary said: "We seek for Jesus who was laid to rest in Joseph's tomb, but he is gone. Do you know where they have taken him?" Then said Jesus: "Did not this Jesus tell you, even in Galilee, that he would die, but that he would rise again?" These words startled the women, but the Master was so changed that they did not yet recognize him with his back turned to the dim light. And as they pondered his words, he addressed the Magdalene with a familiar voice, saying, "Mary." And when she heard that word of well-known sympathy and affectionate greeting, she knew it was the voice of the Master, and she rushed to kneel at his feet while she exclaimed, "My Lord, and my Master!" And all of the other women recognized that it was the Master who stood before them in glorified form, and they quickly knelt before him.

These human eyes were enabled to see the morontia form of Jesus because of the special ministry of the transformers and the midwayers in association with certain of the morontia personalities then accompanying Jesus.

As Mary sought to embrace his feet, Jesus said: "Touch me not, Mary, for I am not as you knew me in the flesh. In this form will I tarry with you for a season before I ascend to the Father. But go, all of you, now and tell my apostles — and Peter — that I have risen, and that you have talked with me."

After these women had recovered from the shock of their amazement, they hastened back to the city and to the home of Elijah Mark, where they related to the ten apostles all that had happened to them; but the apostles were not inclined to believe them. They thought at first that the women had seen a vision, but when Mary Magdalene repeated the words which Jesus had spoken to them, and when Peter heard his name, he rushed out of the upper chamber, followed closely by John, in great haste to reach the tomb and see these things for himself.

The women repeated the story of talking with Jesus to the other apostles, but they would not believe; and they would not go to find out for themselves as had Peter and John.

5. PETER AND JOHN AT THE TOMB

As the two apostles raced for Golgotha and the tomb of Joseph, Peter's thoughts alternated between fear and hope; he feared to meet the Master, but his hope was aroused by the story that Jesus had sent special word to him. He was half persuaded that Jesus was really alive; he recalled the promise to rise on the third day. Strange to relate, this promise had not occurred to him since the crucifixion until this moment as he hurried north through Jerusalem. As John hastened out of the city, a strange ecstasy of joy and hope welled up in his soul. He was half convinced that the women really had seen the risen Master.

John, being younger than Peter, outran him and arrived first at the tomb. John tarried at the door, viewing the tomb, and it was just as Mary had described it. Very soon Simon Peter rushed up and, entering, saw the same empty tomb with the grave cloths so peculiarly arranged. And when Peter had come out, John also went in and saw it all for himself, and then they sat down on the stone to ponder the meaning of what they had seen and heard. And while they sat there, they turned over in their minds all that had been told them about Jesus, but they could not clearly perceive what had happened.

Peter at first suggested that the grave had been rifled, that enemies had stolen the body, perhaps bribed the guards. But John reasoned that the grave would hardly have been left so orderly if the body had been stolen, and he also raised the question as to how the bandages happened to be left behind, and so apparently intact. And again they both went back into the tomb more closely to examine the grave cloths. As they came out of the tomb the second time, they found Mary Magdalene returned and weeping before the entrance. Mary had gone to the apostles believing that Jesus had risen from the grave, but when they all refused to believe her report, she became downcast and despairing. She longed to go back near the tomb, where she thought she had heard the familiar voice of Jesus.

As Mary lingered after Peter and John had gone, the Master again appeared to her, saying: "Be not doubting; have the courage to believe what you have seen and heard. Go back to my apostles and again tell them that I have risen, that I will appear to them, and that presently I will go before them into Galilee as I promised."

Mary hurried back to the Mark home and told the apostles she had again talked with Jesus, but they would not believe her. But when Peter and John returned, they ceased to ridicule and became filled with fear and apprehension.

PAPER 190
MORONTIA APPEARANCES OF JESUS

The resurrected Jesus now prepares to spend a short period on Urantia for the purpose of experiencing the ascending morontia career of a mortal of the realms. Although this time of the morontia life is to be spent on the world of his mortal incarnation, it will, however, be in all respects the counterpart of the experience of Satania mortals who pass through the progressive morontia life of the seven mansion worlds of Jerusem.

All this power which is inherent in Jesus — the endowment of life — and which enabled him to rise from the dead, is the very gift of eternal life which he bestows upon kingdom believers, and which even now makes certain their resurrection from the bonds of natural death.

The mortals of the realms will arise in the morning of the resurrection with the same type of transition or morontia body that Jesus had when he arose from the tomb on this Sunday morning. These bodies do not have circulating blood, and such beings do not partake of ordinary material food; nevertheless, these morontia forms are *real.* When the various believers saw Jesus after his resurrection, they really saw him; they were not the self-deceived victims of visions or hallucinations.

Abiding faith in the resurrection of Jesus was the cardinal feature of the faith of all branches of the early gospel teaching. In Jerusalem, Alexandria,

Antioch, and Philadelphia all the gospel teachers united in this implicit faith in the Master's resurrection.

In viewing the prominent part which Mary Magdalene took in proclaiming the Master's resurrection, it should be recorded that Mary was the chief spokesman for the women's corps, as was Peter for the apostles. Mary was not chief of the women workers, but she was their chief teacher and public spokesman. Mary had become a woman of great circumspection, so that her boldness in speaking to a man whom she considered to be the caretaker of Joseph's garden only indicates how horrified she was to find the tomb empty. It was the depth and agony of her love, the fullness of her devotion, that caused her to forget, for a moment, the conventional restraints of a Jewish woman's approach to a strange man.

1. HERALDS OF THE RESURRECTION

The apostles did not want Jesus to leave them; therefore had they slighted all his statements about dying, along with his promises to rise again. They were not expecting the resurrection as it came, and they refused to believe until they were confronted with the compulsion of unimpeachable evidence and the absolute proof of their own experiences.

When the apostles refused to believe the report of the five women who represented that they had seen Jesus and talked with him, Mary Magdalene returned to the tomb, and the others went back to Joseph's house, where they related their experiences to his daughter and the other women. And the women believed their report. Shortly after six o'clock the daughter of Joseph of Arimathea and the four women who had seen Jesus went over to the home of Nicodemus, where they related all these happenings to Joseph, Nicodemus, David Zebedee, and the other men there assembled. Nicodemus and the others doubted their story, doubted that Jesus had risen from the dead; they conjectured that the Jews had removed the body. Joseph and David were disposed to believe the report, so much so that they hurried out to inspect the tomb, and they found everything just as the women had described. And they were the last to so view the sepulchre, for the high priest sent the captain of the temple guards to the tomb at half past seven o'clock to remove the grave cloths. The captain wrapped them all up in the linen sheet and threw them over a near-by cliff.

From the tomb David and Joseph went immediately to the home of Elijah Mark, where they held a conference with the ten apostles in the upper chamber. Only John Zebedee was disposed to believe, even faintly, that Jesus had risen from the dead. Peter had believed at first but, when he failed to find the Master, fell into grave doubting. They were all disposed to believe that the Jews had removed the body. David would not argue with them, but when he left, he said: "You are the apostles, and you ought to understand these things. I will not contend with you; nevertheless, I now go back to the home of Nicodemus, where I have appointed with the messengers to assemble this morning, and when they have gathered together, I will send them forth on their last mission, as heralds of the Master's resurrection. I heard the Master say that, after he should die, he would rise on the third day, and I believe him." And thus speaking to the dejected and forlorn ambassadors of the kingdom, this self-appointed chief of communication and intelligence took leave of the apostles. On his way from the upper chamber he dropped the bag of Judas, containing all the apostolic funds, in the lap of Matthew Levi.

It was about half past nine o'clock when the last of David's twenty-six messengers arrived at the home of Nicodemus. David promptly assembled them in the spacious courtyard and addressed them:

"Men and brethren, all this time you have served me in accordance with your oath to me and to one another, and I call you to witness that I have never yet sent out false information at your hands. I am about to send you on your last mission as volunteer messengers of the kingdom, and in so doing I release you from your oaths and thereby disband the messenger corps. Men, I declare to you that we have finished our work. No more does the Master have need of mortal messengers; he has risen from the dead. He told us before they arrested him that he would die and rise again on the third day. I have seen the tomb — it is empty. I have talked with Mary Magdalene and four other women, who have talked with Jesus. I now disband you, bid you farewell, and send you on your respective assignments, and the message which you shall bear to the believers is: `Jesus has risen from the dead; the tomb is empty.'"

The majority of those present endeavored to persuade David not to do this. But they could not influence him. They then sought to dissuade the messengers, but they would not heed the words of doubt. And so, shortly before ten o'clock this Sunday morning, these twenty-six runners went forth as the first heralds of the mighty truth-fact of the resurrected Jesus. And they started out on this mission as they had on so many others, in fulfillment of their oath to David Zebedee and to one another. These men had great confidence in David. They departed on this assignment without even tarrying to talk with those who had seen Jesus; they took David at his word. The majority of them believed what David had told them, and even those who somewhat doubted, carried the message just as certainly and just as swiftly.

The apostles, the spiritual corps of the kingdom, are this day assembled in the upper chamber, where they manifest fear and express doubts, while these laymen, representing the first attempt at the socialization of the Master's gospel of the brotherhood of man, under the orders of their fearless and efficient leader, go forth to proclaim the risen Savior of a world and a universe. And they engage in this eventful service ere his chosen representatives are willing to believe his word or to accept the evidence of eyewitnesses.

These twenty-six were dispatched to the home of Lazarus in Bethany and to all of the believer centers, from Beersheba in the south to Damascus and Sidon in the north; and from Philadelphia in the east to Alexandria in the west.

When David had taken leave of his brethren, he went over to the home of Joseph for his mother, and they then went out to Bethany to join the waiting family of Jesus. David abode there in Bethany with Martha and Mary until after they had disposed of their earthly possessions, and he accompanied them on their journey to join their brother, Lazarus, at Philadelphia.

In about one week from this time John Zebedee took Mary the mother of Jesus to his home in Bethsaida. James, Jesus' eldest brother, remained with his family in Jerusalem. Ruth remained at Bethany with Lazarus's sisters. The rest of Jesus' family returned to Galilee. David Zebedee left Bethany with Martha and Mary, for Philadelphia, early in June, the day after his marriage to Ruth, Jesus' youngest sister.

2. JESUS' APPEARANCE AT BETHANY

From the time of the morontia resurrection until the hour of his spirit ascension on high, Jesus made nineteen separate appearances in visible form to his believers on earth. He did not appear to his enemies nor to those who could not make spiritual use of his manifestation in visible form. His first appearance was to the five women at the tomb; his second, to Mary Magdalene, also at the tomb.

The third appearance occurred about noon of this Sunday at Bethany. Shortly after noontide, Jesus' oldest brother, James, was standing in the garden of Lazarus before the empty tomb of the resurrected brother of Martha and Mary, turning over in his mind the news brought to them about one hour previously by the messenger of David. James had always inclined to believe in his eldest brother's mission on earth, but he had long since lost contact with Jesus' work and had drifted into grave doubting regarding the later claims of the apostles that Jesus was the Messiah. The whole family was startled and well-nigh confounded by the news brought by the messenger. Even as James stood before Lazarus's empty tomb, Mary Magdalene arrived on the scene and was excitedly relating to the family her experiences of the early morning hours at the tomb of Joseph. Before she had finished, David Zebedee and his mother arrived. Ruth, of course, believed the report, and so did Jude after he had talked with David and Salome.

In the meantime, as they looked for James and before they found him, while he stood there in the garden near the tomb, he became aware of a nearby presence, as if someone had touched him on the shoulder; and when he turned to look, he beheld the gradual appearance of a strange form by his side. He was too much amazed to speak and too frightened to flee. And then the strange form spoke, saying: "James, I come to call you to the service of the kingdom. Join earnest hands with your brethren and follow after me." When James heard his name spoken, he knew that it was his eldest brother, Jesus, who had addressed him. They all had more or less difficulty in recognizing the morontia form of the Master, but few of them had any trouble recognizing his voice or otherwise identifying his charming personality when he once began to communicate with them.

When James perceived that Jesus was addressing him, he started to fall to his knees, exclaiming, "My father and my brother," but Jesus bade him stand while he spoke with him. And they walked through the garden and talked for almost three minutes; talked over experiences of former days and forecast the events of the near future. As they neared the house, Jesus said, "Farewell, James, until I greet you all together."

James rushed into the house, even while they looked for him at Bethpage, exclaiming: "I have just seen Jesus and talked with him, visited with him. He is not dead; he has risen! He vanished before me, saying, `Farewell until I greet you all together.'" He had scarcely finished speaking when Jude returned, and he retold the experience of meeting Jesus in the garden for the benefit of Jude. And they all began to believe in the resurrection of Jesus. James now announced that he would not return to Galilee, and David exclaimed: "He is seen not only by excited women; even stronghearted men have begun to see him. I expect to see him myself."

And David did not long wait, for the fourth appearance of Jesus to mortal recognition occurred shortly before two o'clock in this very home of Martha and Mary, when he appeared visibly before his earthly family and their friends, twenty in all. The Master appeared in the open back door, saying: "Peace be upon you. Greetings to those once near me in the flesh and fellowship for my brothers and sisters in the kingdom of heaven. How could you doubt? Why have you lingered so long before choosing to follow the light of truth with a whole heart? Come, therefore, all of you into the fellowship of the Spirit of Truth in the Father's kingdom." As they began to recover from the first shock of their amazement and to move toward him as if to embrace him, he vanished from their sight.

They all wanted to rush off to the city to tell the doubting apostles about what had happened, but James restrained them. Mary Magdalene, only, was permitted to return to Joseph's house. James forbade their publishing abroad the fact of this morontia visit because of certain things which Jesus had said to him as they conversed in the garden. But James never revealed more of his visit with the risen Master on this day at the Lazarus home in Bethany.

3. AT THE HOME OF JOSEPH

The fifth morontia manifestation of Jesus to the recognition of mortal eyes occurred in the presence of some twenty-five women believers assembled at the home of Joseph of Arimathea, at about fifteen minutes past four o'clock on this same Sunday afternoon. Mary Magdalene had returned to Joseph's house just a few minutes before this appearance. James, Jesus' brother, had requested that nothing be said to the apostles concerning the Master's appearance at Bethany. He had not asked Mary to refrain from reporting the occurrence to her sister believers. Accordingly, after Mary had pledged all the women to secrecy, she proceeded to relate what had so recently happened while she was with Jesus' family at Bethany. And she was in the very midst of this thrilling recital when a sudden and solemn hush fell over them; they beheld in their very midst the fully visible form of the risen Jesus. He greeted them, saying: "Peace be upon you. In the fellowship of the kingdom there shall be neither Jew nor gentile, rich nor poor, free nor bond, man nor woman. You also are called to publish the good news of the liberty of mankind through the gospel of sonship with God in the kingdom of heaven. Go to all the world proclaiming this gospel and confirming believers in the faith thereof. And while you do this, forget not to minister to the sick and strengthen those who are fainthearted and fear-ridden. And I will be with you always, even to the ends of the earth." And when he had thus spoken, he vanished from their sight, while the women fell on their faces and worshiped in silence.

Of the five morontia appearances of Jesus occurring up to this time, Mary Magdalene had witnessed four.

As a result of sending out the messengers during the midforenoon and from the unconscious leakage of intimations concerning this appearance of Jesus at Joseph's house, word began to come to the rulers of the Jews during the early evening that it was being reported about the city that Jesus had risen, and that many persons were claiming to have seen him. The Sanhedrists were thoroughly aroused by these rumors. After a hasty consultation with Annas, Caiaphas called a meeting of the Sanhedrin to convene at eight o'clock that evening. It was at this meeting that action was taken to throw out of the synagogues any person who made mention of Jesus' resurrection. It was even suggested that any one claiming to have seen him should be put to death; this proposal, however, did not come to a vote since the meeting broke up in confusion bordering on actual panic. They had dared to think they were through with Jesus. They were about to discover that their real trouble with the man of Nazareth had just begun.

4. APPEARANCE TO THE GREEKS

About half past four o'clock, at the home of one Flavius, the Master made his sixth morontia appearance to some forty Greek believers there assembled. While they were engaged in discussing the reports of the Master's resurrection, he manifested himself in their midst, notwithstanding that the doors were securely fastened, and speaking to them, said: "Peace be upon you. While the Son of Man appeared on earth among the Jews, he came to minister to all men. In the kingdom of my Father there shall be neither Jew nor gentile; you will all be brethren — the sons of God. Go you, therefore, to all the world, proclaiming this gospel of salvation as you have received it from the ambassadors of the kingdom, and I will fellowship you in the brotherhood of the Father's sons of faith and truth." And when he had thus charged them, he took leave, and they saw him no more. They remained within the house all evening; they were too much overcome with awe and fear to venture forth. Neither did any of these Greeks sleep that night; they stayed awake discussing these things and hoping that the Master might again visit them. Among this group were many of the Greeks who were at Gethsemane when the soldiers arrested Jesus and Judas betrayed him with a kiss.

Rumors of Jesus' resurrection and reports concerning the many appearances to his followers are spreading rapidly, and the whole city is being wrought up to a high pitch of excitement. Already the Master has appeared to his family, to the women, and to the Greeks, and presently he manifests himself in the midst of the apostles. The Sanhedrin is soon to begin the consideration of these new problems which have been so suddenly thrust upon the Jewish rulers. Jesus thinks much about his apostles but desires that they be left alone for a few more hours of solemn reflection and thoughtful consideration before he visits them.

5. THE WALK WITH TWO BROTHERS

At Emmaus, about seven miles west of Jerusalem, there lived two brothers, shepherds, who had spent the Passover week in Jerusalem attending upon the sacrifices, ceremonials, and feasts. Cleopas, the elder, was a partial believer in Jesus; at least he had been cast out of the synagogue. His brother, Jacob, was not a believer, although he was much intrigued by what he had heard about the Master's teachings and works.

On this Sunday afternoon, about three miles out of Jerusalem and a few minutes before five o'clock, as these two brothers trudged along the road to Emmaus, they talked in great earnestness about Jesus, his teachings, work, and more especially concerning the rumors that his tomb was empty, and that certain of the women had talked with him. Cleopas was half a mind to believe these reports, but Jacob was insistent that the whole affair was probably a fraud. While they thus argued and debated as they made their way toward home, the morontia manifestation of Jesus, his seventh appearance, came alongside them as they journeyed on. Cleopas had often heard Jesus teach and had eaten with him at the homes of Jerusalem believers on several occasions. But he did not recognize the Master even when he spoke freely with them.

After walking a short way with them, Jesus said: "What were the words you exchanged so earnestly as I came upon you?" And when Jesus had spoken, they stood still and viewed him with sad surprise. Said Cleopas: "Can it be that you sojourn in Jerusalem and know not the things which have recently happened?" Then asked the Master, "What things?" Cleopas replied: "If you do not know about these matters, you are the only one in Jerusalem who has not heard these rumors concerning Jesus of Nazareth, who was a prophet mighty in word and in deed before God and all the people. The chief priests and our rulers delivered him up to the Romans and demanded that they crucify him. Now many of us had hoped that it was he who would deliver Israel from the yoke of the gentiles. But that is not all. It is now the third day since he was crucified, and certain women have this day amazed us by declaring that very early this morning they went to his tomb and found it empty. And these same women insist that they talked with this man; they maintain that he has risen from the dead. And when the women reported this to the men, two of his apostles ran to the tomb and likewise found it empty" — and here Jacob interrupted his brother to say, "but they did not see Jesus."

As they walked along, Jesus said to them: "How slow you are to comprehend the truth! When you tell me that it is about the teachings and work of this man that you have your discussions, then may I enlighten you since I am more than familiar with these teachings. Do you not remember that this Jesus always taught that his kingdom was not of this world, and that all men, being the sons of God, should find liberty and freedom in the spiritual joy of the fellowship of the brotherhood of loving service in this new kingdom of the truth of the heavenly Father's love? Do you not recall how this Son of Man proclaimed the salvation of God for all men, ministering to the sick and afflicted and setting free those who were bound by fear and enslaved by evil? Do you not know that this man of Nazareth told his disciples that he must go to Jerusalem, be delivered up to his enemies, who would put him to death, and that he would arise on the third day? Have you not been told all this? And have you never read in the Scriptures concerning this day of salvation for Jew and gentile, where it says that in him shall all the families of the earth be blessed; that he will hear the cry of the needy and save the souls of the poor who seek him; that all nations shall call him blessed? That such a Deliverer shall be as the shadow of a great rock in a weary land. That he will feed the flock like a true shepherd, gathering the lambs in his arms and tenderly carrying them in his bosom. That he will open the eyes of the spiritually blind and bring the prisoners of despair out into full liberty and light; that all who sit in darkness shall see the great light of eternal salvation. That he will bind up the brokenhearted, proclaim liberty to the captives of sin, and open up the prison to those who are enslaved by fear and bound by evil. That he will comfort those who mourn and bestow upon them the joy of salvation in the place of sorrow and heaviness. That he shall be the desire of all nations and the everlasting joy of those who seek righteousness. That this Son of truth and righteousness shall rise upon the world with healing light and saving power; even that he will save his people from their sins; that he will really seek and save those who are lost. That he will not destroy the weak but minister salvation to all who hunger and thirst for righteousness.

That those who believe in him shall have eternal life. That he will pour out his spirit upon all flesh, and that this Spirit of Truth shall be in each believer a well of water, springing up into everlasting life. Did you not understand how great was the gospel of the kingdom which this man delivered to you? Do you not perceive how great a salvation has come upon you?"

By this time they had come near to the village where these brothers dwelt. Not a word had these two men spoken since Jesus began to teach them as they walked along the way. Soon they drew up in front of their humble dwelling place, and Jesus was about to take leave of them, going on down the road, but they constrained him to come in and abide with them. They insisted that it was near nightfall, and that he tarry with them. Finally Jesus consented, and very soon after they went into the house, they sat down to eat. They gave him the bread to bless, and as he began to break and hand to them, their eyes were opened, and Cleopas recognized that their guest was the Master himself. And when he said, "It is the Master — ," the morontia Jesus vanished from their sight.

And then they said, the one to the other, "No wonder our hearts burned within us as he spoke to us while we walked along the road! and while he opened up to our understanding the teachings of the Scriptures!"

They would not stop to eat. They had seen the morontia Master, and they rushed from the house, hastening back to Jerusalem to spread the good news of the risen Savior.

About nine o'clock that evening and just before the Master appeared to the ten, these two excited brothers broke in upon the apostles in the upper chamber, declaring that they had seen Jesus and talked with him. And they told all that Jesus had said to them and how they had not discerned who he was until the time of the breaking of the bread.

PAPER 191
APPEARANCES TO THE APOSTLES AND OTHER LEADERS

RESURRECTION SUNDAY WAS a terrible day in the lives of the apostles; ten of them spent the larger part of the day in the upper chamber behind barred doors. They might have fled from Jerusalem, but they were afraid of being arrested by the agents of the Sanhedrin if they were found abroad. Thomas was brooding over his troubles alone at Bethpage. He would have fared better had he remained with his fellow apostles, and he would have aided them to direct their discussions along more helpful lines.

All day long John upheld the idea that Jesus had risen from the dead. He recounted no less than five different times when the Master had affirmed he would rise again and at least three times when he alluded to the third day. John's attitude had considerable influence on them, especially on his brother James and on Nathaniel. John would have influenced them more if he had not been the youngest member of the group.

Their isolation had much to do with their troubles. John Mark kept them in touch with developments about the temple and informed them as to the many rumors gaining headway in the city, but it did not occur to him to gather up news from the different groups of believers to whom Jesus had already appeared. That was the kind of service which had heretofore been rendered by the messengers of David, but they were all absent on their last assignment as heralds of the resurrection to those groups of believers who dwelt remote from Jerusalem. For the first time in all these years the apostles realized how much they had been dependent on David's messengers for their daily information regarding the affairs of the kingdom.

All this day Peter characteristically vacillated emotionally between faith and doubt concerning the Master's resurrection. Peter could not get away from the sight of the grave cloths resting there in the tomb as if the body of Jesus had just evaporated from within. "But," reasoned Peter, "if he has risen and can show himself to the women, why does he not show himself to us, his apostles?" Peter would grow sorrowful when he thought that maybe Jesus did not come to them on account of his presence among the apostles, because he had denied him that night in Annas's courtyard. And then would he cheer himself with the word brought by the women, "Go tell my apostles — and Peter." But to derive encouragement from this message implied that he must believe that the women had really seen and heard the risen Master. Thus Peter alternated between faith and doubt throughout the whole day, until a little after eight o'clock, when he ventured out into the courtyard. Peter thought to remove himself from among the apostles so that he might not prevent Jesus' coming to them because of his denial of the Master.

James Zebedee at first advocated that they all go to the tomb; he was strongly in favor of doing something to get to the bottom of the mystery. It was Nathaniel who prevented them from going out in public in response to James's urging, and he did this by reminding them of Jesus' warning against unduly jeopardizing their lives at this time. By noontime James had settled down with the others to watchful waiting. He said little; he was tremendously disappointed because Jesus did not appear to them, and he did not know of the Master's many appearances to other groups and individuals.

Andrew did much listening this day. He was exceedingly perplexed by the situation and had more than his share of doubts, but he at least enjoyed a certain sense of freedom from responsibility for the guidance of his fellow apostles. He was indeed grateful that the Master had released him from the burdens of leadership before they fell upon these distracting times.

More than once during the long and weary hours of this tragic day, the only sustaining influence of the group was the frequent contribution of Nathaniel's characteristic philosophic counsel. He was really the controlling influence among the ten throughout the entire day. Never once did he express himself concerning either belief or disbelief in the Master's resurrection. But as the day wore on, he became increasingly inclined toward believing that Jesus had fulfilled his promise to rise again.

Simon Zelotes was too much crushed to participate in the discussions. Most of the time he reclined on a couch in a corner of the room with his face to the wall; he did not speak half a dozen times throughout the whole day. His concept of the kingdom had crashed, and he could not discern that the Master's resurrection could materially change the situation. His disappointment was very personal and altogether too keen to be recovered from on short notice, even in the face of such a stupendous fact as the resurrection.

Strange to record, the usually inexpressive Philip did much talking throughout the afternoon of this day. During the forenoon he had little to say, but all afternoon he asked questions of the other apostles. Peter was often annoyed by Philip's questions, but the others took his inquiries good-naturedly. Philip was particularly desirous of knowing, provided Jesus had really risen from the grave, whether his body would bear the physical marks of the crucifixion.

Matthew was highly confused; he listened to the discussions of his fellows but spent most of the time turning over in his mind the problem of their future finances. Regardless of Jesus' supposed resurrection, Judas was gone, David had unceremoniously turned the funds over to him, and they were without an authoritative leader. Before Matthew got around to giving serious consideration to their arguments about the resurrection, he had already seen the Master face to face.

The Alpheus twins took little part in these serious discussions; they were fairly busy with their customary ministrations. One of them expressed the attitude of both when he said, in reply to a question asked by Philip: "We do not understand about the resurrection, but our mother says she talked with the Master, and we believe her."

Thomas was in the midst of one of his typical spells of despairing depression. He slept a portion of the day and walked over the hills the rest of the time. He felt the urge to rejoin his fellow apostles, but the desire to be by himself was the stronger.

The Master put off the first morontia appearance to the apostles for a number of reasons. First, he wanted them to have time, after they heard of his resurrection, to think well over what he had told them about his death and resurrection when he was still with them in the flesh. The Master wanted

Peter to wrestle through with some of his peculiar difficulties before he manifested himself to them all. In the second place, he desired that Thomas should be with them at the time of his first appearance. John Mark located Thomas at the home of Simon in Bethpage early this Sunday morning, bringing word to that effect to the apostles about eleven o'clock. Any time during this day Thomas would have gone back to them if Nathaniel or any two of the other apostles had gone for him. He really wanted to return, but having left as he did the evening before, he was too proud to go back of his own accord so soon. By the next day he was so depressed that it required almost a week for him to make up his mind to return. The apostles waited for him, and he waited for his brethren to seek him out and ask him to come back to them. Thomas thus remained away from his associates until the next Saturday evening, when, after darkness had come on, Peter and John went over to Bethpage and brought him back with them. And this is also the reason why they did not go at once to Galilee after Jesus first appeared to them; they would not go without Thomas.

1. THE APPEARANCE TO PETER

It was near half past eight o'clock this Sunday evening when Jesus appeared to Simon Peter in the garden of the Mark home. This was his eighth morontia manifestation. Peter had lived under a heavy burden of doubt and guilt ever since his denial of the Master. All day Saturday and this Sunday he had fought the fear that, perhaps, he was no longer an apostle. He had shuddered at the fate of Judas and even thought that he, too, had betrayed his Master. All this afternoon he thought that it might be his presence with the apostles that prevented Jesus' appearing to them, provided, of course, he had really risen from the dead. And it was to Peter, in such a frame of mind and in such a state of soul, that Jesus appeared as the dejected apostle strolled among the flowers and shrubs.

When Peter thought of the loving look of the Master as he passed by on Annas's porch, and as he turned over in his mind that wonderful message brought him early that morning by the women who came from the empty tomb, "Go tell my apostles — and Peter" — as he contemplated these tokens of mercy, his faith began to surmount his doubts, and he stood still, clenching his fists, while he spoke aloud: "I believe he has risen from the dead; I will go and tell my brethren." And as he said this, there suddenly appeared in front of him the form of a man, who spoke to him in familiar tones, saying: "Peter, the enemy desired to have you, but I would not give you up. I knew it was not from the heart that you disowned me; therefore I forgave you even before you asked; but now must you cease to think about yourself and the troubles of the hour while you prepare to carry the good news of the gospel to those who sit in darkness. No longer should you be concerned with what you may obtain from the kingdom but rather be exercised about what you can give to those who live in dire spiritual poverty. Gird yourself, Simon, for the battle of a new day, the struggle with spiritual darkness and the evil doubtings of the natural minds of men."

Peter and the morontia Jesus walked through the garden and talked of things past, present, and future for almost five minutes. Then the Master vanished from his gaze, saying, "Farewell, Peter, until I see you with your brethren."

For a moment, Peter was overcome by the realization that he had talked with the risen Master, and that he could be sure he was still an ambassador of the kingdom. He had just heard the glorified Master exhort him to go on preaching the gospel. And with all this welling up within his heart, he rushed to the upper chamber and into the presence of his fellow apostles, exclaiming in breathless excitement: "I have seen the Master; he was in the garden. I talked with him, and he has forgiven me."

Peter's declaration that he had seen Jesus in the garden made a profound impression upon his fellow apostles, and they were about ready to surrender their doubts when Andrew got up and warned them not to be too much influenced by his brother's report. Andrew intimated that Peter had seen things which were not real before. Although Andrew did not directly allude to the vision of the night on the Sea of Galilee wherein Peter claimed to have seen the Master coming to them walking on the water, he said enough to betray to all present that he had this incident in mind. Simon Peter was very much hurt by his brother's insinuations and immediately lapsed into crestfallen silence. The twins felt very sorry for Peter, and they both went over to express their sympathy and to say that they believed him and to reassert that their own mother had also seen the Master.

2. FIRST APPEARANCE TO THE APOSTLES

Shortly after nine o'clock that evening, after the departure of Cleopas and Jacob, while the Alpheus twins comforted Peter, and while Nathaniel remonstrated with Andrew, and as the ten apostles were there assembled in the upper chamber with all the doors bolted for fear of arrest, the Master, in morontia form, suddenly appeared in the midst of them, saying: "Peace be upon you. Why are you so frightened when I appear, as though you had seen a spirit? Did I not tell you about these things when I was present with you in the flesh? Did I not say to you that the chief priests and the rulers would deliver me up to be killed, that one of your own number would betray me, and that on the third day I would rise? Wherefore all your doubtings and all this discussion about the reports of the women, Cleopas and Jacob, and even Peter? How long will you doubt my words and refuse to believe my promises? And now that you actually see me, will you believe? Even now one of you is absent. When you are gathered together once more, and after all of you know of a certainty that the Son of Man has risen from the grave, go hence into Galilee. Have faith in God; have faith in one another; and so shall you enter into the new service of the kingdom of heaven. I will tarry in Jerusalem with you until you are ready to go into Galilee. My peace I leave with you."

When the morontia Jesus had spoken to them, he vanished in an instant from their sight. And they all fell on their faces, praising God and venerating their vanished Master. This was the Master's ninth morontia appearance.

3. WITH THE MORONTIA CREATURES

The next day, Monday, was spent wholly with the morontia creatures then present on Urantia. As participants in the Master's morontia-transition experience, there had come to Urantia more than one million morontia directors and associates, together with transition mortals of various orders from the seven mansion worlds of Satania. The morontia Jesus sojourned with these splendid intelligences for forty days. He instructed them and learned from their directors the life of morontia transition as it is traversed by the mortals of the inhabited worlds of Satania as they pass through the system morontia spheres.

About midnight of this Monday the Master's morontia form was adjusted for transition to the second stage of morontia progression. When he next appeared to his mortal children on earth, it was as a second-stage morontia being. As the Master progressed in the morontia career, it became, technically, more and more difficult for the morontia intelligences and their transforming associates to visualize the Master to mortal and material eyes.

Jesus made the transit to the third stage of morontia on Friday, April 14; to the fourth stage on Monday, the 17th; to the fifth stage on Saturday, the 22nd; to the sixth stage on Thursday, the 27th; to the seventh stage on Tuesday, May 2; to Jerusem citizenship on Sunday, the 7th; and he entered the embrace of the Most Highs of Edentia on Sunday, the 14th.

In this manner did Michael of Nebadon complete his service of universe experience since he had already, in connection with his previous bestowals, experienced to the full the life of the ascendant mortals of time and space from the sojourn on the headquarters of the constellation even on to, and through, the service of the headquarters of the superuniverse. And it was by these very morontia experiences that the Creator Son of Nebadon really finished and acceptably terminated his seventh and final universe bestowal.

4. THE TENTH APPEARANCE (AT PHILADELPHIA)

The tenth morontia manifestation of Jesus to mortal recognition occurred a short time after eight o'clock on Tuesday, April 11, at Philadelphia, where he showed himself to Abner and Lazarus and some one hundred and fifty of their associates, including more than fifty of the evangelistic corps of the seventy. This appearance occurred just after the opening of a special meeting in the synagogue which had been called by Abner to discuss the crucifixion of Jesus and the more recent report of the resurrection which had been brought by David's messenger. Inasmuch as the resurrected Lazarus was now a member of this group of believers, it was not difficult for them to believe the report that Jesus had risen from the dead.

The meeting in the synagogue was just being opened by Abner and Lazarus, who were standing together in the pulpit, when the entire audience of believers saw the form of the Master appear suddenly. He stepped forward from where he had appeared between Abner and Lazarus, neither of whom had observed him, and saluting the company, said:

"Peace be upon you. You all know that we have one Father in heaven, and that there is but one gospel of the kingdom — the good news of the gift of eternal life which men receive by faith. As you rejoice in your loyalty to the gospel, pray the Father of truth to shed abroad in your hearts a new and greater love for your brethren. You are to love all men as I have loved you; you are to serve all men as I have served you. With understanding sympathy and brotherly affection, fellowship all your brethren who are dedicated to the proclamation of the good news, whether they be Jew or gentile, Greek or Roman, Persian or Ethiopian. John proclaimed the kingdom in advance; you have preached the gospel in power; the Greeks already teach the good news; and I am soon to send forth the Spirit of Truth into the souls of all these, my brethren, who have so unselfishly dedicated their lives to the enlightenment of their fellows who sit in spiritual darkness. You are all the children of light; therefore stumble not into the misunderstanding entanglements of mortal suspicion and human intolerance. If you are ennobled, by the grace of faith, to love unbelievers, should you not also equally love those who are your fellow believers in the far-spreading household of faith? Remember, as you love one another, all men will know that you are my disciples.

"Go, then, into all the world proclaiming this gospel of the fatherhood of God and the brotherhood of men to all nations and races and ever be wise in your choice of methods for presenting the good news to the different races and tribes of mankind. Freely you have received this gospel of the kingdom, and you will freely give the good news to all nations. Fear not the resistance of evil, for I am with you always, even to the end of the ages. And my peace I leave with you."

When he had said, "My peace I leave with you," he vanished from their sight. With the exception of one of his appearances in Galilee, where upward of five hundred believers saw him at one time, this group in Philadelphia embraced the largest number of mortals who saw him on any single occasion.

Early the next morning, even while the apostles tarried in Jerusalem awaiting the emotional recovery of Thomas, these believers at Philadelphia went forth proclaiming that Jesus of Nazareth had risen from the dead.

The next day, Wednesday, Jesus spent without interruption in the society of his morontia associates, and during the midafternoon hours he received visiting morontia delegates from the mansion worlds of every local system of inhabited spheres throughout the constellation of Norlatiadek. And they all rejoiced to know their Creator as one of their own order of universe intelligence.

5. SECOND APPEARANCE TO THE APOSTLES

Thomas spent a lonesome week alone with himself in the hills around about Olivet. During this time he saw only those at Simon's house and John Mark. It was about nine o'clock on Saturday, April 15, when the two apostles found him and took him back with them to their rendezvous at the Mark home. The next day Thomas listened to the telling of the stories of the Master's various appearances, but he steadfastly refused to believe. He maintained that Peter had enthused them into thinking they had seen the Master. Nathaniel reasoned with him, but it did no good. There was an emotional stubbornness associated with his customary doubtfulness, and this state of mind, coupled with his chagrin at having run away from them, conspired to create a situation of isolation which even Thomas himself did not fully understand. He had withdrawn from his fellows, he had gone his own way, and now, even when he was back among them, he unconsciously tended to assume an attitude of disagreement. He was slow to surrender; he disliked to give in. Without intending it, he really enjoyed the attention paid him; he derived unconscious satisfaction from the efforts of all his fellows to convince and convert him. He had missed them for a full week, and he obtained considerable pleasure from their persistent attentions.

They were having their evening meal a little after six o'clock, with Peter sitting on one side of Thomas and Nathaniel on the other, when the doubting apostle said: "I will not believe unless I see the Master with my own eyes and put my finger in the mark of the nails." As they thus sat at supper, and while the doors were securely shut and barred, the morontia Master suddenly appeared inside the curvature of the table and, standing directly in front of Thomas, said:

"Peace be upon you. For a full week have I tarried that I might appear again when you were all present to hear once more the commission to go into all the world and preach this gospel of the kingdom. Again I tell you: As the Father sent me into the world, so send I you. As I have revealed the Father, so shall you reveal the divine love, not merely with words, but in your daily living. I send you forth, not to love the souls of men, but rather to *love men*. You are not merely to proclaim the joys of heaven but also to exhibit in your daily experience these spirit realities of the divine life since you already have eternal life, as the gift of God, through faith. When you have faith, when power from on high, the Spirit of Truth, has come upon you, you will not hide your light here behind closed doors; you will make known the love and the mercy of God to all mankind. Through fear you now flee from the facts of a disagreeable experience, but when you shall have been baptized with the Spirit of Truth, you will bravely and joyously go forth to meet the new experiences of proclaiming the good news of eternal life in the kingdom of God. You may tarry here and in Galilee for a short season while you recover from the shock of the transition from the false security of the authority of traditionalism to the new order of the authority of facts, truth, and faith in the supreme realities of living experience. Your mission to the world is founded on the fact that I lived a God-revealing life among you; on the truth that you and all other men are the sons of God; and it shall consist in the life which you will live among men — the actual and living experience of loving men and serving them, even as I have loved and served you. Let faith reveal your light to the world; let the revelation of truth open the eyes blinded by tradition; let your loving service effectually destroy the prejudice engendered by ignorance. By so drawing close to your fellow men in understanding sympathy and with unselfish devotion, you will lead them into a saving knowledge of the Father's love. The Jews have extolled goodness; the Greeks have exalted beauty; the Hindus preach devotion; the far-away ascetics teach reverence; the Romans demand loyalty; but I require of my disciples life, even a life of loving service for your brothers in the flesh."

When the Master had so spoken, he looked down into the face of Thomas and said: "And you, Thomas, who said you would not believe unless you could see me and put your finger in the nail marks of my hands, have now beheld me and heard my words; and though you see no nail marks on my hands, since I am raised in the form that you also shall have when you depart from this world, what will you say to your brethren? You will acknowledge the truth, for already in your heart you had begun to believe even when you so stoutly asserted your unbelief. Your doubts, Thomas, always most stubbornly assert themselves just as they are about to crumble. Thomas, I bid you be not faithless but believing — and I know you will believe, even with a whole heart."

When Thomas heard these words, he fell on his knees before the morontia Master and exclaimed, "I believe! My Lord and my Master!" Then said Jesus to Thomas: "You have believed, Thomas, because you have really seen and heard me. Blessed are those in the ages to come who will believe even though they have not seen with the eye of flesh nor heard with the mortal ear."

And then, as the Master's form moved over near the head of the table, he addressed them all, saying: "And now go all of you to Galilee, where I will presently appear to you." After he said this, he vanished from their sight.

The eleven apostles were now fully convinced that Jesus had risen from the dead, and very early the next morning, before the break of day, they started out for Galilee.

6. THE ALEXANDRIAN APPEARANCE

While the eleven apostles were on the way to Galilee, drawing near their journey's end, on Tuesday evening, April 18, at about half past eight o'clock, Jesus appeared to Rodan and some eighty other believers, in Alexandria. This was the Master's twelfth appearance in morontia form. Jesus appeared before these Greeks and Jews at the conclusion of the report of David's messenger regarding the crucifixion. This messenger, being the fifth in the Jerusalem-Alexandria relay of runners, had arrived in Alexandria late that afternoon, and when he had delivered his message to Rodan, it was decided to call the believers together to receive this tragic word from the messenger himself. At about eight o'clock, the messenger, Nathan of Busiris, came before this group and told them in detail all that had been told him by the preceding runner. Nathan ended his touching recital with these words: "But David, who sends us this word, reports that the Master, in foretelling his death, declared that he would rise again." Even as Nathan spoke, the morontia Master appeared there in full view of all. And when Nathan sat down, Jesus said:

"Peace be upon you. That which my Father sent me into the world to establish belongs not to a race, a nation, nor to a special group of teachers or preachers. This gospel of the kingdom belongs to both Jew and gentile, to rich and poor, to free and bond, to male and female, even to the little children. And you are all to proclaim this gospel of love and truth by the lives which you live in the flesh. You shall love one another with a new and startling affection, even as I have loved you. You will serve mankind with a new and amazing devotion, even as I have served you. And when men see you so love them, and when they behold how fervently you serve them, they will perceive that you have become faith-fellows of the kingdom of heaven, and they will follow after the Spirit of Truth which they see in your lives, to the finding of eternal salvation.

"As the Father sent me into this world, even so now send I you. You are all called to carry the good news to those who sit in darkness. This gospel of the kingdom belongs to all who believe it; it shall not be committed to the custody of mere priests. Soon will the Spirit of Truth come upon you, and he shall lead you into all truth. Go you, therefore, into all the world preaching this gospel, and lo, I am with you always, even to the end of the ages."

When the Master had so spoken, he vanished from their sight. All that night these believers remained there together recounting their experiences as kingdom believers and listening to the many words of Rodan and his associates. And they all believed that Jesus had risen from the dead. Imagine the surprise of David's herald of the resurrection, who arrived the second day after this, when they replied to his announcement, saying: "Yes, we know, for we have seen him. He appeared to us day before yesterday."

PAPER 192
APPEARANCES IN GALILEE

BY THE TIME the apostles left Jerusalem for Galilee, the Jewish leaders had quieted down considerably. Since Jesus appeared only to his family of kingdom believers, and since the apostles were in hiding and did no public preaching, the rulers of the Jews concluded that the gospel movement was, after all, effectually crushed. They were, of course, disconcerted by the increasing spread of rumors that Jesus had risen from the dead, but they depended upon the bribed guards effectively to counteract all such reports by their reiteration of the story that a band of his followers had removed the body.

From this time on, until the apostles were dispersed by the rising tide of persecution, Peter was the generally recognized head of the apostolic corps. Jesus never gave him any such authority, and his fellow apostles never formally elected him to such a position of responsibility; he naturally assumed it and held it by common consent and also because he was their chief preacher. From now on public preaching became the main business of the apostles. After their return from Galilee, Matthias, whom they chose to take the place of Judas, became their treasurer.

During the week they tarried in Jerusalem, Mary the mother of Jesus spent much of the time with the women believers who were stopping at the home of Joseph of Arimathea.

Early this Monday morning when the apostles departed for Galilee, John Mark went along. He followed them out of the city, and when they had passed well beyond Bethany, he boldly came up among them, feeling confident they would not send him back.

The apostles paused several times on the way to Galilee to tell the story of their risen Master and therefore did not arrive at Bethsaida until very late on Wednesday night. It was noontime on Thursday before they were all awake and ready to partake of breakfast.

1. APPEARANCE BY THE LAKE

About six o'clock Friday morning, April 21, the morontia Master made his thirteenth appearance, the first in Galilee, to the ten apostles as their boat drew near the shore close to the usual landing place at Bethsaida.

After the apostles had spent the afternoon and early evening of Thursday in waiting at the Zebedee home, Simon Peter suggested that they go fishing. When Peter proposed the fishing trip, all of the apostles decided to go along. All night they toiled with the nets but caught no fish. They did not much mind the failure to make a catch, for they had many interesting experiences to talk over, things which had so recently happened to them at Jerusalem. But when daylight came, they decided to return to Bethsaida. As they neared the shore, they saw someone on the beach, near the boat landing, standing by a fire. At first they thought it was John Mark, who had come down to welcome them back with their catch, but as they drew nearer the shore, they saw they were mistaken — the man was too tall for John. It had occurred to none of them that the person on the shore was the Master. They did not altogether understand why Jesus wanted to meet with them amidst the scenes of their earlier associations and out in the open in contact with nature, far away from the shut-in environment of Jerusalem with its tragic associations of fear, betrayal, and death. He had told them that, if they would go into Galilee, he would meet them there, and he was about to fulfill that promise.

As they dropped anchor and prepared to enter the small boat for going ashore, the man on the beach called to them, "Lads, have you caught anything?" And when they answered, "No," he spoke again. "Cast the net on the right side of the boat, and you will find fish." While they did not know it was Jesus who had directed them, with one accord they cast in the net as they had been instructed, and immediately it was filled, so much so that they were hardly able to draw it up. Now, John Zebedee was quick of perception, and when he saw the heavy-laden net, he perceived that it was the Master who had spoken to them. When this thought came into his mind, he leaned over and whispered to Peter, "It is the Master." Peter was ever a man of thoughtless action and impetuous devotion; so when John whispered this in his ear, he quickly arose and cast himself into the water that he might the sooner reach the Master's side. His brethren came up close behind him, having come ashore in the small boat, hauling the net of fishes after them.

By this time John Mark was up and, seeing the apostles coming ashore with the heavy-laden net, ran down the beach to greet them; and when he saw eleven men instead of ten, he surmised that the unrecognized one was the risen Jesus, and as the astonished ten stood by in silence, the youth rushed up to the Master and, kneeling at his feet, said, "My Lord and my Master." And then Jesus spoke, not as he had in Jerusalem, when he greeted them with "Peace be upon you," but in commonplace tones he addressed John Mark: "Well, John, I am glad to see you again and in carefree Galilee, where we can have a good visit. Stay with us, John, and have breakfast."

As Jesus talked with the young man, the ten were so astonished and surprised that they neglected to haul the net of fish in upon the beach. Now spoke Jesus: "Bring in your fish and prepare some for breakfast. Already we have the fire and much bread."

While John Mark had paid homage to the Master, Peter had for a moment been shocked at the sight of the coals of fire glowing there on the beach; the scene reminded him so vividly of the midnight fire of charcoal in the courtyard of Annas, where he had disowned the Master, but he shook himself and, kneeling at the Master's feet, exclaimed, "My Lord and my Master!"

Peter then joined his comrades as they hauled in the net. When they had landed their catch, they counted the fish, and there were 153 large ones. And again was the mistake made of calling this another miraculous catch of fish. There was no miracle connected with this episode. It was merely an exercise of the Master's preknowledge. He knew the fish were there and accordingly directed the apostles where to cast the net.

Jesus spoke to them, saying: "Come now, all of you, to breakfast. Even the twins should sit down while I visit with you; John Mark will dress the fish." John Mark brought seven good-sized fish, which the Master put on the fire, and when they were cooked, the lad served them to the ten. Then Jesus broke the bread and handed it to John, who in turn served it to the hungry apostles. When they had all been served, Jesus bade John Mark sit down while he himself served the fish and the bread to the lad. And as they ate, Jesus visited with them and recounted their many experiences in Galilee and by this very lake.

This was the third time Jesus had manifested himself to the apostles as a group. When Jesus first addressed them, asking if they had any fish, they did not suspect who he was because it was a common experience for these fishermen on the Sea of Galilee, when they came ashore, to be thus accosted by the fish merchants of Tarichea, who were usually on hand to buy the fresh catches for the drying establishments.

Jesus visited with the ten apostles and John Mark for more than an hour, and then he walked up and down the beach, talking with them two and two — but not the same couples he had at first sent out together to teach. All eleven of the apostles had come down from Jerusalem together, but Simon Zelotes grew more and more despondent as they drew near Galilee, so that, when they reached Bethsaida, he forsook his brethren and returned to his home.

Before taking leave of them this morning, Jesus directed that two of the apostles should volunteer to go to Simon Zelotes and bring him back that very day. And Peter and Andrew did so.

2. VISITING WITH THE APOSTLES TWO AND TWO

When they had finished breakfast, and while the others sat by the fire, Jesus beckoned to Peter and to John that they should come with him for a stroll on the beach. As they walked along, Jesus said to John, "John, do you love me?" And when John answered, "Yes, Master, with all my heart," the Master said: "Then, John, give up your intolerance and learn to love men as I have loved you. Devote your life to proving that love is the greatest thing in the world. It is the love of God that impels men to seek salvation. Love is the ancestor of all spiritual goodness, the essence of the true and the beautiful."

Jesus then turned toward Peter and asked, "Peter, do you love me?" Peter answered, "Lord, you know I love you with all my soul." Then said Jesus: "If you love me, Peter, feed my lambs. Do not neglect to minister to the weak, the poor, and the young. Preach the gospel without fear or favor; remember always that God is no respecter of persons. Serve your fellow men even as I have served you; forgive your fellow mortals even as I have forgiven you. Let experience teach you the value of meditation and the power of intelligent reflection."

After they had walked along a little farther, the Master turned to Peter and asked, "Peter, do you really love me?" And then said Simon, "Yes, Lord, you know that I love you." And again said Jesus: "Then take good care of my sheep. Be a good and a true shepherd to the flock. Betray not their confidence in you. Be not taken by surprise at the enemy's hand. Be on guard at all times — watch and pray."

When they had gone a few steps farther, Jesus turned to Peter and, for the third time, asked, "Peter, do you truly love me?" And then Peter, being slightly grieved at the Master's seeming distrust of him, said with considerable feeling, "Lord, you know all things, and therefore do you know that I really and truly love you." Then said Jesus: "Feed my sheep. Do not forsake the flock. Be an example and an inspiration to all your fellow shepherds. Love the flock as I have loved you and devote yourself to their welfare even as I have devoted my life to your welfare. And follow after me even to the end."

Peter took this last statement literally — that he should continue to follow after him — and turning to Jesus, he pointed to John, asking, "If I follow on after you, what shall this man do?" And then, perceiving that Peter had misunderstood his words, Jesus said: "Peter, be not concerned about what your brethren shall do. If I will that John should tarry after you are gone, even until I come back, what is that to you? Only make sure that you follow me."

This remark spread among the brethren and was received as a statement by Jesus to the effect that John would not die before the Master returned, as many thought and hoped, to establish the kingdom in power and glory. It was this interpretation of what Jesus said that had much to do with getting Simon Zelotes back into service, and keeping him at work.

When they returned to the others, Jesus went for a walk and talk with Andrew and James. When they had gone a short distance, Jesus said to Andrew, "Andrew, do you trust me?" And when the former chief of the apostles heard Jesus ask such a question, he stood still and answered, "Yes, Master, of a certainty I trust you, and you know that I do." Then said Jesus: "Andrew, if you trust me, trust your brethren more — even Peter. I once trusted you with the leadership of your brethren. Now must you trust others as I leave you to go to the Father. When your brethren begin to scatter abroad because of bitter persecutions, be a considerate and wise counselor to James my brother in the flesh when they put heavy burdens upon him which he is not qualified by experience to bear. And then go on trusting, for I will not fail you. When you are through on earth, you shall come to me."

Then Jesus turned to James, asking, "James, do you trust me?" And of course James replied, "Yes, Master, I trust you with all my heart." Then said Jesus: "James, if you trust me more, you will be less impatient with your brethren. If you will trust me, it will help you to be kind to the brotherhood of believers. Learn to weigh the consequences of your sayings and your doings. Remember that the reaping is in accordance with the sowing. Pray for tranquillity of spirit and cultivate patience. These graces, with living faith, shall sustain you when the hour comes to drink the cup of sacrifice. But never be dismayed; when you are through on earth, you shall also come to be with me."

Jesus next talked with Thomas and Nathaniel. Said he to Thomas, "Thomas, do you serve me?" Thomas replied, "Yes, Lord, I serve you now and always." Then said Jesus: "If you would serve me, serve my brethren in the flesh even as I have served you. And be not weary in this well-doing but persevere as one who has been ordained by God for this service of love. When you have finished your service with me on earth, you shall serve with me in glory. Thomas, you must cease doubting; you must grow in faith and the knowledge of truth. Believe in God like a child but cease to act so childishly. Have courage; be strong in faith and mighty in the kingdom of God."

Then said the Master to Nathaniel, "Nathaniel, do you serve me?" And the apostle answered, "Yes, Master, and with an undivided affection." Then said Jesus: "If, therefore, you serve me with a whole heart, make sure that you are devoted to the welfare of my brethren on earth with tireless affection. Admix friendship with your counsel and add love to your philosophy. Serve your fellow men even as I have served you. Be faithful to men as I have watched over you. Be less critical; expect less of some men and thereby lessen the extent of your disappointment. And when the work down here is over, you shall serve with me on high."

After this the Master talked with Matthew and Philip. To Philip he said, "Philip, do you obey me?" Philip answered, "Yes, Lord, I will obey you even with my life." Then said Jesus: "If you would obey me, go then into the lands of the gentiles and proclaim this gospel. The prophets have told you that to obey is better than to sacrifice. By faith have you become a God-knowing kingdom son. There is but one law to obey — that is the command to go forth proclaiming the gospel of the kingdom. Cease to fear men; be unafraid to preach the good news of eternal life to your fellows who languish in darkness and hunger for the light of truth. No more, Philip, shall you busy yourself with money and goods. You now are free to preach the glad tidings just as are your brethren. And I will go before you and be with you even to the end."

And then, speaking to Matthew, the Master asked, "Matthew, do you have it in your heart to obey me?" Matthew answered, "Yes, Lord, I am fully dedicated to doing your will." Then said the Master: "Matthew, if you would obey me, go forth to teach all peoples this gospel of the kingdom. No longer will you serve your brethren the material things of life; henceforth you are also to proclaim the good news of spiritual salvation. From now on have an eye single only to obeying your commission to preach this gospel of the Father's kingdom. As I have done the Father's will on earth, so shall you fulfill the divine commission. Remember, both Jew and gentile are your brethren. Fear no man when you proclaim the saving truths of the gospel of the kingdom of heaven. And where I go, you shall presently come."

Then he walked and talked with the Alpheus twins, James and Judas, and speaking to both of them, he asked, "James and Judas, do you believe in me?" And when they both answered, "Yes, Master, we do believe," he said:

"I will soon leave you. You see that I have already left you in the flesh. I tarry only a short time in this form before I go to my Father. You believe in me — you are my apostles, and you always will be. Go on believing and remembering your association with me, when I am gone, and after you have, perchance, returned to the work you used to do before you came to live with me. Never allow a change in your outward work to influence your allegiance. Have faith in God to the end of your days on earth. Never forget that, when you are a faith son of God, all upright work of the realm is sacred. Nothing which a son of God does can be common. Do your work, therefore, from this time on, as for God. And when you are through on this world, I have other and better worlds where you shall likewise work for me. And in all of this work, on this world and on other worlds, I will work with you, and my spirit shall dwell within you."

It was almost ten o'clock when Jesus returned from his visit with the Alpheus twins, and as he left the apostles, he said: "Farewell, until I meet you all on the mount of your ordination tomorrow at noontime." When he had thus spoken, he vanished from their sight.

3. ON THE MOUNT OF ORDINATION

At noon on Saturday, April 22, the eleven apostles assembled by appointment on the hill near Capernaum, and Jesus appeared among them. This meeting occurred on the very mount where the Master had set them apart as his apostles and as ambassadors of the Father's kingdom on earth. And this was the Master's fourteenth morontia manifestation.

At this time the eleven apostles knelt in a circle about the Master and heard him repeat the charges and saw him re-enact the ordination scene even as when they were first set apart for the special work of the kingdom. And all of this was to them as a memory of their former consecration to the Father's service, except the Master's prayer. When the Master — the morontia Jesus — now prayed, it was in tones of majesty and with words of power such as the apostles had never before heard. Their Master now spoke with the rulers of the universes as one who, in his own universe, had had all power and authority committed to his hand. And these eleven men never forgot this experience of the morontia rededication to the former pledges of ambassadorship. The Master spent just one hour on this mount with his ambassadors, and when he had taken an affectionate farewell of them, he vanished from their sight.

And no one saw Jesus for a full week. The apostles really had no idea what to do, not knowing whether the Master had gone to the Father. In this state of uncertainty they tarried at Bethsaida. They were afraid to go fishing lest he come to visit them and they miss seeing him. During this entire week Jesus was occupied with the morontia creatures on earth and with the affairs of the morontia transition which he was experiencing on this world.

4. THE LAKESIDE GATHERING

Word of the appearances of Jesus was spreading throughout Galilee, and every day increasing numbers of believers arrived at the Zebedee home to inquire about the Master's resurrection and to find out the truth about these reputed appearances. Peter, early in the week, sent out word that a public meeting would be held by the seaside the next Sabbath at three o'clock in the afternoon.

Accordingly, on Saturday, April 29, at three o'clock, more than five hundred believers from the environs of Capernaum assembled at Bethsaida to hear Peter preach his first public sermon since the resurrection. The apostle was at his best, and after he had finished his appealing discourse, few of his hearers doubted that the Master had risen from the dead.

Peter ended his sermon, saying: "We affirm that Jesus of Nazareth is not dead; we declare that he has risen from the tomb; we proclaim that we have seen him and talked with him." Just as he finished making this declaration of faith, there by his side, in full view of all these people, the Master appeared in morontia form and, speaking to them in familiar accents, said, "Peace be upon you, and my peace I leave with you." When he had thus appeared and had so spoken to them, he vanished from their sight. This was the fifteenth morontia manifestation of the risen Jesus.

Because of certain things said to the eleven while they were in conference with the Master on the mount of ordination, the apostles received the impression that their Master would presently make a public appearance before a group of the Galilean believers, and that, after he had done so, they were to return to Jerusalem. Accordingly, early the next day, Sunday, April 30, the eleven left Bethsaida for Jerusalem. They did considerable teaching and preaching on the way down the Jordan, so that they did not arrive at the home of the Marks in Jerusalem until late on Wednesday, May 3.

This was a sad home-coming for John Mark. Just a few hours before he reached home, his father, Elijah Mark, suddenly died from a hemorrhage in the brain. Although the thought of the certainty of the resurrection of the dead did much to comfort the apostles in their grief, at the same time they truly mourned the loss of their good friend, who had been their stanch supporter even in the times of great trouble and disappointment. John Mark did all he could to comfort his mother and, speaking for her, invited the apostles to continue to make their home at her house. And the eleven made this upper chamber their headquarters until after the day of Pentecost.

The apostles had purposely entered Jerusalem after nightfall that they might not be seen by the Jewish authorities. Neither did they publicly appear in connection with the funeral of Elijah Mark. All the next day they remained in quiet seclusion in this eventful upper chamber.

On Thursday night the apostles had a wonderful meeting in this upper chamber and all pledged themselves to go forth in the public preaching of the new gospel of the risen Lord except Thomas, Simon Zelotes, and the Alpheus twins. Already had begun the first steps of changing the gospel of the kingdom — sonship with God and brotherhood with man — into the proclamation of the resurrection of Jesus. Nathaniel opposed this shift in the burden of their public message, but he could not withstand Peter's eloquence, neither could he overcome the enthusiasm of the disciples, especially the women believers.

And so, under the vigorous leadership of Peter and ere the Master ascended to the Father, his well-meaning representatives began that subtle process of gradually and certainly changing the religion *of* Jesus into a new and modified form of religion *about* Jesus.

PAPER 193
FINAL APPEARANCES AND ASCENSION

THE SIXTEENTH MORONTIA manifestation of Jesus occurred on Friday, May 5, in the courtyard of Nicodemus, about nine o'clock at night. On this evening the Jerusalem believers had made their first attempt to get together since the resurrection. Assembled here at this time were the eleven apostles, the women's corps and their associates, and about fifty other leading disciples of the Master, including a number of the Greeks. This company of believers had been visiting informally for more than half an hour when, suddenly, the morontia Master appeared in full view and immediately began to instruct them. Said Jesus:

"Peace be upon you. This is the most representative group of believers — apostles and disciples, both men and women — to which I have appeared since the time of my deliverance from the flesh. I now call you to witness that I told you beforehand that my sojourn among you must come to an end; I told you that presently I must return to the Father. And then I plainly told you how the chief priests and the rulers of the Jews would deliver me up to be put to death, and that I would rise from the grave. Why, then, did you allow yourselves to become so disconcerted by all this when it came to pass? and why were you so surprised when I rose from the tomb on the third day?

You failed to believe me because you heard my words without comprehending the meaning thereof.

"And now you should give ear to my words lest you again make the mistake of hearing my teaching with the mind while in your hearts you fail to comprehend the meaning. From the beginning of my sojourn as one of you, I taught you that my one purpose was to reveal my Father in heaven to his children on earth. I have lived the God-revealing bestowal that you might experience the God-knowing career. I have revealed God as your Father in heaven; I have revealed you as the sons of God on earth. It is a fact that God loves you, his sons. By faith in my word this fact becomes an eternal and living truth in your hearts. When, by living faith, you become divinely God-conscious, you are then born of the spirit as children of light and life, even the eternal life wherewith you shall ascend the universe of universes and attain the experience of finding God the Father on Paradise.

"I admonish you ever to remember that your mission among men is to proclaim the gospel of the kingdom — the reality of the fatherhood of God and the truth of the sonship of man. Proclaim the whole truth of the good news, not just a part of the saving gospel. Your message is not changed by my resurrection experience. Sonship with God, by faith, is still the saving truth of the gospel of the kingdom. You are to go forth preaching the love of God and the service of man. That which the world needs most to know is: Men are the sons of God, and through faith they can actually realize, and daily experience, this ennobling truth. My bestowal should help all men to know that they are the children of God, but such knowledge will not suffice if they fail personally to faith-grasp the saving truth that they are the living spirit sons of the eternal Father. The gospel of the kingdom is concerned with the love of the Father and the service of his children on earth.

"Among yourselves, here, you share the knowledge that I have risen from the dead, but that is not strange. I have the power to lay down my life and to take it up again; the Father gives such power to his Paradise Sons. You should the rather be stirred in your hearts by the knowledge that the dead of an age entered upon the eternal ascent soon after I left Joseph's new tomb. I lived my life in the flesh to show how you can, through loving service, become God-revealing to your fellow men even as, by loving you and serving you, I have become God-revealing to you. I have lived among you as the Son of Man that you, and all other men, might know that you are all indeed the sons of God. Therefore, go you now into all the world preaching this gospel of the kingdom of heaven to all men. Love all men as I have loved you; serve your fellow mortals as I have served you. Freely you have received, freely give. Only tarry here in Jerusalem while I go to the Father, and until I send you the Spirit of Truth. He shall lead you into the enlarged truth, and I will go with you into all the world. I am with you always, and my peace I leave with you."

When the Master had spoken to them, he vanished from their sight. It was near daybreak before these believers dispersed; all night they remained together, earnestly discussing the Master's admonitions and contemplating all that had befallen them. James Zebedee and others of the apostles also told them of their experiences with the morontia Master in Galilee and recited how he had three times appeared to them.

1. THE APPEARANCE AT SYCHAR

About four o'clock on Sabbath afternoon, May 13, the Master appeared to Nalda and about seventy-five Samaritan believers near Jacob's well, at Sychar. The believers were in the habit of meeting at this place, near where Jesus had spoken to Nalda concerning the water of life. On this day, just as they had finished their discussions of the reported resurrection, Jesus suddenly appeared before them, saying:

"Peace be upon you. You rejoice to know that I am the resurrection and the life, but this will avail you nothing unless you are first born of the eternal spirit, thereby coming to possess, by faith, the gift of eternal life. If you are the faith sons of my Father, you shall never die; you shall not perish. The gospel of the kingdom has taught you that all men are the sons of God. And this good news concerning the love of the heavenly Father for his children on earth must be carried to all the world. The time has come when you worship God neither on Gerizim nor at Jerusalem, but where you are, as you are, in spirit and in truth. It is your faith that saves your souls. Salvation is the gift of God to all who believe they are his sons. But be not deceived; while salvation is the free gift of God and is bestowed upon all who accept it by faith, there follows the experience of bearing the fruits of this spirit life as it is lived in the flesh. The acceptance of the doctrine of the fatherhood of God implies that you also freely accept the associated truth of the brotherhood of man. And if man is your brother, he is even more than your neighbor, whom the Father requires you to love as yourself. Your brother, being of your own family, you will not only love with a family affection, but you will also serve as you would serve yourself. And you will thus love and serve your brother because you, being my brethren, have been thus loved and served by me. Go, then, into all the world telling this good news to all creatures of every race, tribe, and nation. My spirit shall go before you, and I will be with you always."

These Samaritans were greatly astonished at this appearance of the Master, and they hastened off to the near-by towns and villages, where they published abroad the news that they had seen Jesus, and that he had talked to them. And this was the seventeenth morontia appearance of the Master.

2. THE PHOENICIAN APPEARANCE

The Master's eighteenth morontia appearance was at Tyre, on Tuesday, May 16, at a little before nine o'clock in the evening. Again he appeared at the close of a meeting of believers, as they were about to disperse, saying:

"Peace be upon you. You rejoice to know that the Son of Man has risen from the dead because you thereby know that you and your brethren shall also survive mortal death. But such survival is dependent on your having been previously born of the spirit of truth-seeking and God-finding. The bread of life and the water thereof are given only to those who hunger for truth and thirst for righteousness — for God. The fact that the dead rise is not the gospel of the kingdom. These great truths and these universe facts are all related to this gospel in that they are a part of the result of believing the good news and are embraced in the subsequent experience of those who, by faith, become, in deed and in truth, the everlasting sons of the eternal God. My Father sent me into the world to proclaim this salvation of sonship to all men. And so send I you abroad to preach this salvation of sonship.

Salvation is the free gift of God, but those who are born of the spirit will immediately begin to show forth the fruits of the spirit in loving service to their fellow creatures. And the fruits of the divine spirit which are yielded in the lives of spirit-born and God-knowing mortals are: loving service, unselfish devotion, courageous loyalty, sincere fairness, enlightened honesty, undying hope, confiding trust, merciful ministry, unfailing goodness, forgiving tolerance, and enduring peace. If professed believers bear not these fruits of the divine spirit in their lives, they are dead; the Spirit of Truth is not in them; they are useless branches on the living vine, and they soon will be taken away. My Father requires of the children of faith that they bear much spirit fruit. If, therefore, you are not fruitful, he will dig about your roots and cut away your unfruitful branches. Increasingly, must you yield the fruits of the spirit as you progress heavenward in the kingdom of God. You may enter the kingdom as a child, but the Father requires that you grow up, by grace, to the full stature of spiritual adulthood. And when you go abroad to tell all nations the good news of this gospel, I will go before you, and my Spirit of Truth shall abide in your hearts. My peace I leave with you."

And then the Master disappeared from their sight. The next day there went out from Tyre those who carried this story to Sidon and even to Antioch and Damascus. Jesus had been with these believers when he was in the flesh, and they were quick to recognize him when he began to teach them. While his friends could not readily recognize his morontia form when made visible, they were never slow to identify his personality when he spoke to them.

3. LAST APPEARANCE IN JERUSALEM

Early Thursday morning, May 18, Jesus made his last appearance on earth as a morontia personality. As the eleven apostles were about to sit down to breakfast in the upper chamber of Mary Mark's home, Jesus appeared to them and said:

"Peace be upon you. I have asked you to tarry here in Jerusalem until I ascend to the Father, even until I send you the Spirit of Truth, who shall soon be poured out upon all flesh, and who shall endow you with power from on high." Simon Zelotes interrupted Jesus, asking, "Then, Master, will you restore the kingdom, and will we see the glory of God manifested on earth?" When Jesus had listened to Simon's question, he answered: "Simon, you still cling to your old ideas about the Jewish Messiah and the material kingdom. But you will receive spiritual power after the spirit has descended upon you, and you will presently go into all the world preaching this gospel of the kingdom. As the Father sent me into the world, so do I send you. And I wish that you would love and trust one another. Judas is no more with you because his love grew cold, and because he refused to trust you, his loyal brethren. Have you not read in the Scripture where it is written: `It is not good for man to be alone. No man lives to himself? And also where it says: `He who would have friends must show himself friendly'? And did I not even send you out to teach, two and two, that you might not become lonely and fall into the mischief and miseries of isolation? You also well know that, when I was in the flesh, I did not permit myself to be alone for long periods. From the very beginning of our associations I always had two or three of you constantly by my side or else very near at hand even when I communed with the Father. Trust, therefore, and confide in one another. And this is all the more needful since I am this day going to leave you alone in the world. The hour has come; I am about to go to the Father."

When he had spoken, he beckoned for them to come with him, and he led them out on the Mount of Olives, where he bade them farewell preparatory to departing from Urantia. This was a solemn journey to Olivet. Not a word was spoken by any of them from the time they left the upper chamber until Jesus paused with them on the Mount of Olives.

4. CAUSES OF JUDAS'S DOWNFALL

It was in the first part of the Master's farewell message to his apostles that he alluded to the loss of Judas and held up the tragic fate of their traitorous fellow worker as a solemn warning against the dangers of social and fraternal isolation. It may be helpful to believers, in this and in future ages, briefly to review the causes of Judas's downfall in the light of the Master's remarks and in view of the accumulated enlightenment of succeeding centuries.

As we look back upon this tragedy, we conceive that Judas went wrong, primarily, because he was very markedly an isolated personality, a personality shut in and away from ordinary social contacts. He persistently refused to confide in, or freely fraternize with, his fellow apostles. But his being an isolated type of personality would not, in and of itself, have wrought such mischief for Judas had it not been that he also failed to increase in love and grow in spiritual grace. And then, as if to make a bad matter worse, he persistently harbored grudges and fostered such psychologic enemies as revenge and the generalized craving to "get even" with somebody for all his disappointments.

This unfortunate combination of individual peculiarities and mental tendencies conspired to destroy a well-intentioned man who failed to subdue these evils by love, faith, and trust. That Judas need not have gone wrong is well proved by the cases of Thomas and Nathaniel, both of whom were cursed with this same sort of suspicion and overdevelopment of the individualistic tendency. Even Andrew and Matthew had many leanings in this direction; but all these men grew to love Jesus and their fellow apostles more, and not less, as time passed. They grew in grace and in a knowledge of the truth. They became increasingly more trustful of their brethren and slowly developed the ability to confide in their fellows. Judas persistently refused to confide in his brethren. When he was impelled, by the accumulation of his emotional conflicts, to seek relief in self-expression, he invariably sought the advice and received the unwise consolation of his unspiritual relatives or those chance acquaintances who were either indifferent, or actually hostile, to the welfare and progress of the spiritual realities of the heavenly kingdom, of which he was one of the twelve consecrated ambassadors on earth.

Judas met defeat in his battles of the earth struggle because of the following factors of personal tendencies and character weakness:

1. He was an isolated type of human being. He was highly individualistic and chose to grow into a confirmed "shut-in" and unsociable sort of person.

2. As a child, life had been made too easy for him. He bitterly resented thwarting. He always expected to win; he was a very poor loser.

3. He never acquired a philosophic technique for meeting disappointment. Instead of accepting disappointments as a regular and commonplace feature of human existence, he unfailingly resorted to the practice of blaming someone in particular, or his associates as a group, for all his personal difficulties and disappointments.

4. He was given to holding grudges; he was always entertaining the idea of revenge.

5. He did not like to face facts frankly; he was dishonest in his attitude toward life situations.

6. He disliked to discuss his personal problems with his immediate associates; he refused to talk over his difficulties with his real friends and those who truly loved him. In all the years of their association he never once went to the Master with a purely personal problem.

7. He never learned that the real rewards for noble living are, after all, spiritual prizes, which are not always distributed during this one short life in the flesh.

As a result of his persistent isolation of personality, his griefs multiplied, his sorrows increased, his anxieties augmented, and his despair deepened almost beyond endurance.

While this self-centered and ultraindividualistic apostle had many psychic, emotional, and spiritual troubles, his main difficulties were: In personality, he was isolated. In mind, he was suspicious and vengeful. In temperament, he was surly and vindictive. Emotionally, he was loveless and unforgiving. Socially, he was unconfiding and almost wholly self-contained. In spirit, he became arrogant and selfishly ambitious. In life, he ignored those who loved him, and in death, he was friendless.

These, then, are the factors of mind and influences of evil which, taken altogether, explain why a well-meaning and otherwise onetime sincere believer in Jesus, even after several years of intimate association with his transforming personality, forsook his fellows, repudiated a sacred cause, renounced his holy calling, and betrayed his divine Master.

5. THE MASTER'S ASCENSION

It was almost half past seven o'clock this Thursday morning, May 18, when Jesus arrived on the western slope of Mount Olivet with his eleven silent and somewhat bewildered apostles. From this location, about two thirds the way up the mountain, they could look out over Jerusalem and down upon Gethsemane. Jesus now prepared to say his last farewell to the apostles before he took leave of Urantia. As he stood there before them, without being directed they knelt about him in a circle, and the Master said:

"I bade you tarry in Jerusalem until you were endowed with power from on high. I am now about to take leave of you; I am about to ascend to my Father, and soon, very soon, will we send into this world of my sojourn the Spirit of Truth; and when he has come, you shall begin the new proclamation of the gospel of the kingdom, first in Jerusalem and then to the uttermost parts of the world. Love men with the love wherewith I have loved you and serve your fellow mortals even as I have served you. By the spirit fruits of your lives impel souls to believe the truth that man is a son of God, and that all men are brethren. Remember all I have taught you and the life I have lived among you. My love overshadows you, my spirit will dwell with you, and my peace shall abide upon you. Farewell."

When the morontia Master had thus spoken, he vanished from their sight. This so-called ascension of Jesus was in no way different from his other disappearances from mortal vision during the forty days of his morontia career on Urantia.

The Master went to Edentia by way of Jerusem, where the Most Highs, under the observation of the Paradise Son, released Jesus of Nazareth from the morontia state and, through the spirit channels of ascension, returned him to the status of Paradise sonship and supreme sovereignty on Salvington.

It was about seven forty-five this morning when the morontia Jesus disappeared from the observation of his eleven apostles to begin the ascent to the right hand of his Father, there to receive formal confirmation of his completed sovereignty of the universe of Nebadon.

6. PETER CALLS A MEETING

Acting upon the instruction of Peter, John Mark and others went forth to call the leading disciples together at the home of Mary Mark. By ten thirty, one hundred and twenty of the foremost disciples of Jesus living in Jerusalem had forgathered to hear the report of the farewell message of the Master and to learn of his ascension. Among this company was Mary the mother of Jesus. She had returned to Jerusalem with John Zebedee when the apostles came back from their recent sojourn in Galilee. Soon after Pentecost she returned to the home of Salome at Bethsaida. James the brother of Jesus was also present at this meeting, the first conference of the Master's disciples to be called after the termination of his planetary career.

Simon Peter took it upon himself to speak for his fellow apostles and made a thrilling report of the last meeting of the eleven with their Master and most touchingly portrayed the Master's final farewell and his ascension disappearance. It was a meeting the like of which had never before occurred on this world. This part of the meeting lasted not quite one hour. Peter then explained that they had decided to choose a successor to Judas Iscariot, and that a recess would be granted to enable the apostles to decide between the two men who had been suggested for this position, Matthias and Justus.

The eleven apostles then went downstairs, where they agreed to cast lots in order to determine which of these men should become an apostle to serve in Judas's place. The lot fell on Matthias, and he was declared to be the new apostle. He was duly inducted into his office and then appointed treasurer. But Matthias had little part in the subsequent activities of the apostles.

Soon after Pentecost the twins returned to their homes in Galilee. Simon Zelotes was in retirement for some time before he went forth preaching the gospel. Thomas worried for a shorter period and then resumed his teaching. Nathaniel differed increasingly with Peter regarding preaching about Jesus in the place of proclaiming the former gospel of the kingdom. This disagreement became so acute by the middle of the following month that Nathaniel withdrew, going to Philadelphia to visit Abner and Lazarus; and after tarrying there for more than a year, he went on into the lands beyond Mesopotamia preaching the gospel as he understood it.

This left but six of the original twelve apostles to become actors on the stage of the early proclamation of the gospel in Jerusalem: Peter, Andrew, James, John, Philip, and Matthew.

Just about noon the apostles returned to their brethren in the upper chamber and announced that Matthias had been chosen as the new apostle. And then Peter called all of the believers to engage in prayer, prayer that they might be prepared to receive the gift of the spirit which the Master had promised to send.

PAPER 194
BESTOWAL OF THE SPIRIT OF TRUTH

About one o'clock, as the one hundred and twenty believers were engaged in prayer, they all became aware of a strange presence in the room. At the same time these disciples all became conscious of a new and profound sense of spiritual joy, security, and confidence. This new consciousness of spiritual strength was immediately followed by a strong urge to go out and publicly proclaim the gospel of the kingdom and the good news that Jesus had risen from the dead.

Peter stood up and declared that this must be the coming of the Spirit of Truth which the Master had promised them and proposed that they go to the temple and begin the proclamation of the good news committed to their hands. And they did just what Peter suggested.

These men had been trained and instructed that the gospel which they should preach was the fatherhood of God and the sonship of man, but at just this moment of spiritual ecstasy and personal triumph, the best tidings, the greatest news, these men could think of was the *fact* of the risen Master. And so they went forth, endowed with power from on high, preaching glad tidings to the people — even salvation through Jesus — but they unintentionally stumbled into the error of substituting some of the facts associated with the gospel for the gospel message itself. Peter unwittingly led off in this mistake, and others followed after him on down to Paul, who created a new religion out of the new version of the good news.

The gospel of the kingdom is: the fact of the fatherhood of God, coupled with the resultant truth of the sonship-brotherhood of men. Christianity, as it developed from that day, is: the fact of God as the Father of the Lord Jesus Christ, in association with the experience of believer-fellowship with the risen and glorified Christ.

It is not strange that these spirit-infused men should have seized upon this opportunity to express their feelings of triumph over the forces which had sought to destroy their Master and end the influence of his teachings. At such a time as this it was easier to remember their personal association with Jesus and to be thrilled with the assurance that the Master still lived, that their friendship had not ended, and that the spirit had indeed come upon them even as he had promised.

These believers felt themselves suddenly translated into another world, a new existence of joy, power, and glory. The Master had told them the kingdom would come with power, and some of them thought they were beginning to discern what he meant.

And when all of this is taken into consideration, it is not difficult to understand how these men came to preach *a new gospel about Jesus* in the place of their former message of the fatherhood of God and the brotherhood of men.

1. THE PENTECOST SERMON

The apostles had been in hiding for forty days. This day happened to be the Jewish festival of Pentecost, and thousands of visitors from all parts of the world were in Jerusalem. Many arrived for this feast, but a majority had tarried in the city since the Passover. Now these frightened apostles emerged from their weeks of seclusion to appear boldly in the temple, where they began to preach the new message of a risen Messiah. And all the disciples were likewise conscious of having received some new spiritual endowment of insight and power.

It was about two o'clock when Peter stood up in that very place where his Master had last taught in this temple, and delivered that impassioned appeal which resulted in the winning of more than two thousand souls. The Master had gone, but they suddenly discovered that this story about him had great power with the people. No wonder they were led on into the further proclamation of that which vindicated their former devotion to Jesus and at the same time so constrained men to believe in him. Six of the apostles participated in this meeting: Peter, Andrew, James, John, Philip, and Matthew. They talked for more than an hour and a half and delivered messages in Greek, Hebrew, and Aramaic, as well as a few words in even other tongues with which they had a speaking acquaintance.

The leaders of the Jews were astounded at the boldness of the apostles, but they feared to molest them because of the large numbers who believed their story.

By half past four o'clock more than two thousand new believers followed the apostles down to the pool of Siloam, where Peter, Andrew, James, and John baptized them in the Master's name. And it was dark when they had finished with baptizing this multitude.

Pentecost was the great festival of baptism, the time for fellowshipping the proselytes of the gate, those gentiles who desired to serve Yahweh. It was, therefore, the more easy for large numbers of both the Jews and believing gentiles to submit to baptism on this day. In doing this, they were in no way disconnecting themselves from the Jewish faith. Even for some time after this the believers in Jesus were a sect within Judaism. All of them, including the apostles, were still loyal to the essential requirements of the Jewish ceremonial system.

2. THE SIGNIFICANCE OF PENTECOST

Jesus lived on earth and taught a gospel which redeemed man from the superstition that he was a child of the devil and elevated him to the dignity of a faith son of God. Jesus' message, as he preached it and lived it in his day, was an effective solvent for man's spiritual difficulties in that day of its statement. And now that he has personally left the world, he sends in his place his Spirit of Truth, who is designed to live in man and, for each new generation, to restate the Jesus message so that every new group of mortals to appear upon the face of the earth shall have a new and up-to-date version of the gospel, just such personal enlightenment and group guidance as will prove to be an effective solvent for man's ever-new and varied spiritual difficulties.

The first mission of this spirit is, of course, to foster and personalize truth, for it is the comprehension of truth that constitutes the highest form of human liberty. Next, it is the purpose of this spirit to destroy the believer's feeling of orphanhood. Jesus having been among men, all believers would experience a sense of loneliness had not the Spirit of Truth come to dwell in men's hearts.

This bestowal of the Son's spirit effectively prepared all normal men's minds for the subsequent universal bestowal of the Father's spirit (the Adjuster) upon all mankind. In a certain sense, this Spirit of Truth is the spirit of both the Universal Father and the Creator Son.

Do not make the mistake of expecting to become strongly intellectually conscious of the outpoured Spirit of Truth. The spirit never creates a consciousness of himself, only a consciousness of Michael, the Son. From the beginning Jesus taught that the spirit would not speak of himself. The proof, therefore, of your fellowship with the Spirit of Truth is not to be found in your consciousness of this spirit but rather in your experience of enhanced fellowship with Michael.

The spirit also came to help men recall and understand the words of the Master as well as to illuminate and reinterpret his life on earth.

Next, the Spirit of Truth came to help the believer to witness to the realities of Jesus' teachings and his life as he lived it in the flesh, and as he now again lives it anew and afresh in the individual believer of each passing generation of the spirit-filled sons of God.

Thus it appears that the Spirit of Truth comes really to lead all believers into all truth, into the expanding knowledge of the experience of the living and growing spiritual consciousness of the reality of eternal and ascending sonship with God.

Jesus lived a life which is a revelation of man submitted to the Father's will, not an example for any man literally to attempt to follow. This life in the flesh, together with his death on the cross and subsequent resurrection, presently became a new gospel of the ransom which had thus been paid in order to purchase man back from the clutch of the evil one — from the condemnation of an offended God. Nevertheless, even though the gospel did become greatly distorted, it remains a fact that this new message about Jesus carried along with it many of the fundamental truths and teachings of his earlier gospel of the kingdom. And, sooner or later, these concealed truths of the fatherhood of God and the brotherhood of men will emerge to effectually transform the civilization of all mankind.

But these mistakes of the intellect in no way interfered with the believer's great progress in growth in spirit. In less than a month after the bestowal of the Spirit of Truth, the apostles made more individual spiritual progress than during their almost four years of personal and loving association with the Master. Neither did this substitution of the *fact* of the resurrection of Jesus for the saving gospel *truth* of sonship with God in any way interfere with the rapid spread of their teachings; on the contrary, this overshadowing of Jesus' message by the new teachings about his person and resurrection seemed greatly to facilitate the preaching of the good news.

The term "baptism of the spirit," which came into such general use about this time, merely signified the conscious reception of this gift of the Spirit of Truth and the personal acknowledgment of this new spiritual power as an augmentation of all spiritual influences previously experienced by God-knowing souls.

Since the bestowal of the Spirit of Truth, man is subject to the teaching and guidance of a threefold spirit endowment: the spirit of the Father, the Thought Adjuster; the spirit of the Son, the Spirit of Truth; the spirit of the Spirit, the Holy Spirit.

In a way, mankind is subject to a triple influence of the sevenfold appeal of the universe spirit influences. The early evolutionary races of mortals are subject to the progressive contact of the seven adjutant mind-spirits of the local universe Mother Spirit. Advancing man is influenced by the higher aspects of these seven adjutant mind-spirits, the Seven Ray Energies of the local universe Mother Spirit. As man progresses upward in the scale of intelligence and spiritual perception, there eventually come to hover over him and dwell within him the seven higher spirit influences (and these contain within them the previous double influences). These seven spirits of the advancing worlds are:

1. The bestowed spirit of the Universal Father — the Thought Adjusters.

2. The spirit presence of the Eternal Son — the spirit gravity of the universe of universes and the certain channel of all spirit communion.

3. The spirit presence of the Infinite Spirit — the universal spirit-mind of all creation, the spiritual source of the intellectual kinship of all progressive intelligences.

4. The spirit of the Universal Father and the Creator Son — the Spirit of Truth, generally regarded as the spirit of the Universe Son.

5. The spirit of the Infinite Spirit and the Universe Mother Spirit — the Holy Spirit, generally regarded as the spirit of the Universe Spirit.

6. The mind-spirit of the Universe Mother Spirit — the seven adjutant mind-spirits and their higher aspects, the Seven Ray Energies, of the local universe.

7. The spirit of the Father, Sons, and Spirits — the new-name spirit of the ascending mortals of the realms after the fusion of the mortal spirit-born soul with the Paradise Thought Adjuster and after the subsequent attainment of the divinity and glorification of the status of the Paradise Corps of the Finality.

And so did the bestowal of the Spirit of Truth bring to the world and its peoples the last of the spirit endowment designed to aid in the ascending search for God.

3. WHAT HAPPENED AT PENTECOST

Many novel and strange teachings became associated with the early narratives of the day of Pentecost. In subsequent times the events of this day, on which the Spirit of Truth, the new teacher, came to dwell with mankind, have become confused with the foolish outbreaks of rampant emotionalism. The chief mission of this outpoured spirit of the Father and the Son is to teach men about the truths of the Father's love and the Son's mercy. These are the truths of divinity which men can comprehend more fully than all the other divine traits of character. The Spirit of Truth is concerned primarily with the revelation of the Father's spirit nature and the Son's moral character. The Creator Son, in the flesh, revealed God to men; the Spirit of Truth, in the heart, reveals the Creator Son to men. When man yields the "fruits of the spirit" in his life, he is simply showing forth the traits which the Master manifested in his own earthly life. When Jesus was on earth, he lived his life as one personality — Jesus of Nazareth. As the indwelling spirit of the "new teacher," the Master has, since Pentecost, been able to live his life anew in the experience of every truth-taught believer.

Many things which happen in the course of a human life are hard to understand, difficult to reconcile with the idea that this is a universe in which truth prevails and in which righteousness triumphs. It so often appears that slander, lies, dishonesty, and unrighteousness — sin — prevail. Does faith, after all, triumph over evil, sin, and iniquity? It does. And the life and death of Jesus are the eternal proof that the truth of goodness and the faith of the spirit-led creature will always be vindicated. They taunted Jesus on the cross, saying, "Let us see if God will come and deliver him." It looked dark on that day of the crucifixion, but it was gloriously bright on the resurrection morning; it was still brighter and more joyous on the day of Pentecost. The religions of pessimistic despair seek to obtain release from the burdens of life; they crave extinction in endless slumber and rest. These are the religions of primitive fear and dread. The religion of Jesus is a new gospel of faith to be proclaimed to struggling humanity. This new religion is founded on faith, hope, and love.

To Jesus, mortal life had dealt its hardest, cruelest, and bitterest blows; and this man met these ministrations of despair with faith, courage, and the unswerving determination to do his Father's will. Jesus met life in all its terrible reality and mastered it — even in death. He did not use religion as a release from life. The religion of Jesus does not seek to escape this life in order to enjoy the waiting bliss of another existence. The religion of Jesus provides the joy and peace of another and spiritual existence to enhance and ennoble the life which men now live in the flesh.

If religion is an opiate to the people, it is not the religion of Jesus. On the cross he refused to drink the deadening drug, and his spirit, poured out upon all flesh, is a mighty world influence which leads man upward and urges him onward. The spiritual forward urge is the most powerful driving force present in this world; the truth-learning believer is the one progressive and aggressive soul on earth.

On the day of Pentecost the religion of Jesus broke all national restrictions and racial fetters. It is forever true, "Where the spirit of the Lord is, there is liberty." On this day the Spirit of Truth became the personal gift from the Master to every mortal. This spirit was bestowed for the purpose of qualifying believers more effectively to preach the gospel of the kingdom, but they mistook the experience of receiving the outpoured spirit for a part of the new gospel which they were unconsciously formulating.

Do not overlook the fact that the Spirit of Truth was bestowed upon all sincere believers; this gift of the spirit did not come only to the apostles. The one hundred and twenty men and women assembled in the upper chamber all received the new teacher, as did all the honest of heart throughout the whole world. This new teacher was bestowed upon mankind, and every soul received him in accordance with the love for truth and the capacity to grasp and comprehend spiritual realities. At last, true religion is delivered from the custody of priests and all sacred classes and finds its real manifestation in the individual souls of men.

The religion of Jesus fosters the highest type of human civilization in that it creates the highest type of spiritual personality and proclaims the sacredness of that person.

The coming of the Spirit of Truth on Pentecost made possible a religion which is neither radical nor conservative; it is neither the old nor the new; it is to be dominated neither by the old nor the young. The fact of Jesus' earthly life provides a fixed point for the anchor of time, while the bestowal of the Spirit of Truth provides for the everlasting expansion and endless growth of the religion which he lived and the gospel which he proclaimed. The spirit guides into *all* truth; he is the teacher of an expanding and always-growing religion of endless progress and divine unfolding. This new teacher will be forever unfolding to the truth-seeking believer that which was so divinely folded up in the person and nature of the Son of Man.

The manifestations associated with the bestowal of the "new teacher," and the reception of the apostles' preaching by the men of various races and nations gathered together at Jerusalem, indicate the universality of the religion of Jesus. The gospel of the kingdom was to be identified with no particular race, culture, or language. This day of Pentecost witnessed the great effort of the spirit to liberate the religion of Jesus from its inherited Jewish fetters. Even after this demonstration of pouring out the spirit upon all flesh, the apostles at first endeavored to impose the requirements of Judaism upon their converts. Even Paul had trouble with his Jerusalem brethren because he refused to subject the gentiles to these Jewish practices. No revealed religion can spread to all the world when it makes the serious mistake of becoming permeated with some national culture or associated with established racial, social, or economic practices.

The bestowal of the Spirit of Truth was independent of all forms, ceremonies, sacred places, and special behavior by those who received the fullness of its manifestation. When the spirit came upon those assembled in the upper chamber, they were simply sitting there, having just been engaged in silent prayer. The spirit was bestowed in the country as well as in the city. It was not necessary for the apostles to go apart to a lonely place for years of solitary meditation in order to receive the spirit. For all time, Pentecost disassociates the idea of spiritual experience from the notion of especially favorable environments.

Pentecost, with its spiritual endowment, was designed forever to loose the religion of the Master from all dependence upon physical force; the teachers of this new religion are now equipped with spiritual weapons. They are to go out to conquer the world with unfailing forgiveness, matchless good will, and abounding love. They are equipped to overcome evil with good, to vanquish hate by love, to destroy fear with a courageous and living faith in truth. Jesus had already taught his followers that his religion was never passive; always were his disciples to be active and positive in their ministry of mercy and in their manifestations of love. No longer did these believers look upon Yahweh as "the Lord of Hosts." They now regarded the eternal Deity as the "God and Father of the Lord Jesus Christ." They made that progress, at least, even if they did in some measure fail fully to grasp the truth that God is also the spiritual Father of every individual.

Pentecost endowed mortal man with the power to forgive personal injuries, to keep sweet in the midst of the gravest injustice, to remain unmoved in the face of appalling danger, and to challenge the evils of hate and anger by the fearless acts of love and forbearance. Urantia has passed through the ravages of great and destructive wars in its history. All participants in these terrible struggles met with defeat. There was but one victor; there was only one who came out of these embittered struggles with an enhanced reputation — that was Jesus of Nazareth and his gospel of overcoming evil with good. The secret of a better civilization is bound up in the Master's teachings of the brotherhood of man, the good will of love and mutual trust.

Up to Pentecost, religion had revealed only man seeking for God; since Pentecost, man is still searching for God, but there shines out over the world the spectacle of God also seeking for man and sending his spirit to dwell within him when he has found him.

Before the teachings of Jesus which culminated in Pentecost, women had little or no spiritual standing in the tenets of the older religions. After Pentecost, in the brotherhood of the kingdom woman stood before God on an equality with man. Among the one hundred and twenty who received this special visitation of the spirit were many of the women disciples, and they shared these blessings equally with the men believers. No longer can man presume to monopolize the ministry of religious service. The Pharisee might go on thanking God that he was "not born a woman, a leper, or a gentile," but among the followers of Jesus woman has been forever set free from all religious discriminations based on sex. Pentecost obliterated all religious discrimination founded on racial distinction, cultural differences, social caste, or sex prejudice. No wonder these believers in the new religion would cry out, "Where the spirit of the Lord is, there is liberty."

Both the mother and brother of Jesus were present among the one hundred and twenty believers, and as members of this common group of disciples, they also received the outpoured spirit. They received no more of the good gift than did their fellows. No special gift was bestowed upon the members of Jesus' earthly family. Pentecost marked the end of special priesthoods and all belief in sacred families.

Before Pentecost the apostles had given up much for Jesus. They had sacrificed their homes, families, friends, worldly goods, and positions. At Pentecost they gave themselves to God, and the Father and the Son responded by giving themselves to man — sending their spirits to live within men. This experience of losing self and finding the spirit was not one of emotion; it was an act of intelligent self-surrender and unreserved consecration.

Pentecost was the call to spiritual unity among gospel believers. When the spirit descended on the disciples at Jerusalem, the same thing happened in Philadelphia, Alexandria, and at all other places where true believers dwelt. It was literally true that "there was but one heart and soul among the multitude of the believers." The religion of Jesus is the most powerful unifying influence the world has ever known.

Pentecost was designed to lessen the self-assertiveness of individuals, groups, nations, and races. It is this spirit of self-assertiveness which so increases in tension that it periodically breaks loose in destructive wars. Mankind can be unified only by the spiritual approach, and the Spirit of Truth is a world influence which is universal.

The coming of the Spirit of Truth purifies the human heart and leads the recipient to formulate a life purpose single to the will of God and the welfare of men. The material spirit of selfishness has been swallowed up in this new spiritual bestowal of selflessness. Pentecost, then and now, signifies that the Jesus of history has become the divine Son of living experience. The joy of this outpoured spirit, when it is consciously experienced in human life, is a tonic for health, a stimulus for mind, and an unfailing energy for the soul.

Prayer did not bring the spirit on the day of Pentecost, but it did have much to do with determining the capacity of receptivity which characterized the individual believers. Prayer does not move the divine heart to liberality of bestowal, but it does so often dig out larger and deeper channels wherein the divine bestowals may flow to the hearts and souls of those who thus remember to maintain unbroken communion with their Maker through sincere prayer and true worship.

4. BEGINNINGS OF THE CHRISTIAN CHURCH

When Jesus was so suddenly seized by his enemies and so quickly crucified between two thieves, his apostles and disciples were completely demoralized. The thought of the Master, arrested, bound, scourged, and crucified, was too much for even the apostles. They forgot his teachings and his warnings. He might, indeed, have been "a prophet mighty in deed and word before God and all the people," but he could hardly be the Messiah they had hoped would restore the kingdom of Israel.

Then comes the resurrection, with its deliverance from despair and the return of their faith in the Master's divinity. Again and again they see him and talk with him, and he takes them out on Olivet, where he bids them farewell and tells them he is going back to the Father. He has told them to tarry in Jerusalem until they are endowed with power — until the Spirit of Truth shall come. And on the day of Pentecost this new teacher comes, and they go out at once to preach their gospel with new power. They are the bold and courageous followers of a living Lord, not a dead and defeated leader. The Master lives in the hearts of these evangelists; God is not a doctrine in their minds; he has become a living presence in their souls.

"Day by day they continued steadfastly and with one accord in the temple and breaking bread at home. They took their food with gladness and singleness of heart, praising God and having favor with all the people. They were all filled with the spirit, and they spoke the word of God with boldness. And the multitudes of those who believed were of one heart and soul; and not one of them said that aught of the things which he possessed was his own, and they had all things in common."

What has happened to these men whom Jesus had ordained to go forth preaching the gospel of the kingdom, the fatherhood of God and the brotherhood of man? They have a new gospel; they are on fire with a new experience; they are filled with a new spiritual energy. Their message has suddenly shifted to the proclamation of the risen Christ: "Jesus of Nazareth, a man

God approved by mighty works and wonders; him, being delivered up by the determinate counsel and foreknowledge of God, you did crucify and slay. The things which God foreshadowed by the mouth of all the prophets, he thus fulfilled. This Jesus did God raise up. God has made him both Lord and Christ. Being, by the right hand of God, exalted and having received from the Father the promise of the spirit, he has poured forth this which you see and hear. Repent, that your sins may be blotted out; that the Father may send the Christ, who has been appointed for you, even Jesus, whom the heaven must receive until the times of the restoration of all things."

The gospel of the kingdom, the message of Jesus, had been suddenly changed into the gospel of the Lord Jesus Christ. They now proclaimed the facts of his life, death, and resurrection and preached the hope of his speedy return to this world to finish the work he began. Thus the message of the early believers had to do with preaching about the facts of his first coming and with teaching the hope of his second coming, an event which they deemed to be very near at hand.

Christ was about to become the creed of the rapidly forming church. Jesus lives; he died for men; he gave the spirit; he is coming again. Jesus filled all their thoughts and determined all their new concept of God and everything else. They were too much enthused over the new doctrine that "God is the Father of the Lord Jesus" to be concerned with the old message that "God is the loving Father of all men," even of every single individual. True, a marvelous manifestation of brotherly love and unexampled good will did spring up in these early communities of believers. But it was a fellowship of believers in Jesus, not a fellowship of brothers in the family kingdom of the Father in heaven. Their good will arose from the love born of the concept of Jesus' bestowal and not from the recognition of the brotherhood of mortal man. Nevertheless, they were filled with joy, and they lived such new and unique lives that all men were attracted to their teachings about Jesus. They made the great mistake of using the living and illustrative commentary on the gospel of the kingdom for that gospel, but even that represented the greatest religion mankind had ever known.

Unmistakably, a new fellowship was arising in the world. "The multitude who believed continued steadfastly in the apostles' teaching and fellowship, in the breaking of bread, and in prayers." They called each other brother and sister; they greeted one another with a holy kiss; they ministered to the poor.

It was a fellowship of living as well as of worship. They were not communal by decree but by the desire to share their goods with their fellow believers. They confidently expected that Jesus would return to complete the establishment of the Father's kingdom during their generation. This spontaneous sharing of earthly possessions was not a direct feature of Jesus' teaching; it came about because these men and women so sincerely and so confidently believed that he was to return any day to finish his work and to consummate the kingdom. But the final results of this well-meant experiment in thoughtless brotherly love were disastrous and sorrow-breeding. Thousands of earnest believers sold their property and disposed of all their capital goods and other productive assets. With the passing of time, the dwindling resources of Christian "equal-sharing" came to an *end* — but the world did not. Very soon the believers at Antioch were taking up a collection to keep their fellow believers at Jerusalem from starving.

In these days they celebrated the Lord's Supper after the manner of its establishment; that is, they assembled for a social meal of good fellowship and partook of the sacrament at the end of the meal.

At first they baptized in the name of Jesus; it was almost twenty years before they began to baptize in "the name of the Father, the Son, and the Holy Spirit." Baptism was all that was required for admission into the fellowship of believers. They had no organization as yet; it was simply the Jesus brotherhood.

This Jesus sect was growing rapidly, and once more the Sadducees took notice of them. The Pharisees were little bothered about the situation, seeing that none of the teachings in any way interfered with the observance of the Jewish laws. But the Sadducees began to put the leaders of the Jesus sect in jail until they were prevailed upon to accept the counsel of one of the leading rabbis, Gamaliel, who advised them: "Refrain from these men and let them alone, for if this counsel or this work is of men, it will be overthrown; but if it is of God, you will not be able to overthrow them, lest haply you be found even to be fighting against God." They decided to follow Gamaliel's counsel, and there ensued a time of peace and quiet in Jerusalem, during which the new gospel about Jesus spread rapidly.

And so all went well in Jerusalem until the time of the coming of the Greeks in large numbers from Alexandria. Two of the pupils of Rodan arrived in Jerusalem and made many converts from among the Hellenists. Among their early converts were Stephen and Barnabas. These able Greeks did not so much have the Jewish viewpoint, and they did not so well conform to the Jewish mode of worship and other ceremonial practices. And it was the doings of these Greek believers that terminated the peaceful relations between the Jesus brotherhood and the Pharisees and Sadducees. Stephen and his Greek associate began to preach more as Jesus taught, and this brought them into immediate conflict with the Jewish rulers. In one of Stephen's public sermons, when he reached the objectionable part of the discourse, they dispensed with all formalities of trial and proceeded to stone him to death on the spot.

Stephen, the leader of the Greek colony of Jesus' believers in Jerusalem, thus became the first martyr to the new faith and the specific cause for the formal organization of the early Christian church. This new crisis was met by the recognition that believers could no longer go on as a sect within the Jewish faith. They all agreed that they must separate themselves from unbelievers; and within one month from the death of Stephen the church at Jerusalem had been organized under the leadership of Peter, and James the brother of Jesus had been installed as its titular head.

And then broke out the new and relentless persecutions by the Jews, so that the active teachers of the new religion about Jesus, which subsequently at Antioch was called Christianity, went forth to the ends of the empire proclaiming Jesus. In carrying this message, before the time of Paul the leadership was in Greek hands; and these first missionaries, as also the later ones, followed the path of Alexander's march of former days, going by way of Gaza and Tyre to Antioch and then over Asia Minor to Macedonia, then on to Rome and to the uttermost parts of the empire.

PAPER 195
AFTER PENTECOST

THE RESULTS of Peter's preaching on the day of Pentecost were such as to decide the future policies, and to determine the plans, of the majority of the apostles in their efforts to proclaim the gospel of the kingdom. Peter was the real founder of the Christian church; Paul carried the Christian message to the gentiles, and the Greek believers carried it to the whole Roman Empire.

Although the tradition-bound and priest-ridden Hebrews, as a people, refused to accept either Jesus' gospel of the fatherhood of God and the brotherhood of man or Peter's and Paul's proclamation of the resurrection and ascension of Christ (subsequent Christianity), the rest of the Roman Empire was found to be receptive to the evolving Christian teachings. Western civilization was at this time intellectual, war weary, and thoroughly skeptical of all existing religions and universe philosophies. The peoples of the Western world, the beneficiaries of Greek culture, had a revered tradition of a great past. They could contemplate the inheritance of great accomplishments in philosophy, art, literature, and political progress. But with all these achievements they had no soul-satisfying religion. Their spiritual longings remained unsatisfied.

Upon such a stage of human society the teachings of Jesus, embraced in the Christian message, were suddenly thrust. A new order of living was thus presented to the hungry hearts of these Western peoples. This situation meant immediate conflict between the older religious practices and the new Christianized version of Jesus' message to the world. Such a conflict must result in either decided victory for the new or for the old or in some degree of *compromise*. History shows that the struggle ended in compromise. Christianity presumed to embrace too much for any one people to assimilate in one or two generations. It was not a simple spiritual appeal, such as Jesus had presented to the souls of men; it early struck a decided attitude on religious rituals, education, magic, medicine, art, literature, law, government, morals, sex regulation, polygamy, and, in limited degree, even slavery. Christianity came not merely as a new religion — something all the Roman Empire and all the Orient were waiting for — but as a *new order of human society*. And as such a pretension it quickly precipitated the social-moral clash of the ages. The ideals of Jesus, as they were reinterpreted by Greek philosophy and socialized in Christianity, now boldly challenged the traditions of the human race embodied in the ethics, morality, and religions of Western civilization.

At first, Christianity won as converts only the lower social and economic strata. But by the beginning of the second century the very best of Greco-Roman culture was increasingly turning to this new order of Christian belief, this new concept of the purpose of living and the goal of existence.

How did this new message of Jewish origin, which had almost failed in the land of its birth, so quickly and effectively capture the very best minds of the Roman Empire? The triumph of Christianity over the philosophic religions and the mystery cults was due to:

1. Organization. Paul was a great organizer and his successors kept up the pace he set.

2. Christianity was thoroughly Hellenized. It embraced the best in Greek philosophy as well as the cream of Hebrew theology.

3. But best of all, it contained a new and great *ideal*, the echo of the life bestowal of Jesus and the reflection of his message of salvation for all mankind.

4. The Christian leaders were willing to make such compromises with Mithraism that the better half of its adherents were won over to the Antioch cult.

5. Likewise did the next and later generations of Christian leaders make such further compromises with paganism that even the Roman emperor Constantine was won to the new religion.

But the Christians made a shrewd bargain with the pagans in that they adopted the ritualistic pageantry of the pagan while compelling the pagan to accept the Hellenized version of Pauline Christianity. They made a better bargain with the pagans than they did with the Mithraic cult, but even in that earlier compromise they came off more than conquerors in that they succeeded in eliminating the gross immoralities and also numerous other reprehensible practices of the Persian mystery.

Wisely or unwisely, these early leaders of Christianity deliberately compromised the *ideals* of Jesus in an effort to save and further many of his *ideas*. And they were eminently successful. But mistake not! these compromised ideals of the Master are still latent in his gospel, and they will eventually assert their full power upon the world.

By this paganization of Christianity the old order won many minor victories of a ritualistic nature, but the Christians gained the ascendancy in that:

1. A new and enormously higher note in human morals was struck.

2. A new and greatly enlarged concept of God was given to the world.

3. The hope of immortality became a part of the assurance of a recognized religion.

4. Jesus of Nazareth was given to man's hungry soul.

Many of the great truths taught by Jesus were almost lost in these early compromises, but they yet slumber in this religion of paganized Christianity, which was in turn the Pauline version of the life and teachings of the Son of Man. And Christianity, even before it was paganized, was first thoroughly

Hellenized. Christianity owes much, very much, to the Greeks. It was a Greek, from Egypt, who so bravely stood up at Nicaea and so fearlessly challenged this assembly that it dared not so obscure the concept of the nature of Jesus that the real truth of his bestowal might have been in danger of being lost to the world. This Greek's name was Athanasius, and but for the eloquence and the logic of this believer, the persuasions of Arius would have triumphed.

1. INFLUENCE OF THE GREEKS

The Hellenization of Christianity started in earnest on that eventful day when the Apostle Paul stood before the council of the Areopagus in Athens and told the Athenians about "the Unknown God." There, under the shadow of the Acropolis, this Roman citizen proclaimed to these Greeks his version of the new religion which had taken origin in the Jewish land of Galilee. And there was something strangely alike in Greek philosophy and many of the teachings of Jesus. They had a common goal — both aimed at the *emergence of the individual.* The Greek, at social and political emergence; Jesus, at moral and spiritual emergence. The Greek taught intellectual liberalism leading to political freedom; Jesus taught spiritual liberalism leading to religious liberty. These two ideas put together constituted a new and mighty charter for human freedom; they presaged man's social, political, and spiritual liberty.

Christianity came into existence and triumphed over all contending religions primarily because of two things:

1. The Greek mind was willing to borrow new and good ideas even from the Jews.

2. Paul and his successors were willing but shrewd and sagacious compromisers; they were keen theologic traders.

At the time Paul stood up in Athens preaching "Christ and Him Crucified," the Greeks were spiritually hungry; they were inquiring, interested, and actually looking for spiritual truth. Never forget that at first the Romans fought Christianity, while the Greeks embraced it, and that it was the Greeks who literally forced the Romans subsequently to accept this new religion, as then modified, as a part of Greek culture.

The Greek revered beauty, the Jew holiness, but both peoples loved truth. For centuries the Greek had seriously thought and earnestly debated about all human problems — social, economic, political, and philosophic — except religion. Few Greeks had paid much attention to religion; they did not take even their own religion very seriously. For centuries the Jews had neglected these other fields of thought while they devoted their minds to religion. They took their religion very seriously, too seriously. As illuminated by the content of Jesus' message, the united product of the centuries of the thought of these two peoples now became the driving power of a new order of human society and, to a certain extent, of a new order of human religious belief and practice.

The influence of Greek culture had already penetrated the lands of the western Mediterranean when Alexander spread Hellenistic civilization over the near-Eastern world. The Greeks did very well with their religion and their politics as long as they lived in small city-states, but when the Macedonian king dared to expand Greece into an empire, stretching from the Adriatic to the Indus, trouble began. The art and philosophy of Greece were fully equal to the task of imperial expansion, but not so with Greek political administration or religion. After the city-states of Greece had expanded into empire, their rather parochial gods seemed a bit insignificant. The Greeks were really searching for *one God*, a greater and better God, when the Christianized version of the older Jewish religion came to them.

The Hellenistic Empire, as such, could not endure. Its cultural sway continued on, but it endured only after securing from the West the Roman political genius for empire administration and after obtaining from the East a religion whose one God possessed empire dignity.

In the first century after Christ, Hellenistic culture had already attained its highest levels; its retrogression had begun; learning was advancing but genius was declining. It was at this very time that the ideas and ideals of Jesus, which were partially embodied in Christianity, became a part of the salvage of Greek culture and learning.

Alexander had charged on the East with the cultural gift of the civilization of Greece; Paul assaulted the West with the Christian version of the gospel of Jesus. And wherever the Greek culture prevailed throughout the West, there Hellenized Christianity took root.

The Eastern version of the message of Jesus, notwithstanding that it remained more true to his teachings, continued to follow the uncompromising attitude of Abner. It never progressed as did the Hellenized version and was eventually lost in the Islamic movement.

2. THE ROMAN INFLUENCE

The Romans bodily took over Greek culture, putting representative government in the place of government by lot. And presently this change favored Christianity in that Rome brought into the whole Western world a new tolerance for strange languages, peoples, and even religions.

Much of the early persecution of Christians in Rome was due solely to their unfortunate use of the term "kingdom" in their preaching. The Romans were tolerant of any and all religions but very resentful of anything that savored of political rivalry. And so, when these early persecutions, due so largely to misunderstanding, died out, the field for religious propaganda was wide open. The Roman was interested in political administration; he cared little for either art or religion, but he was unusually tolerant of both.

Oriental law was stern and arbitrary; Greek law was fluid and artistic; Roman law was dignified and respect-breeding. Roman education bred an unheard-of and stolid loyalty. The early Romans were politically devoted and sublimely consecrated individuals. They were honest, zealous, and dedicated to their ideals, but without a religion worthy of the name. Small wonder that their Greek teachers were able to persuade them to accept Paul's Christianity.

And these Romans were a great people. They could govern the Occident because they did govern themselves. Such unparalleled honesty, devotion, and stalwart self-control was ideal soil for the reception and growth of Christianity.

It was easy for these Greco-Romans to become just as spiritually devoted to an institutional church as they were politically devoted to the state. The

Romans fought the church only when they feared it as a competitor of the state. Rome, having little national philosophy or native culture, took over Greek culture for its own and boldly adopted Christ as its moral philosophy. Christianity became the moral culture of Rome but hardly its religion in the sense of being the individual experience in spiritual growth of those who embraced the new religion in such a wholesale manner. True, indeed, many individuals did penetrate beneath the surface of all this state religion and found for the nourishment of their souls the real values of the hidden meanings held within the latent truths of Hellenized and paganized Christianity.

The Stoic and his sturdy appeal to "nature and conscience" had only the better prepared all Rome to receive Christ, at least in an intellectual sense. The Roman was by nature and training a lawyer; he revered even the laws of nature. And now, in Christianity, he discerned in the laws of nature the laws of God. A people that could produce Cicero and Vergil were ripe for Paul's Hellenized Christianity.

And so did these Romanized Greeks force both Jews and Christians to philosophize their religion, to co-ordinate its ideas and systematize its ideals, to adapt religious practices to the existing current of life. And all this was enormously helped by translation of the Hebrew scriptures into Greek and by the later recording of the New Testament in the Greek tongue.

The Greeks, in contrast with the Jews and many other peoples, had long provisionally believed in immortality, some sort of survival after death, and since this was the very heart of Jesus' teaching, it was certain that Christianity would make a strong appeal to them.

A succession of Greek-cultural and Roman-political victories had consolidated the Mediterranean lands into one empire, with one language and one culture, and had made the Western world ready for one God. Judaism provided this God, but Judaism was not acceptable as a religion to these Romanized Greeks. Philo helped some to mitigate their objections, but Christianity revealed to them an even better concept of one God, and they embraced it readily.

3. UNDER THE ROMAN EMPIRE

After the consolidation of Roman political rule and after the dissemination of Christianity, the Christians found themselves with one God, a great religious concept, but without empire. The Greco-Romans found themselves with a great empire but without a God to serve as the suitable religious concept for empire worship and spiritual unification. The Christians accepted the empire; the empire adopted Christianity. The Roman provided a unity of political rule; the Greek, a unity of culture and learning; Christianity, a unity of religious thought and practice.

Rome overcame the tradition of nationalism by imperial universalism and for the first time in history made it possible for different races and nations at least nominally to accept one religion.

Christianity came into favor in Rome at a time when there was great contention between the vigorous teachings of the Stoics and the salvation promises of the mystery cults. Christianity came with refreshing comfort and liberating power to a spiritually hungry people whose language had no word for "unselfishness."

That which gave greatest power to Christianity was the way its believers lived lives of service and even the way they died for their faith during the earlier times of drastic persecution.

The teaching regarding Christ's love for children soon put an end to the widespread practice of exposing children to death when they were not wanted, particularly girl babies.

The early plan of Christian worship was largely taken over from the Jewish synagogue, modified by the Mithraic ritual; later on, much pagan pageantry was added. The backbone of the early Christian church consisted of Christianized Greek proselytes to Judaism.

The second century after Christ was the best time in all the world's history for a good religion to make progress in the Western world. During the first century Christianity had prepared itself, by struggle and compromise, to take root and rapidly spread. Christianity adopted the emperor; later, he adopted Christianity. This was a great age for the spread of a new religion. There was religious liberty; travel was universal and thought was untrammeled.

The spiritual impetus of nominally accepting Hellenized Christianity came to Rome too late to prevent the well-started moral decline or to compensate for the already well-established and increasing political deterioration. This new religion was a cultural necessity for imperial Rome, and it is exceedingly unfortunate that it did not become a means of spiritual salvation in a larger sense.

Even a good religion could not save a great empire from the sure results of lack of individual participation in the affairs of government, from overmuch paternalism, overtaxation and gross collection abuses, unbalanced trade with the Levant which drained away the gold, amusement madness, Roman standardization, the degradation of woman, slavery, physical plagues, and a state church which became institutionalized nearly to the point of spiritual barrenness.

Conditions, however, were not so bad at Alexandria. The early schools continued to hold much of Jesus' teachings free from compromise. Poutaenus taught Clement and then went on to follow Nathaniel in proclaiming Christ in India. While some of the ideals of Jesus were sacrificed in the building of Christianity, it should in all fairness be recorded that, by the end of the second century, practically all the great minds of the Greco-Roman world had become Christian. The triumph was approaching completion.

And this Roman Empire lasted sufficiently long to insure the survival of Christianity even after the empire collapsed. But we have often conjectured what would have happened in Rome and in the world if it had been the gospel of the kingdom which had been accepted in the place of Greek Christianity.

4. THE EUROPEAN DARK AGES

The church, being an adjunct to society and the ally of politics, was doomed to share in the intellectual and spiritual decline of the so-called

European "dark ages." During this time, religion became more and more monasticized, asceticized, and legalized. In a spiritual sense, Christianity was hibernating. Throughout this period there existed, alongside this slumbering and secularized religion, a continuous stream of mysticism, a fantastic spiritual experience bordering on unreality and philosophically akin to pantheism.

During these dark and despairing centuries, religion became virtually secondhanded again. The individual was almost lost before the overshadowing authority, tradition, and dictation of the church. A new spiritual menace arose in the creation of a galaxy of "saints" who were assumed to have special influence at the divine courts, and who, therefore, if effectively appealed to, would be able to intercede in man's behalf before the Gods.

But Christianity was sufficiently socialized and paganized that, while it was impotent to stay the oncoming dark ages, it was the better prepared to survive this long period of moral darkness and spiritual stagnation. And it did persist on through the long night of Western civilization and was still functioning as a moral influence in the world when the renaissance dawned. The rehabilitation of Christianity, following the passing of the dark ages, resulted in bringing into existence numerous sects of the Christian teachings, beliefs suited to special intellectual, emotional, and spiritual types of human personality. And many of these special Christian groups, or religious families, still persist at the time of the making of this presentation.

Christianity exhibits a history of having originated out of the unintended transformation of the religion of Jesus into a religion about Jesus. It further presents the history of having experienced Hellenization, paganization, secularization, institutionalization, intellectual deterioration, spiritual decadence, moral hibernation, threatened extinction, later rejuvenation, fragmentation, and more recent relative rehabilitation. Such a pedigree is indicative of inherent vitality and the possession of vast recuperative resources. And this same Christianity is now present in the civilized world of Occidental peoples and stands face to face with a struggle for existence which is even more ominous than those eventful crises which have characterized its past battles for dominance.

Religion is now confronted by the challenge of a new age of scientific minds and materialistic tendencies. In this gigantic struggle between the secular and the spiritual, the religion of Jesus will eventually triumph.

5. THE MODERN PROBLEM

Modern civilization has brought new problems for Christianity and all other religions to solve. The higher a civilization climbs, the more necessitous becomes the duty to "seek first the realities of heaven" in all of man's efforts to stabilize society and facilitate the solution of its material problems.

Truth often becomes confusing and even misleading when it is dismembered, segregated, isolated, and too much analyzed. Living truth teaches the truth seeker aright only when it is embraced in wholeness and as a living spiritual reality, not as a fact of material science or an inspiration of intervening art.

Religion is the revelation to man of his divine and eternal destiny. Religion is a purely personal and spiritual experience and must forever be distinguished from man's other high forms of thought, such as:

1. Man's logical attitude toward the things of material reality.

2. Man's aesthetic appreciation of beauty contrasted with ugliness.

3. Man's ethical recognition of social obligations and political duty.

4. Even man's sense of human morality is not, in and of itself, religious.

Religion is designed to find those values in the universe which call forth faith, trust, and assurance; religion culminates in worship. Religion discovers for the soul those supreme values which are in contrast with the relative values discovered by the mind. Such superhuman insight can be had only through genuine religious experience.

A lasting social system without a morality predicated on spiritual realities can no more be maintained than could the solar system without gravity.

Do not try to satisfy the curiosity or gratify all the latent adventure surging within the soul in one short life in the flesh. Be patient! be not tempted to indulge in a lawless plunge into cheap and sordid adventure. Harness your energies and bridle your passions; be calm while you await the majestic unfolding of an endless career of progressive adventure and thrilling discovery.

In confusion over man's origin, do not lose sight of his eternal destiny. Forget not that Jesus loved even little children, and that he forever made clear the great worth of human personality.

As you view the world, remember that the patches of evil which you see are shown against a background of ultimate good. You do not view merely patches of good which show up miserably against a background of evil.

When there is so much good truth to publish and proclaim, why should men dwell so much upon the evil in the world just because it appears to be a fact? The beauties of the spiritual values of truth are more pleasurable and uplifting than is the phenomenon of evil.

In religion, Jesus advocated and followed the method of experience, even as modern science pursues the technique of experiment. We find God through the leadings of spiritual insight, but we approach this insight of the soul through the love of the beautiful, the pursuit of truth, loyalty to duty, and the worship of divine goodness. But of all these values, love is the true guide to real insight.

6. MATERIALISM

Scientists have unintentionally precipitated mankind into a materialistic panic; they have started an unthinking run on the moral bank of the ages, but this bank of human experience has vast spiritual resources; it can stand the demands being made upon it. Only unthinking men become panicky about the spiritual assets of the human race. When the materialistic-secular panic is over, the religion of Jesus will not be found bankrupt. The spiritual bank of the kingdom of heaven will be paying out faith, hope, and moral security to all who draw upon it "in His name."

No matter what the apparent conflict between materialism and the teachings of Jesus may be, you can rest assured that, in the ages to come, the teachings of the Master will fully triumph. In reality, true religion cannot become involved in any controversy with science; it is in no way concerned with material things. Religion is simply indifferent to, but sympathetic with, science, while it supremely concerns itself with the *scientist.*

The pursuit of mere knowledge, without the attendant interpretation of wisdom and the spiritual insight of religious experience, eventually leads to pessimism and human despair. A little knowledge is truly disconcerting.

At the time of this writing the worst of the materialistic age is over; the day of a better understanding is already beginning to dawn. The higher minds of the scientific world are no longer wholly materialistic in their philosophy, but the rank and file of the people still lean in that direction as a result of former teachings. But this age of physical realism is only a passing episode in man's life on earth. Modern science has left true religion — the teachings of Jesus as translated in the lives of his believers — untouched. All science has done is to destroy the childlike illusions of the misinterpretations of life.

Science is a quantitative experience, religion a qualitative experience, as regards man's life on earth. Science deals with phenomena; religion, with origins, values, and goals. To assign *causes* as an explanation of physical phenomena is to confess ignorance of ultimates and in the end only leads the scientist straight back to the first great cause — the Universal Father of Paradise.

The violent swing from an age of miracles to an age of machines has proved altogether upsetting to man. The cleverness and dexterity of the false philosophies of mechanism belie their very mechanistic contentions. The fatalistic agility of the mind of a materialist forever disproves his assertions that the universe is a blind and purposeless energy phenomenon.

The mechanistic naturalism of some supposedly educated men and the thoughtless secularism of the man in the street are both exclusively concerned with *things*; they are barren of all real values, sanctions, and satisfactions of a spiritual nature, as well as being devoid of faith, hope, and eternal assurances. One of the great troubles with modern life is that man thinks he is too busy to find time for spiritual meditation and religious devotion.

Materialism reduces man to a soulless automaton and constitutes him merely an arithmetical symbol finding a helpless place in the mathematical formula of an unromantic and mechanistic universe. But whence comes all this vast universe of mathematics without a Master Mathematician? Science may expatiate on the conservation of matter, but religion validates the conservation of men's souls — it concerns their experience with spiritual realities and eternal values.

The materialistic sociologist of today surveys a community, makes a report thereon, and leaves the people as he found them. Two thousand years ago, unlearned Galileans surveyed Jesus giving his life as a spiritual contribution to man's inner experience and then went out and turned the whole Roman Empire upside down.

But religious leaders are making a great mistake when they try to call modern man to spiritual battle with the trumpet blasts of the Middle Ages. Religion must provide itself with new and up-to-date slogans. Neither democracy nor any other political panacea will take the place of spiritual progress. False religions may represent an evasion of reality, but Jesus in his gospel introduced mortal man to the very entrance upon an eternal reality of spiritual progression.

To say that mind "emerged" from matter explains nothing. If the universe were merely a mechanism and mind were unapart from matter, we would never have two differing interpretations of any observed phenomenon. The concepts of truth, beauty, and goodness are not inherent in either physics or chemistry. A machine cannot *know*, much less know truth, hunger for righteousness, and cherish goodness.

Science may be physical, but the mind of the truth-discerning scientist is at once supermaterial. Matter knows not truth, neither can it love mercy nor delight in spiritual realities. Moral convictions based on spiritual enlightenment and rooted in human experience are just as real and certain as mathematical deductions based on physical observations, but on another and higher level.

If men were only machines, they would react more or less uniformly to a material universe. Individuality, much less personality, would be nonexistent.

The fact of the absolute mechanism of Paradise at the center of the universe of universes, in the presence of the unqualified volition of the

Second Source and Center, makes forever certain that determiners are not the exclusive law of the cosmos. Materialism is there, but it is not exclusive; mechanism is there, but it is not unqualified; determinism is there, but it is not alone.

The finite universe of matter would eventually become uniform and deterministic but for the combined presence of mind and spirit. The influence of the cosmic mind constantly injects spontaneity into even the material worlds.

Freedom or initiative in any realm of existence is directly proportional to the degree of spiritual influence and cosmic-mind control; that is, in human experience, the degree of the actuality of doing "the Father's will." And so, when you once start out to find God, that is the conclusive proof that God has already found you.

The sincere pursuit of goodness, beauty, and truth leads to God. And every scientific discovery demonstrates the existence of both freedom and uniformity in the universe. The discoverer was free to make the discovery. The thing discovered is real and apparently uniform, or else it could not have become known as a *thing*.

7. THE VULNERABILITY OF MATERIALISM

How foolish it is for material-minded man to allow such vulnerable theories as those of a mechanistic universe to deprive him of the vast spiritual resources of the personal experience of true religion. Facts never quarrel with real spiritual faith; theories may. Better that science should be devoted to the destruction of superstition rather than attempting the overthrow of religious faith — human belief in spiritual realities and divine values.

Science should do for man materially what religion does for him spiritually: extend the horizon of life and enlarge his personality. True science can have no lasting quarrel with true religion. The "scientific method" is merely an intellectual yardstick wherewith to measure material adventures and physical achievements. But being material and wholly intellectual, it is utterly useless in the evaluation of spiritual realities and religious experiences.

The inconsistency of the modern mechanist is: If this were merely a material universe and man only a machine, such a man would be wholly unable to recognize himself as such a machine, and likewise would such a machine-man be wholly unconscious of the fact of the existence of such a material universe. The materialistic dismay and despair of a mechanistic science has failed to recognize the fact of the spirit-indwelt mind of the scientist whose very supermaterial insight formulates these mistaken and self-contradictory *concepts* of a materialistic universe.

Paradise values of eternity and infinity, of truth, beauty, and goodness, are concealed within the facts of the phenomena of the universes of time and space. But it requires the eye of faith in a spirit-born mortal to detect and discern these spiritual values.

The realities and values of spiritual progress are not a "psychologic projection" — a mere glorified daydream of the material mind. Such things are the spiritual forecasts of the indwelling Adjuster, the spirit of God living in the mind of man. And let not your dabblings with the faintly glimpsed findings of "relativity" disturb your concepts of the eternity and infinity of God. And in all your solicitation concerning the necessity for *self-expression* do not make the mistake of failing to provide for *Adjuster-expression*, the manifestation of your real and better self.

If this were only a material universe, material man would never be able to arrive at the concept of the mechanistic character of such an exclusively material existence. This very *mechanistic concept* of the universe is in itself a nonmaterial phenomenon of mind, and all mind is of nonmaterial origin, no matter how thoroughly it may appear to be materially conditioned and mechanistically controlled.

The partially evolved mental mechanism of mortal man is not overendowed with consistency and wisdom. Man's conceit often outruns his reason and eludes his logic.

The very pessimism of the most pessimistic materialist is, in and of itself, sufficient proof that the universe of the pessimist is not wholly material. Both optimism and pessimism are concept reactions in a mind conscious of *values* as well as of *facts*. If the universe were truly what the materialist regards it to be, man as a human machine would then be devoid of all conscious recognition of that very *fact*. Without the consciousness of the concept of *values* within the spirit-born mind, the fact of universe materialism and the mechanistic phenomena of universe operation would be wholly unrecognized by man. One machine cannot be conscious of the nature or value of another machine.

A mechanistic philosophy of life and the universe cannot be scientific because science recognizes and deals only with materials and facts. Philosophy is inevitably superscientific. Man is a material fact of nature, but his *life* is a phenomenon which transcends the material levels of nature in that it exhibits the control attributes of mind and the creative qualities of spirit.

The sincere effort of man to become a mechanist represents the tragic phenomenon of that man's futile effort to commit intellectual and moral suicide. But he cannot do it.

If the universe were only material and man only a machine, there would be no science to embolden the scientist to postulate this mechanization of the universe. Machines cannot measure, classify, nor evaluate themselves. Such a scientific piece of work could be executed only by some entity of supermachine status.

If universe reality is only one vast machine, then man must be outside of the universe and apart from it in order to recognize such a *fact* and become conscious of the *insight* of such an *evaluation.*

If man is only a machine, by what technique does this man come to *believe* or claim to *know* that he is only a machine? The experience of self-conscious evaluation of one's self is never an attribute of a mere machine. A self-conscious and avowed mechanist is the best possible answer to mechanism. If materialism were a fact, there could be no self-conscious mechanist. It is also true that one must first be a moral person before one can perform immoral acts.

The very claim of materialism implies a supermaterial consciousness of the mind which presumes to assert such dogmas. A mechanism might deteriorate, but it could never progress. Machines do not think, create, dream, aspire, idealize, hunger for truth, or thirst for righteousness. They do not motivate their lives with the passion to serve other machines and to choose as their goal of eternal progression the sublime task of finding God and striving to be like him. Machines are never intellectual, emotional, aesthetic, ethical, moral, or spiritual.

Art proves that man is not mechanistic, but it does not prove that he is spiritually immortal. Art is mortal morontia, the intervening field between man, the material, and man, the spiritual. Poetry is an effort to escape from material realities to spiritual values.

In a high civilization, art humanizes science, while in turn it is spiritualized by true religion — insight into spiritual and eternal values. Art represents the human and time-space evaluation of reality. Religion *is* the divine embrace of cosmic values and connotes eternal progression in spiritual ascension and expansion. The art of time is dangerous only when it becomes blind to the spirit standards of the divine patterns which eternity reflects as the reality shadows of time. True art is the effective manipulation of the material things of life; religion is the ennobling transformation of the material facts of life, and it never ceases in its spiritual evaluation of art.

How foolish to presume that an automaton could conceive a philosophy of automatism, and how ridiculous that it should presume to form such a concept of other and fellow automatons!

Any scientific interpretation of the material universe is valueless unless it provides due recognition for the *scientist*. No appreciation of art is genuine unless it accords recognition to the *artist*. No evaluation of morals is worth while unless it includes the *moralist*. No recognition of philosophy is edifying if it ignores the *philosopher*, and religion cannot exist without the real experience of the *religionist* who, in and through this very experience, is seeking to find God and to know him. Likewise is the universe of universes without significance apart from the I AM, the infinite God who made it and unceasingly manages it.

Mechanists — humanists — tend to drift with the material currents. Idealists and spiritists *dare* to use their oars with intelligence and vigor in order to modify the apparently purely material course of the energy streams.

Science lives by the mathematics of the mind; music expresses the tempo of the emotions. Religion is the spiritual rhythm of the soul in time-space harmony with the higher and eternal melody measurements of Infinity. Religious experience is something in human life which is truly supermathematical.

In language, an alphabet represents the mechanism of materialism, while the words expressive of the meaning of a thousand thoughts, grand ideas, and noble ideals — of love and hate, of cowardice and courage — represent the performances of mind within the scope defined by both material and spiritual law, directed by the assertion of the will of personality, and limited by the inherent situational endowment.

The universe is not like the laws, mechanisms, and the uniformities which the scientist discovers, and which he comes to regard as science, but rather like the curious, thinking, choosing, creative, combining, and discriminating *scientist* who thus observes universe phenomena and classifies the mathematical facts inherent in the mechanistic phases of the material side of creation. Neither is the universe like the art of the artist, but rather like the striving, dreaming, aspiring, and advancing *artist* who seeks to transcend the world of material things in an effort to achieve a spiritual goal.

The scientist, not science, perceives the reality of an evolving and advancing universe of energy and matter. The artist, not art, demonstrates the existence of the transient morontia world intervening between material existence and spiritual liberty. The religionist, not religion, proves the existence of the spirit realities and divine values which are to be encountered in the progress of eternity.

8. SECULAR TOTALITARIANISM

But even after materialism and mechanism have been more or less vanquished, the devastating influence of modern secularism will still blight the spiritual experience of millions of unsuspecting souls.

Modern secularism has been fostered by two world-wide influences. The father of secularism was the narrow-minded and godless attitude of nineteenth- and twentieth-century so-called science — atheistic science. The mother of modern secularism was the totalitarian medieval Christian church. Secularism had its inception as a rising protest against the almost complete domination of Western civilization by the institutionalized Christian church.

At the time of this revelation, the prevailing intellectual and philosophical climate of both European and American life is decidedly secular — humanistic. For three hundred years Western thinking has been progressively secularized. Religion has become more and more a nominal influence, largely a ritualistic exercise. The majority of professed Christians of Western civilization are unwittingly actual secularists.

It required a great power, a mighty influence, to free the thinking and living of the Western peoples from the withering grasp of a totalitarian ecclesiastical domination. Secularism did break the bonds of church control, and now in turn it threatens to establish a new and godless type of mastery over the hearts and minds of modern man. The tyrannical and dictatorial political state is the direct offspring of scientific materialism and philosophic secularism. Secularism no sooner frees man from the domination of the institutionalized church than it sells him into slavish bondage to the totalitarian state. Secularism frees man from ecclesiastical slavery only to betray him into the tyranny of political and economic slavery.

Materialism denies God, secularism simply ignores him; at least that was the earlier attitude. More recently, secularism has assumed a more militant attitude, assuming to take the place of the religion whose totalitarian bondage it onetime resisted. Secularism tends to affirm that man does not need God. But beware! this godless philosophy of human society will lead only to unrest, animosity, unhappiness, war, and world-wide disaster.

Secularism can never bring peace to mankind. Nothing can take the place of God in human society. But mark you well! do not be quick to surrender the beneficent gains of the secular revolt from ecclesiastical totalitarianism. Western civilization today enjoys many liberties and satisfactions as a result of the secular revolt. The great mistake of secularism was this: In revolting against the almost total control of life by religious authority, and after attaining the liberation from such ecclesiastical tyranny, the secularists went on to institute a revolt against God himself, sometimes tacitly and sometimes openly.

To the secularistic revolt you owe the amazing creativity of American industrialism and the unprecedented material progress of Western civilization. And because the secularistic revolt went too far and lost sight of God and *true* religion, there also followed the unlooked-for harvest of world wars and international unsettledness.

It is not necessary to sacrifice faith in God in order to enjoy the blessings of the modern secularistic revolt: tolerance, social service, democratic government, and civil liberties. It was not necessary for the secularists to antagonize true religion in order to promote science and to advance education.

But secularism is not the sole parent of all these recent gains in the enlargement of living. Behind the gains of today are not only science and secularism but also the unrecognized and unacknowledged spiritual workings of the life and teaching of Jesus of Nazareth.

Without God, without religion, scientific secularism can never co-ordinate its forces, harmonize its divergent and rivalrous interests and nationalisms. This secularistic human society, notwithstanding its unparalleled materialistic achievement, is slowly disintegrating. The chief cohesive force resisting this disintegration of antagonism is nationalism. And nationalism is the chief barrier to world peace.

The inherent weakness of secularism is that it discards ethics and religion for politics and power. You simply cannot establish the brotherhood of men while ignoring or denying the fatherhood of God.

Secular social and political optimism is an illusion. Without God, neither freedom and liberty, nor property and wealth will lead to peace.

The complete secularization of science, education, industry, and society can lead only to disaster. During the first third of the twentieth century Urantians killed more human beings than were killed during the whole of the Christian dispensation up to that time. And this is only the beginning of the dire harvest of materialism and secularism; still more terrible destruction may yet come.

9. CHRISTIANITY'S PROBLEM

Do not overlook the value of your spiritual heritage, the river of truth running down through the centuries, even to the barren times of a materialistic and secular age. In all your worthy efforts to rid yourselves of the superstitious creeds of past ages, make sure that you hold fast the eternal truth. But be patient! when the present superstition revolt is over, the truths of Jesus' gospel will persist gloriously to illuminate a new and better way.

But paganized and socialized Christianity stands in need of new contact with the uncompromised teachings of Jesus; it languishes for lack of a new vision of the Master's life on earth. A new and fuller revelation of the religion of Jesus is destined to conquer an empire of materialistic secularism and to overthrow a world sway of mechanistic naturalism. Urantia is now quivering on the very brink of one of its most amazing and enthralling epochs of social readjustment, moral quickening, and spiritual enlightenment.

The teachings of Jesus, even though greatly modified, survived the mystery cults of their birthtime, the ignorance and superstition of the dark ages, and are even now slowly triumphing over the materialism, mechanism, and secularism of today. And such times of great testing and threatened defeat are always times of great revelation.

Religion does need new leaders, spiritual men and women who will dare to depend on Jesus, his incomparable teachings, the Spirit of Truth, and the leadings of their own thought adjusters. If Christianity persists in neglecting its spiritual mission while it continues to busy itself with social and material problems, the spiritual renaissance must await the coming of these new teachers of Jesus' religion who will be exclusively devoted to the spiritual regeneration of men. And then will these spirit-born souls quickly supply the leadership and inspiration requisite for the social, moral, economic, and political reorganization of the world.

The modern age will refuse to accept a religion which is inconsistent with facts and out of harmony with its highest conceptions of truth, beauty, and goodness. The hour is striking for a rediscovery of the true and original foundations of present-day distorted and compromised Christianity — the real life and teachings of Jesus.

Primitive man lived a life of superstitious bondage to religious fear. Modern, civilized men dread the thought of falling under the dominance of strong religious convictions. Thinking man has always feared to be *held* by a religion. When a strong and moving religion threatens to dominate him, he invariably tries to rationalize, traditionalize, and institutionalize it, thereby hoping to gain control of it. By such procedure, even a revealed religion becomes man-made and man-dominated. Modern men and women of intelligence evade the religion of Jesus because of their fears of what it will do *to* them — and *with* them. And all such fears are well founded. The religion of Jesus does, indeed, dominate and transform its believers, demanding that men dedicate their lives to seeking for a knowledge of the will of the Father in heaven and requiring that the energies of living be consecrated to the unselfish service of the brotherhood of man.

Selfish men and women simply will not pay such a price for even the greatest spiritual treasure ever offered mortal man. Only when man has become sufficiently disillusioned by the sorrowful disappointments attendant upon the foolish and deceptive pursuits of selfishness, and subsequent to the discovery of the barrenness of formalized religion, will he be disposed to turn wholeheartedly to the gospel of the kingdom, the religion of Jesus of Nazareth.

The world needs more firsthand religion. Even Christianity — the best of the religions — is not only a religion *about* Jesus, but it is so largely one which men experience secondhand. They take their religion wholly as handed down by their accepted religious teachers. What an awakening the world would experience if it could only see Jesus as he really lived on earth and know, firsthand, his life-giving teachings! Descriptive words of things beautiful cannot thrill like the sight thereof, neither can creedal words inspire men's souls like the experience of knowing the presence of God. But expectant faith will ever keep the hope-door of man's soul open for the entrance of the eternal spiritual realities of the divine values of the worlds beyond.

Christianity has dared to lower its ideals before the challenge of human greed, war-madness, and the lust for power; but the religion of Jesus stands as the unsullied and transcendent spiritual summons, calling to the best there is in man to rise above all these legacies of animal evolution and, by grace, attain the moral heights of true human destiny.

Christianity is threatened by slow death from formalism, overorganization, intellectualism, and other nonspiritual trends. The modern Christian church is not such a brotherhood of dynamic believers as Jesus commissioned continuously to effect the spiritual transformation of successive generations of mankind.

10. THE FUTURE

Christianity has indeed done a great service for this world, but what is now most needed is Jesus. The world needs to see Jesus living again on earth in the experience of spirit-born mortals who effectively reveal the Master to all men. It is futile to talk about a revival of primitive Christianity; you must go forward from where you find yourselves. Modern culture must become spiritually baptized with a new revelation of Jesus' life and illuminated with a new understanding of his gospel of eternal salvation. And when Jesus becomes thus lifted up, he will draw all men to himself. Jesus' disciples should be more than conquerors, even overflowing sources of inspiration and enhanced living to all men. Religion is only an exalted humanism until it is made divine by the discovery of the reality of the presence of God in personal experience.

The beauty and sublimity, the humanity and divinity, the simplicity and uniqueness, of Jesus' life on earth present such a striking and appealing picture of man-saving and God-revealing that the theologians and philosophers of all time should be effectively restrained from daring to form creeds or create theological systems of spiritual bondage out of such a transcendental bestowal of God in the form of man. In Jesus the universe produced a mortal man in whom the spirit of love triumphed over the material handicaps of time and overcame the fact of physical origin.

Ever bear in mind — God and men need each other. They are mutually necessary to the full and final attainment of eternal personality experience in the divine destiny of universe finality.

"The kingdom of God is within you" was probably the greatest pronouncement Jesus ever made, next to the declaration that his Father is a living and loving spirit.

In winning souls for the Master, it is not the first mile of compulsion, duty, or convention that will transform man and his world, but rather the *second* mile of free service and liberty-loving devotion that betokens the Jesusonian reaching forth to grasp his brother in love and sweep him on under spiritual guidance toward the higher and divine goal of mortal existence. Christianity even now willingly goes the *first* mile, but mankind languishes and stumbles along in moral darkness because there are so few genuine second-milers — so few professed followers of Jesus who really live and love as he taught his disciples to live and love and serve.

The call to the adventure of building a new and transformed human society by means of the spiritual rebirth of Jesus' brotherhood of the kingdom should thrill all who believe in him as men have not been stirred since the days when they walked about on earth as his companions in the flesh.

No social system or political regime which denies the reality of God can contribute in any constructive and lasting manner to the advancement of human civilization. But Christianity, as it is subdivided and secularized today, presents the greatest single obstacle to its further advancement; especially is this true concerning the Orient.

Ecclesiasticism is at once and forever incompatible with that living faith, growing spirit, and firsthand experience of the faith-comrades of Jesus in the brotherhood of man in the spiritual association of the kingdom of heaven. The praiseworthy desire to preserve traditions of past achievement often leads to the defense of outgrown systems of worship. The well-meant desire to foster ancient thought systems effectually prevents the sponsoring of new and adequate means and methods designed to satisfy the spiritual longings of the expanding and advancing minds of modern men. Likewise, the Christian churches of today stand as great, but wholly unconscious, obstacles to the immediate advance of the real gospel — the teachings of Jesus of Nazareth.

Many earnest persons who would gladly yield loyalty to the Christ of the gospel find it very difficult enthusiastically to support a church which exhibits so little of the spirit of his life and teachings, and which they have been erroneously taught he founded. Jesus did not found the so-called Christian church, but he has, in every manner consistent with his nature, *fostered* it as the best existent exponent of his lifework on earth.

If the Christian church would only dare to espouse the Master's program, thousands of apparently indifferent youths would rush forward to enlist in such a spiritual undertaking, and they would not hesitate to go all the way through with this great adventure.

Christianity is seriously confronted with the doom embodied in one of its own slogans: "A house divided against itself cannot stand." The non-Christian world will hardly capitulate to a sect-divided Christendom. The living Jesus is the only hope of a possible unification of Christianity. The true church — the Jesus brotherhood — is invisible, spiritual, and is characterized by *unity*, not necessarily by *uniformity*. Uniformity is the earmark of the physical world of mechanistic nature. Spiritual unity is the fruit of faith union with the living Jesus. The visible church should refuse longer to handicap the progress of the invisible and spiritual brotherhood of the kingdom of God. And this brotherhood is destined to become a *living organism* in contrast to an institutionalized social organization. It may well utilize such social organizations, but it must not be supplanted by them.

But the Christianity of today must not be despised. It is the product of the combined moral genius of the God-knowing men of many races during many ages, and it has truly been one of the greatest powers for good on earth, and therefore no man should lightly regard it, notwithstanding its inherent and acquired defects. Christianity still contrives to move the minds of reflective men with mighty moral emotions.

But there is no excuse for the involvement of the church in commerce and politics; such unholy alliances are a flagrant betrayal of the Master. And the genuine lovers of truth will be slow to forget that this powerful institutionalized church has often dared to smother newborn faith and persecute truth bearers who chanced to appear in unorthodox raiment.

It is all too true that such a church would not have survived unless there had been men in the world who preferred such a style of worship. Many spiritually indolent souls crave an ancient and authoritative religion of ritual and sacred traditions. Human evolution and spiritual progress are hardly sufficient to enable all men to dispense with religious authority. And the invisible brotherhood of the kingdom may well include these family groups of various social and temperamental classes if they are only willing to become truly spirit-led sons of God. But in this brotherhood of Jesus there is no place for sectarian rivalry, group bitterness, nor assertions of moral superiority and spiritual infallibility.

These various groupings of Christians may serve to accommodate numerous different types of would-be believers among the various peoples of Western civilization, but such division of Christendom presents a grave weakness when it attempts to carry the gospel of Jesus to the world. Most people do not yet understand that there is a *religion of Jesus* separate, and somewhat apart, from Christianity, which has more and more become a *religion about Jesus*.

The great hope of Urantia lies in the possibility of a new revelation of Jesus with a new and enlarged presentation of his saving message which would spiritually unite in loving service the numerous families of his present-day professed followers.

Even secular education could help in this great spiritual renaissance if it would pay more attention to the work of teaching youth how to engage in life planning and character progression. The purpose of all education should be to foster and further the supreme purpose of life, the development of a majestic and well-balanced personality. There is great need for the teaching of moral discipline in the place of so much self-gratification. Upon such a foundation religion may contribute its spiritual incentive to the enlargement and enrichment of mortal life, even to the security and enhancement of life eternal.

Christianity is an extemporized religion, and therefore must it operate in low gear. High-gear spiritual performances must await the new revelation and the more general acceptance of the real religion of Jesus. But Christianity is a mighty religion, seeing that the commonplace disciples of a crucified carpenter set in motion those teachings which conquered the Roman world in three hundred years and then went on to triumph over the barbarians who overthrew Rome. This same Christianity conquered — absorbed and exalted — the whole stream of Hebrew theology and Greek philosophy. And then, when this Christian religion became comatose for more than a thousand years as a result of an overdose of mysteries and paganism, it resurrected itself and virtually reconquered the whole Western world. Christianity contains enough of Jesus' teachings to immortalize it.

If Christianity could only grasp more of Jesus' teachings, it could do so much more in helping modern man to solve his new and increasingly complex problems.

Christianity suffers under a great handicap because it has become identified in the minds of all the world as a part of the social system, the industrial life, and the moral standards of Western civilization; and thus has Christianity unwittingly seemed to sponsor a society which staggers under the guilt of tolerating science without idealism, politics without principles, wealth without work, pleasure without restraint, knowledge without character, power without conscience, and industry without morality.

The hope of modern Christianity is that it should cease to sponsor the social systems and industrial policies of Western civilization while it humbly bows itself before the cross it so valiantly extols, there to learn anew from Jesus of Nazareth the greatest truths mortal man can ever hear — the living gospel of the fatherhood of God and the brotherhood of man.

PAPER 196
THE FAITH OF JESUS

JESUS ENJOYED a sublime and wholehearted faith in God. He experienced the ordinary ups and downs of mortal existence, but he never religiously doubted the certainty of God's watchcare and guidance. His faith was the outgrowth of the insight born of the activity of the divine presence, his indwelling Adjuster. His faith was neither traditional nor merely intellectual; it was wholly personal and purely spiritual.

The human Jesus saw God as being holy, just, and great, as well as being true, beautiful, and good. All these attributes of divinity he focused in his mind as the "will of the Father in heaven." Jesus' God was at one and the same time "The Holy One of Israel" and "The living and loving Father in heaven." The concept of God as a Father was not original with Jesus, but he exalted and elevated the idea into a sublime experience by achieving a new revelation of God and by proclaiming that every mortal creature is a child of this Father of love, a son of God.

Jesus did not cling to faith in God as would a struggling soul at war with the universe and at death grips with a hostile and sinful world; he did not resort to faith merely as a consolation in the midst of difficulties or as a comfort in threatened despair; faith was not just an illusory compensation for the unpleasant realities and the sorrows of living. In the very face of all the natural difficulties and the temporal contradictions of mortal existence, he experienced the tranquility of supreme and unquestioned trust in God and felt the tremendous thrill of living, by faith, in the very presence of the heavenly Father. And this triumphant faith was a living experience of actual spirit attainment. Jesus' great contribution to the values of human experience was not that he revealed so many new ideas about the Father in heaven, but rather that he so magnificently and humanly demonstrated a new and higher type of *living faith in God.* Never on all the worlds of this universe, in the life of any one mortal, did God ever become such a *living reality* as in the human experience of Jesus of Nazareth.

In the Master's life on Urantia, this and all other worlds of the local creation discover a new and higher type of religion, religion based on personal spiritual relations with the Universal Father and wholly validated by the supreme authority of genuine personal experience. This living faith of Jesus was more than an intellectual reflection, and it was not a mystic meditation.

Theology may fix, formulate, define, and dogmatize faith, but in the human life of Jesus faith was personal, living, original, spontaneous, and purely spiritual. This faith was not reverence for tradition nor a mere intellectual belief which he held as a sacred creed, but rather a sublime experience and a profound conviction which *securely held him.* His faith was so real and all-encompassing that it absolutely swept away any spiritual doubts and effectively destroyed every conflicting desire. Nothing was able to tear him away from the spiritual anchorage of this fervent, sublime, and undaunted faith. Even in the face of apparent defeat or in the throes of disappointment and threatening despair, he calmly stood in the divine presence free from fear and fully conscious of spiritual invincibility. Jesus enjoyed the invigorating assurance of the possession of unflinching faith, and in each of life's trying situations he unfailingly exhibited an unquestioning loyalty to the Father's will. And this superb faith was undaunted even by the cruel and crushing threat of an ignominious death.

In a religious genius, strong spiritual faith so many times leads directly to disastrous fanaticism, to exaggeration of the religious ego, but it was not so with Jesus. He was not unfavorably affected in his practical life by his extraordinary faith and spirit attainment because this spiritual exaltation was a wholly unconscious and spontaneous soul expression of his personal experience with God.

The all-consuming and indomitable spiritual faith of Jesus never became fanatical, for it never attempted to run away with his well-balanced intellectual judgments concerning the proportional values of practical and commonplace social, economic, and moral life situations. The Son of Man was a splendidly unified human personality; he was a perfectly endowed divine being; he was also magnificently co-ordinated as a combined human and divine being functioning on earth as a single personality. Always did the Master co-ordinate the faith of the soul with the wisdom-appraisals of seasoned experience. Personal faith, spiritual hope, and moral devotion were always correlated in a matchless religious unity of harmonious association with the keen realization of the reality and sacredness of all human loyalties — personal honor, family love, religious obligation, social duty, and economic necessity.

The faith of Jesus visualized all spirit values as being found in the kingdom of God; therefore he said, "Seek first the kingdom of heaven." Jesus saw in the advanced and ideal fellowship of the kingdom the achievement and fulfillment of the "will of God." The very heart of the prayer which he taught his disciples was, "Your kingdom come; your will be done." Having thus conceived of the kingdom as comprising the will of God, he devoted himself to the cause of its realization with amazing self-forgetfulness and unbounded enthusiasm. But in all his intense mission and throughout his extraordinary life there never appeared the fury of the fanatic nor the superficial frothiness of the religious egotist.

The Master's entire life was consistently conditioned by this living faith, this sublime religious experience. This spiritual attitude wholly dominated his thinking and feeling, his believing and praying, his teaching and preaching. This personal faith of a son in the certainty and security of the guidance and protection of the heavenly Father imparted to his unique life a profound endowment of spiritual reality. And yet, despite this very deep consciousness of close relationship with divinity, this Galilean, God's Galilean, when addressed as Good Teacher, instantly replied, "Why do you call me good?" When we stand confronted by such splendid self-forgetfulness, we begin to understand how the Universal Father found it possible so fully to manifest himself to him and reveal himself through him to the mortals of the realms.

Jesus brought to God, as a man of the realm, the greatest of all offerings: the consecration and dedication of his own will to the majestic service of doing the divine will. Jesus always and consistently interpreted religion wholly in terms of the Father's will. When you study the career of the Master, as concerns prayer or any other feature of the religious life, look not so much for what he taught as for what he did. Jesus never prayed as a religious duty. To him prayer was a sincere expression of spiritual attitude, a declaration of soul loyalty, a recital of personal devotion, an expression of thanksgiving, an avoidance of emotional tension, a prevention of conflict, an exaltation of intellection, an ennoblement of desire, a vindication of moral decision, an enrichment of thought, an invigoration of higher inclinations, a consecration of impulse, a clarification of viewpoint, a declaration of faith, a transcendental surrender of will, a sublime assertion of confidence, a revelation of courage, the proclamation of discovery, a confession of supreme devotion, the validation of consecration, a technique for the adjustment of difficulties, and the mighty mobilization of the combined soul powers to withstand all human tendencies toward selfishness, evil, and sin. He lived just such a life of prayerful consecration to the doing of his Father's will and ended his life triumphantly with just such a prayer. The secret of his unparalleled religious life was this consciousness of the presence of God; and he attained it by intelligent prayer and sincere worship — unbroken communion with God — and not by leadings, voices, visions, or extraordinary religious practices.

In the earthly life of Jesus, religion was a living experience, a direct and personal movement from spiritual reverence to practical righteousness. The faith of Jesus bore the transcendent fruits of the divine spirit. His faith was not immature and credulous like that of a child, but in many ways it did resemble the unsuspecting trust of the child mind. Jesus trusted God much as the child trusts a parent. He had a profound confidence in the universe — just such a trust as the child has in its parental environment. Jesus' wholehearted faith in the fundamental goodness of the universe very much resembled the child's trust in the security of its earthly surroundings. He depended on the heavenly Father as a child leans upon its earthly parent, and his fervent faith never for one moment doubted the certainty of the heavenly Father's overcare. He was not disturbed seriously by fears, doubts, and skepticism. Unbelief did not inhibit the free and original expression of his life. He combined the stalwart and intelligent courage of a full-grown man with the sincere and trusting optimism of a believing child. His faith grew to such heights of trust that it was devoid of fear.

The faith of Jesus attained the purity of a child's trust. His faith was so absolute and undoubting that it responded to the charm of the contact of fellow beings and to the wonders of the universe. His sense of dependence on the divine was so complete and so confident that it yielded the joy and the assurance of absolute personal security. There was no hesitating pretense in his religious experience. In this giant intellect of the full-grown man the faith of the child reigned supreme in all matters relating to the religious consciousness. It is not strange that he once said, "Except you become as a little child, you shall not enter the kingdom." Notwithstanding that Jesus' faith was *childlike*, it was in no sense *childish*.

Jesus does not require his disciples to believe in him but rather to believe *with* him, believe in the reality of the love of God and in full confidence accept the security of the assurance of sonship with the heavenly Father. The Master desires that all his followers should fully share his transcendent faith. Jesus most touchingly challenged his followers, not only to believe *what* he believed, but also to believe *as* he believed. This is the full significance of his one supreme requirement, "Follow me."

Jesus' earthly life was devoted to one great purpose — doing the Father's will, living the human life religiously and by faith. The faith of Jesus was trusting, like that of a child, but it was wholly free from presumption. He made robust and manly decisions, courageously faced manifold disappointments, resolutely surmounted extraordinary difficulties, and unflinchingly confronted the stern requirements of duty. It required a strong will and an unfailing confidence to believe what Jesus believed and *as* he believed.

1. JESUS — THE MAN

Jesus' devotion to the Father's will and the service of man was even more than mortal decision and human determination; it was a wholehearted consecration of himself to such an unreserved bestowal of love. No matter how great the fact of the sovereignty of Michael, you must not take the human Jesus away from men. The Master has ascended on high as a man, as well as God; he belongs to men; men belong to him. How unfortunate that religion itself should be so misinterpreted as to take the human Jesus away from struggling mortals! Let not the discussions of the humanity or the divinity of the Christ obscure the saving truth that Jesus of Nazareth was a religious man who, by faith, achieved the knowing and the doing of the will of God; he was the most truly religious man who has ever lived on Urantia.

The time is ripe to witness the figurative resurrection of the human Jesus from his burial tomb amidst theological traditions and religious dogmas. Jesus of Nazareth must not be longer sacrificed to even the splendid concept of the glorified Christ. What a transcendent service if, through this revelation, the Son of Man should be recovered from the tomb of traditional theology and be presented as the living Jesus to the church that bears his name, and to all other religions! Surely the Christian fellowship of believers will not hesitate to make such adjustments of faith and of practices of living as will enable it to "follow after" the Master in the demonstration of his real life of religious devotion to the doing of his Father's will and of consecration to the unselfish service of man. Do professed Christians fear the exposure of a self-sufficient and unconsecrated fellowship of social respectability and selfish economic maladjustment? Does institutional Christianity fear the possible jeopardy, or even the overthrow, of traditional ecclesiastical authority if the Jesus of Galilee is reinstated in the minds and souls of mortal men as the ideal of personal religious living? Indeed, the social readjustments, the economic transformations, the moral rejuvenations, and the religious revisions of Christian civilization would be drastic and revolutionary if the living religion of Jesus should suddenly supplant the theologic religion about Jesus.

To "follow Jesus" means to personally share his religious faith and to enter into the spirit of the Master's life of unselfish service for man. One of the most important things in human living is to find out what Jesus believed, to discover his ideals, and to strive for the achievement of his exalted life purpose. Of all human knowledge, that which is of greatest value is to know the religious life of Jesus and how he lived it.

The common people heard Jesus gladly, and they will again respond to the presentation of his sincere human life of consecrated religious motivation if such truths shall again be proclaimed to the world. The people heard him gladly because he was one of them, an unpretentious layman; the world's greatest religious teacher was indeed a layman.

It should not be the aim of kingdom believers literally to imitate the outward life of Jesus in the flesh but rather to share his faith; to trust God as he trusted God and to believe in men as he believed in men. Jesus never argued about either the fatherhood of God or the brotherhood of men; he was a living illustration of the one and a profound demonstration of the other.

Just as men must progress from the consciousness of the human to the realization of the divine, so did Jesus ascend from the nature of man to the consciousness of the nature of God. And the Master made this great ascent from the human to the divine by the conjoint achievement of the faith of his mortal intellect and the acts of his indwelling Adjuster. The fact-realization of the attainment of totality of divinity (all the while fully conscious of the reality of humanity) was attended by seven stages of faith consciousness of progressive divinization. These stages of progressive self-realization were marked off by the following extraordinary events in the Master's bestowal experience:

1. The arrival of the Thought Adjuster.
2. The messenger of Immanuel who appeared to him at Jerusalem when he was about twelve years old.
3. The manifestations attendant upon his baptism.
4. The experiences on the Mount of Transfiguration.
5. The morontia resurrection.
6. The spirit ascension.
7. The final embrace of the Paradise Father, conferring unlimited sovereignty of his universe.

2. THE RELIGION OF JESUS

Some day a reformation in the Christian church may strike deep enough to get back to the unadulterated religious teachings of Jesus, the author and finisher of our faith. You may *preach* a religion *about* Jesus, but, perforce, you must *live* the religion *of* Jesus. In the enthusiasm of Pentecost, Peter unintentionally inaugurated a new religion, the religion of the risen and glorified Christ. The Apostle Paul later on transformed this new gospel into Christianity, a religion embodying his own theologic views and portraying his own *personal experience* with the Jesus of the Damascus road. The gospel of the kingdom is founded on the personal religious experience of the Jesus of Galilee; Christianity is founded almost exclusively on the personal religious experience of the Apostle Paul. Almost the whole of the New Testament is devoted, not to the portrayal of the significant and inspiring religious life of Jesus, but to a discussion of Paul's religious experience and to a portrayal of his personal religious convictions. The only notable exceptions to this statement, aside from certain parts of Matthew, Mark, and Luke, are the Book of Hebrews and the Epistle of James. Even Peter, in his writing, only once reverted to the personal religious life of his Master. The New Testament is a superb Christian document, but it is only meagerly Jesusonian.

Jesus' life in the flesh portrays a transcendent religious growth from the early ideas of primitive awe and human reverence up through years of personal spiritual communion until he finally arrived at that advanced and exalted status of the consciousness of his oneness with the Father. And thus, in one short life, did Jesus traverse that experience of religious spiritual progression which man begins on earth and ordinarily achieves only at the conclusion of his long sojourn in the spirit training schools of the successive levels of the pre-Paradise career. Jesus progressed from a purely human consciousness of the faith certainties of personal religious experience to the sublime spiritual heights of the positive realization of his divine nature and to the consciousness of his close association with the Universal Father in the management of a universe. He progressed from the humble status of mortal dependence which prompted him spontaneously to say to the one who called him Good Teacher, "Why do you call me good? None is good but God," to that sublime consciousness of achieved divinity which led him to exclaim, "Which one of you convicts me of sin?" And this progressing ascent from the human to the divine was an exclusively mortal achievement. And when he had thus attained divinity, he was still the same human Jesus, the Son of Man as well as the Son of God.

Mark, Matthew, and Luke retain something of the picture of the human Jesus as he engaged in the superb struggle to ascertain the divine will and to do that will. John presents a picture of the triumphant Jesus as he walked on earth in the full consciousness of divinity. The great mistake that has been made by those who have studied the Master's life is that some have conceived of him as entirely human, while others have thought of him as only divine. Throughout his entire experience he was truly both human and divine, even as he yet is.

But the greatest mistake was made in that, while the human Jesus was recognized as *having* a religion, the divine Jesus (Christ) almost overnight became a religion. Paul's Christianity made sure of the adoration of the divine Christ, but it almost wholly lost sight of the struggling and valiant human Jesus of Galilee, who, by the valor of his personal religious faith and the heroism of his indwelling Adjuster, ascended from the lowly levels of humanity to become one with divinity, thus becoming the new and living way whereby all mortals may so ascend from humanity to divinity. Mortals in all stages of spirituality and on all worlds may find in the personal life of Jesus that which will strengthen and inspire them as they progress from the lowest spirit levels up to the highest divine values, from the beginning to the end of all personal religious experience.

At the time of the writing of the New Testament, the authors not only most profoundly believed in the divinity of the risen Christ, but they also devotedly and sincerely believed in his immediate return to earth to consummate the heavenly kingdom. This strong faith in the Lord's immediate return had much to do with the tendency to omit from the record those references which portrayed the purely human experiences and attributes of the Master. The whole Christian movement tended away from the human picture of Jesus of Nazareth toward the exaltation of the risen Christ, the glorified and soon-returning Lord Jesus Christ.

Jesus founded the religion of personal experience in doing the will of God and serving the human brotherhood; Paul founded a religion in which the glorified Jesus became the object of worship and the brotherhood consisted of fellow believers in the divine Christ. In the bestowal of Jesus these two concepts were potential in his divine-human life, and it is indeed a pity that his followers failed to create a unified religion which might have given proper recognition to both the human and the divine natures of the Master as they were inseparably bound up in his earth life and so gloriously set forth in the original gospel of the kingdom.

You would be neither shocked nor disturbed by some of Jesus' strong pronouncements if you would only remember that he was the world's most wholehearted and devoted religionist. He was a wholly consecrated mortal, unreservedly dedicated to doing his Father's will. Many of his apparently hard sayings were more of a personal confession of faith and a pledge of devotion than commands to his followers. And it was this very singleness of purpose and unselfish devotion that enabled him to effect such extraordinary progress in the conquest of the human mind in one short life. Many of his declarations should be considered as a confession of what he demanded of himself rather than what he required of all his followers. In his devotion to the cause of the kingdom, Jesus burned all bridges behind him; he sacrificed all hindrances to the doing of his Father's will.

Jesus blessed the poor because they were usually sincere and pious; he condemned the rich because they were usually wanton and irreligious. He would equally condemn the irreligious pauper and commend the consecrated and worshipful man of wealth.

Jesus led men to feel at home in the world; he delivered them from the slavery of taboo and taught them that the world was not fundamentally evil. He did not long to escape from his earthly life; he mastered a technique of acceptably doing the Father's will while in the flesh. He attained an idealistic religious life in the very midst of a realistic world. Jesus did not share Paul's pessimistic view of humankind. The Master looked upon men as the sons of God and foresaw a magnificent and eternal future for those who chose survival. He was not a moral skeptic; he viewed man positively, not negatively. He saw most men as weak rather than wicked, more distraught than depraved. But no matter what their status, they were all God's children and his brethren.

He taught men to place a high value upon themselves in time and in eternity. Because of this high estimate which Jesus placed upon men, he was willing to spend himself in the unremitting service of humankind. And it was this infinite worth of the finite that made the golden rule a vital factor in his religion. What mortal can fail to be uplifted by the extraordinary faith Jesus has in him?

Jesus offered no rules for social advancement; his was a religious mission, and religion is an exclusively individual experience. The ultimate goal of society's most advanced achievement can never hope to transcend

Jesus' brotherhood of men based on the recognition of the fatherhood of God. The ideal of all social attainment can be realized only in the coming of this divine kingdom.

3. THE SUPREMACY OF RELIGION

Personal, spiritual religious experience is an efficient solvent for most mortal difficulties; it is an effective sorter, evaluator, and adjuster of all human problems. Religion does not remove or destroy human troubles, but it does dissolve, absorb, illuminate, and transcend them. True religion unifies the personality for effective adjustment to all mortal requirements. Religious faith — the positive leading of the indwelling divine presence — unfailingly enables the God-knowing man to bridge that gulf existing between the intellectual logic which recognizes the Universal First Cause as *It* and those positive affirmations of the soul which aver this First Cause is *He*, the heavenly Father of Jesus' gospel, the personal God of human salvation.

There are just three elements in universal reality: fact, idea, and relation. The religious consciousness identifies these realities as science, philosophy, and truth. Philosophy would be inclined to view these activities as reason, wisdom, and faith — physical reality, intellectual reality, and spiritual reality. We are in the habit of designating these realities as thing, meaning, and value.

The progressive comprehension of reality is the equivalent of approaching God. The finding of God, the consciousness of identity with reality, is the equivalent of the experiencing of self-completion — self-entirety, self-totality. The experiencing of total reality is the full realization of God, the finality of the God-knowing experience.

The full summation of human life is the knowledge that man is educated by fact, ennobled by wisdom, and saved — justified — by religious faith.

Physical certainty consists in the logic of science; moral certainty, in the wisdom of philosophy; spiritual certainty, in the truth of genuine religious experience.

The mind of man can attain high levels of spiritual insight and corresponding spheres of divinity of values because it is not wholly material. There is a spirit nucleus in the mind of man — the Adjuster of the divine presence. There are three separate evidences of this spirit indwelling of the human mind:

1. Humanitarian fellowship — love. The purely animal mind may be gregarious for self-protection, but only the spirit-indwelt intellect is unselfishly altruistic and unconditionally loving.

2. Interpretation of the universe — wisdom. Only the spirit-indwelt mind can comprehend that the universe is friendly to the individual.

3. Spiritual evaluation of life — worship. Only the spirit-indwelt man can realize the divine presence and seek to attain a fuller experience in and with this foretaste of divinity.

The human mind does not create real values; human experience does not yield universe insight. Concerning insight, the recognition of moral values and the discernment of spiritual meanings, all that the human mind can do is to discover, recognize, interpret, and *choose*.

The moral values of the universe become intellectual possessions by the exercise of the three basic judgments, or choices, of the mortal mind:

1. Self-judgment — moral choice.
2. Social-judgment — ethical choice.
3. God-judgment — religious choice.

Thus it appears that all human progress is effected by a technique of conjoint *revelational evolution*.

Unless a divine lover lived in man, he could not unselfishly and spiritually love. Unless an interpreter lived in the mind, man could not truly realize the unity of the universe. Unless an evaluator dwelt with man, he could not possibly appraise moral values and recognize spiritual meanings. And this lover hails from the very source of infinite love; this interpreter is a part of Universal Unity; this evaluator is the child of the Center and Source of all absolute values of divine and eternal reality.

Moral evaluation with a religious meaning — spiritual insight — connotes the individual's choice between good and evil, truth and error, material and spiritual, human and divine, time and eternity. Human survival is in great measure dependent on consecrating the human will to the choosing of those values selected by this spirit-value sorter — the indwelling interpreter and unifier. Personal religious experience consists in two phases: discovery in the human mind and revelation by the indwelling divine spirit. Through oversophistication or as a result of the irreligious conduct of professed religionists, a man, or even a generation of men, may elect to suspend their efforts to discover the God who indwells them; they may fail to progress in and attain the divine revelation. But such attitudes of spiritual nonprogression cannot long persist because of the presence and influence of the indwelling Thought Adjusters.

This profound experience of the reality of the divine indwelling forever transcends the crude materialistic technique of the physical sciences. You cannot put spiritual joy under a microscope; you cannot weigh love in a balance; you cannot measure moral values; neither can you estimate the quality of spiritual worship.

The Hebrews had a religion of moral sublimity; the Greeks evolved a religion of beauty; Paul and his conferees founded a religion of faith, hope, and charity. Jesus revealed and exemplified a religion of love: security in the Father's love, with joy and satisfaction consequent upon sharing this love in the service of the human brotherhood.

Every time man makes a reflective moral choice, he immediately experiences a new divine invasion of his soul. Moral choosing constitutes religion as the motive of inner response to outer conditions. But such a real religion is not a purely subjective experience. It signifies the whole of the subjectivity of the individual engaged in a meaningful and intelligent response to total objectivity — the universe and its Maker.

The exquisite and transcendent experience of loving and being loved is not just a psychic illusion because it is so purely subjective. The one truly divine and objective reality that is associated with mortal beings, the Thought Adjuster, functions to human observation apparently as an exclusively subjective phenomenon. Man's contact with the highest objective reality, God, is only through the purely subjective experience of knowing him, of worshiping him, of realizing sonship with him.

True religious worship is not a futile monologue of self-deception. Worship is a personal communion with that which is divinely real, with that which is the very source of reality. Man aspires by worship to be better and thereby eventually attains the *best.*

The idealization and attempted service of truth, beauty, and goodness is not a substitute for genuine religious experience — spiritual reality. Psychology and idealism are not the equivalent of religious reality. The projections of the human intellect may indeed originate false gods — gods in man's image — but the true God-consciousness does not have such an origin. The God-consciousness is resident in the indwelling spirit. Many of the religious systems of man come from the formulations of the human intellect, but the God-consciousness is not necessarily a part of these grotesque systems of religious slavery.

God is not the mere invention of man's idealism; he is the very source of all such superanimal insights and values. God is not a hypothesis formulated to unify the human concepts of truth, beauty, and goodness; he is the personality of love from whom all of these universe manifestations are derived. The truth, beauty, and goodness of man's world are unified by the increasing spirituality of the experience of mortals ascending toward Paradise realities. The unity of truth, beauty, and goodness can only be realized in the spiritual experience of the God-knowing personality.

Morality is the essential pre-existent soil of personal God-consciousness, the personal realization of the Adjuster's inner presence, but such morality is not the source of religious experience and the resultant spiritual insight. The moral nature is superanimal but subspiritual. Morality is equivalent to the recognition of duty, the realization of the existence of right and wrong. The moral zone intervenes between the animal and the human types of mind as morontia functions between the material and the spiritual spheres of personality attainment.

The evolutionary mind is able to discover law, morals, and ethics; but the bestowed spirit, the indwelling Adjuster, reveals to the evolving human mind the lawgiver, the Father-source of all that is true, beautiful, and good; and such an illuminated man has a religion and is spiritually equipped to begin the long and adventurous search for God.

Morality is not necessarily spiritual; it may be wholly and purely human, albeit real religion enhances all moral values, makes them more meaningful. Morality without religion fails to reveal ultimate goodness, and it also fails to provide for the survival of even its own moral values. Religion provides for the enhancement, glorification, and assured survival of everything morality recognizes and approves.

Religion stands above science, art, philosophy, ethics, and morals, but not independent of them. They are all indissolubly interrelated in human experience, personal and social. Religion is man's supreme experience in the mortal nature, but finite language makes it forever impossible for theology ever adequately to depict real religious experience.

Religious insight possesses the power of turning defeat into higher desires and new determinations. Love is the highest motivation which man may utilize in his universe ascent. But love, divested of truth, beauty, and goodness, is only a sentiment, a philosophic distortion, a psychic illusion, a spiritual deception. Love must always be redefined on successive levels of morontia and spirit progression.

Art results from man's attempt to escape from the lack of beauty in his material environment; it is a gesture toward the morontia level. Science is man's effort to solve the apparent riddles of the material universe. Philosophy is man's attempt at the unification of human experience. Religion is man's supreme gesture, his magnificent reach for final reality, his determination to find God and to be like him.

In the realm of religious experience, spiritual possibility is potential reality. Man's forward spiritual urge is not a psychic illusion. All of man's universe romancing may not be fact, but much, very much, is truth.

Some men's lives are too great and noble to descend to the low level of being merely successful. The animal must adapt itself to the environment, but the religious man transcends his environment and in this way escapes the limitations of the present material world through this insight of divine love. This concept of love generates in the soul of man that superanimal effort to find truth, beauty, and goodness; and when he does find them, he is glorified in their embrace; he is consumed with the desire to live them, to do righteousness.

Be not discouraged; human evolution is still in progress, and the revelation of God to the world, in and through Jesus, shall not fail.

The great challenge to modern man is to achieve better communication with the divine Monitor that dwells within the human mind. Man's greatest adventure in the flesh consists in the well-balanced and sane effort to advance the borders of self-consciousness out through the dim realms of embryonic soul-consciousness in a wholehearted effort to reach the borderland of spirit-consciousness — contact with the divine presence. Such an experience constitutes God-consciousness, an experience mightily confirmative of the pre-existent truth of the religious experience of knowing God. Such spirit-consciousness is the equivalent of the knowledge of the actuality of sonship with God. Otherwise, the assurance of sonship is the experience of faith.

And God-consciousness is equivalent to the integration of the self with the universe, and on its highest levels of spiritual reality. Only the spirit content of any value is imperishable. Even that which is true, beautiful, and good may not perish in human experience. If man does not choose to survive, then does the surviving Adjuster conserve those realities born of love and nurtured in service. And all these things are a part of the Universal Father. The Father is living love, and this life of the Father is in his Sons. And the spirit of the Father is in his Son's sons — mortal men. When all is said and done, the Father idea is still the highest human concept of God.

Appendix:
A List of Deletions and Changes from the original Urantia Book (for future scholars)

This may seem like a lot of deletions and changes (141 out of 197 papers have been modified) but when you consider how vast the Urantia Book is and how small many of the changes are (sometimes just a few words here or there), these small blemishes on such a magnificent creative project should not be allowed to tarnish the truths and ideas enunciated. I hope these fixes and updates will help the Urantia 2025 to continue to illuminate the minds and spirits of people for many more generations.

A note on how this document was created: in 2006, when the Urantia Book lost it's international copyright I was able to download the entire book in an editable format. This format listed with numbers each paper, section, and paragraph. These numbers you will see below. From 2006 to 2020 I would add to this list any changes or deletions I would make. After 2020 I became a bit lazy and stopped adding to the list, so there are more changes than appear on this list, but the vast majority of changes are contained here.

In preparing for the printing by Spines.com I had to conform to the limit they placed on the length of each book. This lead to me breaking the book up into 6 pieces: Part 1; Part 2; Part 3A; Parts 3B & 4A; Part 4B; and Part 4C. When preparing for Part 3A I had unfortunately made it too long, thus various papers in Part 3A had to be trimmed a bit to keep the book under the limit. So besides all the changes and deletions listed here additional deletions have occurred in papers 63, 66, 68, 69, 70, 71, 83, 84, 85, 86, 87, 88, 89, 90, 91, 92, 97, and 99. But this was just a few sentences or paragraphs in each paper that were deemed to contain nothing of spiritual import and to be not necessary for the overall story.

FOREWORD (PAPER 0)

[0:0.5-6] many changes for new cosmology
[0:3.6] add clarification for new cosmology.
[0:6.2] delete the last 2 sentences on not being able to follow modern terminology as not needed.
[0:6.11] We know from General Relativity that space IS responsive to gravity so change the second sentence to "Pattern is not gravity responsive, and…"
[0:11.9] delete the last 8 words in the first sentence (about the ether hypothesis, because few people, except for those interested in the history of science, even know about this subject anymore.)

PART 1 (PAPERS 1 THROUGH 31)

Paper 1: The Universal Father
[1:5.11] delete last sentence (about only 2 choices – I believe there might be more than 2 choices and this statement is not really needed)

Paper 2: The Nature of God
Add to the 1st sentence of [2:0.1] the words in italics so it reads "Inasmuch as *one of* man's highest possible concept*s* of God…" to make this statement more general and not so restrictive.
[2:7.7] add an "s" onto "universe" in 2nd sentence and drop the "s" on "coheres" to make this more correct in the new cosmology.
[2:7.9] delete reference to "Hebrew" and make this a statement about religions in general; replace "twentieth-century men" with "today".

Paper 3: The Attributes of God
[3:1.7] insert the word "master" before "universe" in the 1st sentence for clarity.
[3:2.4] delete the words "starry hosts composing the" in 4th sentence due to cosmology changes. [3:2.8] delete "an individual race," as not needed in 4th sentence.
Change the words "so stupid" to "such an error" in [3:6.5]. This is not a matter of being stupid, as it has nothing to do with intelligence, it is just an error from the higher spiritual perspective.

Paper 4: God's Relation to the Universe
[4:2.1-2] added galaxy to the lists, twice in 2.1 and once in 2.2 due to cosmology change
[4:5.5] Paragraph modified as follows: substitute the word "ancients" for "Hebrews", and delete the reference to "primitive minds" as not needed.

Paper 6: The Eternal Son
[6:8.3] at the end of the paragraph deleted the numbers "ten million". In making the update to the String Theory cosmology of the revised version, finite numbers like these need to be deleted as obsolete.

Paper 7: Relation of the Eternal Son to the Universe
[7:1.6] delete the word "race," in 2nd sentence as not needed.

Paper 8: The Infinite Spirit
[8:1.11] delete "the race, and" from the 3rd sentence as not needed.

Paper 9: Relation of the Infinite Spirit to the Universe
[9:3.3] deleted last sentence about gyroscopes as not needed, it causes more confusion than it clarifies in my opinion.

Paper 10: The Paradise Trinity

[10:6.5] renumbered Union of Days as number 4, Perfections of Days as number 5, and Recents of Days as number 6. This is required because of the cosmology changes in later papers, see papers 15 and 30 among others.

Paper 11: The Eternal Isle of Paradise

[11:1.3] due to cosmology change delete the phrases "the immensity of the intervening space", "meaning of these enormous distances", and "through the starry realms" and added a few words to make this paragraph clearer.
[11:1.4] delete "trillions upon trillions" and replace with "unlimited number" as more correct.
[11:2.1] delete from the first sentence "the" before the first "material" and add "your local" and then delete the phrase "discernible…systems". Add "Likewise must each superuniverse. Also, must the master universe" and make Ruler plural.
[11:3.4] delete "one billion" and change it to read "all glorified individual working groups now there, or that may arrive, even unto the times of the eternal future." Delete everything else.
[11:4.3] delete the word "enormous" in the first sentence and change "just seven trillion" to "currently an enormous number" in the 2nd sentence. These relatively small finite numbers (like trillions or billions) are no longer relevant with the changes in cosmology due to String Theory.
[11:7.7] delete the 2nd sentence and "of galaxies" in the 3rd, add the word "space" before "procession".
[11:7.9] delete the phrase "of the galaxies". Galaxies exist only in a 4D universe not out in the master universe.
[11:8.1] delete all reference to worlds, stars, and things from our universe and substitute universes and superuniverses, due to cosmology change.

Paper 12: The Universe of Universes

[12:0.3] replace the words "starry realms" with "universe of universes" in 1st sentence.
[12:1.1] delete 3rd sentence as not needed and add the word "master" in front of universe in the 4th sentence. [12:1.6] delete all but the last sentence and add: exist in an expanded 10 or more dimensional space-time which include the universes of which they are composed. Each universe is a hypersurface

or four dimensional membrane (M-brane). These membrane universes are organized around the headquarters of each superuniverse much like flower petals around a flower. If you had higher dimensional vision their beauty is exquisite."

[12:1.7] replace "with an aggregate…seven trillion inhabited planets" with "each a collection of an enormous number of universes" in 1st sentence. In 2nd sentence replace "But" with "Yet" delete "tentative estimate" and insert "the" before "architectural". Delete the word "star" before "students, and delete the last sentence as not needed.

[12:1.8] replace "in space, at an enormous distance from the" with "beyond the", delete the word "inhabited". Delete the last part of 2nd sentence, delete "of these phenomena"; 'about one-half million light-years"; "for over twenty-five million light-years"; and "wheels of energizing".

[12:1.9] delete the phrase "more than fifty million light-years".

[12:2.1-5] Most of this section deleted or modified to incorporate String Theory cosmology ideas of the superuniverses.

[12:4.1-16] Some of this section deleted as obsolete, or modified as above.

[12:5.1] deleted as obsolete. [12:6.8] added "galaxies" to first sentence

Paper 13: The Sacred Spheres of Paradise

[13:1.8] just changed 1900 years ago to "over two thousand"

[13:4.4] added the word "galaxy" to the list in 3rd sentence as per cosmology change.

Paper 14: The Central and Divine Universe

[14:1.7] delete the last clause of last sentence after the comma, because with the String Theory cosmology there is no need for this.

[14:4.4] 2nd sentence, delete "a billion" and add "all of the".

[14:5.1] add the word "galaxy," to the 2nd sentence, as per cosmology change.

Paper 15: The Seven Superuniverses

[15:0.3] added to the last sentence words about the universes.

[15:1.1-6] mostly deleted as obsolete

[15:2.1-12] significantly modified to incorporate the new cosmology

[15:3.1-9] completely deleted as obsolete.

[15:4.4-9] significantly modified and/or deleted
[15:5.1-14] this whole section on “The Origin of Space Bodies” deleted as obsolete.
[15:6.3-10] deleted as obsolete. Last part of the last sentence of [15:6.11] deleted.
[15:7.1] deleted references to nearby suns and the last sentence as obsolete.
[15:7.6-11] changes due to the new cosmology, also deleted [15:7.12] as obsolete.
[15:8.1-2] additions and deleted last sentence; deleted all of [15:8.3] and [15:8.5-7] as obsolete
[15:8.8] deleted the phrase “of the near-by…systems” and parts of [15:8.10]
[15:9.16-17] insert “and galaxies” into last sentence
[15:10.4] deleted the “billions” as too small, rewrote to smooth out the changes
[15:10.6] add to Recents of Days that they are ambassadors to local galaxies. Change all superuniverse to universe; [15:10.7] add “universe and” in front of superuniverse. Change Perfections of Days and Recents of Days to advisors.
[15:10.8] ditto above and delete “of the superuniverse” and “superuniverse”.
[15:12.1] add “galaxies” after constellation
[15:13.1-6] deleted as obsolete
[15:14.6] delete last 2 sentences, change the universe of Nebadon to “your Milky Way galaxy”.
[15:14.7-8] delete as obsolete

Paper 18: The Supreme Trinity Personalities
[18:0.1] reorder 4,5, & 6 for new cosmology. [18:0.2] deleted as obsolete
[18:0.3] added new universe structure
[18:4.1-2] mostly deleted as obsolete
[18:4.1,4,5] minor changes due to new structure
[18:4.8] delete “physical and” and “super” from superuniverse, add “and morontial”.
[18:4.9] deleted as confusing since the cosmology change from String Theory
[18:5.1-5] changes for new cosmology
[18:6.2] delete first sentence [18:6.3] changes due to new cosmology

[18:7.1-5] changes due to new cosmology

Paper 19: The Co-ordinate Trinity-Origin Beings
[19:1.2] delete the last sentence as obsolete. [19:2.1] delete last sentence to avoid actual numbers
[19:3.1] delete last sentence, actual numbers are now way too small with the new cosmology
[19:3.2] modify slightly for the new cosmology
[19:4.1,3,8] delete numbers as too small

Paper 20: The Paradise Sons of God
[20:1.3] Update changes to Vorondadeks from cosmology
[20:2.2] Delete first sentence as too limiting – number of Magisterial Sons
[20:4.1] change "male" to "adult" to avoid sexist language as much as possible
[20:4.4] and [20:6.6] update 1900 years ago to "more than two thousand"
[20:6.2] delete "male" and change "manhood" to "adulthood" to avoid sexism.
[20:7.2] delete as not needed and too limiting
[20:8.2] delete the first sentence as not needed and too limiting

Paper 21: The Paradise Creator Sons
[21:1.4] deleted as not needed and too limiting
[21:3.8] changed 1900 years ago to 2000
[21:4.3] deleted the words "sectors and" from 1st sentence due to cosmology change; deleted the word "higher" and the entire last part of the 2nd sentence as racist.

Paper 22: The Trinitized Sons of God
[22:2.5] last sentence deleted as too limiting for new cosmology
[22:2.8] changed "in the direction of affairs" to "as advisors in" due to cosmology changes
[22:3.2] Second sentence deleted as too limiting for new cosmology
[22:4.2] last sentence deleted as too limiting for new cosmology
[22:5.5] Second sentence deleted as too limiting for new cosmology, also the

number "several billions" as way too small. Changed wording in 2nd sentence due to cosmology change.
[22:6.1] deleted last sentence as too limited
[22:9.3] delete first sentence about number of being as too limited, and change thie paragraph to refer to the High Son Assistants (this makes more sense in the new cosmology).
[22:10.7] delete actual number of beings as before, changed wording for new cosmology.
[22:10.8] change this pathetic description as too negative

Paper 23: The Solitary Messengers
[23:0.2] deleted last 2 sentences dealing with numbers as too limiting for new cosmology.
[23:2.13] deleted last sentence as not making sense with the new cosmology.
[23:2.15] deleted 3rd sentence and the words "Massive stars" as not making sense for new cosmology.

Paper 24: Higher Personalities of the Infinite Spirit
[24:0.3] replace "systems" with "subunits" in 4th sentence to avoid confusion.
[24:1.5] delete second and 3rd sentences as not needed due to cosmology update
[24:2.4-5,7] delete and change actual numbers as far too small and limiting.
[24:3.1] and [24:4.1] delete sentences about actual numbers.
[24:5.1] delete last sentence as too limiting, and also delete "ten thousand" from [24:5.2]
[24:6.8] add after 62 "from the first large stabilized galaxy" for new cosmology.

Paper 25: The Messenger Hosts of Space
[25:1.7] delete last part of 2nd sentence, actual numbers are too small with cosmology change.
[25:3.8-13] Switch the order of these as per the new cosmology and with needed small changes
[25:3.15] deleted as too small in number for the new cosmology

[25:4.1] replace "one million" with "large numbers"; [25:4.3] deleted as numbers too small
[25:4.11] and [25:5.3] update for new cosmology
[25:6.1] delete last part of 1st sentence, many people today would not understand this reference.
[25:6.4] delete 1st sentence as numbers too small for new cosmology

Paper 26: Ministering Spirits of the Central Universe
[26:3.4] just added the word "the" before "system" in first sentence for readability
[26:3.8] replaced "telegraphic" with "communication"

Paper 28: Ministering Spirits of the Superuniverses
[28:4.1] delete the reference to light years and just say where-ever it is
[28:6.2] delete "race" as not needed; [28:6.5] delete the words "and races"

Paper 29: The Universe Power Directors
[29:0.1] replace "your races have" with "mankind has"
[29:0.3] deleted "more than 10 billion" as too limiting, replaced with "an enormous number"
[29:2.1] major cosmology change to 10 groups
[29:2.6] deleted "one thousand" as too limiting, added "the"
[29:2.9] changed to add new cosmology; [29:2.10-12] deleted "one hundred", changed numbers
[29:3.1] deleted "ten billion" as too limiting
[29:4.8-10] changes for new cosmology and deleted actual numbers as too limited
[29:4.12] delete last part of 2nd sentence as not needed and confusing
[29:5.3] changes for new cosmology

Paper 30: Personalities of the Grand Universe
[30:1.4] [30:2.5] reorder Union, Perfections, and Recents of Days as per the cosmology change
[30:2.16] change from 7 to 10 adding major, minor, and galaxy centers and renumbering.
[30:3.2-5] changes due to the new cosmology

[30:3.11] add "of the superuniverse" for clarity.
[30:4.2] delete "of the human races" as not needed
[30:4.11] add "galaxy", [30:4.13 & 15] delete "of the minor sectors" due to cosmology change
[30:4.16] delete first sentence due to cosmology change

Paper 31: The Corps of the Finality
[31:10.9] delete "are actually visible through your telescopes" due to cosmology change
[31:10.12] delete the word "matter" in the last sentence, and replace it with "new types of space-time dimensional structures" due to the new expanded cosmology.

PART 2 (PAPERS 32 THROUGH 56)

Paper 32: The Evolution of Local Universes
[32:0.1], [32:1.2-5] updated for new cosmology; [32:0.4] added "foundations for these"
[32:2.2-4] and [32:2.9] updated for new cosmology; [32:2.11] deleted
[32:2.10] added "Your local system of" and [32:2.12] added higher dimensional viewpoint

Paper 33: Administration of the Local Universe
[33:0.1] and [33:2.5] update for new cosmology
[33:5.3-4] update for new arrangement of Paradise Sons due to cosmology change
[33:6.4-6] and [33:6.8] updates for new cosmology. [33:7.2] replace "system" with "lower".
[33:8.1,3,5] updates for new cosmology

Paper 34: The Local Universe Mother Spirit
[34:1.1] replace "starry and planetary cluster" with "local universe"
[34:3.3] In 2nd sentence delete "either the" and add "any of the major or minor sectors, the galaxies,"; [34:4.7] added 2 sentences and a note about the Seven Ray energies and the books by A.A.B. [34:4.10] deleted as obsolete
[34:6.1] added phrase "including response to the seven ray energies"

[34:7.1-5] deleted the word "race" as much as possible

Paper 35: The Local Universe Sons of God

[35:0.1] delete 1062 and the number of Trinity Teacher Sons as too limiting
[35:2.9] deleted as just too limiting; [35:3.1] minor word changes
[35:3.4,7,10,11,15] updates for new cosmology; [35:4.2] delete ~10 million as too limiting
[35:4.2] delete "approximately ten million" replace with 'a near infinite number'
[35:5-7] add a lot to make Vorondadeks consistent with new cosmology
[35:8.3-6] update for new cosmology, delete [35:8.8] replace with summary
[35:10.1-2] delete 10,000 and last sentence of .2 as not needed

Paper 36: The Life Carriers

[36:1.2] delete first sentence as too limiting
[36:2.4] deleted sentence about 48 pattern control units on Urantia (this was believed to be true back in the 1930's), and added words to make clear that the sequence 12, 24, 48 etc. may be the usual pattern but individual planets may vary, as here on Urantia we have 46.
[36:2.9] delete everything after the first 2 sentences as not needed and confusing
[36:2.11] replace effect with affect
[36:5.13] add several sentences about the seven ray energies
[36:5.15] add "responsive to the seven ray energies and develop the capability to become"
[36:6.1-3] mostly deleted as obsolete, ditto with [36:6.5]

Paper 37: Personalities of the Local Universe

[37:2.1] updates for new cosmology
[37:2.4] delete second sentence as too limiting, ditto last phrase of [37:3.1] and [37:4.1]
[37:2.6] replace 1900 with 2000; [37:3.1] delete last part with actual numbers as too small
[37:4.1] delete last sentence with numbers; [37:4.4] add "sectors, galaxy,"
[37:4.5] add Perfections of Days and Recents of Days; [37:5.5] replace human with planetary

[37:5.6] delete second sentence as too limiting, ditto [37:6.1] third sentence
[37:8.6-9] actual numbers deleted as too limiting
[37:9.3] add "as well as on the capitals of the major and minor sectors"
[37:9.4] add "Each galactic capital and all", delete "one hundred", add "galaxy and" twice
[37:9.8] update for new cosmology; [37:10.1] delete numbers; [37:10.4] add "galaxies and"

Paper 39: The Seraphic Hosts
[39:1.8] replace "racial" with "the struggle against lower"
[39:1.14] add "and the universities and training facilities of the galaxy and the minor and major sectors"; [39:2.3] added "galaxies, minor or major sectors;"
[39:2.15] replace 144,000 with "an incredible number of"
[39:5.4] delete "racial","races", "races of different colors and varies natures" and fill in with peoples, inhabitants, and citizens.

Paper 40: The Ascending Sons of God
[40:5.14] replace "the Urantia races" with "all Urantians"
[40:6.6] replace "Urantia races" with "Urantians"
[40:8.2] add "a galaxy, up through the minor and major sectors" to 2nd sentence.
[40:8.5] delete phrase at end of first sentence on numbers as too limiting
[40:9.2] at the word "to" in the last sentence
[40:10.6] replace "ten million" with "an enormous number of"
[40:10.8] replace "galaxies" in the last sentence with "new space-time universes".

Paper 41: Physical Aspects of the Local Universe
[41:0-2] mostly deleted as obsolete, added stuff about new cosmology
[41:3-9] completely deleted as obsolete
Deleted [41:10.1-2], and much of [41:10.3-4] all as obsolete astronomy info from the 1930's.

Paper 42: Energy – Mind and Matter
[42:0.1] deleted "Force" as not needed and confusing

[42:1.2] replace "nucleus" with "originator", I think that makes more sense
[42:1.4] deleted part of sentence where it says scientists will be powerless to create atoms or originate one flash of energy. Maybe in the 1930's this could still be considered accurate, but today with the Large Hadron Collider (LHC) etc. this is just not correct. We can even create anti-atoms and atoms that no longer appear in nature, i.e. with larger atomic numbers.
[42:1.9] In last sentence added "of universes" so it says "universe of universes".
[42:3.1-13] deleted as obsolete, most of [42:4] deleted as obsolete.
[42:5-9] deleted as obsolete

Paper 43: The Constellations
[43:0.1] updates for new cosmology; [43:0.2] added "at the capitols" to last sentence
[43:2.1] added "one of" and updates for new cosmology
[43:2.2] added "lowest" and long phrase at end for new cosmology
[43:3.1-2] and [43:5.2] add the word tertiary
[43:4.3] replace Union with Recents; [43:4.7] delete "one hundred"
[43:9.5] replace "the Salvington career" with "Zion, the capital of your local galaxy"

Paper 44: The Celestial Artisans
[44:0.1] update for new cosmology; [44:0.14] delete "races" change Urantia to Urantians
Deleted the words "and grotesque" from [44:1.3] as just an unnecessary insult (although I am sure from their vantage point justified). This is just not needed. The same for part of the last sentence in [44:1.6] on "spiritually indolent individuals". I think the Book is better without such statements.
[44:1.8] change "his" to "their" to avoid sexism
Deleted last sentence of [44:4.8] as unnecessary. Ditto with the last two sentences of [44:7.1].
[44:6.1] replace "pitiful" with "crude"

Paper 45: The Local System Administration
[45:3.7] and [45:4.1-2] change 1900 to 2000
[45:3.10] update for new cosmology

[45:4.2-16] delete "race" change the color words by making them in parenthesis
[45:5.4] replaced "Nebadon" in first sentence with "Norlatiadek".
[45:6.3] added paragraphs and footnote about sex fulfillment

Paper 46: The Local System Headquarters
[46:0.1] delete "twentieth-century"; delete [46:1.8] due to cosmology change
[46:3.1] add "Splandon, Ensa, Zion, and Edentia", replace "universe" with galaxy.
[46:5.12] change 1900 to 2000

Paper 47: The Seven Mansion Worlds
[47:3.5] delete several sentences dealing with races as not needed
[47:5.1] delete from last sentence "minor sector of the" due to cosmology change
[47:8.2] add "galaxy and" before universe
[47:8.5] added note about Treatise on Cosmic Fire by A.A.B.

Paper 48: The Morontia Life
[48:1.2] & [48:1.4-5] add galaxies, minor and major sector capitals as per cosmology update
[48:2.7] delete dynamo example as not needed and confusing
[48:3.1] deleted last phrase of actual numbers as too limiting; [48:3.3] ditto
Replaced the words "your races" with "you" and changed "their" to "your" in [48:4.13]. In the 1930's there was still a lot of inherent racism and throughout the Urantia Book I endeavor to remove and replace any possible racist language wherever I notice it.
[48:4.13] replace "your races" with "you"; "their" with "your"
[48:5.6] change universe to galaxy; [48:5.9] add the word "up"
[48:6.11] modified to avoid racist connotations and added "galaxy, constellation, and system"
[48:6.12] changes for new cosmology; JFC footnote added to [48:7.31]

Paper 49: The Inhabited Worlds
Deleted the last sentence in [49:1.6] about mice and elephants. I have no

idea whether this statement is correct or not, but it is just not needed and serves no useful purpose.

Deleted most of [49:2.6] and the statement about the moon in [49:2.7] as possibly creating more unbelief than illumination.

Deleted the word "chemical" in [49:2.15] as not needed and confusing.

Deleted the last sentence in [49:2.16] as useless trivia.

[49:4.2] on colored races deleted as racist – this is one of the major changes

Deleted the word "racial", moved the word "biologic" in [49:5.17] to make the sentence better.

[49:6.14] replace "universe" with "galaxy".

[49:6.18] and [49:6.21] change universe to galaxy as per cosmology update

Paper 50: The Planetary Princes

[50:3.4-5], [50:4.4], and [50:5.6] delete "races" as much as possible

Paper 51: The Planetary Adams

[51:0.3] deleted "race" and replaced with people or inhabitants.

[51:1.1] insert word "directly" before participate and add a several sentences and a footnote about the seven ray energies and how the material sons are 7th ray beings.

[51:1.3] added words to clarify Material Sons appearance on a planet

[51:2.4] added sentences on the end about genetic changes on decimal planets

[51:3.1] and [51:3.3-4] deleted "race" and sentence about origin of the violet race

[51:4] whole section deleted as obsolete

[51:5.1-6] change race to something else, and violet to Adamites.

[51:5.7] deleted as racist

[51:6.1-2] change race and violet as above; [51:6.5] ditto; [51:6.6] drop the "s" on race

Deleted the last seven words of [51:7.5] as unnecessary.

[51:6.3] deleted "in the Levant" as obsolete

Paper 52: Planetary Mortal Epochs

[52:1.1-5] major rewrite with additions of the seven rays

[52:1.8] replace "erect posture" with creature of will and worship

[52:2.1,4,5] replace "race" delete color and orange and green stuff
[52:2.9-12] deleted as obsolete
[52:3.4] deleted as unworthy; [52.3.5] change strains to individuals
[52:3.7] change race to natives and delete last sentence; [52:3.10, 12] change race and violet
[52:4.1] replace race and color; [52:4.5] replace race, delete last sentence
[52:4.4] delete "and all its tributaries" from the end of the sentence and add before "universe" the following "galaxy, minor and major sectors, and the" with "as a whole" after "universe".
[52:4.6] minor changes, delete "of the races".
[52:4.8-9] replace race delete "of the races"
[52:5.1-4] replace race, change 10 million to the entire universe
[52:5.6] delete "normal-minded" to avoid any discrimination in the future
[52:5.9] delete 2nd sentence as eugenic, change delinquency to disharmony
[52:5.10] minor word changes; [52:6.3-4] change or delete race
[52:7.5] delete racial; [52:7.7] replace of the race with people

Paper 53: The Lucifer Rebellion
[53:0.1-2] given numbers deleted as too limiting
[53:4.2,4] and [53:7.3] add new cosmology info
[53:7.1] delete "s" from races
[53:9.1] and [53:9.5] change 1900 to 2000

Paper 54: Problems of the Lucifer Rebellion
Deleted the word 'racial" in [54:1.10] as not needed.

Paper 55: The Spheres of Light and Life
[55:0.3] replace "which" with "whose galaxies", delete "super"; replace but with and.
[55:0.4], [55:2.9], [55:4.26], [55:8.1,7], [55:9.1-3] changes due to new cosmology
[55:3.1] delete racism and senility sentence
[55:3.14-15] updated this to be more realistic
[55:4.8] mostly deleted; [55:4.9] deleted
[55:5.2] deleted most of last two sentences
[55:6.2-3] deleted as not needed. [55:6.4] added seven ray idea

[55:10.1,4] new cosmology updates; deleted [55:10.2-3]; [55:10.5] deleted last part of 1st sentence; [55:10.6-11] and [55:11.1] deleted.
[55:11.2] modified for new cosmology; [55:11.4] deleted first part of 1st sentence
[55:11.7] change 1900 to 2000; [55:11.8] update and deletes for new cosmology
[55:12.1-2] deleted and replaced with material deleted earlier.

Paper 56: Universal Unity
[56:4.4] delete the last part of 2nd sentence; with modern technology it may be possible for someone to have more than one father, i.e. a mix of genes from many fathers.
[56:10.4] add footnote about atheism not always being bad. It can be just another stage of life.

PART 3 (PAPERS 57 THROUGH 119)

Paper 57: The History of Urantia
Deleted [57:0.1] and [57:0.2] about time reckoning as not needed.
Deleted most of the actual time (in years ago) from this whole chapter as well as much of the entire chapter as obsolete. Major rewrite – won't detail every change.

Paper 58: Life Establishment on Urantia
Deleted all of the actual times as above, and once again deleted much of this chapter as obsolete.

Paper 59: The Marine-life era on Urantia
Paper 60: Urantia During the Early Land-Life Era
Paper 61: The Mammalian Era on Urantia
Most of the above three papers have been deleted as obsolete. Look up Paleontology and other related issues on Wikipedia if interested in these subjects.

Paper 62: The Dawn Races of Early Man
Most of this paper deleted as obsolete. But the last few sections on the Life

Carriers are very interesting. Look up Human Evolution on Wikipedia if interested in these early humans.

Paper 63: The First Human Family
[63:2.1,3] delete "of the Primates tribe" as not needed; and "Primates'"
Deleted the last sentence in [63:4.6] as not needed.
Deleted [63:5.1] through [63:5.3] and parts of [63:5.4] as obsolete, and [63:5.7] as not needed.

Paper 64: The Evolutionary Races of Color
Almost totally deleted this whole paper, what remains is mostly new ideas on the seven rays replacing the racism of the original.

Paper 65: The Evolutionary Panorama
Deleted most of [65:2.2] as obsolete.
Deleted the "sudden" appearance of certain types of life (a popular theory of the 1930's) from [65:2.4] and [65:2.12], and other parts of [65:2.5], and all of [65:2.7] as obsolete.
Ditto with parts of [65:2.10] and all of [65:2.11].
[65:3.3] deleted first 6 words of 1st sentence as not needed
[65:4.1] replaced "Nebadon" with "Norlatiadek" which makes more sense
[65:4.7] deleted after first sentence, added response to ray influences.
[65:4.8] replaced Sangik races with colored subgroups; [65:4.9] added the word "and"
[65:4.11] modify as before; [65:6.4] deleted last sentence
[65:6.1,5] deleted as not needed; [65:6.10] and [65:7.3,4] add "the seven ray energies"

Paper 66: The Planetary Prince of Urantia
[66:0.2] replaced "or Sangik races" with "subgroups".
[66:3.7] replaced "colors" with "types" in first sentence.
[66:4.7] replace "skin color" with "physical characteristics"
[66:5.6] deleted last sentence about great fandor birds
[66:5.10] replaced "races" with "groups", deleted end phrase from 2nd sentence

Deleted last part of last sentence in [66:5.29] as an unnecessary and obsolete comparison.
Deleted [66:6.7] as obsolete.; [66:7.5] replaced "Sangik races" with "colored groups"
[66:7.7] deleted as obsolete
[several places] Changed location to Southwestern Africa – deleted several references and sentences about Mesopotamia. Due to modern genetic analysis as to where humans developed.

Paper 67: The Planetary Rebellion
[67:5.1] delete the word "racial" twice
[67:5.5] delete the phrase "the lowest types of the Sangik races of Urantia"
[67:6.1] deleted last half of this long sentence; [67:6.6] replace Sangik races

Paper 68: The Dawn of Civilization
[68:0.1-3] Deleted several "racist" aspects of this chapter, along with sections [68:1.6]. [68:1.7], part of [68:2.1], [68:2.7,9], [68:3.5], [68:4.3], [68:5.5,9], [68:6.8-10], and the last part of [68:6.11]. [68:2.5] changed 20th to 21st century; [68:5.2-4,6] minor changes.
I must say that the Urantia Book deplores racism, but some aspects of the inherent racism of the 1930's seems to seep through in various places (possibly due to the humans who were compiling and editing it), and it's these parts I wish to expunge.

Paper 69: Primitive Human Institutions
Deleted the phrase "of the races" in [69:1.4] as not needed, and last sentence of [69:1.5]
Deleted last part of [69:2.5] and [69:2.6] as not needed.
Deleted sexist remarks from [69:3.2] and [69:3.3].
[69:3.9] deleted last sentence as not needed
Deleted the last sentence in [69:4.3 & 7] as not needed.
[69:5.10] deleted unnecessary racist and eugenic stuff. [69:6.2] deleted last phrase
[69:6.6] deleted unneeded words, deleted [69:6.8]
Deleted [69:7.2] and comments about elephants and dogs as not needed in [69:7.3] and [69:7.4].

Deleted most of [69:8.3] and "racist" comments from [69:8.4] through [69:8.6].
Deleted misguided comments about slavery from [69:8.7] through [69:8.12].
Deleted last sentences in [69:9.5] and [69:9.8,9] [69:9.12,13,16] as not needed.

Paper 70: The Evolution of Human Government
Deleted races in [70:1.1], [70:1.16] and [70:2.16]; deleted most of [70:1.2-3,6] as obsolete.
[70:1.10] replaced superior/inferior; deleted most of [70:1.15,18]
[70:2.4] deleted 4th sentence as eugenic; [70:2.6] delete "already"
[70:2.11] deleted as eugenic
Deleted last sentence from [70:3.2] as obsolete, and parts of [70:3.8] and [70:3.9].
Deleted the last sentence of [70:4.3] and [70:5.1] &[70:5.4,7,9] as obsolete and incorrect.
[70:6.4] and [70:7.9] deleted last sentence; [70:8.6] deleted the word "genetic"
[70:8.11] added word "skin"; [70:8.14] deleted the word "biologic" and [70:8.15] as eugenic
Added to [70:8.16-17] to make them better; deleted from [70:8.18]
Deleted last part of [70:9.4] and all of [70:9.5] through [70:9.7] as unworthy.
Deleted [70:10.3] and [70:10.6] as not needed.
[70:10.11-12] deleted last sentence; [70:10.14,16] deleted
[70:11.2] deleted last sentence.

Paper 71: Development of the State
[71:1.3,7] deleted reference to the Indians; deleted all of [71:1.12]
Deleted 'and backward" in [71:1.13] 6 as not needed.
Deleted the first two sentences in [71:1.14] as obsolete social ideas.
Deleted the last sentence in [71:1.16] as obsolete.
Deleted last sentence in [71:3.5] as obsolete ideas.
[71:4.2] deleted #9 on race and renumbered
Deleted sexist part of [71:8.10] about "specialized service of women".
[71:8.15] replaced "the civilized races" with "you"

Paper 72: Government of a Neighboring Planet

[72:1.1] deleted 3rd and 4th sentences as racist

[72:2.12] replaced "men" with judges to avoid sexism

[72:3.9] replaced "races" with "nations"; [72:4.2] replaced "feeble-minded"

[72:9.8] replaced inferior with criminal

Deleted part of the last sentence, as well as the word "inferior", in [72:5.2] and all of [72:10.3] as being based on old obsolete eugenic concepts.

[72:12.2] minor word changes as above; [72:12.6] added JFC Note

Paper 73: The Garden of Eden

[73:0.1] drop the s on races; [73:1.1] delete "races" add race; [73:1.2] delete "races of the"

[73:1.3] delete last two sentences; [73:1.6] delete part of first sentence on the Sangik

[73:1] This section modified for the African location of Dalamatia

[73:6] changed sentence about the Edentia shrub on migration

[73:7.3] drop the s on races; [73:7.4] delete "racial".

Paper 74: Adam and Eve

[74:0.1] added paragraph on DNA; [74:1.1] added "before rematerializing on Urantia"

[74:1.2] deleted "on Urantia" since I moved that to the previous paragraph.

[74:2.5] replaced Sangik races; [74:3.4] and [74:4.4] replaced fandors with midwayers

[74:3.7] replaced "types of men" with volunteers; [74:5.5] replaced "races" with natives

[74:6.2] replaced races with subgroups; [74:6.5] mostly deleted as not needed

[74:6.7] replaced "races" with "Urantians"

[74:7.3] replaced races with tribes; [74:7.8-10] replaced races with natives, etc.

[74:8.5] deleted last two sentences as not needed; deleted [74:8.11]

[74:8.14] deleted retardation

Paper 75: The Default of Adam and Eve

[75:0.1] replaced race with civilization

Deleted obsolete eugenic concepts from [75:1.1] and [75:1.2].
Deleted first part of 2nd sentence in [75:2.4] as sexist.
[75:3.1] deleted race info as not needed
Deleted last part of last sentence in [75:6.3] as unnecessarily harsh sounding, as not needed.
[75:7.3], [75:8.1] deleted races as not needed
[75:8.2] replaced superior stocks with people, deleted Sangik, replaced with ray info

Paper 76: The Second Garden
[76:0.2] replaced races with tribes; [76:2.4] delete 3rd sentence and parts of the 4th as not needed
[76:2.6] deleted as obsolete ideas; [76:3.1] replace pathetic with sad
[76:4.1] delete last part of 1st sentence; [76:4.2] deleted as not needed
[76:4.4] and [76:4.6] delete last sentence; [76:4.7] replace races with bodies
Also add paragraph on secondary midwayers carrying Adamites; [76:4.8] delete stuff about race

Paper 77: The Midway Creatures
[77:2.3] delete "race mixtures of the" in last sentence; [77:2.4] replace "Sangik"
[77:2.5] delete last sentence; [77:2.8] delete "the eighth race to appear on Urantia"
[77:2.10-12] delete as obsolete; [77:3.1] delete "racial and cultureal" and replace "Sangik"
[77:3.2] replace racial with Nodite; [77:3.8] delete racial; [77:3.9] delete "mixed races of the"
[77:3] This section, on the tower of Babel, deleted as not needed and confusing once the shift to Africa for Dalamatia was implemented, and all subsequent sections renumbered.
[77:4.1] replace "of this race" by Nodites; [77:4.3] delete "or racial" replace stock with people
[77:4.4] replace Sangik, delete last sentence; [77:4.5] replace races with peoples
[77:4.6]delete racial integrity; [77:4.7-9] and [77:4.12] delete as obsolete

[77:5.8] add sentences about midwayer transport; [77:5.9-10] delete last sentence
[77:8.4] replace races with groups

Paper 78: The Violet Race After The Days of Adam
Almost totally deleted from 12 pages down to 4, with a few additions. See the b paper for details.

Paper 79: Andite Expansion in the Orient
This whole paper deleted as obsolete.

Paper 80: Andite Expansion in the Occident
This whole paper deleted as obsolete.

Paper 81: Development of Modern Civilization
[81:0.1-2] replace race, add 7th ray; [8:1.1] delete last sentence add stuff
[81:1.2-6] deleted as obsolete; [81:1.8] delete first sentence; [81:2.3] add massacre
[81:2.8] delete last sentence; [81:2.12] delete "of the more modern races"
[81:2.13-14] deleted as obsolete; [81:2.15] delete last sentence; [81:2.16] deleted
[81:3.1] deleted; [81:3.3] delete all but first sentence; [81:3.4-5] deleted
[81:3.6] delete last sentence; [81:3.8] deleted as obsolete.
All of [81:4] deleted; [81:5.1] deleted; Deleted last few words of [81:5.3]
[81:6.1] delete first 2 sentences and "no Andites". [81:6.4-5,7] deleted
[81:6.11] inset "being", delete "race"; [81:6.18] replace race with nation
[81:6.26] replace "The racial" with "character" and race with people;
[81:6.39] replace race with nation; [81:6.43] add first

Paper 82: The Evolution of Marriage
[82:0.3] drop the s on races; [82:1.2] delete last half; [82:1.5] change to intelligence
[82:1.6,9] deleted; [82:1.7-8] delete race;
Deleted 2nd sentence of [82:2.2] about Pygmies; [82:2.3] free love update
[82:3.3] replace "races" with "groups"

[82:3.5-7] deleted; [82:3.11-12] deleted as obsolete; [82:4.4] delete last sentence
[82:4.5] delete "on the races"; [82:5.4] drop phrase about the Andites;
[82:5.8] deleted; [82:5.9] delete the word "racial"
[82:5.10] deleted; [82:6.1-4] deleted; delete last sentence in [82:6.5];
[82:6.7] deleted
[82:6.9-11] deleted

Paper 83: The Marriage Institution
[83:1.3] delete first part of 2nd sentence; [83:2.5] delete race
[83:2.6] deleted as not needed; deleted last sentences in [83:3.1], [83:4.3-4], [83:4.7], and [83:4.9] as obsolete. [83:5.7] delete most of last sentence;
[83:6.2] delete last sentence.
[83:6.6] add sentence about same sex marriages; [83:6.7] replace husband with spouse
[83:7.2] delete 2nd part of 2nd sentence; [83:7.4] deleted; [83:7.5] delete centuries and last part
Deleted the words Occidental and "racial" from [83:7.7] as not needed.
[83:7.9] deleted
[83:8.8] replace "of a man and a woman" with "between two people"
[83:8.9] deleted as not needed.

Paper 84: Marriage and Family Life
[84:1.5] 21st century; [84:1.9] change to two people; Deleted the last sentence in [84:2.2 and 2.3] [84:2.4-5] deleted as obsolete; Deleted the second to the last sentence from [84:2.6] as sexist. [84:3.2-4] deleted; Deleted the phrase "though slightly less profound" from [84:3.5]
[84:3.6] delete last sentence; [84:3.9] delete barrenness phrase
[84:3.10] delete last 2 sentences; [84:4.3,5,7-9] deleted; [84:4.4] delete the words "and racial"
[84:4.10] delete last sentence; [84:4.11] as obsolete;
[84:5.5] deleted, [84:5.6] delete last phrase, [84:5.10] delete 20th century
[84:5.11-14] deleted as old sexist attitudes that are now obsolete.[84:6.3-4] deleted
Deleted the word "race" from [84:6.8], and [84:7.1] delete last sentence,
Deleted the phrase 'and she obeyed…reason" from [84:7.3] as obsolete.

Added “and daughters” to [84:7.4]. Deleted racial terms from [84:7.6] and [84:7.7].
Deleted obsolete Eskimo material from [84:7.10] and [84:7.21].
Deleted [84:7.22] as racist and renumbered the list. [84:7.29] delete civilized races
[84:8.3] delete Sangik replace with stuff, [84:8.5] delete last sentence

Paper 85: The Origins of Worship
Deleted the 2nd sentence from [85:1.1] and the last sentence in [85:1.2] and parts of [85:1.3-4] as obsolete info about India and Africa. Deleted most of [85:2.4] as obsolete folk information. Deleted sentence about Mongolia in [85:4.1]

Paper 86: Early Evolution of Religion
[86:4.6] delete first sentence; [86:4.8] delete phrase about shadows, and last two sentences
[86:5.1] delete last phrase about Eskimos; [86:5.10] deleted; [86:5.11] delete 3rd sentence
Deleted the first sentence in [86:5.13], about the children of Badanon, as that section was deleted in an earlier paper, and the last sentence about Eskimos as obsolete.
[86:6.3] delete races, replace of with in
Paper 87: The Ghost Cults
Deleted all of [87:1.4-5] as not needed. Deleted last sentence in [87:2.3] as obsolete info on Eskimos. [87:2.7] deleted; deleted sentence about Borneo from [87:2.8], and sentences about the Iroquois from [87:2.10] as obsolete. Deleted last part of [87:6.4] as obsolete.

Paper 88: Fetishes, Charms, and Magic
[88:1.5] delete 3rd and last sentences, deleted obsolete reference to Africa from [88:1.8]. Deleted part of sentence about African tribes from [88:4.5]. Deleted last sentence of [88:5.5] as obsolete info on Bushmen. [88:6.1] delete last sentence; [88:6.4] delete 2nd sentence;
[88:6.7] replace “the race” with man

Paper 89: Sin, Sacrifice, and Atonement

[89:2.3] replace Dilmun with Sumerians, delete "of the dawn of the races"

Deleted last part of last sentence in [89:2.4] as not needed.

[89:3.2] delete "of the races"; [89:3.4] delete last sentence

Deleted last sentence of [89:3.5] as obsolete info about India.

[89:4.8] replace races with peoples; [89:4.9] deleted; [89:5.3] delete last phrase

Deleted much of [89:5.4] and first sentence of [89:5.5]; deleted all of [89:5.7]

Delete last sentence of [89:5.9] as obsolete;

[89:6.1] replace race with evolutionary group, and delete Adamites

Deleted African and Australian from [89:6.2]; delete last sentence from [89:7.3]

delete the words "in Africa" from [89:8.3] as not needed.

[89:8.7] replace "the races" with civilization

Paper 90: Shamanism – Medicine Men and Priests

[90:0.3] add "and daughters"

Delete the 2nd sentence from [90:2.9] as not needed.

Deleted the last sentence in [90:2.11] as obsolete info about Tibet.

[90:2.13] delete last phrase "in the evolution of the race".

Deleted [90:3.6] as obsolete info about Africa.

[90:4.7] delete last sentence about the red man; [90:5.1] delete the word racial

[90:5.3] delete "and selah" as not needed.

Paper 91: The Evolution of Prayer

Deleted the last sentence of [91:0.3] as obsolete info on Australia.

Deleted [91:0.4] and most of [91:0.5] as obsolete.

Deleted the word "racial" in [91:2.6] as not needed; [91:2.8] ditto

Deleted reference to the Toda from [91:3.2] as obsolete.

[91:4.5] replaced races with mankind; [91:5.2] deleted "and whole races"

[91:5.7] deleted the word feeble as a bit insulting, no need for that

Paper 92: The Later Evolution of Religion

[92:0.3] added the seven rays; [92:0.5] replace three with four

[92:1.1] delete last sentence; [92:1.2] replace races with mankind, replace mankind
[92:1.3] replace race with culture; [92:2.2] delete 4th sentence
[92:2.3] add "clearly obsolete or even" before obscene
[92:2.4] replace race with people/prevailing; [92:2.5] delete Races of
[92:3.9] replace "the race" with mankind; [92:4.5] delete last sentence
[92:4.9] delete race; [92:5.3] replace races, delete 2 sentences
[92:5.13] delete "of Satania" as not needed.
Deleted references to specific tribal peoples in [92:6.1] as obsolete
[92:6.2] delete twentieth-century as not needed
[92:6.4] delete last sentence; [92:6.5] replace Ceylon and Burma with south-east Asia
[92:6.9] delete several phrases; [92:7.7] delete sentence about slaves
[92:7.10] delete two, make it thousands of years.
[92:7] deleted sentence about slaves as not needed

Paper 93: Machiventa Melchizedek
[93:1.1] replace "the human races were" with mankind was
[93:5.2] delete sentence about red and yellow men as obsolete
[93:7.2] deleted "by way of the Faroes" and replaced Iceland with Ireland, Iceland was not inhabited until 700 AD or so.
[93:7.3] delete "or race"

Paper 94: The Melchizedek Teachings in the Orient
[94:0.1] delete "and races"; [94:2.1] delete phrase about Sangik peoples
[94:2.2] delete as racist and not needed; [94:2.7] delete last phrase after "it'.
[94:3.2] delete the comma after the word infinite
[94:4.10] replace "white man's" with western;
[94:5.1] replace "See Fuch" with Yibin, "yellow race" with east
[94:5.3] replace the yellow race with they; [94:5.4] replace yellow race phrase with China
[94:5.6] replace yellow and brown races with east; [94:5.7] replace yellow race, and races
[94:6.9] and [94:6.12] replace yellow race with Chinese people
[94:10.1-3] deleted as obsolete; [94:11.1] delete "of the yellow race"
[94:12.5] delete "twentieth-century" as not needed

[94:12.7] delete "nineteen"

Paper 95: The Melchizedek Teachings in the Levant
[95:2.1] delete "superior strains" and phrase about India
[95:2.3] delete last sentence; [95:2.6] delete as not needed
[95:5.13] delete last phrase about dumb animals as not needed
[95:5.15] delete the word racial; [95:6.8] deleted as not needed

Paper 96: Yahweh – God of the Hebrews
[96:2.1] delete last sentence as racist; [96:2.3-4] and [96:3.1] delete the word "racial"
[96:2.5] delete the word "stock"; [96:3.3] "hereditary strains" phrase from 2nd sentence

Paper 98: The Melchizedek Teachings in the Occident
Deleted the words "hordes of inferior" from [98:1.1] as not needed.
[98:1.4] delete "and racial" as not needed;
[98:2.3] deleted "among the higher classes" and "rank and file of the progeny of the slaves of former generations" as racist and not needed. Added two words to complete the sentence.
Deleted the words "white races" in the 2nd sentence of [98:7.11] and replaced it with "west".

Paper 99: The Social Problems of Religion
[99:0.3] replace "in the 20th century" with now
Deleted paragraph [99:3.5] as obsolete Social Darwinist ideas from the 1930's.
[99:4.2] delete 20th century phrase; [99:4.6] delete 20th century phrase and extra "the"s
[99:5.11] delete the words "or racial"; [99:6.1] delete 20th century phrase

Paper 101: The Real Nature of Religion
Deleted "racial tendencies" from paragraph [101:7.1] as obsolete concept.

Paper 102: The Foundations of Religious Faith
[102:8.4] delete the words "or racial" as not needed

[102:8.6] drop the "s" on human races at the end 1st sentence, delete "the" and "of the races" from last sentence.

Paper 103: The Reality of Religious Experience
[103:1.1] replace racial with cultural, delete 20th century
Deleted references to Australians and Bushmen from [103:3.1] as obsolete and not needed.
Replaced the word "man" in [103:8.1] with "being" to avoid sexist language.
Deleted the phrase "and by different races of men" in [103:8.2] as not needed.

Paper 105: Deity and Reality
[105:0.3] added Note about Savitri;
[105:1.5] added Note about HPB's The Secret Doctrine.

Paper 110: Relation of Adjusters to Individual Mortals
[110:1] change "man" to human in last sentence
[110:4] delete last paragraph as unnecessary and negative.

Paper 111: The Adjuster and the Soul
Deleted "eugenics," from [111:4.4] as an obsolete concept put into the Urantia Book only because it was popular back in the 1930's. [111:5] replaced "man" with you in several places. Deleted the first 2 sentences from [111:7.4] as racist and obsolete. Deleted "the ideals of a superior people crossed by the instincts of an inferior race;" from [111:7.5] for the same reason, replaced "race" with brain, and "race" with group.
Paper 112: Personality Survival
[112:7.17] In the 2nd sentence replace "galaxies" with "new creations" to avoid confusion.

Paper 113: Seraphic Guardians of Destiny
[113:1.2] replace "races" with "groups responsive to the different ray energies"
[113:2.2] replace "race" with "subgroup, those human beings most strongly responsive to the first ray energy of will or power".
[113:7.4] rewritten for new cosmology.

Paper 114: Seraphic Planetary Government
[114:0.2] added Note about 1934; [114:5.4] replaced 1900 with 2000
[114:6.9] delete 2nd sentence as obsolete; [114:6.11] delete "and whole races"
[114:7.1] added "when"; [114:7.12] deleted the word "racial".

Paper 115: The Supreme Being
[115:2.1] replace "galaxies" in the 1st sentence with "universe of universes" due to cosmology change.

Paper 117: God the Supreme
[117:3.2] delete the word "galactic" as it is a throwback to the old cosmology where our galaxy was represented as the seventh superuniverse. In the new cosmology this word is just confusing and unnecessary.

Paper 118: Supreme and Ultimate – Time and Space
Deleted the last 2 sentences from [118:3.1] on animal perceptions, as not needed and possibly incorrect. I do not know, but I believe that it may be possible for particularly advanced individual animals to attain near human (or even into the "human") types of perception and personality.
[118:6.2] replace "well-nigh a million" with "the enormous number of" I don't want to limit the number of Creator Sons. [118:8.5] delete the word "racial" in 3rd sentence as not needed.
[118:9.9] replace "galaxies" with universes; [118:10.11] add galaxies to the list in the 4th sentence. [118:10.21] replace "galaxies" with "universes" due to cosmology change.

Paper 119: The Bestowals of Christ Michael
[119:0.5] add galaxies and sectors to 1st sentence.
[119:0.7] delete last part of 2nd sentence on 400 billion years as improbable and obsolete, change 1900 to 2000. [119:1.1] delete "to the Constellation Fathers" due to cosmology change.
[119:1.3] add "major and minor sector, galaxy," due to cosmology change.
[119:2.1] add ", in a galaxy, minor and major sector which I am not at liberty to reveal" ditto

[119:3.1] add "of a particular galaxy which I am again not allowed to name," ditto above
[119:3.3] add "of that galaxy"; [119:4.3] add "in one of the oldest and biggest galaxies"
[119:6.1] add "in one of the newest and smallest galaxies in Nebadon".
[119:6.5] replace constellation with "various"; [119:8.1] add Perfections and Recents of Days
[119:8.8] delete "the chief of ten million inhabited worlds" due to cosmology change

PART 4 (PAPERS 120 THROUGH 196)

Paper 120: The Bestowal of Michael on Urantia
[120:2.7] replace "galaxy" with "universe". [120:3.5] delete "races" insert "people of"

Paper 121: The Times of Michael's Bestowal
[121:3.6] delete the last sentence as not needed and insulting.
[121:5.3] Astrology: replace "in the twentieth century" with "today".

Paper 122: Birth and Infancy of Jesus
[122:0.2] delete the word racial; [122:1.2] delete the word "racial" twice, in the 1st and last sentences. [122:1.3] inset "to", delete "of" in first sentence.

Paper 124: The Later Childhood of Jesus
Deleted the last sentence of [124:6.10] as this breaks the narrative, and is not totally correct. Jesus is probably the greatest, but there is no last prophet. There will always be spiritual teachers and prophets in every generation.

Paper 128: Jesus' Early Manhood
[128:1.13] delete first sentence. Jesus may have accepted worship as a representative of the Father, but this statement is confusing and not needed.

Paper 130: On the Way to Rome
Deleted the phrase "the empire of the yellow race" and replaced with "China' in [130:0.6].

[130:2.8] Added the words "yet" and "individual" and deleted the phrase "anything equivalent to" from this paragraph to leave open the possibility that animals may have a "group soul" and in the far future may transition into the human kingdom.

Paper 131: The World's Religions
[131:1.8] delete the 6th and 7th sentences as redundant and not needed, and the 7th on concealing defects I find weird. Why not fix defects instead of concealing them?

Paper 132: The Sojourn at Rome
[132:0.5] replaced "nineteen" with "twenty" (centuries).

Paper 133: The Return From Rome
Deleted the last part of the last sentence from [133:0.2] about "inferior slaves" etc.
Deleted most of [133:5.12] and reworded to eliminate negative comments about "inferior slaves"

Paper 134: The Transition Years
[134:2.3] deleted parts of 2nd and 3rd sentences about race, replaced with people
[134:5.1] replaced "nineteen hundred" with "two thousand"; [134:5.9] added the word "first" before World War; [134:5.10] added UN etc.
Deleted reference to the 48 states of America in [134:5.13-15] and [134:6.5] as obsolete.
[134:5.17] deleted the word "racially" as not needed.
Deleted one sentence of [134:6.1] about absolute free vs. slave as a false generalization.
Deleted references about the United Kingdom from [134:6.3] as not needed.

Paper 136: Baptism and the Forty Days
[136:1.3] delete the word "racial" in the 1st sentence. Trying to delete this whenever possible, but most other uses of this term in this paper are appropriate I think.

Paper 139: The Twelve Apostles
[139:5.6] delete the word "niggardly" as not needed and possibly offensive.

Paper 140: The Ordination of the Twelve
[140:8.14] Last sentence: delete the words "and advanced". I would not call stringent ideas on divorce necessarily "advanced".
Deleted the phrase "How long shall I bear with you!" from [140:10.4] as not needed and uncharacteristic of Jesus. I don't believe he would say this more than once (in an earlier paper).

Paper 141: Beginning the Public Work
[141:7.10] delete the last sentence; it breaks the flow and has no apparent meaning.

Paper 143: Going Through Samaria
[143:5.11] replaced "nineteen centuries later" with "today".
Deleted the word "white" in [143:6.1] and replace it with " ripe" where Jesus is telling the twelve that "the fields are already white for the harvest", I think "ripe" is what was really intended here.

Paper 146: First Preaching Tour of Galilee
[146:1.1] delete last sentence as not needed, supplies no useful information
[146:1.2] and [146:1.4] deleted as not needed, no idea who Todan was!
[146:3.10-11] deleted as containing no useful new information.

Paper 148: Training Evangelelists at Bethsaida
[148:8] deleted the last part of paragraph 3 and paragraph 4 as unneeded negative details.

Paper 155: Fleeing Through Northern Galilee
Modified the first sentence of [155:3.3] by adding the words in italics so it now reads "The apostles learned that *many of* the Jews were spiritually stagnant and dying…".
Replaced the word "race" with "*culture*" in the first sentence of [155:6.8] and deleted "of mankind" and "racial". Deleted the word "Racial" in the 3rd sentence as not needed and obsolete.

Replaced the words "whole race" with "*group*" in the 2nd sentence of [155:6.10].

Paper 156: The Sojourn at Tyre and Sidon
Deleted the last two sentences from [156:2.8] as offensive, and not needed.

Paper 158: The Mount of Transfiguration
[158:1.1] added footnote reference to "From Bethlehem to Calvary" by A.A.B.

Paper 160: Rodan of Alexandria
Deleted the word "only" in the first sentence of [160:1.5] and added the words *[the lower]* when referring to animals, as I believe it is possible (but very rare) for some of the higher animals to attain equivalent levels of consciousness to man. When they do, they instantly become "primitive men" in spirit. The way it is now worded in the Revised Urantia Book leaves it vague, but more correct in my opinion.
Deleted the words "final, infallible," from the last sentence of [160:1.14] as these words can lead to dogmatic intolerance. Nothing in the worlds of time and space are final or infallible.
Deleted the words "do not" and replaced with *[rarely]* in [160:2.1] and replaced the phrase "the animal" with "most animals"; and inserted the words "the lower" in [160:2.2] all in the same vein to express the possibility that some animals can communicate and attain personality.
[160:2.3] deleted the words "the race" in the last sentence as not needed.
[160:2.4] added "in love, marriage, or as" in 4th sentence; [160:2.6] replace "man and woman" with "two people" in 2 places. Replaced "father-child" with "parent-child". [160:2.10] replaced "race" with civilization
Deleted the word "all" from the 13th sentence of [160:3.1], makes the sentence read better.
Replaced the words "ever known" with "yet known" in [160:5.7] to allow for future expansion, and added the phrase "that is not built on this one" after the phrase "there can never be a higher" to allow for future revelations.
Replaced the word "race" in [160:5.14] with the word "time" which I believe conveys the same idea without inserting the idea of race.

Paper 162: At the Feast of Tabernacles

Deleted the word “racial” in the 3rd sentence of [162:4.2] as not needed.

Paper 167: The Visit to Philadelphia

[167:6.5] deleted the words “of the Creator Sons” from the end of the last sentence, due to the cosmology change.

Paper 170: The Kingdom of Heaven

[170:2.13] in #2 delete the words “racial or” as not needed
[170:2.14] in 2nd sentence delete the words “racial or” as not needed
[170:4.4] deleted the words “Remember that”, “is”, and “periodical” from the 3rd sentence to avoid the old obsolete ideas about Evolutionary Saltation, i.e. sudden and drastic evolutionary changes, and added “can sometimes be”.
[170:5.8] delete the word “, races” as not needed.

Paper 176: Tuesday Evening on Mount Olivet

Deleted the word “hid” from the 4th sentence of [176:3.2] and replaced it with the word “established”; as this seems more positive to me.

Paper 177: Wednesday, The Rest Day

[177:2.6] replace “the twentieth century” with “today”.

Paper 179: The Last Supper

[179:5.2] deleted the word “racial” in 2nd sentence as not needed.

Paper 180: The Farewell Discourse

[180:6.7] replaced the word “man” in the 5th sentence with “baby” to avoid sexist language.

Paper 185: The Trial Before Pilate

Deleted last sentence in [185:8.2] as just not needed and the inclusion of this line tends to incite anti-Semitic feelings.

Paper 186: Just Before the Crucifixion

[186:2.4] deleted, probably OK, but seemed a bit harsh and not really needed.

[186:2.8] deleted the last two sentences as too harsh and not needed. Deleted the word "racial" in the 3rd sentence of [186:5.7] as not needed. The paragraph reads better without that word, and means just as much if not more.

Paper 188: The time of the Tomb

[188:3.12] delete the words "numbering one hundred" due to cosmology change (this number of 100 was from the old identification of the superuniverse with our galaxy with 100 constellations)
[188:4.1] delete the word "racial" in the 1st sentence; [188:4.6] replace "races" with "beings"
[188:5.5] replace "millions of" with "countless" and replace "tens of trillions" with "enormous numbers" due to cosmology change from a single galaxy to the entire observable universe!

Paper 194: Bestowal of the Spirit of Truth

[194:2.12] Add after the 2nd sentence "Advancing man is influenced by the higher aspects of these seven adjutant mind-spirits, the seven ray energies of the local universe Mother Spirit."
[194:2.18] add after mind-spirits "and their higher aspects, the seven ray energies,"
[194:3.1] replace "queer" with "novel"; [194:4.12] In 2nd sentence drop the "t" from "not".

Paper 195: After Pentecost

Deleted the phrase "a little queer" and replaced it with the phrase "a bit insignificant" in the 4th sentence of [195:1.7] in reference to the gods of Greece. "Queer" has too many other connotations in today's English, this rephrasing I think is much better.
Deleted the word "racial" from [195:3.8] and replaced it with "political".
Deleted the phrase "and race decadence" from [195:3.9] as not needed.
[195:5.1] replace "The twentieth century" with "Modern civilization".
Deleted all color words from [195:5.12], i.e. "black" and "white" which are just not needed.
[195:6.9] replace "Nineteen hundred" with "Two thousand"

[195:8.1] replace "twentieth-century" with "modern"; [195:8.5] delete "Twentieth-century"
[195:8.9] replace "the twentieth century" with "today"; [195:8.10] delete ",races," as not needed
[195:8.13] delete the words "is" and "to" and insert the word "may" at end of last sentence.
[195:9.3] replace "the twentieth century" with "today"
[195:9.4] delete the word "solely" and add "the Spirit of Truth, and the leadings of their own thought adjusters". [195:9.8] delete "of the twentieth century"
[195:9.11] delete this whole paragraph as not needed – it adds nothing new.
[195:10.8] replace "the twentieth century" with "today", ditto for [195:10.12]
[195:10.15] replace "Oriental peoples" with "the world"; replace "These races" with "Most people".

Paper 196: The Faith of Jesus

[196:1.2] delete the words "the" and "of nineteen centuries" as not needed in the 1st sentence.

www.ingramcontent.com/pod-product-compliance
Lightning Source LLC
LaVergne TN
LVHW012038160826
845678LV00014B/2633

* 9 7 9 8 8 9 5 6 9 8 9 6 9 *